Review of the Criminal Justice System in Northern Ireland

March 2000

Contents

The Prosecution

Courts and the Judiciary

Restorative and Reparative and Juvenile Justice

Community Safety

Sentences, Prisons and Probation

Victims and Witnesses

Law Reform

Organisation and Research

Structured Co-operation

Recommendations and Appendices

1 Introduction

1.1 The Agreement reached in Belfast on Good Friday 1998 provided for a "... wide-ranging review of criminal justice (other than policing and those aspects of the system relating to the emergency legislation) to be carried out by the British Government through a mechanism with an independent element, in consultation with the political parties and others". This chapter sets out the origins of the review and the approach it has taken.

1.2 The Agreement set out what the participants to the multi-party negotiations believed the aims of the criminal justice system to be, and these formed the starting point for our work, and the touchstone against which we have measured all the proposals we considered and the recommendations we make. These aims "... are to:

- deliver a fair and impartial system of justice to the community;

- be responsive to the community's concerns, and encouraging community involvement where appropriate;

- have the confidence of all parts of the community; and

- deliver justice efficiently and effectively".

The Agreement also noted that "… the British Government remains ready in principle, with the broad support of the political parties, and after consultation, as appropriate, with the Irish Government, in the context of ongoing implementation of the relevant recommendations, to devolve responsibility for policing and justice issues".

OUR TERMS OF REFERENCE

1.3 The Agreement also provided us with our terms of reference, as follows:

"Taking account of the aims of the criminal justice system as set out in the Agreement, the review will address the structure, management and resourcing of publicly funded elements of the criminal justice system and will bring forward proposals for future criminal justice arrangements (other than policing and those aspects of the system relating to emergency legislation, which the Government is considering separately) covering such issues as:

- the arrangements for making appointments to the judiciary and magistracy, and safeguards for protecting their independence;

- the arrangements for the organisation and supervision of the prosecution process, and for safeguarding its independence;

- measures to improve the responsiveness and accountability of, and any lay participation in the criminal justice system;

- mechanisms for addressing law reform;

- the scope for structured co-operation between the criminal justice agencies on both parts of the island; and

- the structure and organisation of criminal justice functions that might be devolved to an Assembly, including the possibility of establishing a Department of Justice, while safeguarding the essential independence of many of the key functions in this area.

> "The Government proposes to commence the review as soon as possible, consulting with the political parties and others, including non-governmental expert organisations. The review will be completed by Autumn 1999."

1.4   The Agreement was put to separate referendums in Northern Ireland and the Republic of Ireland on 21 May 1998. Those referendums endorsed the Agreement and, as a direct result, the Criminal Justice Review Group was established on 27 June 1998 and began its work shortly thereafter.

COMPOSITION OF THE REVIEW GROUP

1.5   The Review Group consisted of four civil servants representing the Secretary of State for Northern Ireland, the Lord Chancellor and the Attorney General, together with five independent assessors who formed the independent element provided for by the Agreement. The membership of the Review Group was as follows:

Jim Daniell, Director of Criminal Justice at the Northern Ireland Office and Chairman of the Review Group;

Glenn Thompson, Director of the Northern Ireland Court Service;

David Seymour, the Legal Secretary to the Law Officers;

Brian White, Head of Criminal Justice Policy Division at the Northern Ireland Office;

Professor Joanna Shapland, Professor of Criminal Justice at Sheffield University and Director of the Institute for the Study of the Legal Profession;

Professor John Jackson, Professor of Public Law and Head of the School of Law at Queen's University, Belfast;

Eugene Grant QC, a barrister in criminal practice in Northern Ireland;

Dr Bill Lockhart, Director of the Extern Organisation in Northern Ireland, and Director of the Centre for Independent Research and Analysis of Crime;

His Honour John Gower QC, a retired English circuit judge.

1.6   The Secretary of the Review Group was Ian Maye of the Northern Ireland Office, who was assisted at various stages by Guy Banim, Rosemary Carson, Coleen Doak, Ernie Hewitt, Rafia Hussain, Bertha Martin, Linda McGookin, and Bridgeen Mullan. We were also assisted by Dr Debbie Donnelly, Principal Statistician at the Northern Ireland Office. We wish to place on record our gratitude to the secretariat. Without their commitment, organisational skills and drafting ability, together with patience and a sense of humour, we could not have completed our task.

The Approach We Adopted

1.7   We met for the first time on 1 July 1998 and held more than 45 days of plenary meetings. We began by briefing ourselves on the background to the criminal justice system in Northern Ireland and on its development in recent years. We received detailed position papers and briefings on current arrangements and procedures from government departments and the criminal justice agencies. We also took account of recent legislative developments, reviews and publications concerning the various aspects of the system that were within our terms of reference. We refer to many of them at appropriate points in our report.

1.8   We were an unusual group in that we were a mix of civil servants representing the Government and independent members who played a full part in all aspects of the review. As a result, we were not wholly a creature of government, nor were we entirely independent, as was the Independent Policing Commission for Northern Ireland. But we were given the freedom to address the task before us in the way we chose.

1.9   We worked from a broad interpretation of what constitutes the criminal justice system in Northern Ireland, which we believe includes the judiciary and the courts, the criminal justice agencies, the legal profession, victims, witnesses and defendants, and those voluntary and community groups who provide criminal justice services. For our purposes the criminal justice system includes the arrangements and procedures for dealing with crime from investigation through prosecution to adjudication. It also includes providing facilities for carrying out sentences imposed by the courts, and policies and structures concerned with the prevention and reduction of crime and criminality, and the fear of crime.

1.10   We committed ourselves from the outset to full consultation. We believed that it was important to gather and test the views of as wide a range of opinion in Northern Ireland as possible. We also believed that we should consider the issues within our terms of reference from a human rights perspective, a perspective that underpins and runs through the Belfast Agreement itself. As a result we have paid a great deal of attention to international and domestic human rights obligations, and considered all of the issues before us from a human rights perspective.

1.11   The focus of our work has been guided by a desire to propose practical confidence building measures for a fresh political climate. We assumed throughout our work that the Belfast Agreement would continue to be implemented and that the political process would continue, leading to devolution of legislative and executive responsibility for economic and social matters to institutions of government within Northern Ireland. We also took account of the statement in the Belfast Agreement that the Government remained "ready in principle, with the broad support of the political parties, and after consultation, as appropriate, with the Irish Government, in the context of ongoing implementation of the relevant recommendations, to devolve responsibility for policing and justice issues". As a result, and because this was the wish of many of those we consulted, our recommendations are made on the assumption that criminal justice matters will be devolved to the Northern Ireland administration. In some cases, however, we have identified matters that can be taken forward which are not dependent on devolution having taken place.

1.12   We recognise also that we report at one point in time and as part of a wider political process which continues to develop, and will develop further as this report is debated and implemented. The extent to which our proposals should be taken forward in any given scenario is a matter for political judgment, and we express no views on transitional or interim arrangements which may prove necessary as a result. We do believe, however, that great care must be taken in implementing any package of agreed changes to ensure that the quality of justice and the efficiency of the system are maintained and enhanced, during the period of implementation and thereafter. Given the breadth and complexity of issues which we address, it is crucial that sufficient time is taken to consult with the criminal justice agencies and those who work within the system and to plan and conduct any process of change in a measured way.

PUBLIC CONSULTATION

1.13   We published a consultation paper on 27 August 1998. Its purpose was to set people thinking. The paper set out a range of issues which we intended to consider, but made it clear that we would be happy to consider other issues raised with us that fell within our terms of reference. It sought written comments, but also encouraged interested organisations and individuals to meet us to make their views known. We distributed over 5,000 copies of the consultation paper to political parties and individual politicians, the churches, the criminal justice agencies and the judiciary, to solicitors and barristers, and to a wide range of voluntary and community organisations known to have an interest in criminal justice issues.

1.14   In the months which followed we met representatives from the following: all of the political parties who wished to make submissions to us; the criminal justice agencies; the judiciary and magistracy, both professional and lay; the Bar Council and Law Society; the major voluntary organisations with an interest in criminal justice; and a wide range of human rights lobby groups. A list of those we met or from whom we received submissions or position papers is set out at Appendix A to this report. We also visited a number of courthouses in Northern Ireland to see how they operated at first hand and to speak to those who worked in them. We visited Antrim courthouse and we observed the proceedings in Belfast Magistrates' Court and Belfast Youth Court. In addition we visited Brighton Magistrates' Court. We also visited Lisnevin Juvenile Justice Centre and HM Prison Maghaberry. In all we held over 70 meetings with interested groups and organisations. We received over 90 written submissions, all of which were thoughtful and constructive.

1.15   We judged that the formal consultation process was successful in drawing out the views of the political parties, the criminal justice agencies, the legal profession, and the major voluntary organisations and lobby groups in the criminal justice field. We published a progress report in April 1999 to set out what we had done and to give a flavour of the issues raised with us. However, we also wanted to hear the views of those who came from the ground level in statutory, voluntary and community organisations, practitioners and those working at the periphery of, or interface with, the criminal justice system. As a result we held a series of nine seminars across Northern Ireland in May and June 1999 to which over 3,000 individuals, groups and organisations were invited ("Your Time to Talk" seminars). The seminars provided an opportunity for practitioners from different agencies and professions and community groups to work together to discuss the issues which we were considering. Around 300 people attended the seminars, from a wide variety of backgrounds, and contributed a great deal to the debate. We learned much from those seminars, and heard a wide range of views. We had feedback from those who attended that they too found the seminars very useful.

1.16   We reflect many of the views presented during the consultation process, but what we say in this report can only be a distillation of what we heard. The views expressed were both thoughtful and genuinely held, and we listened carefully to what people had to say to us. We benefited greatly from them, and we wish to thank all those who contributed to the debate.

RESEARCH AND STUDY PROGRAMME

1.17   From the very beginning of the process we recognised that we should consider experience in Northern Ireland and in other jurisdictions, and that we should find out the views of the public in Northern Ireland on criminal justice issues. We commissioned a programme of comparative research to review the experiences of other jurisdictions on a range of key issues. In addition we put in place an extensive programme of survey research and focus groups to shed light on the views of the public on matters which have an impact on the community's confidence in the criminal justice system. The output of the research is published along with this report, and we draw upon its findings as we examine specific issues within the report. The research reports and their authors are listed in Appendix B. The views and opinions expressed in those reports are those of the authors and do not necessarily reflect those of this Group. Where in the text of this report we mention research which we commissioned, the associated footnote refers to the author(s) and the number of the research report as listed in Appendix B.

1.18   We decided that we should visit some other jurisdictions to see at first hand how other justice systems work, to find out their strengths and weaknesses and to determine what lessons, if any, could be learned for our work. Over the past year the Group, or small teams representing the Group, visited a number of other jurisdictions, including Belgium, Canada, England and Wales, Germany, the Netherlands, New Zealand, the Republic of Ireland, Scotland, South Africa and the United States. Those visits proved invaluable in teasing out the experience of other jurisdictions in delivering criminal justice, and helped us put flesh on the bones of the material we had gathered in the course of our research programme. They assisted us in assessing whether approaches adopted elsewhere might be applicable in the particular circumstances of Northern Ireland. We should like to express our gratitude to those in all the jurisdictions we visited who so willingly gave of their time to assist us in our work.

THE PAST

1.19   In the course of our consultation process, we heard a range of views about how the criminal justice system had performed over the past 30 years. Some thought that it had served Northern Ireland well, in the face of the considerable challenges posed by the security situation; and we heard some suggestions that, if the system was working, change should not be introduced for the sake of it. Others, however, felt differently and expressed strong views about what they believed to be bias against particular parts of the community and a failure adequately to safeguard human rights. There was, of course, a range of opinions between these positions and there was much discussion about the workings of particular parts of the criminal justice system.

1.20   We heard a number of calls for past events to be investigated by the Review Group. Like the Policing Commission we were not set up as a committee of inquiry with all the legal powers to call for papers and question witnesses. That was not within our terms of reference. We were asked to "bring forward proposals for future criminal justice arrangements…". And in that sense we looked forward to the future, not backwards to the past. But we did listen carefully to genuinely and strongly held views, from differing perspectives, about past events. It was important for us to understand these points of view if we were to develop recommendations for arrangements most likely to inspire the confidence of all parts of the community in the future. We do not express any opinion about the validity of views about past events and wish to stress that where we suggest change, this should not in itself be taken as implying criticism of what has gone before.

1.21   We should like to say something about those who have worked in the criminal justice system over the past years, many of whom we have met in the course of our deliberations. We include in this those acting in a judicial capacity, the police, prosecutors, defence lawyers, those agencies whose role it is to ensure that the sentences of the court are carried out, and administrative staff. We are mindful of the sacrifices that they and their families have made over the past 30 years. We pay tribute to those who have paid with their lives the ultimate price for upholding the rule of law and serving the cause of justice, and to those who have been injured or lost loved ones. We recognise and appreciate the challenges and difficulties faced by those in all parts of the criminal justice system at a time of civil strife and division within the community.

POLICING AND EMERGENCY LEGISLATION

1.22   We heard calls during our consultation process for the Review Group to work closely with the Independent Policing Commission, given the obvious overlap between policing and criminal justice. We heard similar calls in respect of emergency legislation. For many, the experience and perceptions of criminal justice were influenced heavily by views on policing and emergency legislation. Some people found it difficult to understand why reviews of policing, criminal justice and emergency legislation were being conducted separately. Our response was always the same: that we could not rewrite the terms of reference that had been agreed by the parties to the Belfast Agreement. We were, however, conscious of the linkages between these three areas, and that our efforts to develop proposals for a fair, rights-based, and effective criminal justice system which inspired the confidence of the community as a whole could not be divorced from the outcome of those separate reviews.

1.23   Much of our work was done at the same time as that of the Independent Commission on Policing for Northern Ireland, but we were expected to report some months after that Commission. The timing of our respective reports was quite deliberate, in that the participants in the multi-party negotiations recognised that it was difficult to separate policing from other aspects of criminal justice, and that we would need time to reflect upon the recommendations which emerged from the Policing Commission in framing our own report. That is not to say, however, that we worked in isolation from the Policing Commission. On the contrary, it was important for this Review Group and the Policing Commission to be aware, in broad terms, of the issues which the other was considering and to ensure that our respective efforts were best directed. We did not, however, believe it appropriate to share our thinking.

1.24   Legislation against terrorism is the subject of a United Kingdom-wide review announced in October 1997, which led to the publication of the consultation paper *Legislation Against Terrorism*,[1] in December 1998. We took the view that where issues raised with us were properly within the remit of that review we would pass such comments on to those responsible. Our terms of reference constrained us from doing or saying anything more in this report on emergency legislation.

THE STRUCTURE OF THIS REPORT

1.25   In the next chapter of our report we consider the nature and extent of crime and criminality in Northern Ireland. We also consider people's experiences of the criminal justice system in Northern Ireland and set out the findings of the attitudinal and focus group research undertaken on our behalf. We contrast the findings, where appropriate, with other jurisdictions.

1.26   In the remainder of the report we have attempted to follow a common pattern, where appropriate, in setting out chapters. In each we consider: the current arrangements in Northern Ireland; the human rights background; what we heard during the consultation process; the available research on the issue and what we know of international experience and trends; and an evaluation of the options for change together with our recommendations.

1.27   In Chapter 3 we address the human rights and guiding principles which should underpin the operation of the criminal justice system in Northern Ireland. In Chapter 4 we consider the arrangements for the prosecution of offences. In Chapters 5, 6, 7 and 8 we examine issues relating to the criminal courts and, importantly, the way in which members of the judiciary

---

1   *Legislation Against Terrorism: A consultation paper* (1998), Home Office and Northern Ireland Office, CM 4178, London: HMSO.

are appointed. In Chapters 9 and 10 we consider the issues of restorative and reparative justice, and juvenile justice. In Chapter 11 we look at the arrangements for crime prevention and community safety in Northern Ireland. In Chapter 12 we consider the arrangements for adult sentences and for prisons and probation in Northern Ireland. Chapters 13 and 14 concern the arrangements for victims and witnesses and for law reform respectively. Chapters 15 and 16 are about the organisation and structure of the criminal justice system in Northern Ireland, and the arrangements for conducting criminal justice research. Finally, Chapter 17 considers the scope for structured co-operation between criminal justice agencies North and South, and within these islands.

1.28   We were essentially a Review Group looking at criminal justice issues, rather than a Royal Commission looking independently into the legal system in Northern Ireland as a whole. Our remit was wide but, given the time and resources available to us, we focused on those issues specified in our terms of reference and on issues raised with us during the consultation process. Criminal justice is where the expertise of our individual members lies. However, a significant number of our proposals, such as those relating to judicial appointments, the role of an Attorney General in Northern Ireland, and mechanisms for law reform, have implications for civil justice and cannot be resolved by criminal justice experts alone. Our proposals are made from a criminal justice perspective, but we recognise that in some areas a civil justice perspective will need to be taken into account when our recommendations are considered.

1.29   Where possible we have given a broad indication of the possible cost implications of our proposals. We have not, however, been able to cost our proposals with any real degree of precision, and in some instances it may not be possible to attach firm resource estimates until the proposals have been fleshed out in the consultation and implementation processes. Taken together, we believe our proposals offer the opportunity to develop an effective and efficient criminal justice system in Northern Ireland that commands the confidence of the community as a whole, at a relatively modest cost.

1.30   We have covered much ground in our review. Some of our proposals relate to things that are already happening or beginning to happen. Taken together, our recommendations represent a major, but measured, programme of change. We welcome and recognise the need for meaningful and inclusive consultation on our proposals, particularly with those whom they will affect, including those who work in the criminal justice system.

1.31   This is the background against which we did our work. You will find our conclusions and recommendations in the ensuing chapters of this report. We commend them to the British and Irish Governments, to the political parties in Northern Ireland, and to the people of Northern Ireland as a whole.

2 Experience of Crime and Criminal Justice in Northern Ireland

Introduction

2.1 This chapter summarises information on the extent of crime in Northern Ireland both as recorded and as perceived by members of the public. It also summarises information on who are the victims of crime, what contact people have with the criminal justice system, and what people think about the system and its constituent parts. Much of the information comes from existing sources. However, we considered it very important to have as full a picture as possible and we therefore commissioned three surveys of the public's views on the criminal justice system and a study that focused on the views of 24 groups of people selected to be reflective of the community.

Extent of Crime

2.2 Northern Ireland is a relatively low crime jurisdiction. Recent findings from the *1998 Northern Ireland Crime Survey*[1] show that around 23% of households experienced at least one crime during 1997. In comparison for the same year the *British Crime Survey*[2] estimated that this applied to 34% of households in England and Wales. Compared to England and Wales people in Northern Ireland experience a lower incidence of most crimes. For example, in Northern Ireland in 1997 13% of households experienced some form of vehicle-related theft or vandalism and 2.5% of households experienced burglary. The equivalent figures for

---

1   Power, Willis and Amelin, *Fear of Crime and Victimisation in Northern Ireland: Findings from the Northern Ireland Crime Survey* (1999), NIO Research Findings 1/99.

2   Mirrlees-Black, Budd, Partridge and Mayhew, *The 1998 British Crime Survey* (1998), Home Office Statistical Bulletin 21/98.

England and Wales were 22% for vehicle crime and 5.6% for burglary. However, experience of violent crimes, such as muggings, woundings and assaults, was similar in the two jurisdictions: 4.4% in Northern Ireland and 4.7% in England and Wales.

2.3 Northern Ireland is also a low crime area in comparison to most European jurisdictions. The most recent international survey of victims of crime, the *International Crime Victimisation Survey,*[3] showed that of the 11 participating countries, Northern Ireland had the lowest proportion of respondents who were victims of crimes covered by the survey. On average, across all the jurisdictions surveyed which included the USA, Canada and several countries from Western Europe, 24% of people reported that they were victims of crime, compared with 17% in Northern Ireland.

2.4 Within this overall picture, however, there are variations in the experience of different types of offence. For example, the *International Crime Survey* showed that car theft in Northern Ireland was at a higher than average rate (1.9% of car owners in Northern Ireland experienced vehicle theft during the twelve months prior to the survey compared with an average of 1.4% in other jurisdictions), whereas the rate of thefts from cars was below average (3.8% compared with 6.1%). A recent comparison with other European jurisdictions[4] showed Northern Ireland as having one of the highest recorded rates for rape.

2.5 The relative risk of being a victim of crime may also be measured by comparing the number of crimes recorded by the police with the size of the population. The recently published *European Sourcebook of Crime and Criminal Justice Statistics*[5] which has standardised definitions for some types of crime shows that annual crime rates per 100,000 population are lower in Northern Ireland for theft (2,000) and burglary (1,001) than in most European jurisdictions, while rates for violent offences such as homicide (6.8), rape (18.1) and armed robbery (40.7) tend to be higher.

2.6 In April 1998 a new system for counting and recording crimes was introduced in England and Wales and in Northern Ireland. As a result current figures for recorded crime are not directly comparable with those of previous years. The new system focuses more on the effect of crime on victims and counts a greater number of minor offences than previously. For example, behaviour resulting in criminal damage to several vehicles might previously have been recorded as one crime, whereas now the figure would be determined by the number of vehicle owners affected. The changes mean that the recorded crime figures now reflect better the amount of crime which victims suffer and with which the police must deal.

2.7 In 1998/99 there were just over 109,000 crimes recorded under this new system in Northern Ireland. This represents a rate of 6,458 per 100,000 population compared to a rate of 9,785 in

3   Mayhew and Van Dijk, *Criminal Victimisation in Eleven Industrialised Countries: Key findings from the 1996 International Crime Victims Survey* (1997), Onderzoek en beleid. Ministry of Justice, Netherlands.

4   *European Sourcebook of Crime and Criminal Justice Statistics*, Council of Europe publication, 2000.

5   *European Sourcebook of Crime and Criminal Justice Statistics*, Council of Europe publication, 2000.

England and Wales under the same counting rules. The majority of crimes were property offences, which include burglary, theft and criminal damage. These accounted for 72% of all recorded crime. Violent offences, including violence against the person, sexual offences, and robbery accounted for almost 20%, and drug offences for 1.3% of all recorded crime.

Recorded Crime in Northern Ireland 1998/99

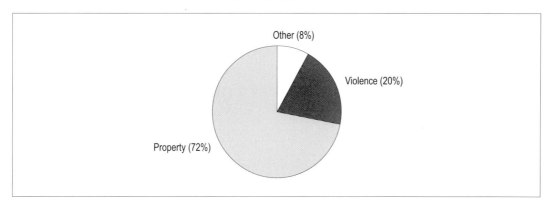

2.8   In order to place 1998/99 in the context of evolving trends in recorded crime, an exercise has been undertaken to produce figures for that year based on the old counting methods. Because of new approaches to the collection of data, the figures are not directly comparable. However, it is noteworthy that the adjusted figures for 1998/99 suggest an increase in recorded crime of around 28% in Northern Ireland when compared with the previous year. Moreover, two important categories of offence, which should not have been affected by the counting rule changes, both showed significant increases in 1998/99: burglary up 13% and sexual offences up 14%. By comparison, the equivalent exercise in England recorded a slight year on year decrease in recorded crime.

2.9   These figures must be interpreted with a degree of caution. In particular, changes in the preparedness of people to report crime, which might be associated with the evolving political and security situation, would affect levels of recorded crime. However, on the basis of available research and anecdotal evidence, we have little doubt that there was a significant increase in recorded crime in Northern Ireland last year. We regard this as important, especially in the light of suggestions made to us during our consultations from sources inside and outside the criminal justice system that the end of civil strife in Northern Ireland might be associated with an increase in ordinary crime. In our view, the figures point up the importance of effective strategies for the reduction of crime and the fear of crime at local and national level (see Chapter 11).

WHERE DOES CRIME OCCUR?

2.10   Levels and patterns of crime vary considerably from area to area and, of course, people are
        most worried about what is happening in their own locality. During our consultations, and
        especially in the seminars, we heard the concerns of people about particular manifestations of
        criminal behaviour in their area, their estate or sometimes even their street.

2.11   The Statistics and Research Branch in the Northern Ireland Office, with the assistance of the
        RUC and working with the Community Safety Centre (see Chapter 11), is developing a model
        for mapping crime in Northern Ireland. Maps 1 and 2 give an indication of the number of
        crimes per thousand of population in each District Council area and within Belfast. (More
        detailed mapping is possible. The figures can be disaggregated into smaller areas and by types
        of crime and work is currently being undertaken to relate them to other variables such as
        employment levels.) Outside Belfast, new and expanding towns tend to have higher crime
        rates than the norm, while places such as Castlereagh and Newtownabbey have lower rates.
        Within Belfast, the areas that experience the highest overall rates of crime tend to be around
        the city centre area where offences such as car theft, shoplifting and assault predominate.

MAP 1 - Recorded Crime Indices for Northern Ireland in 1997
District Council Areas (except Belfast) by Population Density

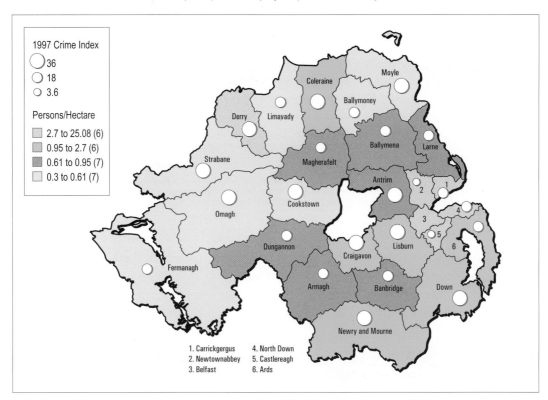

MAP 2 - Recorded Crime Indices for Greater Belfast in 1997
Wards by Population Density

The indices refer to the number of crimes per 1,000 of population

WHO ARE THE VICTIMS OF CRIME?

2.12   The 1998 *Northern Ireland Crime Survey*[6] indicated that people living in the Belfast City
Council area are more likely to be victims of property crime (thefts and burglary) than those
living in other parts of Northern Ireland. Where you live, however, did not seem to affect the
risk of being a victim of a violent crime. The 1998 Survey found that younger people were
more likely to be victims of violent crime than older people (11% of 16-29 year olds
compared to 1% of people 60 years old or over), and men more likely than women (7%
compared to 2.5%). Similar patterns are found in other jurisdictions.[7]

6   Power, Willis and Amelin, *Fear of Crime and Victimisation in Northern Ireland: Findings from the Northern Ireland
Crime Survey* (1999), NIO Research Findings 1/99.

7   Mirrlees-Black, Budd, Partridge and Mayhew, *The 1998 British Crime Survey* (1998), Home Office Statistical Bulletin 21/98.

Views about Crime

2.13   Over the past few years there has been a shift in people's views about the level of crime in their local area, with more people thinking that crime has increased. In the most recent *Northern Ireland Crime Survey* (1998)[8] fewer people thought that the level of crime in their local area had not changed in the previous two years (47% compared to 56% in 1994/95), and more people thought that crime in their local area had increased (41% compared to 30% in 1994/95). There was a greater than average tendency to believe that crime had increased amongst women, people aged between 30 and 59, those living outside Belfast, and Protestant respondents. The *British Crime Survey*[9] indicated that 47% of respondents in England and Wales thought that crime in their local area had increased.

Worry about Crime

2.14   People in Northern Ireland worry about becoming victims of crime,[10] but less so than people in England and Wales.[11] Generally, women worry more than men do and younger people more than older respondents do. Most people feel safe in their own homes, but more women than men, particularly older women, feel unsafe out alone after dark.

2.15   Women and men focus their concerns on different types of crime. Women worry more about becoming victims of physical and sexual attack, whereas men's worries are concerned mainly with car crime. Unsurprisingly, the research shows that fear of crime is greater among those who have been victims.[12]

2.16   Of those who responded to the 1998 *Northern Ireland Crime Survey*,[13] 15% said that they never or hardly ever went out after dark. This group consisted mainly of older people and women. However the reasons given for not going out after dark appear to be more to do with personal preference than specifically about fear of crime. Nevertheless, around 37% of people thought that the quality of their lives was in some way affected by fear of crime, while 6% said that their lives were greatly affected. The tendency to report that their lives have

---

8   Power, Willis and Amelin, *Fear of Crime and Victimisation in Northern Ireland: Findings from the Northern Ireland Crime Survey* (1999), NIO Research Findings 1/99.

9   Mirrlees-Black, Budd, Partridge and Mayhew, *The 1998 British Crime Survey* (1998), Home Office Statistical Bulletin 21/98.

10   Power, Willis and Amelin, *Fear of Crime and Victimisation in Northern Ireland: Findings from the Northern Ireland Crime Survey* (1999), NIO Research Findings 1/99.

11   Mirrlees-Black, Budd, Partridge and Mayhew, *The 1998 British Crime Survey* (1998), Home Office Statistical Bulletin 21/98.

12   Power, Willis and Amelin, *Fear of Crime and Victimisation in Northern Ireland: Findings from the Northern Ireland Crime Survey* (1999), NIO Research Findings 1/99.

13   Power, Willis and Amelin, *Fear of Crime and Victimisation in Northern Ireland: Findings from the Northern Ireland Crime Survey* (1999), NIO Research Findings 1/99.

been affected by crime is greater among women, inhabitants of Belfast, those living in public sector or housing association property (rather than in their own home or rented property), the disabled, and those who have a lower income level.

2.17   There is some evidence that people over estimate the amount of violent crime. They also overestimate the amount of crime "cleared up" by the police (generally taken to mean the amount of crime for which people admit guilt, are prosecuted or are dealt with by the police, for example through caution or warning). People estimate that 53% of all crime is violent, whereas it accounted for 20% of recorded crime in 1998/99. They estimate that 41% of crime is cleared up, whereas the recorded figure for 1998/99 was 29%.[14]

2.18   Respondents were asked about a range of means that could be used to help reduce crime. A small majority, 53%, thought that increased family discipline would help; 51% mentioned neighbourhood/community watch and 48 % more activities for young people. However, only 42% said that they would be willing to become involved in crime prevention initiatives.[15] A study based on group discussion[16] concluded that the preparedness of community members to become involved in crime reduction activities had been influenced by the context of the Troubles. Its authors suggested that the establishment of crime reduction schemes, such as neighbourhood watch, would be difficult to achieve in a context of political violence. In some cases community involvement in crime reduction was perceived as being synonymous with paramilitary involvement, and there was ambivalence as to how welcome the community found this. The authors further suggested that the complexity and sensitivities surrounding community involvement in crime prevention initiatives were compounded by views about the police and the absence of regular policing in some areas.

What Contact do People have with the Criminal Justice System?

2.19   Most people have had no contact with the criminal courts and they feel that they have a poor understanding of the system. However, the majority of people (88%) think that it is important to understand how the courts work.[17] This is an issue we address in Chapter 8.

2.20   Around 33% have had contact with a court at some stage in their lives, although this includes all courts (criminal, civil and family) and contact in any capacity. In any one year about 8% have contact with the courts. Sixty-six per cent say that they do not understand how the courts work. Far fewer people have contact with the criminal courts, 14% at some stage in

---

14   Amelin, Willis Blair and Donnelly, Research Report 1.

15   Amelin, Willis Blair and Donnelly, Research Report 1.

16   Dunn, Morgan and Dawson, Research Report 12.

17   *Community Attitudes Survey Sixth Report*, Central Survey Unit, NISRA Occasional Paper No. 10, 1999.

their lives and, of those, two-thirds have had only one encounter. Contact with the courts is a rare and normally one-off event, with people feeling that they have little knowledge of what the courts do. [18]

2.21   Of those whose most recent contact with a court had been with a criminal court, for 41% this had been in connection with jury service, 23% had been defendants, 14% witnesses, 5% victims, and 10% were there in support of someone else.[19]

2.22   Contact with prisons is also limited. Only 16% of people said that they had ever been inside a prison for any reason at all. In contrast, there is much more familiarity with the police: 32% of people contact the police in any one year and about 10% report a crime to the police at least once a year.

What do People think of the System?

2.23   Despite the lack of direct knowledge of the criminal justice system people generally have a high degree of confidence in the fairness of the system as a whole and in its component parts.[20] Seventy per cent of those surveyed report having confidence in the fairness of the criminal justice system. As to its component parts, 77% of the people surveyed expressed confidence in the fairness of judges and magistrates, 75% juries, 74% the police and 72% lawyers.[21]

2.24   Such views, however, were not held uniformly. There were significant differences between the views of Catholics and Protestants about the fairness of the system overall (61% of Catholics confident in its fairness compared with 77% of Protestants), the fairness of judges and magistrates (69% of Catholics confident in their fairness compared with 82% of Protestants) and the fairness of the police (59% of Catholics confident in their fairness compared with 85% of Protestants). In contrast, confidence in the fairness of juries and lawyers was about the same for both Catholics and Protestants.[22]

2.25   When asked about the sentences given by the courts, most people (around 75%) thought that they were too lenient.[23] Only 1% thought that sentences were too tough, and about 15% thought that sentences were about right. This is similar to the pattern of views expressed in England and Wales.[24] Of the people who thought that crime in Northern Ireland had either

---

18   Amelin, Willis and Donnelly, Research Report 3.

19   Amelin, Willis and Donnelly, Research Report 2.

20   *Community Attitudes Survey Sixth Report*, Central Survey Unit, NISRA Occasional Paper No. 10, 1999.

21   Amelin, Willis and Donnelly, Research Report 2.

22   Amelin, Willis and Donnelly, Research Report 2.

23   Amelin, Willis, Blair and Donnelly, Research Report 1.

increased or decreased almost two-thirds saw these changes as having been affected by the level of sentences offenders received. Indeed, 34% saw sentencing as the most important factor.[25]

2.26   As people get older it is more likely that they think sentences are too lenient, and Protestants are more likely than Catholics to think of sentences as lenient.

2.27   With regard to the treatment of young offenders, 63% thought they were treated too leniently by the courts and 55% too leniently by the police. However, 59% thought that the courts and 42% thought that the police did not have enough ways to deal with young offenders. There was substantial support for the idea that people affected by crime should be involved in decisions about how young people are dealt with by the criminal justice system. Indeed, 75% of people said that they would be willing to attend a meeting to help decide what should happen to a young offender who had stolen something from them.[26] Willingness to undertake this role would be important in a system of justice which involved restitution and restoration by the offender to the victim. Other research suggests that people think a system involving restitution and restoration is more appropriate for young offenders and first time offenders.[27] However, this research also suggests that some people think a system of restoration to be a soft option, a way of avoiding criminals being held to account.

2.28   People were asked how "in touch" they believed parts of the system to be. Overall 66% thought that judges were "out of touch with what ordinary people think", while the figure for resident magistrates was 53%. Opinion on this issue varied and within some groups there was a relatively high proportion of people who did not express an opinion. For example, men, Catholics and those who described themselves as Nationalist or Republican were more inclined to think that judges and resident magistrates were very out of touch.[28] Findings from the *British Crime Survey* also show that most respondents thought that judges and magistrates in England and Wales were out of touch with what ordinary people thought.[29] When reasons for such views in Northern Ireland were explored people felt that judges came from a particular social class and were, therefore, seen as isolated from the community and unable to understand ordinary lives. There was a view that courses and continuous training might remedy the perceived isolation of judges and magistrates. There was also a view that the judiciary, as a group, may benefit from the inclusion of more women on the bench.[30]

---

24   Hough and Roberts, *Attitudes to Punishment: Findings from the British Crime Survey* (1998), Home Office Research Study.

25   Amelin, Willis, Blair and Donnelly, Research Report 1.

26   Amelin, Willis, Blair and Donnelly, Research Report 1.

27   Dunn, Morgan and Dawson, Research Report 12.

28   Amelin, Willis and Donnelly, Research Report 2.

29   Hough and Roberts, *Attitudes to Punishment: Findings from the British Crime Survey* (1998), Home Office Research Study.

30   Dunn, Morgan and Dawson, Research Report 12.

2.29   It is possible that lack of knowledge of and contact with the courts is a factor that affects people's views of judges and magistrates. Also, misconceptions about sentencing practice may be relevant. People who think that sentences are too lenient are also more likely to think that judges and magistrates are "out of touch". This may be of some significance in Northern Ireland given that people have underestimated the proportion of offenders receiving prison sentences for certain types of crime. Respondents estimated that 29% of adult house burglars, 36% of adult muggers, and 61% of male rapists were sent to prison. The actual rate of imprisonment in 1997 was 34% of burglars, 67% of those convicted of robbery, and 90% of those convicted of rape.[31] Research in England and Wales has demonstrated similar relationships between people's perceptions of sentencing practice and their attitudes on leniency.[32]

2.30   Turning to other parts of the criminal justice system, people were fairly evenly divided on whether or not the police were "in touch" or "out of touch". A small majority of Protestant respondents (55%) thought that the police were "in touch" while a small majority of Catholics (52%) thought that the police were "out of touch". Over a quarter of respondents did not express a view about the probation service. Of those who did, there was a fairly even split with 38% of people thinking that the probation service was "in touch" and 35% viewing the service as "out of touch".[33]

Willingness to Participate in the System

2.31   Information on the degree to which people are willing to become involved in the criminal justice system comes from a range of sources. Our commissioned attitudinal surveys and focus group study have been helpful along with existing data from the *Northern Ireland Crime Survey* and the *Community Attitudes Survey*.

2.32   From this research it was apparent that there was little knowledge of how the criminal justice system works and how its component parts link together. The focus group study showed that there was a lack of enthusiasm about becoming involved in the criminal justice system. People's concerns ranged from uncertainty and unease about the process to fear of intimidation or harassment.[34] These are issues dealt with in Chapter 13.

2.33   People were asked about the reporting of crime. Of those who had been victims of crime, 41% said that the crime was reported to the police. People in Northern Ireland most frequently list retribution as the reason for reporting crime (46% of respondents in the 1998

---

31   Amelin, Willis, Blair and Donnelly, Research Report 1.

32   Hough and Roberts, *Attitudes to Punishment: Findings from the British Crime Survey* (1998), Home Office Research Study.

33   Amelin, Willis and Donnelly, Research Report 2.

34   Dunn, Morgan and Dawson, Research Report 12.

Northern Ireland Crime Survey and 43% in the 1996 *International Crime Victimisation Survey*). This is a higher proportion than that found for any of the other countries participating in the 1996 *International Crime Victimisation Survey*.[35] The reasons given for not reporting to the police were mainly because people thought that the crime was too trivial, that the police could not do anything about it, or that it was sorted out privately. The focus group study reported that people could be reluctant to go to the police for help for fear of reprisals and the power and influence of paramilitary groups.[36]

2.34   People's predictions about their willingness to report a crime that they have witnessed are generally much higher than the actual reporting rates of victims.[37] For example, 99% of respondents thought that they would report a burglary if they were the victim - 96% if they were a witness - whereas the proportion of victims who reported their burglary (with loss of property) to the police was 73%.[38] Generally, the nature of the crime determined both the willingness to report the crime and to whom the crime is reported. Social factors such as age, religion and socio-economic group were also shown to be of some significance in people's decision whether or not to report a crime. Overall, the following categories seemed rather less likely to report a crime: younger (16-24) and older (those over 65) people, Catholics, and people in manual occupations.[39]

2.35   Most people would report crimes such as burglary, muggings and thefts to the police, but around 66% would report shoplifting and vandalism to the owner of the property. Although most people (78%) would report a case of child sexual abuse to the police a substantial proportion (27%) would report it to social services, indicating also that some would report it to both authorities.

2.36   There is some evidence that for most types of crime people's willingness to report a crime is not always matched by a preparedness to give a statement to the police and then give evidence in court. This varies according to the nature of the crime, with more people being prepared to follow through from reporting a crime to giving evidence in court in relation to offences such as mugging, child sex abuse and burglary (especially victims of burglary).

2.37   There is evidence that people find appearing in court stressful.[40] Of those who said that they would be willing to give evidence in court, more than 70% said that they would worry about doing so (71% for magistrates' courts and 73% for Crown Court). By far the greatest cause of such concern was fear of intimidation/retaliation (91% for magistrates' courts and 96% for

35   Mayhew and Van Dijk, *Criminal Victimisation in Eleven Industrialised Countries: Key findings from the 1996 International Crime Victims Survey* (1997), Onderzoek en beleid. Ministry of Justice, Netherlands.

36   Dunn, Morgan and Dawson, Research Report 12.

37   Amelin, Willis and Donnelly, Research Report 3.

38   Power, Willis and Amelin, *Fear of Crime and Victimisation in Northern Ireland: Findings from the Northern Ireland Crime Survey* (1999), NIO Research Findings 1/99.

39   Amelin, Willis and Donnelly, Research Report 3.

40   Amelin, Willis and Donnelly, Research Report 3.

Crown Court). Also mentioned were worry about standing up and talking (58% for magistrates' courts and 62% for Crown Court), answering questions (39% for magistrates' courts and 41% for Crown Court), and waiting to be called (35% for magistrates' courts and 37% for Crown Court). In comparison, issues such as taking oaths, Crown symbols and wigs and gowns did not feature prominently. For those who said that they would not be prepared to give evidence the pattern of responses was similar.[41] There was a suggestion in the focus groups [42] that the formality of the system and the language used might put people off and make them nervous and some felt the role of the police in guarding entrances to courts to be off-putting.

2.38   Most people (83%) thought that the courts should offer familiarisation visits to witnesses. Ninety-four per cent who thought that facilities should be made available to ensure that witnesses knew what to expect and have a comfortable place to wait.[42] The focus group study confirmed that people would be helped by the use of clear language, and explanations of the process and what to expect in court.

41   Amelin, Willis and Donnelly, Research Report 3.

42   Amelin, Willis and Donnelly, Research Report 2.

Rights
and
Principles

3 Human Rights and Guiding Principles

"Recognition of the inherent dignity and of the equal and inalienable rights of all members of the human family is the foundation of freedom, justice and peace in the world."

Universal Declaration of Human Rights

Introduction

3.1   In this chapter we explain our view that human rights are central to the criminal justice system. We then examine the principles and values that should underpin the criminal justice system in Northern Ireland and, in the light of these, consider statements of what the criminal justice system should be about and the standards to which it should adhere. We also look at some issues of common applicability across the organisations that make up the criminal justice system and at the role of lawyers, with particular reference to the defence.

3.2   Our starting point is the aims which participants to the talks agreed for the criminal justice system.[1] It was the clear intention of those involved in the talks process, and one which we fully endorse, that these aims should be achieved within an overarching framework of human rights. The fundamental principle is that people have basic rights by virtue of their common humanity. The principles of freedom and justice which spring from this are central to debate on crime and justice. In protecting the lives and property of citizens, or depriving offenders of their liberty, the state upholds the rights of victims or potential victims of crime, just as it has to ensure that it respects the basic rights of offenders.

3.3   Since the *Universal Declaration of Human Rights* (December 1948) there has been a growing recognition of the universality of certain fundamental rights and freedoms. In the

---

1   See Chapter 1 and *The Belfast Agreement,* Policing and Justice, paragraph 4, page 22.

justice sphere a number of important principles are well established. These include the right to liberty and security of person, the right to a fair trial and the prohibition of torture or inhuman or degrading treatment.

3.4   In the research report which we commissioned, two themes that underlie international human rights standards in the field of criminal justice are identified: the protection of the individual against ill-treatment at the hands of law enforcement authorities; and the protection of individuals against arbitrary arrest, detention, trial or punishment.[2] The report goes on to identify a third emerging theme which puts increasing stress on the need for individuals to be protected against threats to their bodily integrity, liberty and dignity from wherever these may emanate. As an example of this, the European Court of Human Rights has indicated that there may be a violation of the right to life where the authorities knew or ought to have known of a real risk to the life of a particular person from the criminal acts of another and they failed to take reasonable precautions against it.[3] The protection owed by states does not just extend to preserving life. The requirement to have sufficient procedures in place to ensure law and order, to properly investigate crimes and bring offenders to justice may also be derived from human rights principles. In another recent case the Court accepted that states were under an obligation to take measures, such as the provision of effective deterrence, to ensure that individuals within their jurisdiction were not subjected to torture or inhuman or degrading treatment or punishment, including that administered by private individuals.[4]

International Instruments

3.5   Basic human rights principles are set out in a number of instruments, notably the *Universal Declaration of Human Rights, the European Convention on Human Rights* (ECHR)[5] and the *1966 International Covenant on Civil and Political Rights* (ICCPR). Building on these are a range of declarations, principles, codes of conduct and guidelines which elaborate on specific areas. For example the *Guidelines on the Role of Prosecutors* were adopted by the Eighth UN Congress on the Prevention of Crime and Treatment of Offenders in 1990.[6]

3.6   The minimum international standards of human rights have guided us throughout our deliberations and we cannot stress too strongly their applicability to all parts of the criminal justice system in Northern Ireland. They do not and cannot provide a template answering all of the questions which we have been addressing. International standards tend to set out the

---

2   Livingstone and Doak, Research Report 14.

3   See Chapter 13 on Victims and Witnesses, *Osman v United Kingdom* 28 October 1998.

4   *A v UK* (1998), Crim LR 892-3.

5   Properly titled the *Council of Europe Convention for the Protection of Human Rights and Fundamental Freedoms*.

6   Livingstone and Doak, Research Report 14.

end to be achieved and the broad framework; they cannot prescribe the detail. This is inevitable given their application to a wide variety of legal systems with very different traditions. It follows that we should view these standards very much as a foundation on which to build.

3.7 The international human rights instruments fall into three categories in terms of their status before domestic courts. First, there are those which have been explicitly incorporated into domestic law by Parliament and which are, or will be, enforceable. Thus as a result of incorporation of the *European Convention on Human Rights* (ECHR) by the Human Rights Act 1998:

- So far as it is possible to do so, all legislation must be read and given effect by the courts in a way that is compatible with the Convention. Subordinate legislation and Acts of the Northern Ireland Assembly (which is governed by the Northern Ireland Act 1998) will be set aside by the courts if incompatible.

- It will be unlawful for any public authority to act in a way that is incompatible with a Convention right, and individuals will be able to challenge acts and decisions by public authorities on grounds of incompatibility.

3.8 The human rights principles set out in the ECHR bear directly on criminal justice and we welcome the fact that preparations for incorporation are being made, for example through the proofing of legislation and training within agencies. Other instruments have been incorporated into domestic law, for example parts of the *UN Convention on the Prevention of Torture.*

3.9 The second category of international instrument comes in the form of binding treaties, which have not been incorporated. *The International Covenant on Civil and Political Rights* (ICCPR) and the *UN Convention on the Rights of the Child* (CRC) fall into this category. While such instruments are not part of domestic law, the UN and other international bodies work to promote compliance. For example, the First Optional Protocol to the ICCPR established a Human Rights Committee whilst Special Rapporteurs and Special Representatives have been appointed by the Secretary-General of the United Nations to report on a variety of topics. These include Special Rapporteurs on the Independence of Judges and Lawyers, the Rights of Women and Children's Rights. Furthermore there has been a trend amongst common law jurisdictions for judicial decisions to take such international norms into account. They are said to have "persuasive authority" before domestic courts. A good example was provided by the landmark ruling on aboriginal land claims in Australia's Supreme Court. In this ruling Justice Brennan stated:

> "The common law does not necessarily conform with international law, but international law is a legitimate and important influence on the development of the common law, especially when international law declares the existence of universal human rights."[7]

---

7   *Mabo v State of Queensland [No 2]* (1992), 175 CLR 1 at 42.

3.10   By their nature, the third category of non-binding instruments, such as the *Guidelines on the Role of Prosecutors,* are not directly applicable before a court of law. They are intended to provide guides to good practice in the areas which they address and are therefore relevant and important as benchmarks for the Northern Ireland system.

3.11   International human rights instruments need to be understood as living texts. As with other bodies of law they require interpretation in the light of different situations and there can be dispute about their practical application, particularly where there is a tension between two principles. For example, Article 8 of the ECHR recognises the need to strike a balance between the right of privacy and the possible need to invade that privacy for the prevention of disorder or crime. Throughout the report, and in making our recommendations, we take full account of, and draw extensively on, the principles enunciated in all three categories of instrument.

Human Rights in the Belfast Agreement

3.12   The Belfast Agreement addressed human rights against the background of Northern Ireland's recent history. It recognised the importance of respect for civil rights and the religious liberties of everyone in the community. The Northern Ireland Human Rights Commission, established on 1 March 1999, has an important role to play in this sphere as the first independent, statutory human rights commission of its type in Western Europe. It is tasked to:

   ▪ keep under review the adequacy and effectiveness in Northern Ireland of law and practice relating to the protection of human rights;

   ▪ advise of legislative or other measures which ought to be taken to protect human rights;

   ▪ advise whether Bills before the Northern Ireland Assembly are compatible with human rights;

   ▪ bring, and assist, proceedings relating to human rights; and

   ▪ to promote understanding and awareness of the importance of human rights.[8]

3.13   The Northern Ireland Act 1998, which established the Northern Ireland Human Rights Commission, defines human rights as including Convention rights, with the result that the remit of the Northern Ireland Human Rights Commission extends to human rights additional to those in the ECHR. The Agreement also allows for a Bill of Rights supplementary to those in the ECHR, to reflect the particular circumstances of Northern Ireland. The Northern Ireland Human Rights Commission has been asked by the Secretary of State to consult and

---

8   Northern Ireland Act 1998, section 69.

provide advice on the scope for defining such rights. The remit of the Commission is such that it will inevitably impact upon the criminal justice system, a state of affairs which we welcome since it means that human rights standards, and their development in the light of changing circumstances, will constantly be on the agenda.

Views Expressed During the Consultation Process

3.14   During our consultation process we gathered views on which principles should guide the criminal justice system and what can be done to ensure that principles espoused are upheld. As a starting point we set out in our consultation document the draft set of guiding principles and values which was produced by the cross-cutting review of the criminal justice system in Northern Ireland, which took place in 1997/98.[9] These principles and values are reproduced below.

GUIDING PRINCIPLES: A DRAFT

The criminal justice system exists to uphold the rule of law. The criminal justice system is concerned with crime in all its elements and the process which brings offenders to account, but constitutes only a part of society's response to crime. The guiding principles of the publicly funded elements of the system are:

- to deliver a fair system of justice to the community;

- to ensure the prompt and just treatment of those suspected, accused or convicted of crime;

- to bring offenders to account;

- where prosecutions ensue, to ensure a fair trial before an independent and impartial tribunal within a reasonable time, and to convict the guilty and to acquit otherwise; and to maintain a proper appellate system;

- to work to prevent individuals from offending and sentence those proven guilty in a just and proportionate manner, while seeking to reduce the risk of further offending;

- to be responsive to the community's concerns, and to encourage community involvement where appropriate;

- to work, in conjunction with the community, to reduce crime, minimise the fear of crime and enhance community safety;

- to have regard to the proper concerns of victims of crime;

- to ensure witnesses and jurors can perform their roles free from harassment or intimidation;

- to act in all instances to enhance the effectiveness, efficiency and economy of the system; and

- to encourage the use of the civil justice system as a remedy in appropriate cases.

---

9   The cross cutting review, instituted as part of the Government's Comprehensive Spending Review, examined the workings, effectiveness and value for money of the criminal justice system as a whole covering services that were the responsibility of the Secretary of State for Northern Ireland, the Lord Chancellor and the Attorney General.

VALUES: A PRELIMINARY DRAFT

The common values to which the publicly funded elements within the criminal justice system adhere are:

- maintenance of the rule of law;

- protection of individual rights and freedoms under the law;

- fairness to all, regardless of gender, ethnic origin, religion, political opinion, age, disability or sexual orientation;

- maintenance of a criminal justice process that is as open, simple, transparent, inclusive, and accessible, as possible;

- respect for the independence of decision making of the police, the prosecuting authorities and the judiciary in relation to operational matters, decisions on whether to prosecute, and judicial functions respectively;

- assurance of public accountability for the performance of the system without compromising that essential independence;

- recognition of the proper independence of action of the various parts of the criminal justice system, including the judiciary;

- partnership between the criminal justice system, the community, and other external bodies; and

- behaviour that promotes public confidence in the criminal justice system.

3.15   There was a variety of responses to the draft principles and values from people we met with and those who attended our consultation seminars. There was widespread support for a statement of the principles or aims of the system. Some approved of the guiding principles and values generally but made specific suggestions for amendments. It was pointed out that noting "proper" concerns of victims of crime implied that some of the concerns were "improper" and it was felt that the rights of victims needed greater emphasis. Some people also wanted a recognition of restorative or reparative principles within the criminal justice system. There was concern that there was an over-emphasis on independence at the expense of accountability and it was suggested that "respect for independence of decision making" sounded like an instruction to the public rather than a value to be upheld by the system. We have been very conscious of such views when addressing issues of independence and accountability in relation to the judicial and prosecution systems in particular.

3.16   Some of those we heard from were unhappy with the form in which the draft guiding principles and values appeared. There was a view that splitting the principles and values was confusing and that they were not presented in an accessible, easily understood way. Particularly during consultation seminars, we found that the principles and values as drafted did not clearly communicate what the criminal justice system was about. Several commented that a shorter clearer statement would be preferable. There was some criticism that the statements were vague, resulting in different people making different interpretations. For example endorsing public accountability left questions about what is meant by accountability,

accountability to whom and how. It was pointed out that acting to enhance effectiveness, efficiency and economy was something that any organisation ought to do, and therefore that stating it as a principle for the criminal justice system seemed unnecessary.

3.17   In our discussions with people about the principles which should be upheld by the criminal justice system some general themes emerged. Here we set out some of the things people understood these themes to mean and what they wanted done as a result:

■ **Fairness**
All should be equal before the law. Being fair and seen to be fair is vital in order to gain people's confidence in the criminal justice system. In part this means treating all those who come into contact with the system equitably. There was a suggestion that the court system was unfair and alienated one side of the community, having "no room for Irishness".

■ **Justice**
A just system would result in the guilty being convicted and the innocent being acquitted. The need for proportionality, with punishment that fits the crime, was raised. Philosophies of justice could be described as retributive, reparative or restorative.[10] For some, freedom from fear of crime was an important aspect of justice which entailed sufficient protection of the public. One view expressed was that justice should mean that those convicted of an offence "lose their rights" but others argued that prisoners had rights.

■ **Respect for Victim**s
There was a feeling that victims "are not high enough on the agenda". It was suggested that victims were ignored and not given a voice in the adversarial system. Victims should not have to prove their case. Many recognised the sensitivities surrounding this area, with the right of the accused to be presumed innocent unless and until proved guilty.[11]

■ **Accountability, Transparency and Accessibility**
The demand that "the system should serve us" was a desire for accountability. One view was that the judiciary lacked respect for ordinary people and a recurrent theme was the need for criminal justice to be open to public view. There was also an emphasis on the need for better communication for a variety of reasons, including the need to counter views such as "the guilty walk free from court." At one consultation seminar there was a call for those in charge of the justice system to get out and explain to the community, rather than "sit in ivory towers". It was variously suggested that accountability required publication of reports, inspection and a good complaints system that "really works".

■ **Independence and Impartiality**
There was a general consensus that judicial and quasi-judicial decision making should not be open to improper outside influence. This raises difficult issues with regard to the need

---

10   See Chapter 9 for a discussion of these concepts.

11   See Chapter 13 for a discussion of issues relating to victims.

to be able to hold people to account for their decisions and the desire for transparency.[12] The question then becomes how to define "improper outside influence". One view was that prisoner releases were governed by political expediency demonstrating too much political control over the criminal justice system.

■ **Prevention**

The maxim "prevention is better than cure" was frequently mentioned with the desire for more emphasis on the causes of crime and effective remedies.[13] It was pointed out that high rates of recidivism or re-offending demonstrated a failure in the system. One suggestion was that success should be measured according to how few people had gone through the system. Many felt that money spent on custody would be better spent on schemes diverting people from crime.

■ **Efficiency**

Efficiency of the system could be defined in terms of cost or the amount of time spent on a case. The maxim "justice delayed is justice denied" sums up the need for justice to be dispensed speedily".[14] Whilst the criminal justice system could be measured in terms of value for money and economy with resources, an alternative was to assess how effective the system was at changing behaviour and rehabilitating offenders.

3.18   These examples are not summaries of our views on these key areas but illustrate a range of opinions that we heard. During the consultation seminars the debate over these principles was not about whether or not they were important to the criminal justice system but what they actually meant in practice. It was noted that concepts such as independence and accountability might be in conflict. There was widespread recognition that there were inevitable tensions in the aims of the system, for example the differing approaches that might be associated with punishing the offender, protecting the community and rehabilitation.

3.19   International human rights principles were widely commented upon in debate over the practical application of abstract principles. Indeed we found a very high degree of awareness of various international instruments and conventions in submissions and during our meetings with groups and at seminars. There were consistent demands that Northern Ireland should use agreed international standards as a benchmark. International principles were seen as allowing for comparisons across jurisdictions and as of particular benefit when they were associated with mechanisms to encourage or enforce their application, thus ensuring that they were more than mere words on paper.

---

12   See Chapter 6 on the judiciary for a discussion of judicial independence, Chapter 4 on the prosecution, and Chapter 15 on the structure and organisation of the criminal justice system.

13   See Chapter 11 on community safety.

14   See Chapter 15 on organisation and structure for more discussion of delay.

3.20   The need for appropriate evaluation was also emphasised. It was argued that a network of indicators should be developed so that data could be published against which the success, or otherwise, of the system could be judged.[15]

3.21   In our consultation document we asked whether principles and values should be enshrined in legislation. Some argued that such a step would be useful, enabling the principles to be used as an aid to judicial interpretation of legislation. One organisation commented "… there is little value in principles being set out for rhetorical effect, what is required is the embodiment of appropriate principles in legislation that confers rights and imposes obligations".

3.22   There are precedents for setting out principles and aims in legislation. For example, in England and Wales the Crime and Disorder Act 1998 established the principal aim of the youth justice system as the prevention of offending by children and young people.[16] We found this approach in other jurisdictions. The Canadian Corrections and Conditional Release Act 1992 outlines the purpose of the Canadian federal correctional system and goes on to set out principles such as the paramountcy of protection of society and that correctional decisions should be made in a forthright and fair manner.[17] Similarly the New Zealand Children, Young Persons and their Families Act 1989 has a list of aims and principles for dealing with young offenders. For example it states that decisions should be made and implemented within a time frame appropriate to the young person's sense of time.

3.23   There was a counter-argument against putting principles into legislation. It was felt that the incorporation of the *European Convention on Human Rights* into domestic law would be a means of ensuring that human rights were protected effectively and of providing appropriate and accessible means of enforcement. It was, therefore, argued that it was unnecessary for an additional list of principles, which might be seen as contrasting with the European Convention, to appear in legislation. There was a danger of causing confusion and of encouraging unproductive litigation if there were too many sources of entrenched rights and principles.

Evaluation and Recommendations

3.24   The criminal justice system exists to uphold the rule of law. The publicly funded elements include the courts and judiciary, the prosecution service, legal aid, the police, probation and prisons. In addition there is the legal profession and a wide range of voluntary groups and agencies working to tackle the effects of crime or reduce criminality.

---

15   See also Chapter 16 on research.

16   Crime and Disorder Act 1998, section 37.

17   Corrections and Conditional Release Act 1992 Part 1, 3-4.

3.25   Respect for human rights and dignity should be the core value of the criminal justice system in all its aspects. There needs to be constant effort to ensure that there is widespread understanding of what this means. The major exercise underway to prepare for the incorporation of the *European Convention on Human Rights* is valuable in this respect. This has included events run by the Judicial Studies Board and a conference organised by the Northern Ireland Office attended by over 200 representatives of key agencies in the criminal justice field, statutory and non-statutory. **We recommend that human rights issues should become a permanent and integral part of training programmes for all those working in criminal justice agencies, the legal professions and the relevant parts of the voluntary sector.**

3.26   During our consultation process and in visits to other jurisdictions we heard a strong case for a shared set of guiding principles or aims for the criminal justice system as a whole. Their publication would serve an important role in allowing the public to judge the system against agreed standards. It is also a mechanism by which those working in criminal justice, in a variety of different services and agencies, can relate to the overall aims towards which they are working and through which those services and agencies can operate in a coherent, co-operative fashion.

3.27   We carefully considered the arguments for including the basic principles of the criminal justice system in legislation. While we strongly endorse the view that the principles and aims expressed should be followed and realised, we do not think that this is best achieved through incorporating them in legislation. Nor do we believe that such legislation would add significant value. Instead we suggest reliance on the human rights framework, which is rapidly increasing in importance and influence, together with enhanced systems of openness and accountability, a theme running through this report.

3.28   While we generally endorse the guiding principles and values identified in our consultation paper, we do not think that such lists provide the necessary clear direction for the criminal justice system. Nor do they communicate to the public in a succinct fashion what the criminal justice system is about. Rather we believe that a statement of aims for the criminal justice system as a whole should be clear, concise, understandable, and in a form which allows the development of measurable indicators. In this context, **we endorse the Criminal Justice Board**[18] **aims for 1999/2000 as a good model for the criminal justice system-wide set of aims:**

---

18   The Criminal Justice Board is an inter-agency strategic body consisting of the directors and chief officers of the main statutory agencies involved in delivering criminal justice.

Aim A

To dispense justice fairly and efficiently and to promote confidence in the criminal justice system

(i)   Provide fair and just criminal processes and outcomes.

(ii)   Improve service delivery by enhancing levels of effectiveness, efficiency and co-operation within the criminal justice system.

(iii) Make the criminal justice system as open, inclusive and accessible as possible and enhance andpromote public confidence in the administration of justice.

Aim B

To contribute to the reduction of crime and the fear of crime

(i)   Work co-operatively to help reduce crime.

(ii)   Reduce numbers of persons re-offending and frequency of re-offending for persistent offenders.

(iii) Reduce levels of fear of crime.

3.29   This set of aims encapsulates those identified by the talks participants (paragraph 1.2 above) and is consistent with the guiding principles and values identified in our consultation document. Such broad aims should stand the test of time and indeed should not be the subject of frequent alteration if progress towards them is to be measured over a meaningful period. However, it is important that the criminal justice system is dynamic and able to adapt to changing circumstances and public opinion. **We recommend that the aims of the criminal justice system be published, together with a criminal justice plan outlining measures to be taken in support of them and appropriate performance indicators.** The plan could cover a three year timeframe but be subject to annual review. It would be the product of consultation between the criminal justice agencies and should take account of views from the community, which might be secured through such mechanisms as the Community Safety and Policing Partnerships (Chapter 11), relevant Assembly committees and elected representatives. **An annual report on progress in implementing the plan should also be published.**

3.30   It is not our wish to see system-wide principles and plans replacing or interfering with the mission statements, ethos and strategic and business plans of individual agencies, all of which we regard as important in themselves. However, it is clear to us that in areas such as tackling delay and acting against particular types of crime, more can be achieved through a co-ordinated approach than if elements of the criminal justice system act in isolation from each other. It follows that the development of the criminal justice plan should be timed in such a way that the planning mechanisms of the individual agencies can take account of it. Particular attention would have to be paid to its relationship with arrangements for developing policing plans, which are also likely to involve an extensive consultative process. Policing is an integral part of the criminal justice system for these purposes.

EQUITY MONITORING

3.31   A core value and objective of the criminal justice system is that it should have the confidence of the community it serves. Another is that it should treat people fairly and equitably regardless of their background. It is in this context that we consider the role of equity monitoring, both in terms of employment in the system and of the impact of the criminal justice process on different sections of the community. We note that section 75 of the Northern Ireland Act 1998 places a statutory duty on public authorities to have due regard to the need to promote equality of opportunity:

(i)   between persons of different religious belief, political opinion, racial group, age, marital status or sexual orientation;

(ii)   between men and women generally;

(iii)   between persons with disability and persons without; and

(iv)   between persons with dependants and persons without.

3.32   From an employment perspective, all criminal justice agencies (but not the judiciary)[19] are subject to the provisions of the Fair Employment Act 1989, which requires them to monitor the religious make-up of their work force and the religion of applicants for jobs and send details to the Equality Commission annually.[20] The Equality Commission publishes a report summarising the returns.

3.33   We regard such monitoring activity as especially important in the criminal justice context for a number of reasons. At one level, commitment to equality of opportunity must be part of the ethos of criminal justice agencies as employers; and from a merit perspective, it is important to ensure that candidates are being attracted from all sections of the community, including those identified in section 75 of the Northern Ireland Act 1998. However, securing a workforce that is as reflective as possible of the community as a whole should also help enhance confidence in the criminal justice system. From another perspective, monitoring applications for posts in the criminal justice system will provide a useful indicator of whether all sections of the community are sufficiently confident in the system to work in it.

3.34   We have had access to figures on the religious background and gender of employees in various of the component parts of the criminal justice system. Overall, Catholics are under-represented in the workforce to a significant extent, although there are large variations between the agencies. For example, while at 1 January 1999 the percentage of Catholic prison officer/governor grades was 6.7%, Catholics accounted for 32.9% of the staff of the Department of the Director of Public Prosecutions and 36.2% of those in the Compensation

---

19   We look at equity monitoring in relation to the judiciary in Chapter 6.

20   The Northern Ireland Act 1998 transferred the functions of the Fair Employment Commission to the Equality Commission.

Agency.[21] From the perspective of gender, women are generally well represented in the "non-operational" parts of the criminal justice system, although we understand that this does not apply to the higher managerial positions.

3.35   The attainment of a workforce that is, at all levels, and in its constituent agencies, broadly reflective of the community in Northern Ireland, by religious background, gender and other categories identified in section 75 of the Northern Ireland Act 1998, is an objective for the criminal justice system which we strongly endorse. It will take time to get there and we do not recommend compromising the merit principle in order to achieve this objective. However, **we recommend that, whatever machinery is devised for administering criminal justice matters after devolution, it should have as a primary task the development of a concerted and proactive strategy for securing a "reflective" workforce in all parts of the system.** The creation of a single Department of Justice (Chapter 15) would be conducive to such an approach. Effective equity monitoring of the workforce and of job applicants will of course be central to the strategy.

3.36   We turn now to the issue of monitoring with a view to recording any potential differential treatment of people who pass through the criminal justice process or are affected by it. The Secretary of State for Northern Ireland has power under Article 56 of the Criminal Justice (Northern Ireland) Order 1996 to publish information to help people in the criminal justice system avoid discrimination on any improper ground. However, data is not yet collected in a way that would allow such monitoring across the system. We believe that this is an important area in the light of the overall values, aims and objectives of the criminal justice system. During our consultation process it was suggested to us variously that Catholics were likely to receive less favourable treatment than Protestants and that the less well off were likely to be treated unfairly in comparison to the affluent. Focus group research which we commissioned identified within the Nationalist community a lack of faith in the criminal justice system as a consequence of the long held beliefs about what they felt to be discrimination, lack of accountability and bias in favour of the Unionist population.[22] The research also noted that an important element in discussion of class was its perceived influence on how people were treated within the criminal justice system. Some women described the experience of being in court as being in an unsympathetic environment.

3.37   We acknowledge that collecting data on the impact of the criminal justice system and process on different categories of people is a major exercise, especially in relation to community background. Given the information systems that are currently in place, it will not be possible for comprehensive information to be collated for some time. In certain cases there may be practical difficulties or human rights objections to the collection of information; for example it would not be appropriate for an individual to be asked his or her community background,

21   It should be borne in mind that in each of these categories a percentage are not classified as either Catholic or Protestant – that figure is as high as 15.1% amongst prison officers and governors.

22   Dunn, Morgan and Dawson, Research Report 12.

although there are proxies for making such classifications. Also this must not interfere with, or have the appearance of interfering with, the essential independence of the judiciary, the prosecution service or other parts of the system where independence of decision making is of importance. However this form of monitoring is necessary if equality and equity issues are to be addressed. Not only does it assist the system in assessing whether it is operating equitably, but, where differential treatment is identified, it enables agencies to research the reasons for such difference of treatment and, where appropriate, take action accordingly.

3.38   We recognise the difficulties and the scale of the task. However, **we recommend that the Criminal Justice Board and its research sub-committee be tasked with developing and implementing a strategy for equity monitoring the criminal justice system, as it affects categories of people, in particular by community background, gender, ethnic origin, sexual orientation and disability, whilst ensuring that this is done in a way that does not compromise judicial independence.** Different approaches may be needed for these categories. Information technology will be central to this, in particular to enable cases to be tracked through the system.

3.39   The question arises of publication of the results of equity monitoring of the criminal justice system, whether in relation to employment or more generally. We heard a variety of opinions on this, especially so far as information on community background was concerned. Some argued for transparency on the basis that such information should be made available provided that it was not disaggregated to such an extent that the background of individuals might be identifiable. The key argument against was that the risk that information could be used selectively to create a distorted picture and, therefore, that it could be damaging to confidence.

3.40   It is our view that it is generally desirable that data from equity monitoring, in all its forms, should be gathered and made publicly available, subject to the need to ensure that a particular individual's community background is not revealed or cannot be deduced.[23] Transparency in the public availability of information of this sort is a confidence booster in itself. Regular publication of data is necessary to demonstrate that problems have been identified and action is being taken, and on occasion to dispel inaccurate and damaging assumptions. Certainly part of the information strategy has to be to avoid misinterpretation of statistics, but we do not believe that the manipulation of statistics carries anything like the risk that is associated with ignorance of the true position.

3.41   We note that a report has been produced on gender in the Northern Ireland criminal justice system under Article 56 of the Criminal Justice (Northern Ireland) Order 1996.[24] A range of

---

23   Handling and disclosure of monitoring information is governed by the Fair Employment (Monitoring) Regulations (Northern Ireland) 1989 and the Fair Employment (Monitoring) (Amendment) Regulations (Northern Ireland) 1991 which make it an offence, subject to narrowly defined exceptions, to disclose, without an individual's consent, information provided for monitoring purposes from which an individual's community background would be revealed or deduced.

24   *Gender in the Northern Ireland Criminal Justice system.* (1997) Northern Ireland Office: HMSO.

publications has been produced in England and Wales under similar powers.[25] **We recommend that the outcome of equity monitoring should be published on a regular basis, to the maximum extent possible without risking the identification of the community background of individuals.**

ETHICS, CONFLICT OF INTEREST AND MEMBERSHIP OF EXCLUSIVE OR SECRET OATH BOUND ORGANISATIONS

3.42   During the course of our consultations, while it did not feature as one of the strongest issues, concerns were raised with us about membership of various organisations, including the Loyal Orders, the Ancient Order of Hibernians and Freemasons. Some were worried that if judges or prosecutors in particular belonged to such groups, there could at the very least be a perception that it might affect decision making in individual cases. Others felt that it was inappropriate for an employee of any criminal justice agency to be associated with such organisations. There was, however, another view that precautions to deal with possible conflict of interest in individual cases should be sufficient to address the problem, without putting restrictions on or monitoring membership of the organisations.

3.43   This is a difficult area. We are conscious of the recommendation of the Independent Commission on Policing that all police officers should be obliged to register their associations; and we are aware of the view of the Northern Ireland Affairs Committee on the matter.[26] We do not think that other criminal justice agencies are entirely analogous to the police, with their very direct relationship with the public, but we have an unease about those employed in the criminal justice system being members of organisations such as those described at paragraph 3.42 above. However, we are conscious that freedom of expression (Article 10 ECHR) and freedom of association (Article 11 ECHR) are fundamental human rights. We also reflect that the *Basic Principles on the Role of Lawyers* note the right of lawyers to freedom of expression and association and that the *Basic Principles on the Independence of the Judiciary* state:

> "In accordance with the Universal Declaration of Human Rights, members of the judiciary are like other citizens entitled to freedom of expression, belief, association and

---

25   Publications under Section 95 of the Criminal Justice Act 1991 include: *Race and the Criminal Justice System 1992, 1994, 1995, 1997 and 1998*; *Gender and the Criminal Justice System, 1992*; *Costs of the Criminal Justice System, 1992*; *Briefing Paper for the Ethnic Minorities Advisory Committee at the Judicial Studies Board 1997*; *Does the Criminal Justice System treat men and women differently?* Research findings No 10 1994; *The Sentencing of Women*, No 58 1997.

26   The Northern Ireland Affairs Committee, in its July 1998 Report on *"the Composition, Recruitment and Training of the RUC"* concluded that membership of organisations such as Loyal Orders, the Ancient Order of Hibernians or other exclusive groups who generally prohibit membership on religious grounds was incompatible with membership of public organisations, especially the RUC.

assembly, provided, however, that in exercising such rights judges shall always conduct themselves in such a manner as to preserve the dignity of their office and the independence and impartiality of the judiciary."[27]

3.44   We take into account that we are looking ahead to a period when we hope that membership of these organisations, and expressions of cultural identity associated with them, will not arouse the concerns that might have been the case in the past. We do not recommend that membership of exclusive or oath bound organisations should be regarded as incompatible with employment in or holding office within those parts of the criminal justice system that are the concern of our review. We have thought about the idea of registers of membership. Such a device would enable information to be made public about the extent of membership within various agencies, and could be used in order to allocate work so as to avoid any possible conflict of interest. Care would have to be taken to ensure the confidentiality of any register. Registers of membership of specified exclusive organisations could be considered further by the Government, but we are not satisfied that the benefits of such an approach would be sufficient to justify the exercise, with all the practical and definitional issues that would be involved.

3.45   Particular issues arise over the membership of these organisations on the part of people exercising judicial or quasi-judicial functions. The issue of perception of bias contrary to Article 6(1) of the ECHR when judges are Freemasons arises in *Salaman v UK*, a case currently before the European Court of Human Rights.[28] We believe that these matters are best dealt with through self-regulation in the context of existing policies on ensuring the actuality and appearance of impartiality and addressing conflict of interest. **As part of our strategy for developing transparency and accountability mechanisms, we recommend the publication of statements of ethics for each of the criminal justice agencies covering all those employed or holding office in the criminal justice system.** In some cases such a statement might be incorporated in other published documents.

3.46   When conflict of interest might be at issue in decision making, with the judiciary and prosecution for example, a statement of ethics would reflect existing practice by making clear that it was the responsibility of the individual concerned to ensure that this did not arise, where necessary by declining to take particular cases. A statement of ethics would of course include other matters appropriate to the circumstances of the particular agency or group. The recent decision of the Court of Appeal in *Locabail (UK) Ltd v Bayfield Properties and another and related appeals*[29] gives important guidance on conflict of interest in a judicial context.

---

27   *Basic Principles on the Independence of the Judiciary,* Article 8.

28   *Salaman v United Kingdom* (App. No. 43505/98).

29   The Times, 19 November 1999.

3.47 We can of course envisage circumstances where membership of a particular organisation would be incompatible with employment in the criminal justice system. **If an organisation were, by its policy or its actions, clearly committed to acting contrary to the law or the interests of the criminal justice system, then it would be for the criminal justice agencies to make clear that their employees were not permitted to belong to such an organisation.**

DEFENCE SAFEGUARDS AND THE LEGAL PROFESSION

3.48 Many of the values and human rights norms that underpin the criminal justice system are concerned with safeguards for defendants and the protection of their rights. For such rights and safeguards to be deployed effectively, defendants need to have access to a competent legal profession.

3.49 Article 5 of the *European Convention on Human Rights* refers specifically to the right of persons arrested to be informed promptly in a language which is understood of the reasons for their arrest and of any charge against them, the right to be brought promptly before a judge and the right to be entitled to trial within a reasonable period of time or to release pending trial. Article 6 refers to the right of everyone charged with a criminal offence to be entitled to a fair and public hearing within a reasonable time by an independent and impartial tribunal established by law. The Article goes on to guarantee everyone charged with a criminal offence to be presumed innocent until proved guilty according to law. It lays down a number of "minimum rights", which include the right to be informed promptly in language which is understood of the nature and cause of the accusation, the right to have adequate time and facilities for the preparation of a defence, the right to defend oneself in person or through legal assistance of one's own choosing, the right to free legal assistance if one has not sufficient means to pay for it, the right to examine and cross-examine witnesses and the right to have the free assistance of an interpreter in court.

3.50 We also endorse a number of specific rights which are provided in the *International Covenant on Civil and Political Rights* (ICCPR) and other international instruments, including the right of all persons deprived of their liberty to be treated with humanity and with the respect for the inherent dignity of the human person,[30] to have access to doctors,[31] to be visited by and to correspond with members of their family and to be given adequate opportunity to communicate with the outside world.[32]

---

30 Article 10(1) of the ICCPR.

31 Human Rights Committee General Comment 20, paragraph 11.

32 Principle 19 of the *Body of Principles for the Protection of all Persons under Any Form of Detention or Imprisonment* (Body of Principles).

3.51   We want to emphasise that one of the most important defence safeguards is for persons to have access to a lawyer throughout the criminal process. The assistance of a lawyer is a primary means of ensuring the protection of the human rights of people accused of criminal offences.[33] Lawyers play a vital role in ensuring a defendant's right to a fair trial as they have a duty to put their client's case before the court, whatever the nature of the crime with which he or she is charged. It is vital that there is public understanding of this role and that there is no confusion between the client and the lawyer. Later in this chapter we outline a strategy for making the public better informed about the criminal justice system. This must include education on the role of the defence lawyer.

3.52   Lawyers also play an important role in protecting their clients in custody. We endorse principle 1 of the *United Nations Basic Principles on the Role of Lawyers* that all persons are entitled to call upon the assistance of a lawyer of their choice to protect and establish their rights and to defend them in all stages of criminal proceedings. We also endorse principle 5 of the Basic Principles that every person who is arrested, detained or charged must be informed of their right to have the assistance of legal counsel.

3.53   Principle 16 of the Basic Principles also provides that governments shall ensure that lawyers are able to perform all of their professional functions without intimidation, hindrance, harassment or improper interference. In his report on his mission to the United Kingdom in 1998, the Special Rapporteur on the Independence of Judges and Lawyers, Mr Param Cumaraswamy, expressed particular concern about the fact that lawyers in Northern Ireland who had represented those accused of terrorist offences had been subjected to intimidation, harassment or improper interference and had been identified with their clients or with their clients' causes. The Special Rapporteur welcomed the Northern Ireland Law Society's decision to establish a complaints procedure to enable solicitors to complain to the Society about any agency within either the criminal or civil justice system which had allegedly impugned or threatened their independence, professionalism and integrity. **We agree with the Special Rapporteur on the Independence of Judges and Lawyers that government has a responsibility to provide the machinery for an effective and independent investigation of all threats made against lawyers and note the role of the Police Ombudsman if such allegations relate to the actions of police officers. Further, we endorse his recommendation that training seminars should be organised to enable police officers and members of other criminal justice agencies to appreciate the important role that defence lawyers play in the administration of justice and the nature of their relationship with their clients.**

3.54   It is crucial to the health of the criminal justice system that there should be effective legal professions. We note this passage from the 1970 report of the Committee on the Supreme Court of Judicature of Northern Ireland:

---

33   See Amnesty International, *Fair Trials Manual* (1998), page 103.

"The administration of justice and the maintenance of the rule of law depend on the quality and strength of the legal profession more than any other single factor. The best laws and the best procedures must fail to produce the best results if those who practise the law are less learned and competent or less willing and able to bear their professional responsibilities than they should be."[34]

3.55   Under current arrangements, unique to Northern Ireland, the Department of Further and Higher Education, Training and Employment funds a number of bursaries for those who have completed undergraduate law degrees and who wish to continue their study to become barristers or solicitors. The situation was last reviewed by the Committee on Professional Legal Education in Northern Ireland,[35] which reported in 1985 under the chairmanship of Professor P M Bromley. The report noted that "there is a strong public interest in securing the most suitable training of members of the legal profession which should extend to providing financial support for those in training... we believe it necessary to ensure that students, qualified to do so, should have the opportunity to enter the profession irrespective of their financial position".[36] This is of particular importance in ensuring that the legal profession as a career is accessible to people from all parts of the community, based on merit. We heard that the bursary scheme had been effective in helping maintain the quality of the legal profession in Northern Ireland and ensuring that entry to it was not determined by wealth. **We recommend the continuation of bursaries to ensure that entry to the legal profession is open to people of talent from all sections of the community, regardless of means.**

3.56   The *UN Basic Principles on the Role of Lawyers* state the need for government, professional associations of lawyers and educational institutions to ensure that lawyers have appropriate education and training and are made aware of the ideals and ethical duties of the lawyer and human rights and fundamental freedoms recognised by national and international law.[37] We have discussed above the impact of the Human Rights Act 1998 and some of the preparations that have been made by the Government and judiciary. **We recommend that lawyers should receive appropriate training in human rights principles before starting to practise.**

3.57   As we were finalising our report two barristers sought leave for a judicial review of the form of the declaration required on appointment as a Queen's Counsel. We do not address this issue in our report, and note that the matter is now being considered by the court. Nor do we address other aspects of the internal structures and organisation of the legal profession, which we believe go beyond our remit.

---

34   *Report of the Committee on the Supreme Court of Judicature of Northern Ireland* (1970).

35   *Report of the Committee on Professional Legal Education in Northern Ireland* (1985).

36   *Report of the Committee on Professional Legal Education in Northern Ireland* (1985) paragraph 7.7.

37   *Basic Principles on the Role of Lawyers,* Article 9.

LEGAL AID

3.58   Accessibility to justice regardless of ability to pay is an important principle and if the right to legal assistance is to be effective, it must be provided free to those who do not have sufficient means to pay for it. We note that the Government published a consultation paper on arrangements for the administration of legal aid in Northern Ireland on 14 June 1999.[38] Consultation finished on 29 October 1999 and the Government is considering its response. As noted in the consultation document, the provision of publicly funded criminal legal services is a necessary function of a free and democratic society governed under the rule of law and is a means of ensuring fairness and confidence in the system. Article 3(3)(c) of the *European Convention on Human Rights* recognises the right of free legal aid provided it is in the interests of justice for it to be granted.

3.59   One of the principles of legal aid is that suspects and defendants can state their case on an equal footing with the prosecution. The European Court has developed this principle to require that the defence have equal access to material information and expert assistance before and at the trial. In particular it has been established that the defendant must be able to secure the attendance and examination of experts on his or her behalf under the same conditions as apply to experts against him or her.[39] This means that legal aid provision must enable the defence to draw upon experts of equal standing to those called for the prosecution.

3.60   It is important that there should be adequate availability of expert witnesses, such as forensic psychiatrists or fingerprint experts, both for the prosecution and the defence. We have not heard evidence of any difficulties in the availability of such witnesses in Northern Ireland. However, **we suggest that there would be some benefit in the compilation by the Law Society of a list of experts in particular fields that could be drawn on by the defence.**

THE RIGHT OF SILENCE

3.61   A number of individuals and groups raised with us particular aspects of current criminal procedure and practice which in their view did not protect the interests of defendants sufficiently. Some of these, such as the arrangements for disclosure of evidence to the defence and the length of time defendants are having to wait in custody before trial, are dealt with later in our report.[40] One area that we deal with here is the law on the right of silence. Under the Criminal Evidence (NI) Order 1988 a court or jury is able to draw an adverse inference from a suspect's failure to answer police questions in certain circumstances and

---

38   *Public Benefit and the Public Purse: Legal Aid Reform in Northern Ireland*, a consultation paper issued by the Northern Ireland Court Service, 1999: HMSO, Chapter 12.

39   *Bonisch v Austria* (1985) Series A No 92.

40   See Chapter 15 on the organisation and structure of the criminal justice system.

from a failure to testify at trial.[41] A number of groups have raised doubts about the legislation on human rights grounds. There was a more specific concern over the impact of the cautions given by police officers about the consequences of remaining silent upon vulnerable suspects such as children and people with a learning disability.

3.62   Although the European Convention does not explicitly guarantee the right of silence, Article 14(3)(g) of the ICCPR states that in the determination of any criminal charge against a person, everyone shall be entitled to a guarantee not to be compelled to testify against himself or herself or to confess guilt. This fundamental right has been considered to be inherent in Article 6 of the European Convention even though it is not expressly set out there. In *John Murray v United Kingdom*, the European Court of Human Rights stated that the right to remain silent under police questioning and the privilege against self-incrimination were generally recognised international standards which lay at the heart of the notion of a fair procedure under Article 6.[42] The Court held that the right of silence was not absolute and that a court could draw inferences from an accused's failure to provide an explanation for facts that clearly called for an explanation. However, certain safeguards had to be in place before this could be done and the Court put particular emphasis on the weight of the evidence against the accused, the discretion vested in the judge as to whether to draw inferences or not and the availability of reasons for drawing them. The Court held on the facts that there was no violation of Article 6 in this case by reason of the application of the law on permitting the drawing of inferences from silence. The Court, however, found that the drawing of inferences from an accused's silence in the first 48 hours of detention during police questioning, when the accused was denied access to legal advice, was a violation of Article 6. We note that there are other applications currently before the Court from Northern Ireland and other parts of the United Kingdom raising this same issue, and that it will be necessary for the Government to monitor the outcome of these cases and, if necessary, take remedial action.

3.63   A recent survey of the use made of the 1988 Order suggests that although the courts have considerable latitude to draw whatever inferences appear proper from an accused's silence, the Order has been used much more often to strengthen an already strong prosecution case than to fill any large evidential gaps.[43] The Government has taken administrative steps to prevent the drawing of inferences from silence when a suspect is questioned in the police station while denied access to legal advice. It has also prepared the legislation necessary to amend the 1988 Order to this effect and is preparing for the consultation process required to amend the Code of Practice governing police questioning issued under the Police and Criminal Evidence (NI) Order 1989 (PACE). However, given the concerns raised with us,

---

41   Articles 3-6 of the Criminal Evidence (Northern Ireland) Order 1988.

42   [1996] 22 EHRR 29.

43   Jackson, Wolfe and Quinn, *Legislating Against Silence: The Northern Ireland Experience* (2000) forthcoming.

and in particular worries about the lack of understanding which vulnerable people can have of the cautions which are issued to them, **we recommend research into the impact of PACE at the stage of police questioning.**

3.64   In the interests of a healthy criminal justice system which enjoys the support of the whole community it is essential that the rights of both defendants and victims are upheld. We deal with issues relating to victims in greater detail in Chapter 13.

PUBLIC UNDERSTANDING AND ACCOUNTABILITY

3.65   A very clear message from our consultation process was the need for more effort to be made on the part of those working within the criminal justice system to explain their work to those outside. Securing a clear understanding on the part of the community about the way in which criminal justice operates and is structured is an essential component of a strategy of enhancing public confidence in the system and is an important contribution to transparency and accountability. Throughout our consultation process and in the research we commissioned we found that a lack of knowledge of the system proved a barrier to the necessary public confidence in and interaction with the system. We hope that our consultation process and this report will help in this respect by improving awareness of key aspects of the system.

3.66   We believe that each criminal justice agency has a responsibility to explain its activities to the public in an accessible manner. In principle, accountability must lie not just to government,[44] but to the public and individuals affected by the criminal justice system as well. A variety of creative means, such as the internet and schools programmes, can be used, taking account of the target audience in order for information to be widely disseminated. Government has an overarching responsibility for promoting the dissemination of information about criminal justice and its operation. This would be a function of any newly created Department of Justice.

3.67   **We recommend a public information and education strategy for the criminal justice system. This might include the following features, some of which are already in place:**

- **The production and distribution of guides to various aspects of criminal justice, targeting specific groups such as witnesses, victims, children, minority groups and defendants.**

- **The prominent display of mission statements for each criminal justice agency.**

- **The publication of statements of principles showing how the system as a whole will address specific issues, such as the treatment of victims, racial discrimination or cross-agency working.**

- **The publication by all agencies of codes of practice in accessible language.**

---

44   See Chapter 17 for a discussion of accountability through political structures, complaints and inspection.

- The publication by all agencies of annual reports, which include objectives, indicators and an account of performance.

- The publication of statistical and research material in accessible form.

- Consideration of innovative methods for increasing public understanding such as open days at courts for schools, colleges and the public,[45] and the creation of videos explaining aspects of the criminal justice system.

- The inclusion of a criminal justice module in the school civics curriculum.

3.68   In relation to this last point, the teaching pack *Law in Our Lives*,[46] supported by Queen's University, the Law Society and the Bar Council, has been distributed to all schools in Northern Ireland. However, criminal justice does not have a place in the curriculum. We note the report of the Citizenship Taskforce in England, which recommended that 5% of curriculum time should be devoted to education for citizenship.[47] In Northern Ireland a pilot project has been established by the University of Ulster (with the support of the Northern Ireland Council for the Curriculum, Examinations and Assessment, the Citizenship Foundation and Nuffield) to develop this area of the curriculum. We understand that, as part of the current review of the Northern Ireland curriculum, the Northern Ireland Council for the Curriculum, Examinations and Assessment plan to issue proposals in April 2000 for consultation on specific provisions for education in democratic citizenship. **The need for awareness of criminal justice issues should be considered as part of the current review of the Northern Ireland curriculum.**

3.69   We believe that mechanisms of the sort outlined above will enhance the accountability of the criminal justice system to the public. Also, the publication of relevant data, including codes of practice, statements of principles, standards and performance indicators, will help provide benchmarks against which the success of the system can be measured and against which its component parts can be inspected. Recommendations on inspection arrangements are made in Chapter 15.

3.70   Another important aspect of accountability is the existence of satisfactory complaints mechanisms. We deal with this in ensuing chapters relating to specific agencies. However, we wish here to make the general point that **all parts of the criminal justice system should be covered by complaints mechanisms that are well publicised, easily accessible and understood, administered with due sensitivity and expedition and which, where appropriate, have an independent element. The workings of the complaints mechanisms should receive coverage in annual reports and, in those parts of the system subject to inspection, be inspected.**

---

45   See Chapter 8 on the courts.

46   *Law in Our Lives* (1993), Northern Ireland Curriculum Council.

47   *Final Report of the Advisory Group on Citizenship*, QCA 22 September 1998.

The Prosecution

4 The Prosecution

Introduction

4.1 Our terms of reference invite us to address "the arrangements for the organisation and supervision of the prosecution process, and for safeguarding its independence".

4.2 In this chapter we consider whether in Northern Ireland the police should continue to prosecute the majority of cases heard in the magistrates' courts, with the Director of Public Prosecutions being responsible for the more serious cases at that level and for all prosecutions in the Crown Court, or whether an independent prosecuting authority should be responsible for all criminal prosecutions. We look at the point in a case prior to a decision to prosecute when an independent prosecutor could become involved and the nature of any such involvement, for example whether it should be supervisory or advisory in relation to the police. The relationship between the investigative and prosecution processes is also examined.

4.3 We examine the nature of prosecutorial discretion and the grounds on which it might be exercised, including the extent to which a prosecutor might have a role in diverting offenders away from the court process. We also address accountability, including the relationship between the prosecutor and the executive arm of government, and how it can be reconciled with the concept of independence.

4.4 Prosecution is pivotal in the criminal justice system. It is the gateway through which cases are brought to court following investigation by the police or other investigative agency. We concur with the view of the Director of Public Prosecutions that the independence of the prosecution function stands at the heart of the rule of law. In a common law environment the prosecutor stands between the state and the individual and it is critical therefore that the prosecuting authority is independent from the executive. That theme will run through our recommendations in this area.

4.5 Public confidence demands that decisions on whether to prosecute are taken in a fair, objective and consistent manner, taking account of the likelihood of securing a conviction and any public interest considerations. Just as people need to be confident that cases are prosecuted firmly, fairly and competently, in a wholly impartial manner, so it is also important that decisions to prosecute are not taken lightly. The very act of bringing a prosecution against an individual, even for a relatively minor offence and followed by discontinuance or acquittal, is liable to cause distress and damage to reputation.

Human Rights Background

4.6 The arrangements for prosecuting offences differ widely in jurisdictions around the world, reflecting differing legal systems and cultures. There is therefore no one template to draw from. Research carried out for the Review[1] notes that while few international human rights instruments deal specifically with the prosecution, the prosecutorial authorities have an important role to play in relation to a range of human rights issues at the pre-trial stages. These include ensuring that detained suspects are promptly brought before a judicial authority and that the trial takes place within a reasonable time,[2] together with provisions in support of the requirement for a fair trial with due regard to the rights of the defence.[3] Also, as an independent body having early contact with the police investigative process, the prosecuting authority can have a role in assessing the adequacy of investigations into criminal violations of human rights and in identifying and acting upon any misconduct by the investigators.[4]

4.7 We did pay particular attention to the *UN Guidelines on the Role of Prosecutors* and the *Standards and Statement of Essential Duties and Rights of Prosecutors* adopted by the International Association of Prosecutors (IAP). While not a human rights instrument as such, the IAP Standards are clearly heavily influenced by the UN Guidelines and were produced with full regard to the human rights context.

4.8 The UN Guidelines and IAP Standards recognise the importance of the prosecutor being in a position objectively to assess the evidence before deciding whether to prosecute. They require that prosecutions should not be initiated, or should be discontinued, if the evidence shows charges to be unfounded, while the IAP Standards (Article 4.2d) provide that a case should be proceeded with only when it is well founded upon evidence reasonably believed to be reliable and admissible. Where there is a reasonable belief that evidence is obtained unlawfully, especially if a suspect's human rights are violated, it is not to be deployed and the prosecutor is enjoined to take steps to ensure that those responsible are brought to justice (UN Guideline 16 and IAP Standards 4.3(g) and 4.3(h)). Prosecutors are expected to give due attention to the prosecution of crimes committed by public officials, especially where violations of human rights are involved (UN Guideline 15).

1   Livingstone and Doak, Research Report 14, section 4.2.

2   ECHR Article 5(3), ICCPR Article 9(3), BOP Principle 37, CRC Article 37(d).

3   ECHR Article 6(1) and 6(3), ICCPR Articles 14(1) and 14(3).

4   ECHR Articles 2(2), 3, ICCPR Articles 6(1) and 7, UNDHR Articles 3 and 5, UNCAT Article 15.

4.9   The Guidelines and Standards give an indication of the contribution to be made by the prosecutor in support of the fair trial and minimum defendants' rights requirements of the European Convention and the International Covenant on Civil and Political Rights. UN Guideline 13b provides that prosecutors should "take account of the position of the suspect and the victim and pay attention to all relevant circumstances, irrespective of whether they are to the advantage or disadvantage of the suspect". The IAP Standards talk of seeking "to ensure that all necessary and reasonable enquiries are made and, in accordance with the law or the requirements of a fair trial, the result disclosed, whether that points towards the guilt or innocence of the suspect" (IAP Standard 3.1e).

4.10   The Guidelines and Standards encourage prosecutors to consider action to divert appropriate cases away from the formal criminal justice system, especially where juveniles are involved. But they stress that this should be addressed in accordance with national law, with full respect for the rights of suspects and victims. Prosecutors are required in all that they do to consider and take account of the views and concerns of victims and to keep them informed (UN Guidelines 17 and 18, IAP Standard 4.3(i)), in accordance with the *UN Declaration of Basic Principles of Justice for Victims of Crime and Abuse of Power*.

4.11   Impartiality, fairness and objectivity are themes that recur frequently in these instruments and which can only be safeguarded if prosecutors are enabled to act with independence. UN Guideline 4 places a duty on states to ensure that the prosecution can act "without intimidation, hindrance, harassment, improper interference or unjustified exposure to civil, penal or other liability". They and the IAP Standards also recognise the importance of conditions of service, remuneration and tenure being organised in a way that reinforces independence. The Standards say that prosecutors should "remain unaffected by individual or sectional interests and public or media pressures and shall have regard only to the public interest". They refer to prosecutorial discretion being exercised independently and free from political interference.

4.12   In stressing the importance of independence, the Standards recognise that non-prosecutorial authorities may have the right to issue general or specific instructions to prosecutors – in that event such instructions should be transparent, lawful and within established guidelines drawn up to safeguard the prosecutor's independence. Similar strictures apply where there is provision for prosecutors to be instructed by another authority on whether to proceed with or discontinue individual cases, although it is stressed that this should be exceptional.

4.13   In highlighting the importance of independence, that does not imply isolation or detachment from the rest of society or other criminal justice agencies. UN Guideline 19 and IAP Standard 5 view co-operation with the police, the courts, the legal profession and other government agencies as necessary in order to ensure fairness and effectiveness.

4.14   We have taken the principles enunciated in these human rights instruments and the IAP's Statement of Professional Standards into full account when addressing prosecution arrangements in Northern Ireland.

The Structure and Organisation of the Prosecution Process

BACKGROUND TO CURRENT ARRANGEMENTS

4.15   The Office of Director of Public Prosecutions was created by the Prosecution of Offences (Northern Ireland) Order 1972. This Order, made at the outset of Direct Rule, has its origins in the Hunt Report,[5] which called into question the practice of the police undertaking almost all prosecutions (98%) in the magistrates' courts (the police also conducted the bulk of committal proceedings for cases going on to the higher courts). It did so on the ground that the impartiality of the police might be questioned if they were to investigate, decide who was to be prosecuted and then conduct cases in court; there was also concern about the impression given of an over-close relationship between the police and the courts. In the light of this, Hunt called for consideration to be given to the establishment of an independent prosecution service along the lines of the Scottish procurators fiscal.

4.16   Following Hunt, a Working Party on Public Prosecutions was established under the chairmanship of the (then) Hon J C MacDermott (subsequently to become Lord Justice MacDermott) to examine whether the Scottish system should be adopted for summary prosecutions in Northern Ireland. The MacDermott Report,[6] while focusing on summary trials, noted the use of part-time Crown Solicitors, appointed by the Attorney General, in Assize and Quarter Session cases. It adopted the view of the Royal Commission on the Police in 1962 that "it is undesirable that police officers appear as prosecutors except for minor cases. In particular we deplore the regular employment of the same police officers as advocates for the prosecution. Anything which tends to suggest to the public mind the suspicion of alliance between the police and the court cannot but be prejudicial".[7] The Working Party was also influenced by the burden which court work placed on the police, diverting them from their mainstream duties, but made clear their view that the police had carried out this role with complete integrity and competence.

---

5   *Report of the Advisory Committee on Police in Northern Ireland* (1969), Belfast: HMSO Cmnd 535.

6   *Report of the Working Party on Public Prosecutions* (1971), Belfast: HMSO, Cmnd 554.

7   Cmnd 1728, paragraph 381.

4.17   In the event the MacDermott Working Party did not recommend adoption of the Scottish system (on the ground that grafting it onto a completely different system of criminal jurisprudence would not work) and came to the view that it would be a retrograde step if "trifling" cases could not be processed through the courts expeditiously by the police. However, it did reach the conclusion that, as a matter of general principle, prosecutions should be conducted by public prosecutors, independent of the investigating process and of political influence. It recommended the establishment of a Department of Public Prosecutions, staffed with full-time lawyers that would be responsible for prosecutions brought in all courts, other than minor summary cases.

THE PROSECUTION OF OFFENCES (NORTHERN IRELAND) ORDER 1972

4.18   The Prosecution of Offences Order gives the Director of Public Prosecutions an overview of all prosecutions in Northern Ireland. The Director has a role in ensuring that all prosecutions are carried out properly and he can take over prosecutions being conducted by any other individual or agency. Article 5(1)(c) provides that the Director shall, where he thinks proper, initiate and undertake on behalf of the Crown proceedings for indictable offences (tried in the Crown Court) and for any summary offence or class of summary offence that he considers should be dealt with by him. Article 6(3) of the Order places a corresponding duty on the Chief Constable to inform the Director of indictable offences and any other offences specified by the Director.

4.19   Article 6(3) places a duty on the Chief Constable to respond to a request from the Director for information necessary for the discharge of his functions under the Order and in particular information on "any matter which may appear to the Director to require investigation on the ground that it may involve an offence against the law of Northern Ireland... ". This could be interpreted as giving the DPP the opportunity to ensure that a full and proper investigation has taken place. However, he has emphasised to us that he and his staff have no locus in supervising or participating in police investigations. In practice Article 6(3) is formally invoked on the rare occasions when the facts of an alleged crime are reported directly to the DPP; but it also underpins the routine requests for further information or enquiries frequently made of the police by the Director when considering whether to prosecute. The Order also makes provision for the appointment of the Director and his staff and for the relationship between the Director and the Attorney General, matters which we will address later.

4.20   The Police (Northern Ireland) Act 1998 provides that where, as a result of investigations of a complaint against the police, the Police Ombudsman believes that a criminal offence may have been committed, he or she is required to send the papers to the Director. It also enables the Director to seek further information from the Ombudsman to assist in deciding whether there should be a prosecution.

WHICH CASES ARE PROSECUTED BY THE DPP AND WHICH BY THE RUC?

4.21   Other than indictable only offences (serious offences such as murder, manslaughter, rape and robbery), which must be referred to him, it is for the Director to determine which type of case his Department will take on. The offences which the police are required to refer to the Director for decision on whether to initiate prosecution, and subsequently to prosecute in court, are listed in Appendix 5D to the RUC Manual. In addition to indictable only offences, those requiring to be referred to the DPP are selected for a variety of reasons including: seriousness; complexity both of substantive law and of evidential issues; political, racial or sectarian sensitivity; the fact that the offences are against children; in some cases the sexual nature of the offences; the fact that the accused is a police officer etc. The DPP keeps the list of cases to be referred to him under review and in recent years has added to it indecent assaults, offences of gross indecency between men and "stalking" offences.

4.22   It remains the case that, while the DPP does prosecute the more serious cases in the magistrates' courts as well as virtually all cases in the Crown Court, the large majority of prosecutions are undertaken by police officers. In 1997 there were 1,128 prosecutions carried out by the DPP in the Crown Court, 7,262 by the DPP in magistrates' courts and 27,209 by the RUC in the magistrates' courts. It is noteworthy that some 20,233 RUC prosecutions were for motoring offences of which 11,093 would be classified as minor (failure to wear a seat belt, excess speed, failure to produce documents etc). Overall, 76% of cases were prosecuted by the police including 79% of those in the magistrates' courts.

4.23   In addition to most road traffic offences, police prosecutions would typically include burglary, theft, assault, some disorder offences, criminal damage, and some offences of indecency. As already pointed out, the decision on whether to prosecute in such cases can have major implications for the parties involved and its significance should not be down-played simply because the offending behaviour is not as serious as in those cases where the DPP is involved.

CHARGE OR SUMMONS?

4.24   Defendants may be proceeded against by way of charge or summons. This is the case whether they are prosecuted by the police or by the DPP, and whether they are tried summarily in a magistrates' court or on indictment in the Crown Court. A suspect may be charged at any point in the investigation, often but not invariably following arrest by the police. At this stage he or she is subject to a "holding charge" which may be revised once the investigation is complete and at the point where it is decided to prosecute.

4.25   A summons to appear in court, normally deployed in less serious cases, is sought after the investigation is complete and it has been decided to proceed. The summons is presented by the police to a justice of the peace (or a clerk of petty sessions) who exercises judicial discretion in determining whether to sign or refuse it. It is then usually served at the defendant's usual or last known home address a reasonable time before the court hearing. Service of summonses by post has been piloted and consideration is being given to extending this practice more widely.

PROSECUTIONS CONDUCTED BY THE POLICE

4.26   The opening of Central Process Offices (CPOs) in Armagh and Londonderry in January 2000 completes a process of change through which all police prosecutions throughout Northern Ireland are the responsibility of such offices. Under these arrangements, the investigating officer passes the completed file through his or her line manager to the sub-divisional commander (SDC). The SDC, or an officer not below the rank of inspector to whom he or she has delegated the responsibility, then has the options of taking no further action, authorising a caution or recommending prosecution to the CPO. At the CPO, police inspectors dedicated to the task, using specific criteria, determine whether to prosecute and the terms of a summons (or whether to amend the holding charge). The prosecution is then conducted by an inspector from the CPO.

4.27   If the inspector does not believe that a case for prosecution is made, he or she must refer it to the chief inspector in command of the CPO or his deputy. Only they can direct "no prosecution". It is open to them to consult with the DPP's Department. The criteria used by the CPO in determining whether to prosecute are set out in a Force Order and mirror the evidential and public interest tests used by the DPP. However, in the course of discussions with the police we did gain the impression that the application of such criteria by police officers might not always be as rigorous as would be the case if carried out by trained lawyers within the Department of the DPP. The accountability arrangements for the RUC, while extensive, do not focus on their role as prosecutors and publicly available information about this part of their work is limited.

4.28   Prior to the introduction of CPOs, police prosecutions were carried out by local sub-divisional process offices. Under these arrangements an investigating officer would submit a prosecution file, through his line manager, to the sub-divisional commander or a designated officer not below the rank of inspector who assessed the evidence and directed prosecution or no prosecution. In the event of a prosecution, the case was presented by the local duty inspector.

4.29   Replacing these local arrangements with the CPO structure should promote objectivity and consistency in decision making. It should also encourage the development within the police of a body of expertise in this area, while providing some degree of structural separation of the prosecutorial and investigative processes. However, it is too soon to evaluate the impact of this change. At the time of writing it was estimated that around 25 to 30 police officers of inspector or chief inspector rank, seven sergeants and 80 to 90 administrative support staff would be employed in the CPOs, once they were fully operational throughout Northern Ireland.

PROSECUTIONS CONDUCTED BY THE DIRECTOR OF PUBLIC PROSECUTIONS

4.30   In addition to the Director and his deputy, the Department of the DPP consists of 41 lawyers and 114 support staff. The DPP's staff work under the supervision of a Senior Assistant Director and six Assistant Directors, respectively responsible for the Belfast/Eastern circuit, the Northern/Southern circuit, Belfast Crown Court (which includes scheduled offences), special and complex cases, fraud cases and High Court matters including appeals and judicial review. The Department's offices are located primarily in Belfast, although staff from the Northern/Southern circuit work out of Coleraine and Omagh, each with a complement of eleven staff.

4.31   Decisions as to prosecution may be taken by any of the Director's legally qualified staff. However, there are internal instructions requiring that files of a particular nature, or involving particular offences, be referred upwards for decision, some to the Director or Deputy Director. There are restrictions on the decision making capacity of some members of the professional staff, normally as a result of their grade or because they are not fully trained.

4.32   The DPP adopts a two-step test in determining whether to prosecute. The first requirement is that the evidence which can be adduced in court is sufficient to provide a reasonable prospect of conviction, i.e. that a jury (or other tribunal), properly directed in accordance with the law, might reasonably be expected to find proved beyond reasonable doubt that the accused committed the offence in question. The second requirement is that it is in the public interest to prosecute. The Director starts from a presumption that the public interest requires prosecution where there has been a breach of the criminal law, especially when the offence is of a serious nature. However, there are instances when this might not be the case, for example where the defendant is ill or elderly, the offence is technical or is about to be repealed, the offence is stale, or where prosecution would involve disproportionate expense.

4.33   The nature of the decision on prosecution is significant. The DPP is more than a reviewer of a decision to prosecute already taken by the police and formally takes the decision to prosecute or "directs" on cases referred to him. This results in a proactive involvement by the DPP. It is why, when the police charge, it is accepted as a "holding charge" pending direction by the DPP. Other than in the simplest of cases, the police do not purport to charge the accused with all the offences for which he or she might be prosecuted, leaving it to the DPP to determine the exact nature and extent of the charges.

4.34   Where holding charges are preferred in serious cases, the early involvement of a DPP lawyer through a screening process provides an important safeguard to ensure that there is sufficient evidence to warrant the charge and to seek a remand; this happens within one day and before the first court appearance in Belfast, while in other courts for resource reasons it may happen up to a week later. If it is judged that there is insufficient evidence to support the charge then the DPP directs that the charge be withdrawn at the first court appearance.

4.35   Where a DPP case is proceeding by way of summons, the police submit a file to the Director and, unless time limits come into play, only take out a summons after a direction to prosecute has been issued.

4.36   The DPP has no formal involvement in the conduct of police investigations, prior to charge or summons, or between the charge and the submission to him of the police investigation file. It is however open to the police to seek the advice of the DPP's staff in the course of their investigations, especially where it is apparent that complex issues of law or evidence are likely to be involved.

4.37   The Director has provided the police with detailed instructions on what should be included in an investigation file, which is transmitted by the police manually rather than electronically. The DPP will normally await receipt of the complete file before making a decision. Having received the file, in deciding whether or not to prosecute, his staff may consult with the police, victims and witnesses and visit the scene of the crime. Consultation has been found particularly useful in cases where sexual offences are involved, identification is at issue, where the credibility or reliability of witnesses is in question, and in complex fraud cases. The DPP views early contact with victims and witnesses as important, not only in the context of deciding whether to prosecute, but also in pursuance of his Department's policy on victims and witnesses, as a means of reassuring them that their interests are being taken into account.

4.38   The DPP seeks further information from the police before coming to a decision on whether to prosecute in about 30% of cases. While this relatively proactive approach may add to the time taken to process cases at the earlier stages, it is the DPP's view that it improves the quality of decision making and is less likely to result in problems, such as discontinuance, at later stages. This is especially so, given the increasing complexity of cases.

4.39   Once a decision is taken to prosecute, a lawyer on the DPP's staff collates the evidence to be used in summary proceedings, or at committal where the trial is to be conducted on indictment. The DPP instructs independent counsel to conduct cases in the Crown Court and, often, to take business through the magistrates' courts, including summary trials, remand hearings and committals. In the magistrates' courts, both a police prosecutor and a DPP representative may therefore be present at the same time. Were it not for pressure of work, we understand that the Department's own staff would be doing much more of the court business. The DPP's professional staff have rights of audience in the magistrates' courts, county courts and Crown Court.

4.40   We should record that there are increasing workload pressures on the DPP's Department.
We have already referred to the extension of the number of cases triable summarily which
have to be reported to the DPP. Recently enacted legislation has also had a significant effect.
The Criminal Procedure and Investigations Act 1996 came into force in Northern Ireland in
January 1998 and has resulted in an as yet unquantifiable increase in legal and administrative
work associated with disclosure. The Director has responsibilities under the Proceeds of
Crime (Northern Ireland) Order 1996 in applying to the High Court for restraint orders to
freeze a defendant's assets prior to a confiscation hearing in the Crown Court. There will also
be considerable implications for the DPP, as for other parts of the criminal justice system,
arising from the incorporation of the *European Convention on Human Rights.*

SPEED OF PROCESSING CASES

4.41   The DPP and RUC have played their part in efforts to tackle delay in the criminal justice
system and are currently implementing new systems to reduce the time taken to bring cases
to trial (see Chapter 15). This applies to cases prosecuted by the RUC and to those that are
for the DPP. In relation to the latter, there are arrangements for joint case management
which were put in place following an analysis, undertaken in 1996/97, of the reasons for
delay in processing indictable cases from charge through to committal. The associated report
highlighted the problems that could arise if post-investigative preparation of cases was seen
as two distinct processes, police file preparation and DPP case file review, and argued that
the necessary independence of police and prosecutor would not be compromised by
administrative compatibility between them. From comments made to us during our
consultations, it is clear that while progress has been made in reducing delay, there remains
scope for considerable further improvement.

ACCOUNTABILITY AND THE PROSECUTION PROCESS –
CURRENT ARRANGEMENTS

4.42   Both accountability and independence are crucial in relation to the prosecution process, but
there are inevitable tensions between them. For example, in what way can a prosecution
service be held accountable to a Minister, yet retain its independence? The current position is
set out in Article 4 of the Prosecution of Offences (NI) Order 1972, which provides for the
appointment of the Director of Public Prosecutions and the deputy DPP by the Attorney
General for Northern Ireland. The Director and his deputy may be removed from office by
the Attorney on grounds of inability or misbehaviour; their retirement age is 65.

4.43   Under Article 3(2) of the Order, the Director operates under the superintendence and
direction of the Attorney General in all matters. Article 5(2) makes him responsible to the

Attorney for the performance of his functions under the Order. This means that in law the Attorney may require that any particular case or class of case should be brought to his attention before any direction is given; and the Attorney could direct that a particular case be prosecuted or not. The prosecution of certain offences, such as those relating to official secrets, explosive substances or corruption, requires the consent of the Attorney General.

4.44   It is clear from the terms of the Order, a piece of legislation drafted during the time of the Stormont Parliament but with significant amendment (in respect of accountability arrangements) made in the early days of direct rule, that it envisaged the DPP operating in the context of a local administration, with a locally appointed Attorney General. However, under direct rule, the Attorney General for England and Wales has also been appointed Attorney General for Northern Ireland; and the Director's line of accountability has therefore been to the Attorney General at Westminster.

4.45   Given the Attorney's position as a member of the Government, his power of "superintendence and direction" could have implications for the essential independence of the Director in carrying out his functions. However, successive Attorneys have placed emphasis on not allowing political considerations to interfere with their position as guardians of the public interest, one aspect of which is their role in relation to prosecutions. The Director has emphasised to us that there has been no political interference in the exercise of his functions by the Attorney General. The classic statement of the constitutional position of the Attorney General in relation to prosecutions was given by Attorney General Sir Hartley Shawcross to the House of Commons in 1951 where he said that:

> "It is the duty of an Attorney General... to acquaint himself with all the relevant facts, including, for instance, the effect which the prosecution, successful or unsuccessful as the case may be, would have upon public morale and order, and with any other consideration affecting public policy. He may, although I do not think he is obliged to, consult with any of his colleagues in the government, and indeed, as Lord Simon once said, he would in some cases be a fool if he did not... the assistance of his colleagues is confined to informing him of particular considerations which might affect his own decision and does not consist, and must not consist, of telling him what the decision ought to be. Responsibility for the eventual decision rests with the Attorney General and he is not to be put, and is not put, under pressure by his colleagues in the matter... it is the Attorney General, applying his judicial mind, who has to be the sole judge of those considerations."

That is the principle to which the Law Officers, both in Northern Ireland and England and Wales, have long adhered when applying considerations of public interest.

4.46   While the Director maintains his independence of action, he does consult the Attorney from time to time on various matters, including difficult or sensitive cases, or cases which give rise to public interest considerations. That ability to consult and seek views from the Law Officer, if used by both parties with due respect for the need to maintain the Director's independence, is an element of accountability which should enhance the quality of the decision making process. However, we do recognise that significant disquiet has been expressed by groups in Northern Ireland about the possibility of political interference occurring under the current arrangements, especially in relation to a small number of high profile cases. Given the difficulties associated with making public the details of any communication between the DPP and the Attorney on an individual case, there is the scope for speculation which can be damaging to confidence.

4.47   It is for the incumbents of the posts of Attorney General and Director of Public Prosecutions to ensure that this most important and sensitive relationship works in a way that promotes and safeguards the administration of justice. The management of this relationship is an issue which has been addressed in many other common law jurisdictions.

4.48   As a government Minister the Attorney General answers in Parliament for matters falling within his or her own responsibilities. This includes superintendence of the Director of Public Prosecutions for Northern Ireland. Occasionally, the Attorney General will make a statement on a particular prosecution decision if it is properly a matter of great public interest.

4.49   The Prosecution of Offences (Northern Ireland) Order 1972 laid responsibility for funding the DPP's office, staffing it and providing its accommodation on the Ministry for Home Affairs. Since direct rule these functions have been carried out by the Secretary of State for Northern Ireland. This means that the Secretary of State and the Permanent Secretary of the Northern Ireland Office have a proper concern for the expenditure of the Department of the DPP, and internal accountability mechanisms reflect that position. However, the Secretary of State and the Northern Ireland Office have no locus in relation to the discharge of the Director's prosecution functions. We do not know why responsibility for resource issues was allocated in this way, but it is likely that the size of the Director's Department was not considered sufficient to justify establishing separate finance and personnel functions for it.

4.50   The Director's decisions on whether to prosecute or not are subject to judicial review although, on the basis of a recent House of Lords judgment,[8] decisions to prosecute are amenable to review only when there is dishonesty, bad faith or some other exceptional circumstance. A handful of applications for review of decisions not to prosecute have been made, of which one was successful when a decision not to prosecute for intimidation was sent back for consideration of whether there was a reasonable prospect of conviction for an alternative offence of criminal damage. The Director and his Department constitute a public authority within the terms of section 6 of the Human Rights Act 1998, and as such will be subject to its provisions; it is unlawful for them to act in a way that contravenes a right contained in the European Convention.

---

8   *R v Director of Public Prosecutions, Ex Parte Kebilene and Others*, House of Lords, 28 October 1999.

4.51   Another aspect of accountability lies in the DPP's relationship with victims of crime in particular, and the public at large, who have a clear interest in the effective prosecution of crime. Opportunities for contact between the Director's Department and the wider community have been inhibited by the existence of a state of civil strife since the inception of the office in 1972. However, there has always been close contact between the Director's Department and victims of crime. Consulting victims in advance of trial can provide reassurance for the victim that all aspects of the case will be fully examined and that their interests will be properly taken into account, and gives the victim the opportunity to raise any concerns about the trial.

4.52   The Director and his staff have been taking steps to build upon and develop the service which they provide to victims. The DPP's circular to staff, *Victims, Witnesses and the Prosecution* (September 1997), provides a statement of what victims and witnesses can expect from the DPP at various stages in the process. Provision of information on the progress of cases is a high priority, as is the matter of special assistance for vulnerable witnesses and victims; and the guidelines say that the position of victims is to be taken into account in addressing the public interest element of decisions on whether to prosecute. In addition, the Director's office has lent valuable support to various inter-agency working groups in the whole area of victim care.

4.53   *Victims, Witnesses and the Prosecution* sets out the Director's policy on the giving of reasons for decisions not to prosecute. Given that this is an aspect of accountability which arouses considerable interest, we reproduce the relevant passage in full:

> "The Director, when giving reasons for decisions as to prosecution, will do so in general terms. The Director will indicate, when requested, whether the decision was based on evidential or public interest considerations. The requirements of justice and fairness militate against giving detailed reasons. If detailed reasons are given in one or more cases, they must be given in all. Otherwise, wrong conclusions will inevitably be drawn in relation to those cases where detailed reasons are not given, resulting either in unjust implications regarding the guilt of the suspect or former accused, or suspicions of malpractice, or both. If, on the other hand, reasons are given in all cases and those reasons are in more than general terms, the unjust consequences are even more obvious. For example, to state that the absence of a particular proof was the sole reason for non-prosecution would amount to conviction without trial in the eyes of the public at large and would deprive the person concerned of the careful public analysis of the evidence that the trial procedure affords."

If a decision is taken at the trial stage to reduce the charge or accept a plea to a lesser offence, then the DPP's guidance requires that the reasons be explained to the victim, if he or she wishes, and that counsel or the DPP's representative should listen to anything which the victim wishes to say.

4.54   In the event of a written complaint being made against his Department in relation to the exercise of its professional functions, the Director or one of his senior staff determines the level at which it should be dealt with and from which a response should issue. Written procedures require that complaints be dealt with promptly and courteously, normally within 15 working days, and copies of all relevant correspondence are archived, with a view to the nature and volume of complaints being reviewed annually by the Board of Management.[9] Serious complaints against the DPP would be addressed by the Attorney General. There is no independent element in this process, but most complaints are about decisions on prosecution and it would be difficult to involve people from outside the Department in dealing with them.

4.55   The existence of human rights norms constitutes an increasingly important accountability mechanism, in that they provide a benchmark against which to measure the performance of the prosecution system. In this context we would also draw attention to the significance of conferences of prosecutors and international organisations of which the present Director is a member. Such organisations foster the development of international standards drawing on human rights instruments such as the UN Guidelines. We have already mentioned the International Association of Prosecutors, which is dedicated to promoting the highest standards in the administration of justice and to ensuring that the duties and responsibilities of prosecutors are recognised and protected. The Director is also a member of the Heads of Prosecution Agencies Conference. Consisting of prosecutors from Commonwealth countries and the Republic of Ireland, the Conference fosters co-operation and the exchange of ideas and is also concerned with "assisting in preserving the vital independence of prosecutors in member countries and at the same time promoting a balance between independence and public accountability".

Views Expressed During the Consultation Process

4.56   The role of the police in prosecuting minor offences received considerable attention in the consultation process. The proposition that responsibility for initiating and undertaking all prosecutions should rest with an independent prosecuting authority attracted widespread support from a broad range of political parties, NGOs representing human rights interests, some practitioners and other individuals and organisations.

4.57   Most of those advocating change focused on the desire to enhance public confidence by distancing the quasi-judicial decision to prosecute from the investigative function. It was argued that the police, as investigators, were not best placed to determine objectively whether the outcome of an investigation justified prosecution. Scrutiny by an independent prosecutor

---

9   The Board of Management comprises the Senior Assistant Director, Assistant Directors and the Head of the Financial Control and Resources section, under the chairmanship of the deputy Director. Its primary function is to ensure that the aims and objectives of the Department, set by the Director, are met.

was also seen by some as providing a safeguard against mistakes or malpractice on the part of the police; and indeed others saw it as a means of protecting the police against unjustified complaints and allegations. There were concerns that police prosecutors were not as well placed as qualified lawyers to deal with the increasing complexity of criminal justice legislation and the growing importance of human rights issues, when presenting cases in court.

4.58   It is important to record that some of those who argued for this change made clear that they were not doing so out of a sense of criticism of the police. Indeed there were some favourable comments about the expertise of police officers working in this field, although practitioners talked of variable competence. Some, who were equivocal about the need for change, pointed to the local knowledge that a good police prosecutor could bring to a case and expressed concern at the lack of authority given to counsel employed by the DPP in summary cases. We were told that court business could be held up as counsel telephoned the DPP's office in order to obtain instructions. There was one suggestion that responsibility for prosecuting minor offences might be retained by the police but with greater scope for supervision by the DPP. The RUC did not have strong views about retaining the prosecution function in relation to minor offences and could appreciate the public confidence arguments for making all prosecutions the responsibility of an independent prosecutor. However, they did point to the advantage of developing a cadre of expertise in evidential and court related issues within the police service.

4.59   The minority who argued for retention of the police prosecuting role did so for a variety of reasons: the police were doing a good job; the involvement of a prosecution service in minor cases would increase delay; and cost considerations.

4.60   There was debate about the relationship between investigation and prosecution and the stage in a case when an independent prosecutor should become involved. Some argued for the complete separation of the investigative and prosecution processes, in order to safeguard the independence of the prosecutor, thus preventing the objectivity of the prosecution service from being compromised by the investigative ethos. Others, including practising lawyers, saw advantage in the early involvement of the prosecutor well before the police submitted the investigation file for a decision on prosecution. This would help ensure that evidential issues were addressed at an early stage, thus reducing delay further down the line, lessening the likelihood of holding charges being changed at a later stage, and, in some cases, identifying at the outset weaknesses in a case which might result in it being dropped. Care would have to be taken to ensure that the prosecutor did not get too close to the police in these circumstances. The RUC pointed out that, particularly in serious cases, they valued the opportunity to seek the advice of the DPP at an early stage and that sometimes they sought his input prior to charge.

4.61   There was a significant and broad based body of opinion that an independent prosecution service should have a much more "hands on" role in the investigative process. Some talked of the ability of the prosecutor to direct or supervise investigations, attend interviews of suspects and visit scenes of crime, and there was one suggestion that the prosecutor should be given the responsibility of drafting warrants of arrest and charging suspects. The Scottish system of procurators fiscal was often mentioned, as was the role of District Attorneys in the United States. Those expressing these views came to them from a number of different perspectives. There was the public confidence dimension in the sense of subjecting the police to external supervision to ensure that human rights were respected and that all cases were investigated fairly and impartially, including offences committed by public officials and members of law enforcement agencies. There was also a view that enabling the prosecutor to become involved in investigations, particularly of the more serious cases, made for a more effective approach to dealing with crime.

4.62   Delay was a concern of practising lawyers and some of the human rights organisations, especially in relation to the more serious cases where custody was involved. Reference was made to the time taken for the RUC to present files to the DPP and to the length of time taken by his Department in determining whether to prosecute, especially in cases where further information had to be sought from the police. There was a feeling that it should take a matter of days for the police to submit a file to the DPP, unless the case was especially complex, and days or weeks, rather than months, for the DPP to direct. A long term objective might be to aim for time limits along the lines of those operating in Scotland, although it was recognised that in present circumstances this could place the defence in some difficulties. Concern was expressed about the Criminal Procedure and Investigations Act 1996 which some felt placed complex decisions on disclosure to the defence in the hands of the police, with police officers being required to make the initial judgement on what might undermine the prosecution case.

4.63   The possibility of the prosecutor having a central role in diverting cases (e.g. in relation to young people or mentally disordered offenders) away from the criminal justice system did not receive a great deal of attention. Those who did comment were broadly in favour, especially if there were suitable schemes, and options involving restorative justice, available to the prosecutor. However, there were differing views about the concept of prosecutorial fines as operated in Scotland and some civil law jurisdictions. Some saw this as a useful diversionary measure enabling the speedy resolution of straightforward cases (similar in principle to fixed penalties), while others felt that disposals of this sort should be left to the judiciary.

4.64   As for the performance of the DPP's Department, many of those whom we consulted did not express a view, some were critical and some commented favourably on the performance of the criminal justice system as a whole. We were left with a sense that some at least of those who said they wanted lawyers to take on all prosecutions were influenced by a positive view of the way in which the Department had conducted itself over the years. The Attorney General emphasised to us that, on the basis of his experience and that of his predecessors, he had complete confidence in the professionalism of the DPP and the Department.

4.65   Some concerns were expressed about the handling of particular types of case. Organisations representing the Nationalist perspective and some human rights groups said that the DPP's Department had not demonstrated the necessary objectivity, independence and rigour in pursuing cases where Nationalists had been the victims, especially where the security forces were implicated. A number of cases were quoted in some detail, giving rise to allegations of partiality and/or political influence on the prosecution process. There was concern that no public explanation was ever offered about why prosecutions had not taken place or charges were withdrawn in such cases and that private enquiries of the DPP were invariably met with the response that it was not policy to give reasons.

4.66   On the same theme, comment was made by these groups about the very small number of successful prosecutions resulting from deaths caused by security force actions. There were similar concerns about what they felt was lack of action following allegations of police misconduct. It was said that the DPP gave the appearance of being in business in order to secure convictions on behalf of the RUC. Those expressing these views felt that there was not the constructive tension between the RUC and the DPP that was so crucial if the public were to have confidence in the prosecution system.

4.67   A range of views was expressed about the future shape of an independent prosecutors' office, from some who saw no need for change at all through to those who effectively wanted to replace the DPP's Department with a new organisation having no connection with previous arrangements. Clearly, if the DPP's Department were to assume significant additional responsibilities, it would at the very least require substantial change in structure and organisation. A wide body of opinion, from across the political spectrum, favoured a move towards a new office responsible for all prosecutions. A submission made from the Unionist perspective supported the creation of a single independent prosecution service, responsible for all prosecutions, with a sufficiently independent chief to ensure the degree of cross-community acceptance necessary for its effective functioning. This would necessitate the recruitment through open advertisement of high calibre staff with a long-term strategy of developing a cadre of highly skilled senior prosecutors able to manage a case from scene of crime through to prosecution in the Crown Court. The service would have a key role in developing public confidence. During the consultation process, there were a number of references to the procurator fiscal model and a suggestion that posts in the prosecution service should be open to defence lawyers.

4.68   We should record that a number of people stressed the importance of learning from the experiences associated with the early years of the Crown Prosecution Service (CPS) in England and Wales. Under-funding at the start, over-centralisation and bureaucratic procedures, together with lawyers appearing in court insufficiently briefed, were mentioned in that context as pitfalls to be avoided.

4.69   As for where political responsibility for prosecutions should lie, most who commented envisaged devolution of the function sooner or later, although some expressed reservations about whether this should happen before local institutions of government had proved themselves. There was recognition of the difficulties associated with getting the balance right between independence and accountability. The concern to distance the prosecution service from political influence meant that there was little support for a Minister of Justice having any role in relation to prosecutions.

4.70 There were suggestions that a local Attorney General might be appointed. Some felt that such a person ought not to be a member of the Assembly or Executive, but rather would be drawn from the ranks of senior lawyers and would be essentially a non-political figure. A local Attorney would have an oversight function in relation to prosecutions, but there was a view in some quarters that he or she should not be in a position to issue directions on whether or not to prosecute or require the discontinuance of prosecutions. There was a suggestion that an independent prosecution service might be accountable to Parliament or the Assembly for matters of financial probity and administration but not in respect of decisions on whether or not to prosecute. A common theme was the desire to insulate the prosecutor from political influence.

4.71 On wider issues of accountability, there was a general desire to see a prosecution service that was more answerable to the public. Suggestions included an annual report and publication of factors taken into account in deciding whether to prosecute, as well as a more open and proactive role in communicating with the public at large. On the difficult question of reasons, there was one suggestion that full reasons should be required for the initiation of criminal proceedings or the refusal to do so. Others recognised the difficulties of spelling out reasons, especially given the implications for the rights of the suspect. There were calls for a clear, accessible and open complaints procedure, with an independent element.

4.72 A number of people stressed the importance of accountability to victims through providing them with information and taking their views into account. There was some support for the idea of external scrutiny of the work of prosecutors. For example, the Northern Ireland Human Rights Commission might be invited to examine papers in cases of disquiet. Another idea was that an international agency might be invited to send individuals of standing to review the operation of an independent prosecution service, perhaps after two years of its operation.

Research and Experience of Other Jurisdictions

4.73 Through our visits and with the benefit of research conducted on our behalf[10] we examined with great interest prosecutorial arrangements in a range of common and civil law jurisdictions. There are considerable variations in the systems and in ways of dealing with such issues as the relationship between investigation and prosecution and between

10 Bryett and Osborne, Research Report 16.

independence and accountability. Such differences are influenced by cultural and historical background and by what is best suited to the particular political and legal systems of the jurisdictions concerned. This is not the place for a comprehensive survey, but we do seek to identify aspects of experience elsewhere that may be relevant to a debate about a prosecution system suited to the particular circumstances of Northern Ireland.

WHETHER THE POLICE SHOULD HAVE A ROLE IN THE PROSECUTION PROCESS

4.74   Internationally the trend, while not universal, has been towards giving responsibility for all aspects of prosecution to a prosecution agency independent of the police. There is a long tradition in civil law systems of public prosecutors taking responsibility for prosecutions in the public interest, which pre-dates the creation of police forces. Although the inquisitorial process originated in an inquiry by a judge, specialised officials acting on behalf of the court later became charged with building the case against the defendant long before police forces came in to existence. In the common law tradition by contrast prosecutorial functions remained mainly in the hands of private individuals until police forces developed in the nineteenth century. The notion of a separate prosecution agency emerged in most common law countries, after police forces had already been established, and is not so embedded within the common law culture. During the course of the last century, however, independent prosecution services have been establishing themselves and taking responsibility for all prosecutions.

4.75   England and Wales provide a useful starting point. Until 1986 the police were responsible for investigating crime and for the prosecution of cases through the courts, with the exception of the most complex and serious which were prosecuted by the DPP. As in Northern Ireland today, prosecutions for minor offences were often conducted in magistrates' courts by police officers; the police instructed lawyers to act on their behalf in the more serious cases. By 1980, most county and metropolitan councils had prosecuting solicitors' departments and the range of offences prosecuted by lawyers was increasing. The Royal Commission on Criminal Procedure, reporting in 1981 under the chairmanship of Sir Cyril Philips,[11] recommended the establishment of a separate service responsible for the prosecution of all offences. In doing so the Royal Commission took account of the following main considerations:

- concerns that combining the role of investigation and prosecution invested too much power and responsibility in one organisation;

- the inherent desirability, from a public confidence perspective and in order to secure a balanced criminal justice system, of separating the investigative and prosecutorial functions;

---

11   *The Royal Commission on Criminal Procedure* (1981), London: HMSO, Cmnd 8092.

- inconsistencies in prosecution policy across the country and concerns that too many cases were being prosecuted on the basis of insufficient evidence; and

- a desire for greater accountability and openness and common standards on the part of prosecutors.

4.76   Following on from the Philips Report, the Prosecution of Offences Act 1985 established the Crown Prosecution Service as a national agency responsible for reviewing police decisions to prosecute and for conducting all prosecutions in the courts. Thus England and Wales moved from a situation where almost all prosecutions were carried out by or at the behest of the police to one where responsibility was vested in an independent prosecution service.

4.77   In Scotland, all prosecutions are the responsibility of procurators fiscal working under the authority of the Lord Advocate. In considering the applicability or otherwise of the Scottish experience to Northern Ireland, it is worth bearing in mind some of the features of the inquisitorial system associated with Scottish criminal procedure and the historical context. The office of procurator fiscal emerged during the late 16th to 18th centuries, when it took over the investigative and prosecutorial functions of the medieval sheriff who was left primarily with a judicial function. The fiscal in Scotland therefore predates the police and has developed as an integral part of the Scottish system and culture over the centuries.

4.78   Prosecutorial arrangements in Ireland have similar roots to those in England and Wales and in Northern Ireland. They have evolved with the Irish State and are governed to a large extent by the provisions of the Irish Constitution (Article 30.3) and by statute, in particular the Prosecution of Offences Act 1974, which established the office of Director of Public Prosecutions. In summary, it is for the DPP to determine whether to prosecute cases that are tried on indictment (except for a small number of offences where the consent of the Attorney General is required). He nominates barristers from the private bar to present such cases in court. He takes the decision based on papers submitted to him by the Garda Síochána through the State Solicitor Service. However, he has little involvement in summary cases heard before the district courts and which form the bulk of criminal business. Many of these cases are prosecuted by the Garda investigating officer. In Dublin, Garda court presenters are being introduced on a phased basis and one of their duties includes the prosecution of summary offences. In summary cases outside Dublin a superintendent or inspector determines whether to prosecute and presents the case in court; in Dublin, the Chief State Solicitor's Office prosecutes the more serious cases heard in the district courts.

4.79   These arrangements have been the subject of considerable scrutiny in recent years, most recently by a Study Group, working under the auspices of the Office of the Attorney General and chaired by Mr Dermot Nally, former Secretary to the Government. Included, amongst other things, in the Group's terms of reference was the question of "whether there is a continuing role for the Garda to prosecute as well as to investigate crime". Its report last year concluded that while there was scope for improvement in co-ordination and effectiveness, the existing system should not be replaced with a unified prosecution service. The Group reached this conclusion largely on grounds of financial considerations and general confidence in the current arrangements expressed during the course of its consultations.

4.80   As for common law systems outside these islands, the system in the United States is well known. There, the US Attorney in federal cases and the District Attorney (who is directly elected) at local level are responsible for deciding whether to prosecute almost all cases (we understand that in some areas the police have a role in the prosecution of very minor traffic infractions). This system and culture is so well established that the question of police involvement in prosecutions is simply not an issue. Similarly in Canada, while detailed arrangements vary between the various jurisdictions, executive responsibility for all prosecutorial matters is vested in the relevant Attorney General operating through Crown Counsel. In South Africa the Constitution and the National Prosecuting Authority Act 1998 established a single body with responsibility, inter alia, for deciding whether or not to institute criminal proceedings. During our visit to South Africa it was apparent that this Authority was intended to take an increasingly high profile in prosecution work in order to enhance public confidence, improve efficiency, safeguard individual rights and enhance consistency of approach.

4.81   In Australia and New Zealand, the police still retain a substantial role in deciding upon and conducting prosecutions of less serious or summary cases and, in some cases, in processing indictable offences through the committal stage. One significant factor behind this may be the existence in country areas of widely scattered communities where, for practical reasons, police involvement in less serious cases is seen as the most efficient approach. In Australia, the trend seems to be towards reducing police involvement in prosecutions.[12] In New Zealand, however, the Law Commission has considered and rejected the idea of a single unified prosecution service but has recommended instead a dedicated national career oriented prosecution function within the police, responsible for prosecuting all summary cases in court. This would impose an internal separation between the investigation and prosecution of crime and seems to be a rather more advanced form of the Central Process Office approach being adopted by the RUC.

4.82   The Netherlands is a fairly typical example of prosecutorial arrangements in a civil law jurisdiction. There are some 450 prosecutors and 2,500 support staff, organised on a regional basis, but under the central direction of a Board of Prosecutors. The prosecutors have responsibility for the investigation of crime, although in practice they become involved only in the more serious cases at this stage, and for determining whether to prosecute in all cases. Their decision on whether to prosecute is based on evidential and public interest grounds, in accordance with guidelines laid down at the centre. Such guidelines might specify types of crime to which priority should be given or procedures for handling sensitive cases such as

---

12   Bryett and Osborne, Research Report 16.

those involving sex abuse. On our visit it was apparent that the ability to settle cases out of court, for example through diversion or a prosecutorial fine, was valued by prosecutors and that effective co-operation with the police and local authorities was a key priority.

THE INTERFACE BETWEEN INVESTIGATION AND PROSECUTION

4.83   In earlier parts of this chapter, we have referred to the idea of separating the investigative from the prosecutorial function. It will be apparent from what we say in this section that, based on the experience of other jurisdictions, the matter is not quite so simple.

4.84   One of the key factors behind establishing the Crown Prosecution Service in England and Wales was the desire to draw a clear line between functional responsibility for investigation and prosecution. Under the 1985 Act, the police retained the power to investigate and to decide what charge to bring. The CPS took over the conduct of all criminal proceedings instituted by the police, defined as meaning from the time of the issue of a summons or warrant or from the time of charge. The police assembled the evidence for review by the CPS. The responsibility of the CPS was to determine whether the evidence was sufficient to prove the charge and, if not, what other evidence might be needed. If such evidence was not available, then it was for the CPS to decide whether to discontinue the case. The CPS has no role in supervising investigations although it advises on legal issues if asked; nor can it direct that lines of enquiry be pursued. In commenting on the working of these arrangements in the early years, the Glidewell Report[13] quoted the evidence of Sir Alan Green, the then DPP, to the Public Accounts Committee:

> "In many ways the very convenient relationship between the police and their County Prosecuting Solicitors disappeared. I think that suddenly a steel curtain came down between the two services and this went a bit too far. People in both services, both the police and ourselves, felt that we must keep our distance, we must not talk to each other, we must not communicate, the CPS is independent of the police and must be seen to be so."

The Glidewell Report noted that in practice the police had retained several important functions post-charge, including preparation of the case file and making arrangements for the initial court appearance.[14] This meant that on occasion the CPS would not become aware of a case for as long as 14 days after a prosecution was initiated.

4.85   It is apparent to us from our reading and discussions held in London that effective joint management of the interface between investigation and prosecution is of critical importance to the efficiency and effectiveness of the criminal justice system as a whole. The Royal

---

13   *The Review of the Crown Prosecution Service* (1998), London: HMSO, Cmnd 3960 (The Glidewell Report).

14   *The Review of the Crown Prosecution Service* (1998), London: HMSO, Cmnd 3960 (The Glidewell Report), page 127.

Commission on Criminal Justice[15] considered the issue of whether it was more appropriate for the prosecuting authority (rather than the police) to initiate proceedings but did not recommend such a change largely because of the practical implications. However, the thrust of recent thinking, evidenced in such reviews as Glidewell and the *Review of Delay in the Criminal Justice System* conducted for the Home Office by Martin Narey in 1997, has been to place the emphasis on co-ordination, partnership and integrated working between the police and CPS with the prosecutor being fully involved from the point of charge.

4.86   The arrangements in Scotland are rather different, and we mention them in some detail here as a number of people have suggested to us that they are worthy of consideration in the Northern Ireland context. Procurators fiscal have a common law duty to investigate crime and section 17(3) of the Police (Scotland) Act 1967 places Chief Constables under a statutory duty to comply with the lawful instructions of the fiscal. In terms of their relationship with the police, the fiscals are in some ways in a position more akin to their counterparts in civil law jurisdictions than to their CPS colleagues.

4.87   In practice it is only in the more serious or complex cases that the fiscal would become heavily involved at the investigative stage, for example through attendance at the scene of a murder to take charge of the evidential aspects of the investigation and autopsy arrangements. In serious cases, the police will consult with the fiscal at an early stage and positively welcome his or her assistance and direction. Another factor militating in favour of this early involvement is that in some respects the fiscal has more investigative powers than the police, for example in seeking arrest or search warrants or authorisation to take blood samples. In the large majority of cases, however, the fiscal's formal involvement starts at the point of considering a report by the police with a view to determining whether or not to institute criminal proceedings.

4.88   The critical importance and benefits of effective working arrangements between prosecution and police are demonstrated by the timetable to which the prosecutor has to work in Scottish custody cases. The 110-day rule relates to cases prosecuted under the solemn procedure, i.e. those heard in the High Court or before a sheriff sitting with a jury. In summary custody cases in the district or sheriff court, the time limit for commencement of trial is 40 days. Following arrest, the defendant must be brought before a court on the next working day, by which time the fiscal will have decided whether there is reasonable suspicion to support a charge and seek remand in custody. The fiscal then has eight days to complete initial enquiries with a view to committing accused persons on his or her own authority. In murder cases, and cases involving accused persons under the age of 16, the fiscal must seek authority from the Crown Counsel to have the accused fully committed at the next appearance in court. The committal process in Scotland does not constitute any form of preliminary hearing or consideration of the papers supporting the case; rather it involves the fiscal exercising a quasi-judicial function in assessing whether the evidence is sufficient to secure a conviction as

---

15 *Royal Commission on Criminal Justice. Report by Viscount Runciman of Doxford* (1993), London: HMSO, Cmnd 2263.

charged. If the fiscal is not so convinced, then the defendant is "liberated", which leaves open the possibility of indictment within one year. From the point of committal, trial must start within 110 days during which time evidence is assembled, witnesses precognosed (a procedure whereby the fiscal interviews witnesses), the case put to Crown Counsel, who makes the decision as to proceedings and issues instructions to the fiscal accordingly. It is, however, important to emphasise that some aspects of Scottish criminal procedure, relating to disclosure for example, are very different from Northern Ireland.

4.89   Evidence of a complaint, including witness statements obtained by the police, is e-mailed by the police to the fiscal in a standard form, with information fields and data transfer arrangements set out in joint protocols. In less serious cases, this usually enables a quick decision to be taken on whether to proceed by way of summary trial before a district court or sheriff. It is then for the fiscal to issue the complaint to the accused and arrange a court hearing. In summary matters there is a target, which is currently being met, to have 75% of cases in court within nine weeks of receipt of the report.

4.90   From what we heard on our visits, it is worth recording that the participants in these processes in Scotland seemed comfortable with the arrangements (although comments were made about the tightness of the time limits). The independence of the fiscal was fully respected, relations and the level of co-operation between the fiscal and police seemed good and cases were generally processed speedily and efficiently without impairment of the quality of justice. At the same time, the Crown Office and Procurator Fiscal Service are very much alive to their responsibilities in respect of Convention rights, which have applied in relation to actions of the Scottish Executive (and therefore to the actions of prosecutors, since they act on behalf of the Lord Advocate) since May 1999. They have been conducting an extensive review to ensure that their policies, practices and procedures are closely aligned to the requirements of the Convention.[16]

4.91   In civil law jurisdictions, the prosecutor invariably has a role in supervising investigations, certainly those of more serious criminal behaviour; in some countries, France for example, judges play a supervisory role in the most serious cases. In the inquisitorial environment it is not surprising that the distinction between investigation, prosecution and adjudication should be more blurred than is the case in common law systems. We did hear some concerns from defence lawyers that the involvement of prosecutors with the police in an investigation might compromise their ability to make dispassionate judgements and process cases in court further down the line. In some jurisdictions this problem is addressed by ensuring that where a prosecutor is involved at the investigative stage, different personnel review the case and appear in court.

4.92   The FBI and local police services in the United States have a tradition of involving the US Attorney or District Attorney at an early stage in the investigation of serious crime.

---

16   *Crown Office and Procurator Fiscal Service Annual Report* 1998-1999, Edinburgh: HMSO, page 14.

Prosecutors might be involved in the planning of major operations and in the development of long-term strategies to deal with organised crime. This ensures the availability of early advice on evidential issues and such matters as timing of arrest. The prosecutor also has a role in giving specialist advice and seeking judicial authorisation of the use of certain investigative tools such as wiretaps. The early involvement of prosecutors was represented to us as helping to avoid legal difficulties further down the line, reducing the need for requests for supplementary information and facilitating the efficient processing of cases at the later stages. We were left in no doubt nevertheless that the need for the prosecutor to remain independent from the police was crucial and indeed we heard some opposition to the concept of co-location of police and prosecutor. In such systems it was apparent that much depended on the standards and integrity of individual prosecuting attorneys.

4.93   In Manhattan we were told that the District Attorney's office was expected to make the decision whether to charge within hours of arrest or detention. In the less serious cases the police were left to investigate with relatively limited prosecutorial involvement. However, to facilitate the decision making process within such a short time-frame, extensive use was made of pagers and video-conference facilities, while in around 35% of cases the police faxed a pro forma provided by the prosecutor containing the information on which a decision to charge could be based.

4.94   In South Africa it is for the prosecutor to determine whether to charge, based on consideration of a police "docket", which is a standard form file. It was clear to us that one benefit of the development of the independent prosecution service was that it reduced the capacity of suspects to put pressure on the police to withdraw charges. Early prosecutorial involvement in investigations was seen as important in assisting the police in developing their investigative techniques, in accordance with evidential requirements. We were told of legislation enabling the establishment of a limited number of investigating directorates, headed by prosecutors, to facilitate partnerships with the police and other agencies in dealing with particular types of serious crime such as urban terrorism and car-jacking.

4.95   To sum up on the investigation/prosecution interface, the international trends we observed were towards:

- greater prosecution involvement at the investigative stage (in an advisory and sometimes supervisory role), especially in relation to serious crime giving rise to complex evidential issues;

- early involvement of the prosecutor in deciding whether to proceed further;

- recognition of the importance of partnership between police, prosecutor and other agencies, and effective procedures for getting information and evidence from the police to the prosecutor to enable speedy and informed decisions to be taken (IT, protocols and effective communications were critical); and

- appreciation of the need to safeguard the independent role of the prosecutor.

DIVERSION

4.96   In several jurisdictions covered in the research programme and visited by the Group, the prosecution has the discretion to divert cases away from the court process, notwithstanding that there is sufficient evidence to prosecute. This tends to be more prevalent in countries where the prosecutor has responsibility for all prosecutions (diversion is less likely to be an issue where such responsibility is limited to serious cases) and is involved relatively early in the process.

4.97   In England and Wales, where the prosecution role is one of review after proceedings are instituted by the police, it is the police who have the discretion to issue warnings and cautions, and who can embark upon initiatives such as restorative justice. However, the CPS can, and do in appropriate cases referred to them, suggest to the police that they take such action.

4.98   In Scotland there is a fairly sophisticated diversionary package available to the procurators fiscal, including fiscal warnings, conditional offers for fixed penalties, fiscal fines and diversionary schemes (e.g. supervision by a social worker, referral to drug treatment, restorative interventions etc). During our visit to Scotland it was clear that fiscals valued their diversionary role, both as an effective response to dealing with certain types of offender and as a means of avoiding congestion in the court system. Members of the fiscal service emphasised the importance of having diversionary schemes available across the jurisdiction so that maximum advantage could be taken of this approach and for the sake of fairness and consistency.

4.99   The fiscal fine[17] (accounting for almost 20,000 cases in 1998) is available where there is sufficient evidence to support a prosecution for offences triable before a district court and in circumstances determined by internal guidelines. In issuing it, at levels between £25 and £100, the fiscal renounces the right to prosecute and it does not appear on criminal records. The offender does have the option of asking for the case to be heard in court, thus complying with human rights requirements.

4.100   The prosecutorial fine is a disposal employed in the Netherlands, where other forms of diversion can also be considered by the prosecutor. Interestingly there the prosecutors have agreed that the police can divert young people to the "Halt" project, a nationwide scheme for young people combining some of the features of community service and restorative justice. Giving this responsibility to the police enables action to be taken in suitable cases within hours of arrest, the immediacy of the intervention being seen as a critical factor in ensuring the right impact.

---

17   Section 56 of the Criminal Justice (Scotland) Act 1987, as amended by section 61 of the Criminal Justice (Scotland) Act 1995.

4.101   It was apparent that, where they had this option, prosecutors had a range of criteria in determining the types of cases to be diverted, for example: admission of guilt by the offender; lack of previous convictions; the nature of the offending behaviour; triviality or otherwise of the offence; and the age of the offender. In some cases, there was the option to resume prosecution if the offender failed to co-operate with the process after having agreed to it.

ACCOUNTABILITY AND INDEPENDENCE

4.102   Safeguarding the independence of the prosecutor, while at the same time providing for accountability and transparency, is one of the most important issues considered by the review. In the following paragraphs we look at how this has been addressed in a range of other jurisdictions. We examine how others have handled the relationship between the prosecutor and the political process, since the independence of the prosecutor from political influence is an issue which received considerable attention during the consultative stage of our review. In doing so, we are conscious of the different forms of accountability identified by our researchers, in particular the subordinate/obedient relationship and the explanatory/answerability models.[18] We focus primarily, but not exclusively, on the experiences of those common law jurisdictions most likely to be relevant in the Northern Ireland context.

4.103   In England and Wales, section 3(1) of the Prosecution of Offences Act 1985 provides that "the Director of Public Prosecutions shall discharge his functions ... under the superintendence of the Attorney General". Interestingly, and unlike the current position in Northern Ireland, the Attorney General is given no explicit power to "direct" the DPP. This appears to have been a conscious decision of the legislators, given that earlier legislation had made a specific reference to a power of direction. In practice rarely, if ever, did an Attorney General formally exercise the power of direction while these provisions were in force, although according to the Glidewell Report, it seems that on occasion some did in all but name.[19]

4.104   As for what is meant by "superintendence", the issue is examined in some depth by the Glidewell Report.[20] In short, the relationship between Attorney General and DPP is in practice primarily consultative in nature, enabling the Attorney to retain a general overview of prosecution policy and be aware of potentially contentious or important cases; also, the DPP is expected to provide sufficient information to the Attorney General to enable the Attorney to answer to Parliament for the performance of the Crown Prosecution Service. Successive Attorneys have made the point that they are not in the business of directing or managing the day-to-day conduct of individual prosecutions. However, while there is some uncertainty over

---

18   Bryett and Osborne, Research Report 16.

19   Page 194, paragraph 8.

20   *The Review of the Crown Prosecution Service* (1998), London: HMSO, Cmnd 3960 (The Glidewell Report), pages 193-196.

whether in law the Attorney General for England and Wales does have a power of direction over the DPP in the handling of individual cases, there seems to be acceptance that in the (unlikely) event of a stark divergence of view on whether or not to prosecute, then the Attorney's view would prevail. Under common law the Attorney does have the power to end a prosecution through entering a *"nolle prosequi"*.

4.105   In England and Wales, as in other jurisdictions, it is not only the relationship between the prosecutor and the Attorney General, but also the position of the Attorney General in relation to the Government and Parliament that is significant. The conventions surrounding the office of Attorney General are important in assessing the independence of the prosecution system. While the Attorney is invariably either a member of the House of Commons or House of Lords, and as a Law Officer is the Government's principal adviser on legal matters, convention requires that when exercising functions in relation to prosecution decisions he or she does not act as a representative of Government but in a separate capacity as guardian of the public interest. In this capacity the Attorney should not take into account political considerations but may take into account public interest considerations in accordance with the Shawcross doctrine. The Attorney's accountability to Parliament (and therefore that of the DPP through him) is one of general answerability for prosecution matters and the policy applied in particular cases. The Attorney answers parliamentary questions, written and oral, appears before select committees and may be involved in adjournment debates. However, he would not answer for "the 'intrinsic merits of individual decisions' or the 'nitty gritty' of each and every one of the 1.3 million cases conducted annually by the prosecution authorities that [he superintends]".[21] As permanent head of the Crown Prosecution Service, the DPP is accountable to Parliament for the efficient administration of the CPS and has on a number of occasions appeared before select committees.

4.106   In Scotland, the Lord Advocate is in a clear supervisory role in relation to the Procurator Fiscal Service in that fiscals are subject to his directions contained in a Book of Regulations, Crown Office circulars and specific instructions which may be issued in particular cases. However, section 48(5) of the Scotland Act 1998 explicitly states that any decision of the Lord Advocate, in his capacity as head of the Prosecution Service, shall continue to be taken by him independently of any other person. Section 27 is also of interest in that it envisages the possibility of a Lord Advocate not being a Member of the Scottish Parliament (indeed, neither of the current Law Officers is an elected Member); in such circumstances the holder of the office could be enabled by Standing Orders to participate in parliamentary business, but not vote. This would enable the Lord Advocate to answer questions and make statements. Section 27 also deals with the issue of MPs asking questions about the conduct of

---

21   Mr John Morris, Attorney General, House of Commons, 5 March 1998.

particular cases in that it enables the Lord Advocate to decline to answer such questions if to do so might prejudice criminal proceedings or would otherwise be against the public interest. By virtue of section 44 both Law Officers are *ex officio* Ministers of the Government.

4.107　　Other Commonwealth jurisdictions have variations on the relationship between an Attorney General and a chief prosecutor. In Australia each state DPP is accountable to a politically appointed Attorney General. However, we understand that while in constitutional terms the relationship could be described as supervisory, and prosecutorial decisions can be debated in state parliaments, no decision by a DPP has ever been overruled by an Attorney General. We note with interest the view of Australian DPPs quoted in the research report[22] that so long as the Attorney General's power is not exercised with any regularity and never in respect of individual cases, it can be a valuable safeguard rendering the DPP accountable for the considerable power with which he or she is vested. We also note the views of the DPP of Western Australia: "The high responsibility given to an unelected official (DPP or chief prosecutor) to wield great power carries with it the duty to be accountable for its exercise."[23]

4.108　　Canadian jurisdictions contain a range of models. In Alberta we were told that while the Attorney General was a working politician and oversaw the prosecution service, this had not caused significant difficulties. He would be informed of high profile prosecutions and might be called to account in the legislature but did not exercise control or play any decision making role in relation to individual prosecutions.

4.109　　During our visit to South Africa, our attention was drawn to what in Southern Africa was seen as a landmark judgment on the relationship between the Government Minister responsible for prosecution and the permanent head of the prosecution service - a case brought by the Attorney General of Namibia in the Supreme Court[24] to determine whether he had the power to direct the Prosecutor General on whether to initiate a prosecution or discontinue it. The judgment contains a review of the position in other Commonwealth jurisdictions and of legal and academic authorities on the subject. The Supreme Court concluded that the "final responsibility for the Office of Prosecutor General" assigned by the Namibian Constitution to the Attorney General did not of itself amount to the ability to "superintend and direct" and did not therefore give the Attorney the power to direct in individual cases. It rejected as unconstitutional a provision of a 1977 Act, enacted by the South African Government during its administration of Namibia, which gave the Minister (i.e. the Attorney) express power to direct the prosecutor and reverse any decision taken by him. In doing so, the Court took account of the intention of the Constitution that the Office of DPP should be truly independent, subject only to the duty of the Prosecutor General to keep the Attorney General properly informed.

22　Bryett and Osborne, Research Report 16.

23　Bryett and Osborne, Research Report 16, page 3, Chapter 3.

24　*Ex parte Attorney-General, Namibia: In Re: The Constitutional Relationship between the Attorney General and the Prosecutor General* - 1995(8) BCLR 1070 (No 5).

4.110   Of all the jurisdictions visited, the Republic of Ireland has perhaps the most clearly defined statutory safeguards for the independence of the prosecutor, contained in the Prosecution of Offences Act 1974. Section 2(5) states that the DPP shall be independent in the performance of his or her functions, while section 6 makes it unlawful to communicate with the DPP or others involved in the prosecution process in order to influence them not to prosecute or to withdraw proceedings; this provision does not, however, apply to the defendant, the defendant's professional advisers, the defendant's family or to a social worker or anyone personally involved in the case. The Attorney General in the Republic is appointed by the President on the nomination of the Taoiseach in accordance with Article 30 of the Irish Constitution, but is not necessarily an elected politician. The relationship with the DPP is set out in section 2(6) of the 1974 Act which provides that the Attorney and the Director shall consult from time to time in relation to matters pertaining to the functions of the Director. We understand that statutory consultations are very rare, but that consultations on an informal basis, often at the request of the Director, are more frequent.

OTHER ACCOUNTABILITY ISSUES

4.111   Whether or not reasons for prosecutorial decisions should be given, and if so, in what detail, are current issues in several jurisdictions. They have important implications for accountability, in the explanatory/answerability sense, both in relation to individuals affected by a case and in relation to cases where there is a high degree of public interest.

4.112   In the United Kingdom jurisdictions, as in many others, there has been some reluctance on the part of prosecutors to give reasons for decisions in any but the most general terms. The considerations taken into account by the DPP for Northern Ireland were generally endorsed by those to whom we spoke, with particular concerns about the need to protect the rights of the suspect. Other considerations militating against giving reasons were concern about releasing witness related material outside the controlled environment of the court and resource implications.[25] It would be a significant additional burden if prosecutors had to consider in individual cases how far they could go in releasing reasons without infringing the rights of witnesses and suspects or contravening other public interest considerations.

4.113   The DPP in the Republic of Ireland has also come out strongly against giving reasons for his decisions in individual cases.[26]

4.114   Outside the United Kingdom and the Republic of Ireland we detected a greater willingness to contemplate giving reasons in individual cases. In Canada the presumption is against doing so but there are important exceptions. For example, where a decision is taken not to prosecute in a case of misconduct by a public servant, a press release might be issued giving the broad

---

25   *Annual Report of the Crown Office and Procurator Fiscal 1998/99,* Edinburgh: HMSO, paragraphs 24-25.

26   *Annual Report of the Department of the Director of Public Prosecutions, 1998 (1999) Dublin* - Appendix 7.

reasons for the decision. In the United States it was apparent during our visit that District Attorneys were prepared to be very open in explaining publicly their approach to some cases, provided that their intervention would not be seen as prejudicial. In South Africa, we were told that attempts would be made to give reasons in general terms, but this approach invariably led to pressure for more detail. The draft Code of Conduct for prosecutors there sounds a word of caution: "reasons for the exercise of prosecutorial discretion should not be supplied where any individual rights, such as those of victims, witnesses or accused, might be compromised or where it might not be in the public interest to do so." On our visits to the Netherlands and Germany we noted that there was a mechanism whereby aggrieved victims could learn of reasons for non-prosecution by appealing to the courts against the prosecutor's decision.

4.115   Despite the caution in this area, we did detect a feeling in some quarters that a more flexible approach to giving reasons might be inevitable. We note the postscript to the Butler Report[27] where the observation is made that, while it would be absurd to suggest that in every case the CPS should give reasons for a decision not to prosecute, there may well be cases where it would be right to do so. Also, while it is not the practice of the CPS to divulge detailed reasons for its decisions, in cases where a victim has died prosecutors will meet relatives to discuss the basis on which a decision to drop a case was taken.[28]

4.116   Especially if reasons are not given as a general rule, public confidence could be enhanced if there were more widespread understanding of the process and the considerations that go into decisions on whether or not to prosecute. In this context, the CPS is required to furnish an annual report to the Attorney General, which is laid before Parliament; also the DPP in England and Wales is required to produce a code giving guidance on general principles to be applied by prosecutors, and which must be included in the annual report.[29] The code gives useful guidance on the sorts of considerations that are taken into account in assessing evidence and rehearses some of the public interest considerations that might militate in favour of or against prosecution. Similarly, the annual report of the Crown Office and Procurator Fiscal Service provides a readable and informative guide on the work of the Service. The DPP in the Republic of Ireland produced his first annual report in 1998.

4.117   During our visit to South Africa we were interested to see that the National Prosecution Authority was engaged in a public consultation process about the development of a prosecution policy document, similar in some aspects to the CPS Code, and a Code of Conduct for members of the Authority. According to the draft policy document, its purpose is to make sure that everyone knows the principles that prosecutors apply when they do their work. Similar initiatives are taking place elsewhere. We should add, however, that the development of a prosecution policy document did not include making publicly available

---

27   *Inquiry into Crown Prosecution Service. Decision making in Relation to Deaths in Custody and Related Matters* (1999), London: HMSO.

28   *Statement on the Treatment of Victims and Witnesses by the Crown Prosecution Service* (1993), London: HMSO, page 4.

29   Prosecution of Offences Act 1985, sections 9 and 10.

detailed manuals of instructions on the circumstances when prosecutions could take place; to do so was argued to be against the public interest in that such information would be of value to potential offenders and its widespread availability might have the effect of fettering the discretion of the prosecutor.

4.118   It was apparent to us that in several jurisdictions accessibility and involvement in community issues on the part of prosecutors were having a positive impact in increasing understanding and transparency. Outreach programmes in the United States, carried out by District Attorneys and the US Attorney, were being given high priority and it was clear that in the Netherlands the involvement of prosecutors, jointly with other agencies, in managing local responses to crime was viewed positively. The Procurator Fiscal Service in Scotland participates to the full in the development of local inter-agency initiatives which can involve attendance at meetings with community councils during evenings and weekends. The Glidewell Report[30] commented on the need for the CPS to adopt a higher public profile, whilst taking care not to compromise its independence; it recommended CPS involvement in community safety initiatives being developed by local authorities in partnership with the police, under the auspices of the Crime and Disorder Act.

4.119   One other important accountability instrument is that of an inspectorate. In the CPS an internal inspectorate was formed in 1997. The Glidewell Report commented positively on its work and made recommendations to enhance its effectiveness and public standing, in particular through the introduction of an independent element into inspectorate activity.[31] The inspectorate was seen as enhancing public confidence in providing assurances about efficiency and quality of performance and in spreading best practice. Legislation establishing a statutorily based independent inspectorate for the CPS is currently before Parliament.

4.120   To sum up on the issue of independence and accountability as it is viewed in various jurisdictions around the world, if there are discernible trends they seem to be in the direction of:

- independence of prosecutorial decision making from political influence;

- the enhancement of transparency and public understanding through the development of "explanatory" mechanisms; and

- the provision of some form of insurance or redress against the (unlikely) possibility of misconduct or incapacity on the part of the senior prosecutor.

30   Pages 204 onwards.

31   Pages 199-203.

Evaluation and Recommendations

4.121   In this part of the report, we make recommendations for the development of a prosecution service in Northern Ireland that will assume responsibility for deciding on and undertaking all prosecutions currently undertaken by the police. We go on to deal with accountability issues and conclude with an assessment of the organisational and resource implications of our proposals.

4.122   We have taken account of the wide range of views that we have heard about all aspects of the prosecution process, including those that were critical of the present arrangements and of the DPP's Department. Some of those critical of the Department cited particular cases to illustrate their concerns. However, we should also record that we met with the DPP and his senior staff on a number of occasions in the course of our work and we were left in no doubt as to their commitment to professionalism, objectivity and above all to sustaining the independence of the office.

RESPONSIBILITY FOR PROSECUTIONS

4.123   We considered carefully the important question of whether responsibility for all criminal prosecutions should lie with a single unified prosecution service. This would mean the police no longer taking the decision to prosecute in less serious cases and presenting them in magistrates' courts.

4.124   There are arguments on both sides. Those in favour of retaining the current arrangements for police prosecutions of summary cases argued that the system appeared to work; we did not detect a strength of feeling on the part of practitioners or others that the arrangements for police prosecutions were fatally flawed in some way. The introduction of Central Process Offices throughout Northern Ireland means that, within the police, there is some degree of separation between the investigative and prosecution processes. We were also reminded of the view that processing trivial cases through a prosecution service might be wasteful, unnecessary and add to delay; this was a factor clearly in the minds of the MacDermott Working Party. Making a change would inevitably have significant resource implications.

4.125   The case in favour of change, supported by most who commented and in line with international trends, is founded largely on the desire to separate the prosecutorial function from the organisation responsible for carrying out investigations. This was the rationale behind the original recommendation of the MacDermott Report to create an independent prosecution service in Northern Ireland and reduce the role of the police in prosecutions. Securing the independence of the prosecution process for cases at all levels of seriousness should assure the public that decisions on whether to proceed are made against consistently applied criteria by legally qualified staff. In saying this, we are conscious that decisions on whether to prosecute the most trivial cases can have a major impact on the parties concerned. On the question of the local knowledge of police prosecutors, we have noted the point made to us by prosecutors in some other jurisdictions that this can leave police officers open to influences which could impair their objectivity in deciding whether to prosecute. We are also mindful of the increasing complexity even of less serious cases and the increasing significance of human rights issues. Such considerations militate in favour of lawyers appearing in court for the prosecution to deal with difficult legal issues as they arise. The human rights instruments seem to us, in the Northern Ireland context, to point in the direction of having a separate service responsible for all prosecutorial decisions.

4.126   It is of course possible for the prosecutor to have an overview of prosecutions carried out by the police and to use the process currently available to the DPP to call cases in for consideration. However, it is not, in our view, likely that a prosecution service would be able to monitor the prosecutorial function within the police with sufficient rigour; nor do we believe that such an arrangement would be consistent with the sort of relationship between police and prosecution service that we envisage. Later in this chapter we make recommendations about public accountability in relation to the prosecution process and we think that these are likely to be more effectively implemented if all or most prosecutions are the responsibility of one independent body.

4.127   Public confidence in the future criminal justice system in Northern Ireland is of critical importance. We believe that the independence of key parts of the process from each other, and from influence by government, is central to this. Investigation, prosecution and adjudication are the key components of the process in this context. The clear separation of such functions provides an assurance of objective, dispassionate decision making, and of checks and balances. This is important if the rights of the parties, including defendants, victims and witnesses, are to be protected and seen to be protected. **We recommend that in all criminal cases, currently prosecuted by the DPP and the police, responsibility for determining whether to prosecute and for undertaking prosecutions should be vested in a single independent prosecuting authority.** Thus the police would no longer have a role in prosecuting less serious cases before the magistrates' courts.

4.128   We did consider whether there might be a class of trivial cases, minor regulatory traffic offences for example, where prosecutorial responsibility should be left with the police. We decided against such an option as it would dilute the principle of independence, which we believe to be so important, for little practical gain. However, we do not suggest any change to the current arrangements whereby prosecution for TV licence offences under the Wireless Telegraphy Act and motor tax offences are brought by the Regional TV Licensing Centre and the Driver and Vehicle Licensing Agency respectively. Nor do we propose any change in the arrangements for other prosecutions currently carried out under the auspices of government departments or agencies, many of which are presented by the DPP. We also see the right to bring private prosecutions continuing as at present.

THE INTERFACE BETWEEN INVESTIGATION AND PROSECUTION - GENERAL

4.129   We considered whether the prosecution service should have a supervisory role in relation to police investigation, perhaps by making it responsible for the conduct of investigation into crime as in Scotland and other jurisdictions. We understand the argument that this might provide reassurance against possible excesses by investigators and improve the quality of investigations by ensuring that evidential issues are fully addressed at the earliest possible point. However, such an arrangement would seriously compromise the independence of the prosecution and investigative processes from each other, which in Northern Ireland we believe to be an important safeguard and confidence building measure in itself. Against the background of Northern Ireland, having a prosecution service that is objective in its approach and able to take full account of the rights of the suspect in accordance with human rights norms might not sit easily with it being given a supervisory or participatory role in investigation. We share the view of the MacDermott Working Party that introducing the Scottish model of prosecutorial supervision of investigation into a very different criminal justice system and culture would constitute a fundamental change, which is not necessary and might well not work or produce the desired outcomes.

4.130   **We recommend that the investigative function should remain the responsibility of the police and not be subject to external supervision.** However, our recommendations below, many of them influenced by what we have seen in Scotland, the United States and other jurisdictions, do, we believe, go a long way towards meeting the concerns of those who were attracted to the idea of giving the prosecution service a supervisory role in relation to investigations.

4.131   On the basis of submissions made to us, it was apparent that some saw a role for the prosecutor in ensuring a full and rigorous investigation of all cases no matter what the circumstances or who might be involved. As noted above, Article 6(3) of the Prosecution of Offences (Northern Ireland) Order 1972 already places a duty on the Chief Constable to respond to a request from the DPP for information on any matter requiring investigation on the ground that it may involve a criminal offence and to provide the DPP with any information necessary for the discharge of his functions. **We recommend that the powers contained in Article 6(3) of the Prosecution of Offences (Northern Ireland) Order 1972 be retained and that the head of the prosecution service should make clear publicly the service's ability and determination to prompt an investigation by the police of facts that come into its possession, if these appear to constitute allegations of the commission of a criminal offence, and to request further information from the police to assist it in coming to a decision on whether or not to prosecute.**

4.132   This last recommendation would underline the central point that, while it is no part of the prosecutor's function to supervise investigations, it is the prosecutor's concern to prosecute crime and when allegations of criminal offences come into his or her domain, the prosecutor has a duty to see that such allegations are investigated. The question arises of what happens in the event that the prosecutor is dissatisfied with the response to a request for matters to be investigated and believes that they have not been pursued with sufficient vigour by the police. We note that under the Police (Northern Ireland) Act 1998 the Secretary of State and the Police Authority of Northern Ireland may refer a case to the Police Ombudsman after consultation with the Chief Constable where it is desirable to do so in the public interest. **We recommend that Article 6(3) of the 1972 Order be supplemented with a provision enabling the prosecutor to refer a case to the Police Ombudsman for investigation where he or she is not satisfied with an Article 6(3) response.**

4.133   The early involvement of the prosecutor in a case raises the question of his or her role if he or she were to suspect malpractice on the part of the police investigators. **We recommend that a duty be placed on the prosecutor to ensure that any allegations of malpractice by the police are fully investigated.** This would be consistent with human rights guidelines and is in line with present practice. As for whether evidence secured in such circumstances should be deployed in court, that is a matter for the prosecutor who would take account of the human rights imperative of a fair trial and the need to avoid abuse of process. It would not necessarily be in the interests of justice for all such evidence to be excluded in all circumstances. The prosecutor, in deciding whether to use evidence obtained through malpractice or unlawful means, would make a judgement on whether it was likely to be regarded as admissible in court and on whether it would be proper in all the circumstances to use it.

4.134   We should emphasise that recommendations such as those in the previous paragraphs are not intended to place the prosecution in a position of authority over the police investigator. They are intended to ensure that the prosecutor has the necessary powers to exercise his or her prosecutorial duties effectively and in conformity with human rights obligations.

4.135   While we do not envisage prosecutorial supervision of investigation, we were impressed by the strength of the arguments for early involvement of a prosecuting lawyer in police investigations in the more complex and serious cases. This came through strongly in our visits to Scotland, the United States and many of the civil law jurisdictions. The involvement of prosecuting lawyers might amount to providing advice on whether there is sufficient evidence to justify an arrest and charge or it could be more proactive in contributing to the planning of a complex operation in a way that was likely to secure admissible evidence. Such advice is already given on occasion in Northern Ireland. **We recommend that it be a clearly stated objective of the prosecution service to be available at the invitation of the police to provide advice on prosecutorial issues at any stage in the investigative process.**

4.136   This last recommendation raises the question of whether a prosecutor who has given advice at the investigative stage, especially if closely involved in the case on a regular basis, is in a position to make an objective decision on whether to prosecute. In some jurisdictions which we visited, in such circumstances another prosecutor would take the decision on whether to prosecute or the decision would be the subject of scrutiny by a supervisor. That would not always be easy or practical in a jurisdiction the size of Northern Ireland, and we do not believe that the nature of the relationship we envisage between prosecution and police should give rise to many problems of this sort. **We suggest that, where a prosecutor has been extensively involved in advising the police on prosecutorial matters at the investigative stage, in order fully to safeguard the independence of the prosecution process consideration should be given to the possibility of arranging for the decision to prosecute to be made or scrutinised by another member of the prosecution service.**

4.137 For the sake of clarity, we wish to say that we fully appreciate the need for the police to have access to legal advice from their own lawyers on such matters as employment issues, operational matters and civil claims. These are not matters for the prosecution.

THE INTERFACE BETWEEN INVESTIGATION AND PROSECUTION – RESPONSIBILITY FOR CHARGING

4.138 In the more serious cases where the suspect is subject to a charge, we gave careful thought to the point at which the prosecutor should assume responsibility. In particular, should the prosecutor be responsible for initiating proceedings by taking the decision to charge following an arrest? This would involve a legal professional input at an early stage and appears to provide a valuable safeguard. However, we have considered relevant provisions of the Police and Criminal Evidence (Northern Ireland) Order 1989 (PACE) and associated codes as they apply to the detention, treatment and questioning of suspects by police officers. We have also looked at the practicalities and resource implications. These considerations, and in particular our concern to interfere as little as possible with the current PACE procedures, militate against giving prosecutors a role immediately after the point of arrest, as would be necessary if it were to be their responsibility to prefer the initial charge. In order to maintain a clear distinction between investigation and prosecution, we believe that the police are best left with the responsibility of deciding what charges to bring initially in the light of their investigation and after interviewing suspects, but that a professional prosecutor should be involved at an early enough stage to take responsibility for deciding which charges should be presented to the court and for presenting the case in court. **We recommend that where the police prefer a "holding" charge under Article 38(7) of the Police and Criminal Evidence (Northern Ireland) Order 1989, a prosecutor should be seized of and be responsible for the presentation of the case before a magistrates' court in accordance with the provisions of Article 47 of the Order.[32] It should be the prosecutor's sole responsibility to formulate and determine the charge that is presented to the court.**

---

32   Article 47 requires that a person charged and detained in custody shall be brought before a magistrates' court as soon as is practicable and in any event not later than the following day, or where that day is a Sunday, Christmas or Good Friday, the next following day that is not one of these days.

The prosecutor should have legal responsibility for the application to the magistrates' court for remand, including the presentation of all supporting evidence. This will require legislative change.

4.139　Under Article 47 of the Police and Criminal Evidence (Northern Ireland) Order 1989 once a person is charged, he or she must be brought before a magistrates' court within the required timescale. It is not possible to drop the charges before the court appearance, although they can of course be withdrawn at the hearing. **We recommend that consideration be given to amending the Police and Criminal Evidence (Northern Ireland) Order 1989 to enable a prosecutor, on reviewing the case, to withdraw the charges before the court appearance.** Further we appreciate that publicity surrounding the charging of an individual can be distressing and damaging to reputation. Accordingly **we recommend that (if the law is changed in the way we suggest), until the prosecutor has determined whether to proceed with the remand application, the fact of the arrest and the name of the person detained should not be publicised.**

4.140　We recognise that the arrangements recommended in the previous paragraphs will require prosecutors to be available to receive papers and appear in court outside normal working hours and at weekends before the first remand hearing takes place. In the event of police bail being granted, the time limits are less stringent but the same principles would apply.

4.141　We have considered carefully the present position and the relationship between the police and prosecutor in relation to the preparation and presentation of cases between charge and trial. Following charge, it will continue to be for the police to produce evidence to enable the prosecutor to direct on whether to proceed with the prosecution and to put together material to enable the prosecutor to take decisions on disclosure. However, **we recommend that the prosecutor should assume full responsibility for the case between the point of charge (or summons) and trial, including tracking progress of the case, advising the police on the evidence required to secure conviction and deciding on what matters should be disclosed to the defence.** On the basis of discussions in Northern Ireland and of what we have seen elsewhere, we see the prosecution as having the key role at this stage of the process in ensuring the timely management of cases and focusing attention on evidential issues. Close co-operation with and, on evidential matters, direction of the police on the part of the prosecutor is crucial if cases are to be processed efficiently and to a high standard. This does not mean the prosecutor having responsibility for investigation or the direction of police resources and we are satisfied that it can be pursued without impairing the essential independence of the two organisations.

4.142　We recognise that the approach as suggested in the preceding paragraphs would place significant additional responsibilities on the prosecution and that there would be practical and resource implications. We are also aware of the scale of change in organisation and process that would be associated with implementation of the totality of our recommendations. The lesson from other jurisdictions is that change should be carefully planned and properly resourced if the integrity of the prosecution process is to be safeguarded and not put under unacceptable pressure. With that thought in mind, **we suggest that the timing of commencement of legislation that will flow from our recommendations should be planned so as to ensure that all necessary resources, preparation and training are in place and completed before procedural changes are introduced.**

4.143   As regards disclosure, it is for the prosecution to take full responsibility for deciding what matters should be disclosed to the defence. But we note the concerns raised by practising lawyers that the police act as a filter by making judgements in the first place as to what material may undermine the prosecution case. In fact the disclosure code issued under the Criminal Procedure and Investigations Act 1996 states that the police disclosure officer must also provide the prosecutor with schedules listing all material which may be relevant to an investigation. However, **we believe that the present disclosure provisions should be reviewed and suggest in Chapter 14 that this might be one of the matters for consideration by a Law Commission.**

4.144   The issue of the time taken to bring cases to trial is dealt with in Chapter 15. In this context the period between first remand and committal for trial is critical. At present the average time taken to progress non-scheduled custody cases through this period is about 30 weeks of which 16 weeks account for the time taken for the police to submit a file to the DPP. Through joint case management, between the police and DPP, efforts are being made to reduce these periods, although it is recognised that sufficient time taken to prepare properly can reduce the likelihood of problems later on, including the risk of miscarriages of justice. We believe that our recommendations, which should mean a closer involvement of the prosecutor throughout, will aid further progress. However, we view with interest the Scottish system where it is for the fiscal to make a motion for committal, on being satisfied that there is sufficient evidence for a jury to convict. This process does not involve a preliminary consideration of the evidence by the court. We also note the trend in England and Wales towards simplified procedures for transferring cases to the Crown Court. **We recommend that consideration be given to introducing simplified procedures for transferring cases to the Crown Court in Northern Ireland, while ensuring safeguards for a defendant who wishes to argue that there is no case to answer. Such a development could be accompanied by a major effort further to reduce time taken to bring cases to trial.**

THE INTERFACE BETWEEN INVESTIGATION AND PROSECUTION – SUMMONS CASES

4.145   The less serious cases, which form the bulk of criminal business, are normally processed by way of summons. Most of these are currently prosecuted by the RUC but, if our recommendations are accepted, they will in future be processed by an independent prosecution service. That service will continue of course to prosecute the more serious cases tried before magistrates' courts. In considering how this might work, we have been concerned to ensure proper scrutiny of the case before issue of summons, to avoid unnecessary additional costs and not to add to delay.

4.146 The Scottish and Manhattan experiences were instructive. There should normally be no need for any prosecutorial involvement until a decision is required on whether to proceed in these cases. **We recommend that once the police at divisional level decide that they wish to proceed and judge that they have sufficient evidence to warrant prosecution, the facts of the case should be sent to the prosecutor. In order to facilitate the process, consideration should be given to the development of standard forms, with the information fields necessary for purposes of issuing a summons, which could be e-mailed or faxed to the prosecutor.** We understand that the criminal justice integrated IT project, currently being developed, would support such a mechanism.

4.147 Where these cases are submitted by the police to the prosecutor, it would be appropriate for them to be endorsed by or routed through a supervisory level within the police, in order to provide safeguards and quality control. However, prosecutors in some other jurisdictions stressed the importance of their being able to deal with material prepared by the police officer most involved and being able to discuss issues directly with the investigator when questions arose. The more remote the point of police interface was from the actual investigation, the greater was the danger of misunderstanding and delay. **We recommend that in summons cases arrangements be made to ensure that the facts of the case are passed to the prosecutor by a police officer who is close to and familiar with the investigation.** There should be no need for cases to be processed through several levels within the police and, in particular, we would counsel against retaining any form of Central Process Office to act as a link with the prosecutor. We see the prosecution service as taking over the role of the Central Process Office; the additional cost of expanding the prosecution service accordingly to deal with the caseload should to a considerable extent be offset by ending this function within the police.

4.148 The prosecutor, having examined the case and decided to prosecute, would be responsible for drawing up the summons, deciding when the case was to be heard, submitting the summons to a JP or clerk of petty sessions for consideration and signature, and arranging for it to be served.

4.149 As for prosecution in court, **we envisage moving towards a position where it is the norm for legally qualified staff of the prosecution service to present cases at magistrates' courts (including committals), while retaining the option of briefing independent counsel when appropriate.** This is an approach which would help enhance the quality and diversity of work available to the prosecutor's staff while providing value for money. We do not at this stage recommend using non-qualified staff from the prosecution service to prosecute routine cases as we see the involvement of lawyers in all aspects of prosecution work as an important confidence-builder.

DIVERSION AND THE COMMUNITY

4.150   It is currently the police who, in Northern Ireland, determine whether to divert offenders away from the court process - for example by way of warning or caution. In the case of juveniles they are advised by juvenile liaison bureaux (in those areas where they exist), which may in some cases recommend intervention by other agencies such as social services or education as part of a proposal to caution. We do not wish to disturb these arrangements which are consistent with the role of the police in the community; moreover, if all such cases were to be processed through the prosecutor's office for decision it would add significantly to costs and delay. In 1994/95 some 3,900 offenders were the subject of an official caution in respect of notifiable offences, 60% of those in respect of theft.

4.151   Considerations of equity require that decisions on whether to caution are taken on a consistent basis across Northern Ireland; and, given the role which we envisage for the prosecution service in relation to decisions on prosecution for all offences, it must have an input into policy on cautioning. **We recommend that caution guidelines should be agreed between the police and the prosecution service. Statistics should be kept and the practice kept under review, with particular attention being paid to consistency of approach and to ensuring that cases are dealt with expeditiously.**

4.152   As to whether the prosecution service should have the option of diverting offenders away from the court process in cases submitted to it by the police, we are conscious that this is less likely to be an issue at present, given that the DPP is only involved in the more serious cases. On rare occasions the DPP might refer a case back for police caution. However, we noted that in other jurisdictions, where the prosecution had responsibility for deciding on all prosecutions, there was often a presumption that every effort would be made to divert offenders away from the courts if at all possible. In the scheme of things that we are proposing, **we recommend that prosecutors be enjoined positively to consider the diversion option in their consideration of cases. The options available to them might be:**

- **referral back to the police with a recommendation to caution;**

- **diversionary options, for example mentally disordered offenders or drug users being referred to treatment or young offenders being offered programmes to address offending behaviour; and**

- **the making of arrangements for restorative interventions.**

If prosecutorial diversion is to develop in a meaningful way, it will of course be dependent on the availability of diversionary schemes.

4.153   The cases to be considered for prosecutorial diversion are likely to be more serious than those where a police caution is issued, given that the police will have passed them to the prosecutor for a decision on whether to prosecute. In the circumstances **we think it right** for the prosecutor to have the ability to review the decision not to prosecute if the offender fails to follow through the arrangements for diversionary activity, treatment or restorative agreements.

4.154   We thought carefully about the possibility of prosecutorial fines. It might be argued that they involve the imposition of punishment, or putting pressure on a suspect to accept punishment without recourse to due process. However, provided that in issuing a fine it is made very clear that the recipient has the option of fighting the case in court, there should be no human rights objections to this course. It would be a means of expediting some of the less serious cases, while giving the alleged offender the opportunity of avoiding a criminal record. In principle the concept is little different from a fixed penalty. **We recommend that consideration be given to introducing the prosecutorial fine in Northern Ireland.** Consideration would have to be given to whether it should be possible to cite a prosecutorial fine in any further court proceedings, as is the case with cautions.

4.155   A well-structured approach to diversion, on the part of the police and the prosecutor, has the dual benefit of avoiding criminalisation in suitable cases and reducing the volume of business in the courts. It is important, however, that the community understand the process if confidence is to be retained that effective action is being taken in respect of criminal behaviour. **It will be necessary for the prosecution service, together with the police, to engage with the community and other agencies and service providers about what is involved in the diversionary process and to seek to arrive at a clear understanding of what diversionary schemes and options may be available at the local level.**

4.156   This last recommendation brings us into an important area. It opens up the prospect of prosecutors engaging at the local level with other agencies and the community in a way that has not hitherto been possible. From our visits to other jurisdictions we are conscious of the enhanced and positive contribution that prosecutors can make to the criminal justice system and the community at large through such engagement, without compromising their independence. It is not just about issues of diversion, but also involvement in community safety matters, court user issues and helping familiarise the public with criminal justice processes. **We recommend that outreach to the community and inter-agency working be a stated objective of the prosecution service.**

POLITICAL ACCOUNTABILITY

4.157   We were asked in our terms of reference to safeguard the independence of the prosecution process; and it is clear from comments made to us throughout the consultation period that independence from political influence is what is sought above all else. Yet the prosecution service which we envisage will be bigger than at present, spend more money, have a greater role in the criminal justice system and have a higher profile in the community. In the circumstances, some form of political accountability is inevitable and we did not come across any jurisdiction where the prosecutor was able to act entirely without reference to government and/or legislature. The challenge is how to develop a meaningful relationship between prosecution, the executive and the legislature without compromising the essential independence of the process.

4.158   The weight of opinion, though by no means unanimous, was that responsibility for prosecutions should be devolved to local Northern Ireland institutions sooner or later. Some felt that it could be delayed until local institutions of government had had time to prove themselves. Given the discrete nature of the function, it would be possible for the prosecution service to remain accountable to an Attorney General in London for a period after other criminal justice functions had been devolved. However, **we recommend that political responsibility for the prosecution system should be devolved to local institutions along with other criminal justice functions, or as soon as possible after devolution of such functions.** We so recommend because the prosecution service, whilst sustaining its independence, will need to work effectively in partnership with other local criminal justice agencies and interact rather more with local communities than in the past; this does not fit well with a system where the service looks to London for its political focus at a time when other domestic functions are run from Northern Ireland.

4.159   After devolution, one possible solution would be for the prosecution service to be accountable to a Minister for Justice. That does occur in some other jurisdictions. However, given the potential sensitivities of Northern Ireland and the need for the prosecution to be seen to be independent, we recommend against such a line of accountability to any departmental Minister with operational responsibilities. Nor do we believe that it is right for the prosecution service to be dependent for finance, accommodation or other corporate services on another department; it should be a self-sufficient organisation. We thought about other possibilities including an entirely free standing service, one which reports to the First Minister and Deputy First Minister or the retention of a role for the Attorney in London. But none of these is ideal.

4.160   A number of people have suggested that the head of the prosecution service might be accountable to a local Attorney General. We regard the creation of such a post as raising many issues beyond our terms of reference. But we note that such a figure might have responsibilities as senior legal adviser to the Northern Ireland Executive, be responsible for the legislative draftsmen, be the Executive's link with the Law Commission, and take responsibility for human rights-proofing legislation. **We recommend that consideration be given to establishing a locally sponsored post of Attorney General who, inter alia, would have oversight of the prosecution service. We see the Attorney General as a non-political figure drawn from the ranks of senior lawyers and appointed by the First Minister and Deputy First Minister. We would suggest a fixed term appointment, with security of tenure, say for five years, which would not be affected by the timing**

of Assembly terms. The appointment process should be transparent, enabling people to declare themselves as candidates. We would see such a position as carrying significant status, equivalent to that of a High Court judge, and attracting candidates of the highest possible calibre.

4.161   The question of political accountability arises in the event that this proposal is adopted. **We recommend that the formulation in section 27 of the Scotland Act 1998 be adopted in that, although not a member of the Assembly, the Attorney should be enabled by Standing Orders to participate in Assembly business, for example through answering questions or making statements, but without voting rights.**

4.162   An Attorney General appointed along the lines envisaged above would be less "political" than almost all counterparts in other common law jurisdictions, where the post holder is a member of the Government or at the very least an appointee of the governing party. This would, in itself, help insulate the prosecution process from political pressure. However, in the particular circumstances of Northern Ireland, we believe that this independence should be further strengthened, by ensuring that the relationship between the Attorney General and the head of the prosecution service, while containing elements of oversight, is consultative and not supervisory. In other words, **there should be no power for the Attorney General to direct the prosecutor, whether in individual cases or on policy matters.** Our impression is that in some other common law jurisdictions the relationship between Attorney and prosecutor works well in practice and that the independence of the prosecutor in decision making is respected; but ultimately, if there were disagreement between the Attorney and the prosecutor on an individual case, then in law the Attorney's will would probably prevail. We do not believe that such an arrangement would be suitable in the Northern Ireland context.

4.163   We are attracted to aspects of the model in the Republic of Ireland. **We recommend that legislation should: confirm the independence of the prosecutor; make it an offence for anyone without a legitimate interest in a case[33] to seek to influence the prosecutor not to pursue it; but make provision for statutory consultation between the head of the prosecution service and the Attorney General, at the request of either.** The Attorney General would be answerable to the Assembly for the work of the prosecution service in general terms but **we recommend that it be made clear on the face of legislation, as in section 27 of the Scotland Act 1998, that the Attorney could decline to answer questions on individual cases where to do so might prejudice criminal proceedings or would be contrary to the public interest.** It may be that the prosecutor and Attorney General would conclude that in no circumstances should they be expected to answer such questions. Nevertheless we do not think that this should be ruled out for all time, as will be apparent from our views on the giving of reasons for decisions. **We recommend that the head of the prosecution service should be accountable to the appropriate Assembly**

---

33   People with a legitimate interest could be the defendant, his or her medical or legal advisers, his or her family, professionals with an interest in the case such as teachers or social workers, and the victim. Section 6 of the Republic of Ireland's Prosecution of Offences Act 1974 contains a possible formulation.

Committee for financial and administrative matters relating to the running of service. In this event it would be important that Standing Orders made clear the limitations on questioning which might impinge on individual cases.

OTHER ACCOUNTABILITY MEASURES

4.164   Giving reasons for decisions to the public or interested stakeholders such as victims or the relatives of victims is the most direct form of accountability in the explanatory sense. We have noted the submissions of human rights groups that prosecutors should be more responsive to victims and their families when they raise concerns about the investigation of their case. We think it right that victims should be given as much information about their case as they request, so far as is possible, and we can see that there might be circumstances where public confidence would be enhanced by providing explanations for decisions in individual cases.

4.165   However, this is a difficult area and we note the reluctance of prosecutors in many jurisdictions to give detailed reasons. It would be inimical to the interests of justice if conclusions were drawn about the guilt of an individual, not on the basis of a trial before an independent tribunal, but rather because it appeared from reasons given for non-prosecution that the case had to be abandoned due to some technicality or concern for the welfare of a particular witness. There would also be a damaging effect on witnesses whose credibility was called into question. We can think of other instances where giving detailed reasons would not be in the public interest.

4.166   However, we are also of the view that there will be occasions when it should be possible to give quite detailed reasons to victims in such a way as would not be prejudicial to the interests of justice or the reputations of others. In some cases where there are evidential difficulties, for example, it should be possible to explain what these are without impugning in any way the reputation of an individual. We note that in the United States District Attorneys tend to be very open in explaining their approach in cases of major public concern, perhaps in part because of their elected status. The experience in Germany and the Netherlands has also shown that it is possible to formulate a system of giving reasons without prejudicing the cause of justice.[34]

4.167   **We recommend that, where information is sought by someone with a proper and legitimate interest in a case on why there was no prosecution, or on why a prosecution has been abandoned, the prosecutor should seek to give as full an explanation as is possible without prejudicing the interests of justice or the public interest. It will be a matter for the prosecutor to consider carefully in the circumstances of each individual case whether reasons can be given in more than**

---

34   Fionda, *Public Prosecutors and Discretion: A Comparative Study* (1993), page 211.

general terms and, if so, in how much detail, but the presumption should shift towards giving reasons where appropriate. We appreciate that this could impose a significant additional burden on the prosecution service. We suggest that those regarded as having a legitimate interest in a case be confined for the most part to victims and their families. There may be the occasional high profile case, where it might be appropriate to respond to public concerns and make reasons for prosecutorial decisions more widely available, but this will be the exception rather than the rule.

4.168 We should stress that we do not envisage reasons for prosecutorial decisions being made available to public representatives on a routine basis. If such a practice were to become the norm, the independence of the prosecution service would be liable to be compromised.

4.169 Giving reasons might be slightly less of an issue if there were greater public understanding of the work of the prosecution service. This is also an important element of accountability, from what we have seen in other jurisdictions. **We recommend that the head of the prosecution service be required by statute to publish the following:**

- **an annual report;**

- **a code of practice outlining the factors to be taken into account in applying the evidential and public interest tests on whether to prosecute; and**

- **a code of ethics, based in part on the standards set out in UN Guidelines.**

It would also be beneficial for the service to publish good practice guidelines on such matters as the treatment of witnesses and refer to them in its annual report. Publications of the sort outlined above, together with a programme of outreach, would in our view remove much of the mystery in the process which was apparent to us during the public consultations that we carried out. We also believe that a policy of transparency and openness would enhance public confidence and the quality of work satisfaction for those in the service.

4.170 Greater public understanding of the way in which the prosecution system works, achieved through a policy of transparency and openness as outlined above, should have a significant impact in confidence building terms. However, particularly given that it will not always be possible for prosecutors to give detailed explanations for their decisions, there remains an issue about providing assurances on the quality of prosecutorial decision making. **We recommend that the prosecution service should be subject to inspection, with a significant independent input.**

4.171 The scale of the prosecution service in Northern Ireland will not be sufficient to warrant a standing inspectorate. For the same reason, it would not be feasible for inspections to be carried out by teams made up primarily of members of the service. **We recommend that the Criminal Justice Inspectorate, which we propose in Chapter 15, be given the responsibility for buying in the professional expertise necessary to carry out inspections.** The source of expertise might be prosecutors or independent lawyers from other jurisdictions, the Crown Prosecution Service inspectorate, for example. Inspection activity would not be limited to covering the quality of professional decision making on prosecution matters but should also embrace other aspects of service provision such as contact with victims and management issues. **We recommend that the Criminal Justice Inspectorate be under a statutory duty to arrange for the inspection of the prosecution service, report to the Attorney General on any matter to do with the service which the Attorney refers to it and also report the outcome of inspections to the Attorney General. We recommend that the Criminal Justice Inspectorate should include in its annual report a review of inspection activity and its outcomes in relation to the prosecution service.** All of this would be consistent with what is proposed for the CPS.

4.172   The handling of complaints is an essential part of effective accountability mechanisms. **Details of complaints procedures for the prosecution service should be publicly available and included in the service's annual report, along with an account of the handling of complaints throughout the year.** Given the increased role of the prosecution service, there may be a greater volume of complaints and **we recommend that an independent element be introduced into the procedures where the complainant is not satisfied with the initial response and where the complaint is not about the exercise of prosecutorial discretion. The Criminal Justice Inspectorate should audit the operation of the prosecution service's complaints procedures on a regular basis.**

THE PROSECUTION SERVICE

4.173   So far in this section of the report, our recommendations have been concerned with where responsibility for prosecutions should lie, the role of a prosecution service and accountability mechanisms. We now address the issue of the nature of the organisation that will deliver the service that we envisage.

4.174   In functional terms, what we are recommending entails building upon the responsibilities and work of the existing Department of the Director of Public Prosecutions. However, our recommendations entail taking on new work, a different approach to aspects of its existing work and substantial organisational change. We feel that this should be reflected in the name of the prosecution service. **We recommend that the Department of the Director of Public Prosecutions be renamed the Public Prosecution Service for Northern Ireland.**

4.175   As for the professional head of the service, we considered the case for a new title, perhaps "Chief Public Prosecutor". We envisage major changes in the prosecutorial arrangements in Northern Ireland, which we believe will enhance the system and public confidence in it. A new title for the head of the organisation would help to demonstrate to those outside it, as well as those inside, that the remit and responsibilities of the organisation have changed considerably. On the other hand, the term "Director of Public Prosecutions" is used in many common law jurisdictions throughout the world and within these islands. It is widely understood and indicates a position of standing and status, as befits the head of an independent prosecution service. The arguments are finely balanced. We make no recommendation on the title of the head of the Public Prosecution Service.

4.176   It is particularly important that the process of appointing the head of the Public Prosecution Service is insulated from any possibility or appearance of political influence. The same applies to procedures for dismissal in the event of incapacity or misconduct. **We recommend that the appointment process for the head of the Public Prosecution Service and deputy be through open competition, with a selection panel, in accordance with procedures established by the Civil Service Commissioners for Northern Ireland. These appointments would be made by the Attorney General for Northern Ireland. Appointments would be for a fixed term, or until a statutory retirement date. There should be statutory safeguards to ensure that removal from office by reason of misconduct or incapacity would be possible only after a recommendation to that effect coming from an independent tribunal.**

4.177   The new organisation will be larger than the present Department. A substantial number of additional legal staff, together with support staff, will be needed to undertake the prosecution work that is currently the responsibility of the police. The corporate functions of the Service will need to be strengthened if it is to assume full responsibility for its own finance, personnel and administration, which we regard as particularly important.

4.178   If the Public Prosecution Service is to work as envisaged in our recommendations, it will require good accessibility to local courts and the police at divisional level together with the ability to interface with the communities which it will be serving. This points to a significant degree of decentralisation. Accordingly, **we recommend that the Public Prosecution Service should establish local offices from which the bulk of prosecutorial work in their respective areas would be conducted. The boundaries of such offices should be coterminous with police and court boundaries, which in turn are based on district council areas.** We make no recommendation about the precise number of such local offices. We think that five, including Belfast, may be about right but suggest that this should be the subject of detailed consideration, based on such factors as caseload and accessibility. **We recommend that each of these offices should be headed by a senior prosecutor of sufficient status for decisions on most prosecutions to be delegated to the local offices.**

4.179   In looking at the nature of the transition that will be involved in moving from the present arrangements to the new, we took account of a number of considerations. We need above all to consider the importance of sustaining the quality of justice through the period of change. The experience of others suggests to us that a measured approach to organisational change is likely to produce the best results in the Northern Ireland context.

4.180   We were given access to information on the religious and gender balance of the Department of the DPP. While the religious and gender balance is reasonably reflective of that in the community, we do recognise the views of those who would like to see a staffing complement that is diverse in terms of professional background and experience and which will help sustain an environment of measured change. While some support staff from the Central Process Offices might be encouraged to transfer into the Public Prosecution Service, there will remain the need to recruit substantial additional numbers of people at a range of levels, both professional lawyers and administrative staff. **External recruitment of new staff should be subject to open competition, in accordance with fair employment and equal opportunities best practice. A substantial recruitment exercise would provide the opportunity to attract applicants from a range of diverse backgrounds, including defence lawyers and people from all parts of the community, with a geographical spread across Northern Ireland. Consideration should be given to some posts being the subject of fixed-term contracts and to offering financial assistance to a limited number of students seeking professional qualifications, on the basis that they might start their career within the Public Prosecution Service.** This exercise, together with the expanded role for the Public Prosecution Service and implementation of others of our recommendations, will herald a period of significant change. However, we should stress the importance of sustaining the quality and efficiency of the service's work throughout this time.

4.181   **We recommend the appointment of a senior manager as head of Corporate Services to work to, and alongside, the head of the Public Prosecution Service. This post would have particular responsibility for driving the change agenda and ensuring the efficient and effective management of what will be a larger and more dispersed organisation than is the case at present.**

4.182   The influx of newly recruited staff, increasingly complex legislation, the human rights dimension and the change in operating environment will place a big premium on training. We noted the emphasis placed on training by the Procurator Fiscal Service during our visit to Scotland, especially in relation to human rights. **We recommend that at the earliest possible stage in establishing the Public Prosecution Service training needs should be identified and the necessary resources deployed to meet them.**

4.183   In the course of our work, we considered in some detail whether there were lessons to be derived from the *Review of the Crown Prosecution Service in England and Wales* that reported in 1998 under the chairmanship of the Rt. Hon Sir Iain Glidewell. Indeed we have already referred to some of the issues identified in this report. That review examined the development of the CPS since its formation in 1986 and contained much useful material about the management of structural change and the interface between the CPS, police and other agencies. There are many differences between the scenario that we envisage and that which was associated with the formation of the CPS. For example, the introduction of the CPS meant that, almost overnight, police responsibility for the vast bulk of prosecutions was transferred to an independent service, whereas in Northern Ireland it is already the case that a substantial number of cases are the responsibility of the DPP. In addition, the scale of the operation in England and Wales was and remains totally different. We are aware that the DPP has already considered the applicability of Glidewell to his Department. However, **we recommend that those who are considering the resource implications and the organisational issues arising from our proposals in respect of the prosecution function should examine the Glidewell Report, with a view to seeing whether there are lessons to be learnt from the experience of England and Wales.**

RESOURCE ISSUES

4.184   One of the clear lessons coming out of the Glidewell Report is the importance of ensuring that any new structures in this field are properly resourced from the outset. We employed consultants to produce a broad indication of the possible cost implications of our recommendations for the prosecution system. We are grateful to them and to the RUC and the DPP for their co-operation in enabling the work to be done.

4.185   The consultants produced a model based on a number of assumptions drawn from our report. These included the Public Prosecution Service assuming responsibility for all prosecutions currently carried out by the police, with the consequential need for more staff, to some extent offset by the closure of the Central Process Offices. They worked on the basis of the Public Prosecution Service being a stand-alone agency, with its own corporate structure and decentralised offices. They also took account of the need for out of hours cover and made assumptions about the time that would be needed to process cases of differing degrees of complexity. In short their broad estimate of the additional annual costs of the proposed arrangements was in the region of £1.5 million to £2 million, with additional start-up costs of about £2 million. This does not take account of any redundancies that might be associated with the process. The DPP's budget for 1998/99 was just over £7.5 million.

4.186   We should emphasise that much more detailed work will be required to produce a firmer estimate of the costs of our proposals in this chapter. The emphasis on outreach, involvement in inter-agency working, working with victims and training will carry some additional resource implications.

Courts and the Judiciary

5 The Structure of the Courts and the Judicial System

5.1　The three chapters that follow will deal with issues relating to the judiciary and the courts. We thought that it would be useful, before examining these areas in detail, to give readers a brief overview of the court system and of the way in which the judiciary is organised. In doing so, we are conscious that we will include material that relates to the civil jurisdiction, which is not within our terms of reference. This is necessary if readers are to gain a full picture of how the whole system might be affected by our recommendations on judicial appointments and court matters. Most of the commentary in this introductory chapter is, however, written from the perspective of how criminal cases are processed through the courts.

5.2　Court of Appeal and High Court cases are heard in the Royal Courts of Justice in Belfast, but cases before the Crown Court, county courts and magistrates' courts take place at venues throughout Northern Ireland. The petty sessions (i.e. magistrates' court) boundaries coincide with district council areas. The frequency of sittings of courts varies largely according to caseload. For example, in most major towns the magistrates' court sits between five and 20 times per month, while in Belfast there are 53 sittings and in Kilkeel and Clogher only one per month. At most Crown Court venues there are around 120 to 150 sittings each year; the figure for Belfast, however, is 744.

Table 1: The Court Structure in Northern Ireland

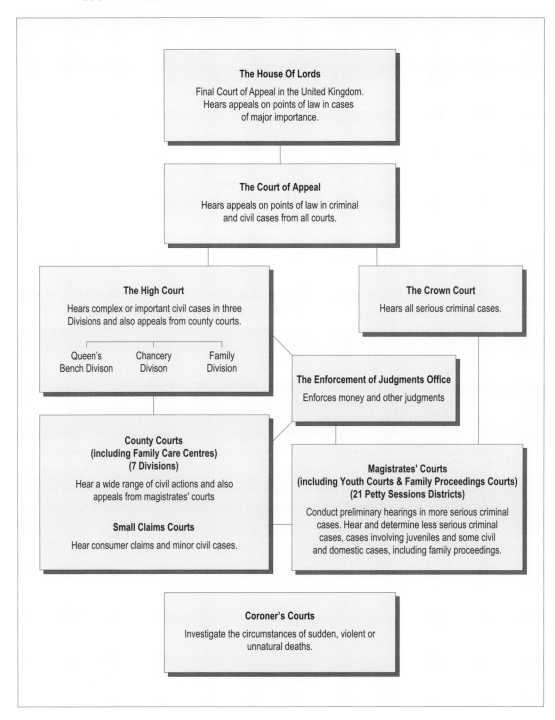

The House Of Lords

Final Court of Appeal in the United Kingdom.
Hears appeals on points of law in cases
of major importance.

The Court of Appeal

Hears appeals on points of law in criminal
and civil cases from all courts.

The High Court

Hears complex or important civil cases in three
Divisions and also appeals from county courts.

Queen's
Bench Divison

Chancery
Divison

Family
Division

The Crown Court

Hears all serious criminal cases.

The Enforcement of Judgments Office

Enforces money and other judgments

**County Courts
(including Family Care Centres)
(7 Divisions)**

Hear a wide range of civil actions and also
appeals from magistrates' courts

Small Claims Courts

Hear consumer claims and minor civil cases.

**Magistrates' Courts
(including Youth Courts & Family Proceedings Courts)
(21 Petty Sessions Districts)**

Conduct preliminary hearings in more serious criminal
cases. Hear and determine less serious criminal
cases, cases involving juveniles and some civil
and domestic cases, including family proceedings.

Coroner's Courts

Investigate the circumstances of sudden, violent or
unnatural deaths.

5.3   The full-time judicial complement in Northern Ireland at 31 March 1999 was 58, made up of the following:

Lord Chief Justice	1
Lords Justices of Appeal	3
High Court Judges	7
County Court Judges	14
District Judges	4
Resident Magistrates	17
Masters of Supreme Court	7
Principal Secretary and Legal Secretary to the LCJ	1
Official Solicitor	1
Chief Social Security and Child Support Commissioner	1
Social Security and Child Support Commissioner	1
Coroner	1

At that date there were 40 deputy county court judges, seven deputy district judges, 20 deputy resident magistrates, six part-time coroners and five deputy coroners. There were over 1,400 judicial and quasi-judicial posts, including 930 justices of the peace, 126 members of tribunals, and 148 juvenile court lay panellists. [1]

5.4   For criminal cases, the magistrates' courts hear and determine the less serious cases, that is those where the offences are classified as summary, or those which may be tried either summarily or on indictment but where it is decided to try them summarily. Around 50,000 adult and juvenile criminal cases are dealt with by magistrates each year. In addition, these courts conduct preliminary proceedings in respect of the more serious cases that go to the Crown Court.

5.5   Youth courts, usually consisting of a resident magistrate sitting with two lay panellists, try summary and indictable offences (other than homicide) where the defendant is a child aged from 10 to 16 inclusive. These courts dealt with 1,952 defendants in 1998.

5.6   The criminal jurisdiction of county courts is limited to hearing appeals from magistrates' courts and youth courts against conviction and/or sentence - some 3,000 cases in 1998.

5.7   The Crown Court was established in 1979 under the Judicature (NI) Act 1978 on the recommendation of a committee chaired by Lord Justice Jones[2] which reviewed the jurisdiction of the magistrates' courts and county courts in Northern Ireland. It recommended doing away with the old Assize Courts and replacing their criminal jurisdiction, and that of the county courts, with a single Crown Court that would sit in the

---

1   *Northern Ireland Court Service Annual Report 1998/99* (1999), Belfast: HMSO

2   *Report of the Committee on County Courts and Magistrates' Courts in Northern Ireland* (1974), Cmnd 5824.

principal cities and towns. The Crown Court has exclusive jurisdiction to try the more serious indictable cases, for example, murder, manslaughter and rape. It also tries a variety of other offences, such as burglary, fraud and indecent assault, which come before it as a result of defendants having elected jury trial or because magistrates consider them too serious to be dealt with summarily. The Crown Court disposed of 1,080 cases in 1998. The Jones Report recommended leaving appeals from magistrates' courts to be heard by county court judges in the county court on the basis that they would be experienced in criminal matters through regular sittings in the Crown Court.

5.8   Two levels of judiciary sit in the Crown Court: Supreme Court judges (High Court and above) and county court judges, with the allocation of cases between them being determined in accordance with Lord Chancellor's Directions on classes of case. The most serious cases (Class 1), such as murder, must be tried by a Supreme Court judge. The Lord Chief Justice has discretion in allocating the remainder (Classes 2 to 4) between the two judicial levels, which he exercises taking account of complexity, seriousness and judicial availability.

5.9   The Court of Appeal hears appeals in criminal matters from the Crown Court and in civil matters from the High Court. It also hears appeals on points of law from the county courts, magistrates' courts and certain tribunals.

5.10   The highest appellate court in the United Kingdom on matters that are not devolved is the House of Lords sitting in its judicial capacity. Decisions of the Northern Ireland Court of Appeal can be the subject of appeal to the House of Lords, with the leave of that Court or the House. Leave cannot be granted unless the Court of Appeal certifies that there is a point of law of general public importance and either that Court or the House views it as one which the Lords ought to consider.

5.11   Under the Northern Ireland Act 1998, the Judicial Committee of the Privy Council is the final appeal court for devolved issues, including questions of compatibility with the *European Convention on Human Rights*. The Committee comprises the Law Lords and other Privy Councillors who hold or have held high judicial office.

6 The Judiciary

Introduction

6.1 Our terms of reference invite us to address "… the arrangements for making appointments to the judiciary and magistracy, and safeguards for protecting their independence".

6.2 In this chapter we consider appointments procedures and the related issues of tenure, conditions of service, disciplinary procedures and judicial training. All of these matters impact upon the crucial issues of judicial independence and public confidence. For purposes of definition, unless we explicitly say otherwise, references to the judiciary should be taken as including the magistracy. Issues concerning JPs, lay panellists and lay involvement in adjudication are addressed in Chapter 7.

The Role of the Judge

6.3 An effective and impartial judiciary is crucial to the well-being of any society, especially one where there have been divisions and conflict such as have been experienced in Northern Ireland. All parts of the community must have confidence that judges and magistrates are adjudicating on disputes and dispensing justice fairly and objectively in accordance with the law, without being subject to influence from the Government, politicians or other interest groups. In the criminal justice system it is the judiciary above all others who ensure that two of its critical aims, fairness and due process, are, and are seen to be, achieved.

6.4 Objectivity, fairness, knowledge, the ability to command respect and the intellectual capacity to analyse and adjudicate upon an increasingly complex body of law have been and will remain of central importance for the judiciary. The same goes for such qualities as humanity and an understanding of people. However, we believe that the role of the judge has developed rapidly in recent years, in a trend that is set to continue and accelerate. This has implications for selection procedures, judicial training and the crucial issue of judicial independence. If we are to address these issues, as required in our terms of reference, we do of course have to take account of the work of the judiciary in the civil sphere and all its aspects, as well as in relation to criminal matters.

6.5   There is nothing new in judges interpreting statutes where the literal meaning is unclear or developing case law where statute and precedent are silent, taking account of changing economic and social circumstances; that is how the common law developed over the centuries. However, over the past two decades judges have been called upon to interact increasingly with executive and legislative decisions. Judicial review, where judges determine whether decisions of public authorities have been taken in accordance with proper procedures, has developed to such an extent that the courts have frequently held the executive to account for unlawful acts. Accession to the European Union and developments in the field of human rights have also resulted in more frequent challenge to legislative provisions and have ended the presumption that international legal instruments are separate from and outside the competence of domestic courts.

6.6   Incorporation of the *European Convention on Human Rights* will have an impact at all levels of court. It will mean judges being empowered to declare primary Westminster legislation incompatible with the Convention and to set aside lesser legislation, including Acts of a Northern Ireland Assembly. They will be called upon to determine whether individuals have been treated in accordance with Convention rights and whether acts of public authorities are in contravention of such rights. In many cases the courts will be required under the terms of the Convention to carry out a proportionality exercise which requires balancing the protection of individual rights against the general interest of the community, and to consider whether the protection of such rights is necessary in a democratic society.[1] This is likely to mean not only weighing the merits of competing rights but also considering arguments about their economic and social impact; it will involve giving meaning to fundamental human rights, approaching the Convention as a "living instrument" to be "interpreted in the light of present day conditions".[2] Such considerations also arise in relation to rights and equality legislation in Northern Ireland, and with the prospect of a Bill of Rights as envisaged in the Belfast Agreement. Devolution will bring its own challenges, focusing attention on constitutional matters concerning the relationship between and competence of various organs of government, other organisations and individuals.

6.7   Taken together, these developments point increasingly in the direction of judges, especially but by no means exclusively at the higher levels, hearing high profile cases in which one party at least is a public authority or part of government. They will be addressing rights issues and taking account of the economic and social impact of their decisions. If recent experience in England and Wales is anything to go by, there will be heightened interest in their background. All of this reinforces the need to ensure judicial independence from the executive and to

---

1   *Rights Brought Home, The Human Rights Bill*, Home Office, London: HMSO, Cm 3782, paragraph 2.5.

2   *Tyrer v United Kingdom* (1978) 2 EHRR 1.

enable the judiciary to act, and be seen to act, in a dispassionate way, free from any sectoral influence, real or perceived. This is especially important in a small jurisdiction. That is not to say however that judges should be distant from the community. Quite the reverse; we attach great importance to their having an understanding of all aspects of the society that is so dependent on them for its well-being.

6.8   Independence and awareness of the social context apply as much to judicial involvement in criminal justice matters as to other parts of the legal system; and human rights issues, especially those arising out of the Convention, will come into play in all of the criminal courts. If informed decisions on sentencing are to be made, it makes sense for judges and magistrates to take an interest in the development of custodial and community-based programmes, crime trends and the social and economic background against which crime is committed. This can be achieved through visits, training, informal contacts and participation in inter-agency groups dealing with criminal justice issues.

6.9   Judges have an important role in helping safeguard the interests of all those who appear in court, including vulnerable witnesses and defendants, and children. This has implications for the management of proceedings in court, but judges and magistrates are also well placed to encourage the managers of court premises to run the facilities in a way that meets the needs of different categories of user. Further, they can help educate the public in the workings of the legal system, for example through participating in the arrangements for court visits by schools and other groups and by talking to groups in the community.

6.10   On both the criminal and civil sides, organisational and case management skills are required, as is demonstrated by the active involvement of the judiciary in current initiatives to reduce delay and generally improve the efficiency of the legal process.

Human Rights Background

6.11   The international human rights instruments, to which the Government is committed, give some clear benchmarks on issues relating to the judiciary. Article 6 of the *European Convention on Human Rights* provides that "in the determination of his civil rights and obligations, or of any criminal charge against him, everyone is entitled to a fair and public hearing within a reasonable time by an independent and impartial tribunal established by law." Article 14 of the *International Covenant on Civil and Political Rights* states: "in the determination of any criminal charge against him, or of his rights and obligations in a suit of law, everyone shall be entitled to a fair and public hearing by a competent, independent and impartial tribunal established by law." In the words of the preamble to the *Siracusa Principles*,[3] an independent judiciary is indispensable for the implementation of this right.

---

3   Livingstone and Doak, Research Report 14, Appendix 10.

6.12   Other international instruments set out matters to be addressed in order to secure and safeguard judicial independence, in particular the *UN Basic Principles on the Independence of the Judiciary*.[4] These start by requiring the state to guarantee the independence of the judiciary and to provide that judicial decisions will be taken without improper influence or interference from any source. One facet of independence is that the assignment of cases to judges should be determined by the judicial administration, independently of the executive. The Principles stress the importance of selection and career management of judges based on objective considerations of merit such as integrity, ability and efficiency, with no discrimination on grounds (inter alia) of race, colour, sex, religion or political opinion. The importance of judicial training and proper remuneration is also identified.

6.13   In order to reinforce the judiciary's ability to act without fear or favour, the Basic Principles lay emphasis on security of tenure until mandatory retirement age or expiry of a fixed term of office. Complaints against judges are required to be processed expeditiously and fairly under an appropriate procedure, against established standards of judicial conduct; suspension or removal of judges is permitted only on grounds of incapacity or behaviour rendering them unfit to discharge their duties. Emphasis is placed on freedom of expression and association for judges, provided that in exercising their rights they act in such a manner as to preserve the dignity of their office, impartiality and independence.

6.14   Other instruments, such as the *Siracusa Principles* and the *Procedures for the Effective Implementation of the Basic Principles on the Independence of the Judiciary*[5] go into matters in rather more detail. For example the *Siracusa Principles*, in qualifying the entitlement to freedom of expression and association, state that judges should not express public criticism or approval of government or pronounce on controversial political issues, in order to avoid the impression of partisanship. The involvement of a government Minister in making or recommending appointments does not of itself pose a problem in terms of judicial independence.[6] However, it is noteworthy that the recommendations of the Committee of Ministers of the Council of Europe in 1994[7] suggested that where appointments were made by government (as opposed to an independent authority) there should be measures to ensure transparency and independence, for example "a special independent and competent body to give the government advice which it follows in practice" or "the right for an individual to appeal against a decision to an independent authority".

---

4   Livingstone and Doak, Research Report 14, Appendix 7.

5   Livingstone and Doak, Research Report 14, Appendix 8.

6   But see *Starrs v Procurator Fiscal,* 11 November 1999 (unreported judgment of the High Court of Justiciary concerning the appointment of temporary sheriffs).

7   Recommendation No R (94) 12 of the Committee of Ministers to Member States on the Independence, Efficiency and Role of Judges.

Current Arrangements

APPOINTMENTS

6.15 The complement of judges and magistrates in Northern Ireland and the arrangements for their appointment are set out in the table following, which includes only those judicial posts relevant to the criminal courts.

6.16 Prior to direct rule, the Governor of Northern Ireland made appointments of county court judges and resident magistrates, on the advice of the Minister of Home Affairs. Appointments of High Court judges, Lords Justices of Appeal and the Lord Chief Justice were made by Her Majesty The Queen by Letters Patent on the advice of the Lord Chancellor. Since 1973 the Lord Chancellor has been responsible for making or advising on all judicial appointments in Northern Ireland, while the 1978 Judicature Act also gave him responsibility for the unified courts administration. We understand that the transfer of these responsibilities to the Lord Chancellor was driven mainly by a desire to secure and demonstrate the independence of judicial matters and courts administration from any political office that was closely associated with political and security developments in Northern Ireland.

6.17 Under the Northern Ireland Act 1998, the appointment and removal of judges, magistrates and other holders of judicial office in Northern Ireland are classified as "excepted". In other words the Lord Chancellor's responsibility for judicial appointments in Northern Ireland could not be devolved to the Assembly other than by primary legislation at Westminster. This contrasts with most other justice functions, including courts administration, which are in the "reserved" category; they can be devolved by an Order in Council laid before Parliament in accordance with section 4(2) of the Northern Ireland Act 1998.

Judicial Appointments in Northern Ireland

Office	Eligibility	Present Complement	Procedure
Lord Chief Justice	A Lord Justice of Appeal [or qualified for appointment as] or a Lord of Appeal in Ordinary having practised for not less than 10 years at the Bar in Northern Ireland.	1	Appointment by The Queen on the recommendation of the Prime Minister following advice from the Lord Chancellor.
Lord Justice of Appeal	A judge of the High Court or any person who has practised for not less than 15 years at the Bar of Northern Ireland.	3	Appointment by The Queen on the recommendation of the Prime Minister following advice from the Lord Chancellor.
High Court Judge	Not less than 10 years' practice at the Bar of Northern Ireland.	7	Appointment by The Queen on the recommendation of the Lord Chancellor following advice from the Lord Chief Justice on applicants who respond to an advertisement in the journal of the Law Society and in the Bar Library or persons whom he considers most suitable whether they have submitted an application form or not.
County Court Judge	Not less than 10 years' practice as a barrister or solicitor or not less than 3 years as a deputy county court judge.	14	Appointment by The Queen on the recommendation of the Lord Chancellor following advice from the Lord Chief Justice on applicants who respond to an advertisement in the journal of the Law Society and in the Bar Library and are successful at interview.
Resident Magistrate	Not less than 7 years' practice as a barrister or solicitor.	17	Appointment by The Queen on the recommendation of the Lord Chancellor on applicants who respond to an advertisement in the journal of the Law Society and in the Bar Library and are successful at interview.
Deputy Resident Magistrate (part-time)	Not less than 7 years' practice as a barrister or solicitor.	20	Applicants who respond to an advertisement in the journal of the Law Society and in the Bar Library and are successful at interview are appointed by the Lord Chancellor.

6.18   Eligibility for judicial appointments is set out in a variety of statutes and is governed by the length of time that lawyers have been in active practice (i.e. working as a solicitor or barrister) or their standing (the period since they were admitted as solicitors or called to the Bar). For purposes of the appointments that concern us, length of time in active practice is currently the key consideration. For example to be considered for appointment as a resident magistrate, a barrister or solicitor must have practised for not less than seven years, while appointment as a High Court judge is open to barristers who have practised for not less than 10 years. In Northern Ireland the definition of practice includes lawyers employed by government departments.

6.19   In discharging his duties in relation to judicial appointments in Northern Ireland, the Lord Chancellor receives administrative support from the Northern Ireland Court Service. Three principles underpin the operation of the procedures at all levels of the judiciary.

- Appointments are made on merit, regardless of ethnic origin, gender, marital status, sexual orientation, political affiliation, religion or disability.

- Significant weight is placed upon the views of serving members of the judiciary and heads of the legal profession who have knowledge of the candidates' legal expertise.

- Experience as a part-time judicial office holder is considered desirable as a prerequisite to appointment to full-time office.

6.20   In recent years there has been a trend towards greater openness in the procedures for selecting people to be recommended for appointment. Other than the appointments of the Lord Chief Justice and Lords Justices of Appeal, which are regarded as internal promotions, all vacancies for judicial office are advertised in the Journal of the Law Society of Northern Ireland and the Bar Library, inviting written applications. Application forms include a section requiring candidates to indicate whether they have been the subject of disciplinary proceedings by their professional bodies. The application pack contains information on the selection criteria covering the skills, ability, legal knowledge and experience and personal qualities required for appointment. Typical selection criteria are as follows:

- Legal knowledge and experience.

- Intellectual and analytical ability.

- Decisiveness.

- Communication skills.

- Authority.

- Integrity.

- Fairness.

- Understanding of people and society.

- Maturity and sound judgement.

- Courtesy and humanity.

- Commitment to public service.

6.21   Below county court level, applications are sifted and then those who are successful at that stage will undergo a structured interview by a panel consisting of three members: one from the judicial tier to which the appointment is being made; a representative of the Lord Chancellor's Department; and a senior representative of the Northern Ireland Court Service who is normally in the chair. Applicants are asked to name referees, one of whom should be a serving full-time member of the judiciary familiar with their work and practice. Further references can be sought. The panel then makes a recommendation for appointment to the Lord Chancellor.

6.22   Where, at present, High Court (and previously county court) appointments are concerned, vacancies are advertised inviting applications, but there is no system of interview and references are not sought from applicants. In coming to a decision on whether to recommend a candidate for appointment by Her Majesty The Queen, the Lord Chancellor receives advice from the Lord Chief Justice. In formulating advice, the Lord Chief Justice consults with judges of the Supreme Court, the Chairman of the Council of Her Majesty's County Court Judges, the Chairman of the Bar Council and the President of the Law Society. This a formal written process, and the written views of those consulted go forward to the Lord Chancellor along with the Lord Chief Justice's own written assessment. We were advised that the Lord Chancellor had decided in principle that in future structured interviews would become part of the appointments process for county court judges. The precise details of how future consultation would be carried out for this category of appointments had not been determined.

6.23   Prior to confirmation of appointment, details of any disciplinary proceedings declared on the application form are sought from the Bar Council or Law Society. Other forms of screening are carried out, for example criminal record checks and, for full-time appointments, financial checks with the Inland Revenue, Customs and Excise and the Enforcement of Judgments Office Register of Judgments. Those appointed to full-time office also undergo a medical examination.

6.24   On appointment, judges and magistrates (and JPs and lay panellists) are required by legislation to take the Oath of Allegiance and the Judicial Oath. The Oath of Allegiance takes the following form:

> "I, [ ], do swear that I will be faithful and bear true allegiance to Her Majesty Queen Elizabeth The Second, her heirs and successors, according to law. So help me God."

The Judicial Oath is intended to bind the appointee to perform his or her functions under the law independently and impartially in respect of all citizens. Section 4 of the Promissory Oaths Act 1868 prescribes the form of the Judicial Oath as follows:

> "I, [ ], do swear that I will well and truly serve our Sovereign Lady Queen Elizabeth The Second in the office of [ ], and I will do right to all manner of people after the laws and usages of this realm, without fear or favour, affection or illwill. So help me God."

For those who do not wish to swear an Oath, there is also the option of making solemn affirmations in similar terms.

JUDICIAL TRAINING

6.25   The Judicial Studies Board for Northern Ireland was formed in 1993. Its aims and objectives are to provide suitable and effective programmes of practical studies for members of the judiciary and to improve upon the system of disseminating information to them. In order to protect judicial independence, and in particular to ensure that sectional interests are not brought to bear on the judiciary through training programmes, the Board is "judge driven". It is chaired by a Lord Justice of Appeal and its membership includes representation from each judicial tier and the Director of Servicing the Legal System Ltd (SLS).[8] The Northern Ireland Court Service provides secretarial support for the Board and finances its work directly from the Court Service vote.

6.26   Seminars and talks arranged by the Board fall into the following categories:

- New legislation.

- Induction/refresher training.

- Sentencing seminars.

- Special interest and topical issues.

6.27   In 1998/99 the Board held a total of 10 seminars and lectures which included presentations on the Criminal Justice (Children) (NI) Order 1998, the Northern Ireland Act 1998 and the *European Convention on Human Rights*. In addition there was judicial representation from Northern Ireland at 39 conferences, courses and seminars, mostly held in other jurisdictions. The Board has compiled and produced publications on such matters as sentencing guidelines through synopses of judgements in particular classes of case and a Crown Court bench book consisting of specimen directions designed to assist judges in directing juries.

6.28   The Board enjoys good working relationships with the Judicial Studies Board for England and Wales. This is of considerable value in that it enables the Northern Ireland Board to draw on experience and advice from its much larger English counterpart in devising seminars and programmes of work; and there are places available in England for Northern Ireland judges on induction and refresher courses which could not be run in Northern Ireland on a cost effective basis. It is working closely with the English and Welsh Board and the Scottish Board in developing and taking advantage of training opportunities in the priority area of the *European Convention on Human Rights* and the implications of incorporation. In one respect the small scale of the operation in Northern Ireland does have an advantage in that mentoring and work shadowing arrangements can be made for new appointees based on their individual needs.

---

8   SLS was established in 1980 to promote publications, seminars and training on aspects of the law and legal system in Northern Ireland.

6.29   Attendance at Board events is not mandatory, although lists of attendees are kept. The attendance rate is around 66%.

TENURE

6.30   Full-time judges and magistrates have tenure, during good behaviour, until the statutory retirement age of 70.[9] Deputies are appointed for a fixed term of three years, renewable up until the age of 70. Procedures for the removal of judges and magistrates are governed by statute. Judges of the Supreme Court hold office during good behaviour subject to the power of removal by Her Majesty The Queen on an address by both Houses of Parliament. All other appointees may be removed by the Lord Chancellor on the grounds of incapacity or misbehaviour.

STANDARDS

6.31   It is necessary to stress that while the Lord Chancellor does have a disciplinary role in relation to the judiciary, he is not in any sense their line manager and does not have a supervisory or directing role. This is of importance in addressing the independence issue. Moreover, while the Lord Chief Justice is President of the High Court, Court of Appeal and Crown Court, he does not fulfil that function in relation to county courts and magistrates' courts for which there is no such position.

6.32   There is no formal code or statement of judicial ethics. However, memoranda on conditions of appointment and terms of service comprise statements on a range of issues including conduct and the circumstances in which the Lord Chancellor might consider exercising his powers to remove from office on grounds of misbehaviour. These include criminal offences of violence, dishonesty and moral turpitude and substantiated complaints of behaviour which might cause offence on racial or religious grounds or amount to sexual harassment.

6.33   Complaints are received from time to time about members of the judiciary. To the extent that they relate to the exercise of judicial discretion in a particular case, considerations of judicial independence are such that it is not considered appropriate for comment to be made on the substance of the issue in response to a complainant. It may be possible to use the avenue of appeal to address such matters. However, if a complaint relates to the conduct of a judge or magistrate and is not obviously trivial or misconceived, then it would be normal practice for officials, acting on behalf of the Lord Chancellor, to seek comments from the office holder in question and take them into account in replying to the complainant. Further steps, including the personal involvement of the Lord Chancellor, or in practice more likely the Lord Chief

---

9   The statutory retirement date of 70 was set by the Judicial Pensions and Retirement Act 1993. Judges and magistrates in office when that legislation was enacted retained their existing retirement dates.

Justice, would be considered only if a serious complaint were seen to have been substantiated. In such circumstances, the Lord Chancellor or Lord Chief Justice would be in a position to counsel or guide a judge whose behaviour was in question. Where the matter is particularly serious but action short of dismissal is considered appropriate, such as a rebuke or warning, it is open to the Lord Chancellor to make a public statement.

Views Expressed During the Consultation Period

6.34   Almost all those who participated in the consultative process had something to say about the judicial system. There was a range of views, from those who believed that the current arrangements on the whole worked reasonably well to those who thought them flawed and sought radical change. Given the fundamental importance of securing confidence in the judiciary throughout the community, we wish to take full account of all of those perspectives in our recommendations.

6.35   One of the strongest messages to come across was a desire for transparency in judicial appointments. In some cases, the advertising of vacancies for example, suggestions were made which have already been adopted in Northern Ireland (which might in itself be indicative of the need for more public information). At some of the seminars there were calls to demystify the process, perhaps through publishing a guide on judicial appointment mechanisms. Published criteria for appointments were called for. Openness was seen as of critical importance in demonstrating fairness and that improper influence was not being brought to bear. In this context some doubts were expressed about the way in which consultation with the senior judiciary and professional bodies was being undertaken; there was little knowledge about this and some felt that it flew in the face of the requirement of transparency.

6.36   On the criteria for appointment, merit was seen by most as the overriding governing principle. Within that context the qualities most often mentioned were legal ability, integrity, experience and fairness. Some consultees stressed that appointment criteria should be broadly drawn so as not unduly to restrict the pool of potential applicants. Managerial ability was mentioned as being increasingly important. Opening up appointments at all levels to solicitors was a common theme and, in terms of experience, the Law Society argued that litigation was as relevant as advocacy.

6.37   Impartiality, fairness, independence and freedom from political influence were themes that recurred throughout the consultation process.

6.38   There was little support for the idea of a career judiciary along the lines of that found in civil law jurisdictions (i.e. judges being appointed in their 20s and progressing through the various tiers of judiciary). Indeed some expressed concern that an entirely promotion-based structure might appear to compromise the independence of judicial decision making, with the impact on promotion prospects coming into play when difficult or controversial cases were being considered. Rather, there was support for the retention of the current system of being able to recruit people with substantial legal experience. There was, however, significant support for movement between judicial tiers being much more the norm than has so far been the case, in order to make the best use of available talent and to remove a possible disincentive for some applicants to judicial office.

6.39   There was much debate about the representativeness of the judiciary in terms of community background, gender and class. There was a widespread view amongst those who commented that judges and magistrates should be representative of society as a whole. One group suggested that "the development of a judiciary reflective of modern societal values as a whole should enable better judicial understanding of the perspective of court users of all types, without loss of legal quality".

6.40   From some quarters we heard serious concern about what was believed to be the unrepresentative nature of the bench in Northern Ireland in terms of community background. Those expressing this view felt that it was not sufficient to point to the existence of Catholic judges and magistrates, many of whom it was believed could be Unionist by inclination. They saw a need to secure a fair balance of Nationalist representation amongst the judiciary. There was one suggestion that a target of three years be set in which to bring this about. In confidence terms the current position was said to be exacerbated by the association of judges with the Diplock Courts. Those expressing these views, and others, suggested that there was a disproportionate tendency to appoint prosecuting lawyers and Crown Counsel as judges, contributing to a perception of the judiciary as a body being too close to the state and favouring the police and prosecution. A number of submissions indicated a clear feeling that the judicial system had not delivered justice to the Nationalist community.

6.41   From another perspective, we heard suggestions that it was policy to maintain a particular proportion of the two communities on the bench; and that there was a tendency to appoint Catholic and Protestant judges alternately, with the implication that the merit principle was being compromised.

6.42   There was considerable concern from many different groups about the under-representation of women at all levels in the judiciary (two out of 17 resident magistrates are women, one out of four district judges, one out of 14 county court judges and no Supreme Court judges). While the increasing numbers of women at the Bar and in the solicitors' branch of the profession might be expected to feed through into judicial appointments, there remained obstacles to their securing preferment. Career breaks and family commitments sometimes made it difficult to get the right sort of experience and there was one suggestion that women tended to gravitate towards family law, with client resistance to employing them in, for example, the commercial and criminal fields. The nature of their experience and economic considerations sometimes militated against women seeking or obtaining silk (appointment as QC), which appeared in practice currently to be a necessary hurdle to surmount before appointment to the senior judiciary.

6.43   We also received comments to the effect that the judiciary was unrepresentative from a class perspective and it was observed that there was no-one from an ethnic minority on the bench.

6.44   There was not widespread pressure from those who commented to compromise the merit principle in order to secure a more representative judiciary. However, a programme of affirmative action and outreach was advocated by several groups and organisations in order to maximise the pool of applicants and help redress apparent imbalances. In relation to community background this would be associated with a strategy for addressing any "blockages" in the way of potential applicants and removing perceived "chill factors" which might inhibit Nationalists from seeking judicial office - for example, oaths requiring allegiance to Her Majesty The Queen, Royal Crests in courthouses, the use of the term "Royal" etc. Some advocated an open system of equity monitoring, with figures on the community background, gender balance and ethnic origin of the judiciary being made publicly available on a regular basis.

6.45   There were differing views on where political responsibility for judicial appointments should lie, although, as an issue, this did not feature strongly in the consultation process. Some favoured retention of the Lord Chancellor's present role, largely in order to maintain a distance between judicial appointments and local political pressures. However unease was expressed in other quarters about the Lord Chancellor's involvement in view of his political role in government. Others suggested delaying devolution of such an important responsibility until the new institutions of government in Northern Ireland had had time to settle. On the other hand, a significant body of opinion favoured a clear commitment to giving the responsibility to local political institutions, perhaps retaining a role for the Prime Minister in relation to the most senior appointments (as is now the case in Scotland).

6.46   A strong and broad-based body of opinion (from most parts of the political spectrum) favoured the establishment of some form of Judicial Appointments Commission, an independent body to appoint or make recommendations on appointments to the appointing authority. Two main strands of thinking lay behind this. There was a belief that such an independent body, with a demonstrably transparent approach, would help secure the independence of the appointments process from political manipulation. Also, with appropriate lay involvement, it would be a means of ensuring that every effort was seen to be made to open up the appointments process to qualifying candidates from as broad a base as possible - in other words, a component of an affirmative action strategy.

6.47   As for the make-up of such a body, there was general agreement on the need for a substantial judicial element and nominees from professional bodies were also mentioned. Most favoured a strong lay element in the membership, although there were differences between some who wanted the inclusion of elected representatives or their nominees and others who stressed the importance of minimising any political influence. Lay members of a Commission were seen as bringing a range of qualities including the perspective of court users, recruitment expertise and an ability to assess the non-legal qualities required of prospective judges and magistrates.

6.48   The importance of judicial training was mentioned in many of the submissions that we received and at seminars. Human rights issues and technical legal matters were frequently identified but other subjects for inclusion in training programmes included the needs of victims and vulnerable witnesses, children, women's issues, domestic violence, conflict resolution through mediation, the position of minority groups and cultural awareness. Some believed that training (particularly induction training) should be mandatory and there were suggestions that it should be the responsibility of a Judicial Appointments Commission. However there was also a view that the drive and impetus for training should come from the judiciary and that care should be taken to ensure that judicial independence was not compromised by an interventionist approach in this area on the part of the executive or other groups.

6.49   Terms and conditions and tenure did not feature strongly in the consultation process, although a view was expressed that salaries and other conditions of service should be determined by a procedure which did not allow for political influence to be brought to bear on the judiciary. There was some interest in the idea of a published code of conduct or standards for the judiciary and a suggestion that a statement of judicial ethics might be enshrined in law. To be meaningful, this would need to be supplemented by a published procedure for administering such standards and dealing with complaints. Those expressing these views suggested that such a procedure should be devised in a way that did not compromise judicial independence; and, in this context, the Canadian Judicial Council was mentioned. A suggestion was made that the Lord Chief Justice should take on this responsibility, perhaps assisted by a representative from each branch of the legal profession.

Research and Experience in Other Jurisdictions

6.50   From the research conducted on our behalf and our study visits, it is apparent that the issues raised about judicial appointments and terms and conditions in Northern Ireland have in recent years been a major pre-occupation in both the common and civil law traditions. It follows that there is a wealth of material and debate to draw on in our examination of this topic; but equally there is no model package of universal applicability to be taken off the shelf and also little evidence of the extent to which changes made elsewhere have impacted upon the quality of justice. The arrangements for judicial appointments in Northern Ireland need to be framed in a way that complies with certain key principles, for example those established in human rights instruments, and are suited to the particular circumstances of our jurisdiction. In the following paragraphs we therefore focus on particular experiences and systems elsewhere which seem to us to be relevant to Northern Ireland.

6.51   In democratic systems there is a universal commitment to promote an independent judiciary in accordance with human rights norms. The principle can be enshrined in written constitutions as in Canada (Articles 96-101 of the Constitution supplemented by the Charter of Rights and Freedoms), the Republic of Ireland and in South Africa, where Article 165 of the Constitution states "the Courts are independent and subject only to the Constitution and the law", and goes on to require organs of the state to assist and protect that independence through legislative and other measures. The separation of powers is perhaps most clearly provided for in the United States Constitution.

6.52   Whatever provisions may be in place to protect the independence of the judiciary in its operation, the manner in which judges are appointed has clear implications for the independence of the judicial system and for public confidence. The trend in recent years has been to dilute the direct involvement of governments and ministries in appointments through the establishment of Independent Boards or Commissions that appoint directly or recommend appointment to the appropriate Minister. We examine this trend in a range of jurisdictions and look at different approaches to the "representativeness" issue.

6.53   The civil law jurisdictions of Europe are characterised by the establishment of higher judicial councils, whose membership typically includes judges at various levels, a prosecutor and sometimes nominees of the government and/or legislature. In these systems, usually with career judiciaries recruited direct from university or law school, it is not uncommon for appointments and promotions to be made under the auspices of the council (as opposed to being recommended to a political authority), for all but the most senior positions.

ENGLAND AND WALES

6.54   The experience of common law jurisdictions, with their judiciary usually appointed after years of working as practitioners, is of more applicability in the Northern Ireland context. England and Wales share many of the features of the Northern Ireland legal system. They have not followed the path of establishing a board or commission responsible for making or recommending appointments, and the Lord Chancellor remains responsible for making or recommending to Her Majesty The Queen most judicial appointments. The Prime Minister advises Her Majesty The Queen on the appointments of Law Lords, the Lord Chief Justice and Lords Justices of Appeal. The details of the arrangements are set out in the research paper on judicial appointments[10] published along with this report.

---

10   Blair, Research Report 5.

6.55   It is noteworthy that in recent years a number of steps have been taken in England and Wales to enhance transparency (in itself an important factor in securing accountability and demonstrating the reality of independence) and demystify the process. For example there are published criteria for appointment. High Court judicial posts are advertised. Posts up to and including circuit judges are advertised (except for recorderships where posts are filled on promotion from assistant recorder) and there is lay representation on panels that conduct structured interviews. The panels have the opportunity to see and take account of the outcome of consultations with judges and practitioners about applicants. Of particular value is the detailed guide to all aspects of the appointments process published by the Lord Chancellor's Department in March 1999.[11] Northern Ireland is moving in much the same direction and we will return to some of these themes in making our recommendations.

6.56   In the summer of 1999 the Lord Chancellor appointed Sir Leonard Peach to conduct an independent scrutiny of the assessment and selection systems used for judicial and Queen's Counsel appointments in England and Wales, and of safeguards in the system to prevent discrimination on grounds of gender or ethnic origin. His terms of reference focused on how appointments were made, rather than by whom. Sir Leonard's report was published on 3 December 1999.[12]

6.57   Within its terms of reference, the report commented favourably on the selection procedures and their execution as compared with those adopted by other organisations in the public and private sectors. The report's recommendations included the establishment of an independent Commission for Judicial Appointments tasked with keeping the appointments system under review and dealing with complaints and grievances about the process. The report examined many aspects of the appointments process, including the role of consultation with the judiciary and the professions on the merits of candidates. The report also made a number of comments and recommendations for enhancing equal opportunities and the monitoring of applications and appointments on the basis of gender and ethnic background. The Lord Chancellor welcomed the report and accepted its principal recommendation for a Commissioner for Judicial Appointments to provide independent monitoring of the procedures. He indicated that he would consider the report's further recommendations in detail along with other comments and reactions to the report.

SCOTLAND

6.58   Scotland is of particular relevance in that it provides an existing model of devolved arrangements within the United Kingdom context. Prior to devolution the Lord Advocate, in addition to his roles as head of the Prosecution Service and Scottish Law Officer, had a

---

11   *Judicial Appointments*, (1999), Judicial Group, Lord Chancellor's Department, London: HMSO.

12   *An Independent Scrutiny of the Appointment Processes of Judges and Queen's Counsel in England and Wales: A Report to the Lord Chancellor by Sir Leonard Peach*, (1999), London: HMSO (The Peach Report).

pivotal role in judicial appointments. We understand that, although there was some expectation that this would continue after devolution, there has been a degree of public comment on whether such a role is appropriate for the head of the Prosecution Service. This issue is likely to be addressed in a forthcoming consultation paper on judicial appointments procedures. In the meantime, the Scotland Act 1998 places on the First Minister constitutional responsibility for recommending judicial appointments to Her Majesty The Queen or the Prime Minister. The responsibilities of the Lord Advocate in this area are not specified, thus giving the Scottish Executive and Parliament the ability to determine their own approach. One feature of interest is the division of responsibility between Edinburgh and London, with the Prime Minister recommending the appointment of the two most senior judges on the nomination of the First Minister, while the latter recommends directly to Her Majesty The Queen the appointment of judges of the Court of Session, sheriffs principal and sheriffs.

REPUBLIC OF IRELAND

6.59   Articles 13.9 and 35.1 of the Irish Constitution provide for the appointment of judges by the President, acting on the advice of the Government. A Judicial Appointments Advisory Board was established under the Courts and Courts Officers Act 1995. It is made up of the Chief Justice, the Court Presidents, the Attorney General, a barrister, a solicitor and three lay people representing business interests and court users. Appointments are advertised and candidates are shortlisted. The Board provides the Minister for Justice, Equality and Law Reform with a list of at least seven names for consideration by the Government. In advising the President in relation to an appointment, the Government must firstly consider for appointment the persons whose names have been recommended by the Board.

SOUTH AFRICA

6.60   In South Africa, the Judicial Services Commission (JSC) is established by the Constitution. It is made up of the Chief Justice (in the chair), the President of the Constitutional Court, the President of the High Court, two barristers, two solicitors, one teacher of law, the Minister of Justice, six members of the Legislative Assembly (including three from opposition parties), four members of the Council of Provinces and four designated by the President after consultation with the political parties. There is therefore a substantial majority of lay/political appointees. There are special procedures for the President to appoint the four most senior judges, after consultation with the JSC. Vacancies for the Constitutional Court are filled by the President from a list (containing three names more than the number of vacancies) provided by the JSC. If dissatisfied with the list, the President may ask for a further list, giving reasons for his dissatisfaction, but he must fill the vacancies from this second list. The President must appoint judges of all other courts on the advice of the JSC.

6.61　The position of the judiciary and the courts in South Africa was the subject of considerable debate during the transition from apartheid when, of 165 judges, 163 were white males, one was a white female and there was one judge of Asian origin who is now Chief Justice. We were told that the system had previously been unashamedly manipulated to ensure that judges unsympathetic to apartheid were not allocated sensitive and important cases. In these circumstances, it is not surprising that the issue of representativeness was addressed and Article 174(2) of the Constitution provides that: "the need for the judiciary to reflect broadly the racial and gender composition of South Africa must be considered when judicial officers are being appointed".

6.62　Given the need to secure and sustain a high quality judiciary and the time that it was going to take to develop a representative profession, a conscious decision was taken not to force the pace of change. The pre-transition judges were re-appointed and, of the appointments made since, around 50% have been non-white while there remains a significant under-representation of women. The significance and benefits of such a measured approach were mentioned in a submission to us and this was confirmed during our visit. It was apparent that at a time of major change the judicial system had made the transition into the new dispensation remarkably well and had the confidence of the community at large.

6.63　The JSC has adopted a very public procedure. It advertises for vacancies and, while there are no published criteria for appointment, the application form gives an indication of the breadth of qualities being sought with a focus on published works, experience as practitioner and then acting judge (service as acting judge is a pre-requisite for appointment), as well as involvement in community and voluntary organisations. The shortlist is prepared by the Chief Justice in consultation with judicial colleagues followed by interviews conducted in public by the full JSC.

6.64　We sat in on three such interviews. There was detailed questioning of candidates about their legal experience and competence, largely orchestrated by the judicial and professional members of the Commission. There were also some questions about candidates' activities outside the working environment and their awareness of societal issues, some of which could be interpreted as coming from a political perspective. The Commission takes its decisions on which candidate to select in private, although there is pressure to open up these deliberations to public scrutiny. In discussion with a variety of interests in South Africa, it appeared that the system was broadly accepted and welcomed; but it was believed by some that the public nature of the proceedings and the possible impact on professional reputations might put off some good candidates and there was concern in some quarters that on occasion merit took second place to political and gender considerations.

UNITED STATES

6.65 In the United States, the myriad of jurisdictions does not have a convenient template of appointment procedures and it remains the case that in some states judges are elected. In short, most appointments at the federal and state levels involve an interaction between the executive and legislature, including nominations and confirmatory hearings, together with a major input from the respective bar associations which screen candidates for professional competence. While in a system governed by separation of powers such procedures do provide checks and balances, the extent of the political input required is such that they are unlikely to find favour in Northern Ireland.

6.66 However, the increasing use of nominating committees or commissions in the United States is of some interest. Senators, in making nominations to the President for appointments to the federal district judgeships, will often appoint nominating committees, representative of interest groups in the community, to broaden the field of potential nominees and encourage nominations from under-represented groups. At state level elections have gradually been replaced by the use of "merit commissions".

6.67 During our visit Connecticut was commended to us as offering a good example of a commission. It consists of 12 members, two from each congressional district; the Governor appoints six Attorneys, one from each district, and the remaining (lay) members are appointed, one each by the presiding officer of the Senate and the House of Representatives and the majority and minority leaders of the two Houses. The American Judicature Society, in promoting the development of these commissions, has stressed that "all appointing authorities shall make reasonable efforts to ensure that the Commission substantially represents the gender, ethnic and racial diversity of the jurisdiction". The Commission in Connecticut is tasked with evaluating incumbent judges for reappointment and seeking qualifying candidates for nomination to the Governor; the Governor is required to appoint from the list produced by the Commission. In the spirit of openness and transparency, each January the Commission reports to the State Standing Committee on the Judiciary covering such matters as the numbers interviewed for appointment, numbers recommended for appointment, statistics on race, gender, years of experience etc. Reporting in this way on the workings of recruitment procedures, without going into individual appointments, may be an idea worth developing for Northern Ireland.

6.68 In the United States we asked about attitudes to merit and representativeness. With the strong history of elected judges and politically dominated nomination procedures it is perhaps not surprising that merit, in terms of legal competence, was not always seen as the sole criterion for appointment. It was clear that in some US jurisdictions it would be regarded as reasonable for a candidate from an under-represented group to be appointed ahead of others with similar qualifications; and on one occasion it was argued that "representativeness" was an aspect of merit in the sense that if the judiciary was not being demonstrably chosen from as broad a pool as possible, then some of the best candidates were being lost to the system.

CANADA

6.69   In Canada a significant factor in the move to establish appointments committees in the 1980s was the expansion of the judiciary's public policy role associated with the enactment of the Charter of Rights and Freedoms in 1982. This contributed to pressure for greater openness and wider participation in a process of executive appointment with many similarities to that found in the United Kingdom. The federal committees, appointed by the Minister of Justice, consist of three lay people, three lawyers and one judge. In appointing the committees, the Minister is required to ensure that they are reflective of the gender, geographical, language and cultural make-up of the province concerned. The functions of these committees are relatively limited in that on the basis of application papers and interviews, they classify the candidates' level of suitability for appointment in advising the Minister. It remains the case that the Prime Minister is responsible for senior judicial appointments, operating without an advisory committee.

6.70   At provincial level such committees tend to be more proactive. The Ontario committee, for example, consists of a majority of lay members appointed by the Attorney General – seven, together with three lawyers, two judges and a member of the Judicial Council. They engage in the full process of recruitment, seeking views from the bench and bar, interviewing and assessing candidates; they then submit a ranked list to the provincial Attorney General who must select from it or request another list to be drawn up. In its work the Ontario committee is required by statute to have regard to: "assessment of the professional excellence, community awareness and personal characteristics of candidates and recognition of the desirability of reflecting the diversity of Ontario society in judicial appointments." Within this framework it has considerable freedom to set criteria for particular appointments. In 1990, it used this freedom to focus attention on under-represented groups through an outreach programme, while at the same time the Attorney General wrote to 1200 women lawyers asking them to apply.

NEW ZEALAND

6.71   The administration of judicial appointments in New Zealand is the responsibility of a Judicial Appointments Unit that at the time of our visit was located within the Ministry of Justice. This system is of interest in that at district court level, a standing list is kept of qualified candidates (barristers or solicitors of seven years experience who are considered fit and proper for appointment) who respond to advertisements inviting expressions of interest. At the same time as advertising, nominations are sought from a range of groups inside and outside the legal system with a view to ensuring that this initial pool of candidates is socially diverse. Appointments are made from the list in a process that involves sifts, interviews and consultation with professional bodies.

JUDICIAL TRAINING

6.72   It was stressed to us in a number of jurisdictions that judicial training is most effective and independence best safeguarded when the training is judge-driven. That is the case in England and Wales, where the Judicial Studies Board is a non-departmental public body and where judges are course directors; this does not of course preclude the use of academic and other experts to provide training in specialist areas. Our visit to the United States Federal Judicial Centre provided an example of judicial training and court administration in general being the sole responsibility of judges who managed a large administrative machine; their independence was bolstered by arrangements which ensured that they had sufficient finance, subject to their appearing before the Appropriations Committee every three years.

6.73   We found a positive approach to judicial training in Canada, where there has been a tradition of judicially managed training institutes that determine course content and arrange delivery. The National Judicial Institute was established in 1988 with a mission to foster a high standard of judicial performance through programmes that stimulate continuing professional and personal growth and engender a high level of social, gender and multi-cultural awareness, ethical sensitivity and pride of excellence, within an independent judiciary, thereby improving the administration of justice. The Institute organises approximately 40 programmes a year covering substantive law, skills training and social context issues. It undertook a project in 1992, which resulted in the development and publication of standards for judicial education. This recommended that every new judge should take approximately 10 days of intensive judicial education as soon as possible after appointment, with refresher training each year. It was apparent that cultural and social awareness, together with an appreciation of factors surrounding social problems such as domestic violence, was a key priority.

6.74   New Zealand has a recently established Judicial Studies Institute reporting to the Chief District Court Judge. There is an expectation that all newly appointed judges will embark upon a training process which involves sitting with mentor judges, visits to prisons and briefing from other criminal justice agencies. In their first year, they undertake a one-week residential course in which newly appointed Australian and Pacific Island judges are also involved. The Institute also has responsibilities for updating the bench book on an annual basis and for developing a sentencing information system.

TERMS AND CONDITIONS OF SERVICE

6.75   In most common law jurisdictions, tenure was recognised as of critical importance in safeguarding judicial independence. US Federal judges are appointed for life (removable only by impeachment proceedings) but in most cases there is a statutory retirement age of 70 or 75.

6.76   The characteristics of procedures for the removal of judges tend to centre around ensuring safeguards against arbitrary action by any one authority. For example, the Scotland Act 1998 provides that a judge of the Court of Session may be removed by Her Majesty The Queen on the recommendation of the First Minister, which in turn may only be made if agreed by Parliament on the basis of a report from a judicial tribunal concluding that the person in question is unfit for office by reason of inability, neglect of duty or misbehaviour. Such a tribunal may be established on the initiative of the First Minister or the Lord President (the most senior judge in Scotland). In South Africa the President's power to remove a judge may be used only on the advice of a two-thirds majority of the Judicial Services Commission and on the basis of a two-thirds majority secured in the National Assembly; grounds for dismissal are incapacity, incompetence or misconduct.

6.77   In Canada, removal can be secured only following an independent inquiry by the Canadian Judicial Council, a recommendation for removal from the Council to the Governor and a joint address by the two Houses of Parliament. The Canadian Judicial Council comprises the Chief Justices of the Supreme Courts and is the responsible body for federally appointed judges. It is tasked with the responsibility of enquiring into and investigating situations where there are allegations against a judge of: incapacity through age or infirmity, misconduct, a failure to execute his or her duties or having placed himself or herself in a position incompatible with the execution of his or her office. Such arrangements balance the need to safeguard independence with the public interest in having a degree of accountability.

6.78   Another feature of independence is that the judiciary should not feel beholden to government in terms of remuneration or proper resourcing. The South African Constitution provides that the salaries, allowances and benefits of all holders of judicial office may not be reduced. In Canada, since the early 1980s there has been increasing dependence upon independent commissions to advise the executive and Parliament on judicial salaries. At the time of our visit, a judicial review was in progress at provincial level challenging the Alberta Government's decision to reject a commission's recommendation on pay.

Evaluation and Recommendations

6.79   As we pointed out in the introductory paragraphs of this chapter, judges and magistrates are at the heart of the criminal justice system. It is they who ensure due process and who, without fear or favour, are expected to secure the fair treatment of all parties who appear before them. Their role is developing, especially in the context of human rights, and in ways that serve to emphasise the importance of that part of our terms of reference that requires us to safeguard and protect their independence.

6.80   We said in the introductory chapter to this report that our concern was with the future rather than making judgements about the past. We have, of course, listened to what people have said about the way the judicial system has worked over the past decades; that helps in determining what arrangements will best ensure public confidence in the future. We also take account of the difficulties and challenges that have been faced by judges and magistrates in dispensing justice against a backcloth of civil disturbance and division in the community. The capacity of the judicial system to come through such a period in the way that it has should be borne in mind when considering any future arrangements. While in recent public attitude surveys a significant proportion of respondents described the judiciary as "out of touch",[13] a sizeable majority from both parts of the community was very confident or fairly confident in the fairness of judges and magistrates.[14]

JUDICIAL APPOINTMENTS: KEY PRINCIPLES

6.81   We start by addressing the key principles that should apply, whichever system of judicial appointments is adopted.

6.82   Our terms of reference, the human rights instruments, those who have expressed views to us and international practice point to the independence and impartiality of the judiciary as of paramount importance. The principle is enshrined in the European Convention through its reference to "an independent and impartial tribunal". We noted above that a commitment to judicial independence is enshrined in the constitutions of many countries. **We recommend that primary Westminster legislation should make explicit reference to the requirement for an independent judiciary and place a duty on the organs of government to uphold and protect that independence.**

6.83   Adherence to the concept of independence should not detract from the key requirements of transparency and openness in the administration of appointments and other judicial matters. This is a facet of accountability and we have no doubt that knowledge and understanding of institutions and processes enhance confidence in them. A number of our recommendations are made with this in mind.

6.84   The *International Covenant on Civil and Political Rights* makes specific reference to the entitlement to be heard by a competent tribunal, as well as referring to the qualities of

---

13   Amelin, Willis and Donnelly, Research Report 2.

14   Community Attitudes Survey, Central Survey Unit, NISRA, Occasional Paper No 10, 1999.

independence and impartiality. **Merit, including the ability to do the job, thus providing the best possible quality of justice, must in our view continue to be the key criterion in determining appointments**. There is of course room for discussion about the attributes that determine merit and we address this later. Our recommendations will also take account of the importance of training in contributing to competence and quality.

6.85 It is clear that the extent to which the composition of the judiciary reflects the society which it serves is a confidence issue and has implications for its legitimacy in the eyes of many in the community. If there is a perception that judges come predominantly from a narrow pool, then there is liable to be concern that the way in which the law as a whole is developed may be unduly influenced by one particular set of values. This is of particular significance in the light of the developing judicial role. For example, the incorporation of the *European Convention on Human Rights*, a living instrument to be interpreted in the light of present day conditions and changing social values, makes it increasingly important that the judiciary should be as reflective as possible of society in its diversity. Moreover the larger the field from which members of the judiciary is chosen, and the more demonstrable the commitment to equality of opportunity, the greater can be the confidence that the best possible candidates are being appointed. It follows that, while merit should be the deciding factor in individual appointment decisions, **it should be a stated objective of whoever is responsible for appointments to engage in a programme of action to secure the development of a judiciary that is as reflective of Northern Ireland society, in particular by community background and gender, as can be achieved consistent with the overriding requirement of merit.** Some detailed recommendations on aspects of affirmative action and equity monitoring are made at various points in this chapter.

6.86 During the consultation process and in our visits to other jurisdictions the idea of securing a judiciary that was so far as possible representative of society arose frequently. In some cases, South Africa and Ontario for example, this objective was given statutory effect, while in others, such as some of the nominating committees in the United States, administrative machinery was established in order to help secure greater representativeness.

6.87 In our view this concept should be addressed with great care in Northern Ireland. We have used the word "reflective" as opposed to "representative" advisedly. Individual judges and magistrates, in carrying out their functions, do not "represent" any particular section of society; rather they should apply objective and impartial consideration to the facts of the case before them, regardless of the background of the parties. If judges were to believe that a factor contributing to their appointment was the extent to which they represented one part of society, this would have serious implications for their impartiality. In looking at this issue we are also mindful of fair employment legislation in Northern Ireland and the human rights instruments which prohibit discrimination (even if the intention of the discriminatory act is to secure a more representative body) and demand selection arrangements based on objective considerations of merit.

6.88   We have given careful thought to the argument that political affiliation (in the sense of Nationalist or Unionist), as opposed to religious background, should be an issue in any consideration of the extent to which the judiciary reflects society. We understand the thinking that lies behind this view. However, it raises in sharp relief the points we make about representativeness. Given the importance of distancing the judiciary from political issues, it would in our view be inappropriate in the context of Northern Ireland to expect candidates for appointment or incumbents to provide information about their political beliefs.

ELIGIBILITY

6.89   Eligibility requirements are significant in that they clearly define the field from which appointments are made. **We endorse the view that extensive experience of advocacy should not be regarded as a prerequisite of success in a judicial capacity and recommend that practice and/or standing requirements for recruitment to all levels of the bench should not differentiate between barristers and solicitors.** Experience and ability as an advocate may well be an indicator of suitability for judicial office but litigation would be of equal significance. There is a perception that acquisition of silk (appointment as a QC) is a pre-requisite of appointment to the High Court bench; we see no good reason why this should be so.

6.90   Northern Ireland's approach to defining practice, enabling employed lawyers to apply for posts, is one that which we would endorse. However the emphasis on practice as opposed to standing in determining eligibility, while increasing (though not guaranteeing) the prospects of a candidate having secured relevant legal experience over a period of years, may in our view serve to limit the field of applicants unduly. We have in mind suggestions made to us in the consultation process and evidence from other jurisdictions that the appointment of legally qualified academics should be allowed. Also, some (particularly women) who have had career breaks or have entered part-time employment for family reasons, might have much to offer yet could fall foul of the practice requirements. If the eligibility criteria were relaxed, candidates would still of course be required to demonstrate that they had the capacity and competence to perform judicial functions and relevant experience would be an important factor in this. **We recommend that consideration be given to consolidating and amending the legislation relating to eligibility criteria for judicial appointments with a view to shifting the emphasis to standing (i.e. period since being called to the Bar or admitted as a solicitor) rather than practice. Time spent in lower judicial posts should also be recognised for eligibility purposes.**

6.91   We are not recommending a career judiciary along the lines of that found in many civil law jurisdictions and envisage that, below the level of Lord Justice of Appeal, most appointments will continue to be made from the ranks of solicitors and barristers. However, we did consider whether there might be more movement upwards from one judicial tier to another than is the case at present. The main arguments against are that this could compromise the independence of decision making by causing judges (perhaps subconsciously) to contemplate the impact of their decisions on promotion prospects; and that it might inhibit talented practitioners from applying for higher tier posts later in their careers. On the other hand, it is argued that if the best use of available talent is to be made, promotion from one tier to another should be a normal feature. **In our view it should be clear that progression from one judicial tier to another is regarded as an accepted form of appointment, provided that it takes place on the basis of merit as part of open competition.**

POLITICAL RESPONSIBILITY FOR JUDICIAL APPOINTMENTS

6.92   We are conscious of the range of views expressed during the consultation process on where political responsibility for judicial matters should lie and on whether this was a suitable matter for devolution at an early stage or later. In some quarters there was unease about whether judicial appointments, which are at the heart of the justice system, should be put in the hands of new and untried institutions of government. Others firmly believed that devolution of such responsibilities was necessary if other justice matters were to be devolved, thus enabling local institutions to address such matters in a responsible and co-ordinated manner.

6.93   The judiciary, whilst independent in their judicial functions, are nevertheless part of a justice system which needs to be viewed and developed as a coherent whole. This cannot easily be achieved if political responsibility for judicial and related matters is permanently detached from that for the rest of the justice system in Northern Ireland. We are of course mindful of the position in Scotland where responsibility for judicial appointments rests with the Scottish Executive. To contemplate something different for Northern Ireland would, we believe, convey an unfortunate message about our confidence in the ability of devolved institutions of government to operate effectively.

6.94   We take account of the passage in the Belfast Agreement which states that the Government remains ready in principle to devolve policing and justice matters. Once devolution of criminal justice matters has taken place, we do not believe that responsibility for such a crucial aspect of domestic administration as judicial appointments should be retained in London for longer than necessary. Indeed, our preference would be for all justice matters to be devolved at the same time. However, we understand the views of those who emphasise the importance of devolved institutions of government having established and proved themselves before responsibility for such a critical issue as the judiciary is transferred from Westminster. We would not, therefore, rule out the possibility of political responsibility for the judiciary being devolved as part of a staged process, thus allowing for a degree of flexibility over timing.

6.95 For the sake of ensuring confidence and stability, we think it important that the details of the appointments machinery should be included in the legislation that brings about devolution. **We recommend the enactment of legislation enabling responsibility for judicial appointments in Northern Ireland to be devolved on an agreed basis at a date to be determined by the Government in the light of the prevailing circumstances. This would of necessity be primary Westminster legislation. The legislation would include provisions establishing the machinery and procedure by which appointments were to be made.**

6.96 As for where in Northern Ireland administrative responsibility for judicial appointments should lie in the event of devolution, we are conscious that in many jurisdictions the Minister of Justice has this role, although often with mechanisms such as an appointments commission to insulate the process from direct political influence. However, in Northern Ireland we do not feel that the independence of the judiciary would be best served by allocating responsibility for the appointments process to a highly "political" department with operational responsibility for such issues as police, prisons and the criminal law. **On devolution, political responsibility and accountability for the judicial appointments process should lie with the First Minister and the Deputy First Minister.** We believe that it would be sensible to adopt the Scottish model that retains a role for Westminster in the most senior appointments. **For the appointment of the Lord Chief Justice and Lords Justices of Appeal, responsibility for making recommendations to Her Majesty The Queen would lie with the Prime Minister, as now, but on the basis of recommendations from the First Minister and the Deputy First Minister.**[15]

6.97 Throughout our consultation process people stressed the importance of, and the need to protect, judicial independence. Given the importance of this in terms of the constitution and public confidence, **we suggest that consideration be given to including in the primary Westminster legislation that provides for the transfer of judicial matters of a provision that no vote, resolution or Act of the Assembly on judicial matters should be valid unless it has cross community support, as defined by section 4(5) of the Northern Ireland Act 1998.**[16] In addition, we see the *European Convention on Human Rights* as providing an important safeguard against any action that might compromise judicial independence.

---

15 See paragraphs 6.106 - 6.109 for a detailed description of the responsibilities we propose for the First Minister and Deputy First Minister in relation to judicial appointments.

16 Cross community support means that a vote should have the support of a majority of designated Unionists present and voting, and a majority of designated Nationalists present and voting; or 60% of all members present and voting, including at least 40% of each of the designated Nationalists and designated Unionists present and voting.

A JUDICIAL APPOINTMENTS COMMISSION?

6.98   We now consider the procedure and machinery for judicial appointments in the context of devolution, in particular the desirability or otherwise of establishing an independent body (which we shall call a judicial appointments commission) to be responsible for the process. In examining the case for a commission, we envisage a body responsible for making or recommending appointments. This goes further than the recommendations of the Peach Report[17] which focuses on a commission with responsibility for keeping procedures under review and dealing with complaints and grievances.

6.99   Given that significant progress has already been made, especially in rendering the judicial appointments system more transparent, and that we have further suggestions to make in this context, we considered carefully whether an independent judicial appointments commission would add value to the process. Such an innovation does have potential drawbacks. For example, if judges and/or senior lawyers predominate on a commission, then there is a danger that they might tend to appoint in their own image. On the other hand a predominance of lay people could detract from the critical importance of legal ability in assessing merit and there might be fears that they could bring a political element into the deliberations; or at the very least that they might see themselves as representing particular interest groups. There would be the possibility of appointments being made or recommended by compromise. There would also be issues about accountability and what action would be taken if the commission did not meet with expectations.

6.100   However, we are mindful that a recurring theme in many countries has been the need to ensure that judicial appointments arrangements are immune from partisan political pressure, while at the same time made more open and accountable. This has been addressed in a number of instances by some kind of independent judicial appointments body, although, as we have seen, there is a variety of different models to suit different legal and political cultures. There is little research evidence to shed light on what impact appointments commissions have had, but a recent study has indicated a strong link between the creation of such bodies and growing judicial activism.[18] The argument runs that as the role of judges grows and develops, so there is a greater need than ever to insulate the appointments process from any possible suspicion of political influence; a way of doing this is by creating an independent appointments commission.

6.101   We have noted the strong local support for the creation of an independent appointments commission, especially among a number of the political parties. In the Northern Ireland context, the highly developed "rights" legislation and culture, taken with devolution and the prospect of litigation involving the individual and different organs of government (both

---

17   *An Independent Scrutiny of the Appointment Processes of Judges and Queen's Counsel in England and Wales: A Report to the Lord Chancellor by Sir Leonard Peach* (1999), London: HMSO (The Peach Report).

18   Malleson, 1999 - The New Judiciary.

devolved and Westminster based), point us in the direction of an independent appointments commission. Such a body could be established in a way that would ensure transparency and accountability, while meeting many of the concerns outlined above. The right balance of lawyers and lay people on a commission would ensure that proper account was taken of legal and judicial ability and of the need for a broader awareness of issues in society. Also it could become a public focus of good practice and of measures to ensure a fair system which ensured appointment on merit from a wide pool of candidates reflecting, so far as possible, Northern Ireland in its diversity.

6.102   We believe that in Northern Ireland an appointments commission would enhance public confidence. But the factor which, above all, sways us in favour of recommending such a body is the imperative that if political responsibility for judicial appointments is to be devolved, the appointments process must be transparent and responsive to society's needs on the one hand, but on the other it must be clearly seen to be insulated from political influence. Given the political and community divisions that exist in Northern Ireland, we do not believe that it would be feasible, particularly from the perspective of judicial independence, to leave significant discretion on appointments matters in the hands of Ministers on the Executive Committee. **We recommend that legislation enabling responsibility for judicial appointments to be devolved should include provision for the establishment of a Judicial Appointments Commission.**

6.103   **As for membership of the Commission, we envisage a strong judicial representation drawn from all tiers of the judiciary (including a representative of the lay magistracy – see Chapter 7) and nominated for appointment by the Lord Chief Justice after consultation with each of those tiers. The Lord Chief Justice or his nominee would chair the Commission. In line with practice elsewhere, there would be one representative nominated by the Law Society and one by the Bar Council. In total the Commission might consist of around five judicial members, two from the professions and four or five lay members.**

6.104   We do not envisage that the lay membership would include members of the Assembly or political nominees such as are to be found on the Judicial Services Commission in South Africa and in other jurisdictions. In the Northern Ireland context it is important to keep any hint of political input out of the appointments process. The lay members would be selected on the basis of the additional value which they would bring to the Commission's deliberations, including such qualities as experience of selection processes, the court users' perspective and the ability to assess the personal qualities of candidates. **The lay members of the Commission should be drawn from both sides of the community, including both men and women. This could be achieved through a legislative provision along the lines of section 68(3) of the Northern Ireland Act 1998 which provides that the Secretary of State should, so far as practicable, secure that the Northern Ireland Human Rights Commission is representative of the community in Northern Ireland.**

The First Minister and Deputy First Minister would appoint the nominees of the Lord Chief Justice and the professions and would secure the appointment of lay members through procedures in accordance with the guidelines for public appointments (the Nolan procedures).

6.105   **The Commission should be responsible for organising and overseeing, and for making recommendations on, judicial appointments from the level of High Court judge downwards**, that is over 1,000 appointments. We do not envisage the full Commission conducting interviews as in South Africa and nor do we believe it necessary that each interview panel should consist only of members of the Commission, although that may well be the case for the more senior appointments. **Working through an Appointments Unit, the Commission would organise its selection panels which, for appointments at deputy resident magistrate and above, would always include at least one member of the judiciary at the tier to which the appointment was to be made and a lay person. The selection panel would shortlist, take account of the available information on the candidates, and conduct interviews with a view to making recommendations to the Commission.** While procedures for appointments to the lay magistracy and other positions, such as tribunal members, would be the responsibility of the Commission, it would not be practicable for members of the Commission to participate in the detailed arrangements for all such appointments.

6.106   We considered whether the Commission should make appointments as suggested by some consultees, thus emphasising the independence of the process from political influence, or whether it should recommend appointments to a political authority. If its role is to recommend then, as we have seen in other jurisdictions, there is a variety of models to be considered including the submission of one name or a list of names which might be ranked or unranked. The desirability of an element of political accountability and the involvement of Her Majesty The Queen in making many of these appointments point in the direction of the Commission making recommendations to the First Minister and Deputy First Minister. However we are conscious that in giving a political figure the opportunity to choose from a list or to reject recommendations, as is the case in a number of other jurisdictions, there would be a danger of neutralising much of the purpose of establishing a Commission which is to reduce the scope for political influence. **We recommend that for all judicial appointments, from lay magistrate[19] to High Court judge, and all tribunal appointments, the Commission should submit a report of the selection process to the First Minister and Deputy First Minister together with a clear recommendation. The First Minister and Deputy First Minister would be required either to accept the recommendation or to ask the Commission to reconsider, giving their reasons for**

---

19   See the next chapter for our proposals regarding juvenile lay panel members, who we recommend should be re-titled lay magistrates.

doing so; in the event of their asking for a recommendation to be reconsidered, they would be bound to accept the second recommendation. **The First Minister and Deputy First Minister would then:**

- in respect of High Court and county court judges, and resident magistrates, advise Her Majesty The Queen to appoint the recommended candidate; and

- in respect of appointment of deputy county court judges and deputy resident magistrates, and of appointments below the level of resident magistrate, make the appointment.

6.107 As outlined above we envisage that it should be open to the First Minister and Deputy First Minister to refer an initial recommendation for appointment back to the Commission for reconsideration; this could happen at the instigation of one or both of the Ministers. In that event, the Commission would again apply considerations only of merit in reconsidering the case and might well re-submit the same name, which would then have to be accepted. The capacity to refer back must be viewed not as a means of putting indirect pressure on the Commission to take factors other than merit into account, but rather as a safeguard to ensure that recommendations made by the Commission are fully justified.

6.108 We have given some thought to the role of the Commission in relation to the most senior appointments (that is those of the Lords Justices of Appeal and the Lord Chief Justice), when it would be for the Prime Minister to make the recommendation to Her Majesty The Queen, following advice from the First Minister and Deputy First Minister. In doing so, we were conscious that the judiciary at this level are important in constitutional terms and have responsibilities going beyond Northern Ireland in that they are members of the Privy Council. Also in certain circumstances there might be difficulties in convening an appropriate panel from the Judicial Appointments Commission, especially given the small size of the jurisdiction. We are aware too that the position of Lord Chief Justice requires particular skills in the field of organisation and management.

6.109 We note that in some other jurisdictions procedures for the top judicial appointments vary from the rest; in South Africa for example the President consults with the Judicial Services Commission over the appointment of the most senior judges, whereas he is required to accept the Commission's advice for other judicial appointments. In all the circumstances, **we recommend that the First Minister and Deputy First Minister should consult with the Judicial Appointments Commission over the procedure to be adopted in appointments to the positions of Lord Chief Justice and Lord Justice of Appeal and submit such procedure to the Prime Minister for approval. The same principles of transparency and appointment on merit should apply as with other appointments.**

APPOINTMENTS PROCEDURES

6.110   In order to appoint on merit it is necessary to secure a pool of applicants with the right qualities from across the professions and to have in place procedures that will ensure the selection of the highest qualified, based on clearly articulated criteria. That means building on progress already made and applying best practice in selection procedures for judicial appointments. We endorse such features as advertising posts, published criteria for appointment, selection panels, structured interviews and the use of other transparent and open means of securing the necessary information to assess the suitability of candidates for appointment. It also means having in place an organisational structure dedicated to achieving these ends and focused on the appointments process.

6.111   In order to operate effectively, **the Judicial Appointments Commission would require a fully resourced administrative structure in the form of a Judicial Appointments Unit separate from the Court Service (or Department of Justice) but staffed by officials drawn from it. This Unit, under the supervision of the Commission, would assist the Commission in:**

- **establishing criteria for appointment which provide for the level of technical and legal competence required by particular posts and the personal qualities necessary for members of the judiciary, including an awareness of social and human rights issues;**

- **organising the selection processes which would include open advertising, published criteria for appointment and structured interviews for all appointments from High Court judges downwards;**

- **ensuring that selection panels had before them all the information on which to base decisions, including the results of consultation with the senior judiciary and professional associations;**

- **publishing detailed information on all aspects of the appointments system in Northern Ireland, along the lines of *Judicial Appointments*, the Lord Chancellor's Department publication for England and Wales;**

- **publishing an annual report on the appointments process;**

- **developing a strategy of equal opportunity and outreach designed to broaden the pool of potential applicants in a way that maximised the opportunity for men and women from all parts of the community to secure appointments; and**

- **identifying and, where possible, addressing factors which might make it more difficult, or constitute a disincentive, for qualified candidates from particular parts of the community to apply for appointment.**

6.112   Given the importance of judicial appointments, and that there is security of tenure, we believe that those responsible for selection or making recommendations for appointment should have relevant information from a variety of sources. **There should remain a role for formal written consultation with the senior judiciary and the heads of the legal profession in respect of candidates for appointment as county court judge and above. For the sake of ensuring transparency and fairness, the results of such consultation should be made available to the selection panels for these posts, who would consider them along with all other relevant information. We consider that the present practice of asking for named referees for lower tier appointments should be extended to include candidates for appointment as High Court or county court judges and suggest that consideration be given to including an element of self-assessment in application forms for judicial appointments.** The Peach Report contained suggestions for linking the format of application forms, references and consultations more closely to the specific appointment criteria. We suggest that this be examined further in the Northern Ireland context.

EQUAL OPPORTUNITY

6.113   In developing an equal opportunity strategy, we have a number of initiatives to suggest. The extent to which candidates drawn from the ranks of practising barristers and solicitors can demonstrate their suitability for preferment will be largely dependent upon their relevant experience within the profession. We received some suggestions that there might be factors inhibiting the progress of women through the professions (and which therefore impacted upon the pool of candidates qualified for appointment to the judiciary) which would be worthy of attention. **We recommend that those responsible for judicial appointments should engage in discussions with the Bar Council and Law Society about equal opportunity issues and their implications for the judicial appointments process. The Equality Commission should be asked to assist with these discussions.**

6.114   **Efforts should be made to stimulate interest in becoming a judge, especially in sectors which are under-represented or where historically applications have been disproportionately low.** Considerations of gender, geography and community background might come into this. The approach to targeting groups adopted by the Ontario authorities may be worth examining further although we should stress that we are not recommending positive discrimination in the appointments process itself; merit should continue to be the deciding factor.

6.115   **We are attracted to the idea of developing a database of qualified candidates interested in securing judicial appointment, and we recommend that this idea be considered further.** People who have expressed an interest would receive, on a personal basis, details of all posts being advertised and might be invited to familiarisation seminars at which judges and magistrates would participate. This would also complement an outreach strategy in that it would help in assessing the pool of likely future applicants to establish whether there was the potential for under-representation of particular groups in the future.

PART-TIME APPOINTMENTS AND DEPUTIES

6.116   Part-time appointments to the judiciary are made in a number of jurisdictions. They can be beneficial for equal opportunities purposes and in bringing a breadth of experience and expertise into the judiciary. Such appointments would be made on merit and subject to the same eligibility criteria as full-time appointments and, while part-timers might undertake other work (such as academic teaching), they would not be allowed to practice. This is not the same concept as that of deputies. **We recommend that consideration be given to introducing a small number of part-time appointments.** This would need careful examination from the perspective of the efficient administration of the court system.

6.117   We should say at this point that we gave some thought to the appointment of deputies. The practice enables possible candidates for future full-time appointment to determine whether they are suited to the role. It is also of importance from an administrative perspective in giving the courts' administration the flexibility to cover court sittings and facilitate the efficient despatch of business. Some concerns have however been expressed about the prospect of deputy judges or magistrates, usually lawyers in private practice, presiding in a court where parties are represented by lawyers with whom they have dealings in their practices; this is a particular issue in a small jurisdiction. Another issue is that the involvement of the executive in appointing deputies on a renewable fixed term basis might be taken as compromising their independence. This was recently the subject of litigation in Scotland where arrangements for appointing temporary sheriffs were found to be in contravention of Article 6 of the *European Convention on Human Rights*.[20] Given the need to consider the implications of this judgment, we make no recommendation on the issue of deputies.

EQUITY MONITORING

6.118   We gave careful thought to whether the judiciary should be monitored by gender, ethnicity and community background. Clearly gender does not create a difficulty and parliamentary questions have been answered in which the gender balance of the various tiers of judiciary has been given.[21] However, the question of community background, assessed on the basis of religious affiliation, is more problematic.

---

20   *Starrs v Procurator Fiscal,* 11 November 1999 (unreported judgment of the High Court of Justiciary).

21   Hansard - 27 July 1999.

6.119   On balance we do not wish to recommend that fair employment legislation be applied to the judiciary, as to do so would have implications for their independence; but we do believe that the principles underpinning that legislation should be applied and be seen to be applied. We are conscious that this is a matter of considerable concern and that there are perceptions in a number of quarters about an imbalance, perceptions which may not be entirely well founded. We do not propose that existing members of the judiciary be asked about their religion although we believe that, if ways could be found to give an indication of the religious balance of the bench, this would help boost public confidence.

6.120   We do understand the reluctance of some to contemplate a situation where applicants for judicial posts are asked for information about their religious or ethnic background. It could be taken as implying a "representative" role for judges of the type that we have made clear is not appropriate; and this might be seen as having implications for judicial independence. On the other hand this form of monitoring and good practice for employment purposes is accepted throughout Northern Ireland and does not compromise the merit principle; and monitoring of this kind is carried out in England and Wales in relation to ethnic background.[22] Having such information would assist the Judicial Appointments Commission in judging the effectiveness of its outreach programme and in assessing the fairness and impact of the selection procedures. **We recommend that consideration be given to finding a satisfactory way, with the assistance of proxy indicators if necessary, of assessing for statistical purposes the religious background of applicants for judicial posts and of those who wish to be included in the database. There would also need to be assessment for statistical purposes of the ethnic background of applicants. This information would not be available to those involved in the selection process.** Particular care should be taken to devise monitoring procedures that do not, and are seen not to, compromise the overriding principles of judicial independence and appointment on merit.

6.121   Consistent with normal fair employment practice, there would be no question of publishing information about community background in a way that would enable individuals to be identified. However, we would expect the annual report of the Judicial Appointments Commission to make reference in general terms to the background of applicants to posts by reference to religion, gender, ethnicity, disability and geographical location.

IMPLEMENTATION OF JUDICIAL APPOINTMENTS PROCEDURES

6.122   We recognise that it may be some time before our recommendations on the devolution of justice matters and the establishment of a Judicial Appointments Commission are implemented. However, many of our recommendations on appointments procedures do not depend on these; in some cases they build upon changes already in train. We think it is

---

22   *An Independent Scrutiny of the Appointment Processes of Judges and Queen's Counsel in England and Wales: A Report to the Lord Chancellor by Sir Leonard Peach,* (1999), London: HMSO (The Peach Report).

important, in order to increase transparency, openness and confidence, that our recommendations on procedure and outreach are implemented as soon as possible. Hence, **we recommend that those elements of our appointments strategy which do not require legislative change be adopted for implementation at an early stage and be operated within the existing structures. Early steps should also be taken to establish a dedicated Judicial Appointments Unit within the Northern Ireland Court Service to assist the Lord Chancellor and the Lord Chief Justice in their duties within the current judicial appointments process.** The Judicial Appointments Commission which we have recommended[23] would thus be served by an already established Judicial Appointments Unit (which would be separated from the Court Service on devolution) and be in a position to continue with a strategy already in train.

6.123   Further, we believe that there is scope for enhancing confidence, openness and transparency by introducing an element of independent oversight of the existing appointments process. **We recommend the early appointment of a person or persons of standing to oversee and monitor the fairness of all aspects of the existing appointments system and audit the implementation of those measures that can be introduced before devolution. Such a person or persons should not be a practising member of the legal profession, should be independent of the judicial system and government, and should have the confidence of all parts of the community. They should have access to all parts of the appointments process and report annually to the Lord Chancellor. That report should be published.** Although the thrust of our thinking on this is similar to that which underpins the Peach Report,[24] the detailed arrangements would have to be tailored to the specific circumstances of Northern Ireland.

OATH OF ALLEGIANCE AND JUDICIAL OATH

6.124   We have already referred to one of the tasks of a Judicial Appointments Commission as having to identify and, where possible deal with, any blockages which might inhibit people from applying for judicial appointments. It has been represented to us by some that the Judicial Oath and Oath of Allegiance (or equivalent affirmation) required to be taken by judges, magistrates, JPs and lay panellists on appointment, could constitute such a blockage.

6.125   We recognise that a substantial element of the community in Northern Ireland aspires to the unification of Ireland. That they should do so has no bearing on their suitability or otherwise for judicial office and we can envisage circumstances where members of the Nationalist community would feel uncomfortable with being required to swear allegiance to or to serve Her Majesty The Queen. We also note the recognition in the preamble to the Belfast

---

23   See paragraph 6.102.

24   *An Independent Scrutiny of the Appointment Processes of Judges and Queen's Counsel in England and Wales: A Report to the Lord Chancellor by Sir Leonard Peach,* (1999), London: HMSO (The Peach Report).

Agreement of the equal legitimacy of differing political aspirations. On the other hand we realise that such oaths, sworn elsewhere in the United Kingdom, are of significance and importance to others.

6.126　We do not believe that maintaining the status quo in this area would show sufficient regard to the position of the Nationalist community. At the same time there should be recognition of the fact of the constitutional position. We considered a number of options:

- no longer requiring the Oath of Allegiance, but retaining the Judicial Oath;

- replacing both Oaths with a new oath which focuses on the judicial function, while including a reference to the fact of the Crown's constitutional position; and

- replacing both Oaths with a politically neutral judicial oath in modern language with no reference to Her Majesty The Queen.

6.127　We have taken advice on the constitutional implications of this and understand that there is no legal or constitutional impediment to any of the options outlined above. We note in particular that the constitutional status of the judiciary is underpinned by its origins in the Royal Prerogative with members of the judiciary being deemed to be doing justice on behalf of Her Majesty. However modern constitutional doctrine now focuses on the impartiality of the judiciary and its independence from the executive.

6.128　In all the circumstances we favour the third option outlined above. **We recommend that, on appointment, members of the judiciary be required to swear on oath along the following lines:**

> **I, [ ], do swear [or do solemnly and sincerely and truly affirm and declare] that I will well and faithfully serve in the office of [ ], and that I will do right to all manner of people without fear or favour, affection or illwill according to the laws and usages of this realm.**

JUDICIAL TRAINING

6.129　We wish to emphasise the importance that we attach to judicial training. Human rights instruments referring to the need for competent tribunals, the views expressed in the consultation exercise and the evidence from other jurisdictions all reinforce our view. The increasing complexity of legislation, the incorporation of the European Convention and the rapidly changing political and social context in which judges operate all point to the need not just for induction training but also for regular refresher exercises. New principles of interpretation arising out of human rights legislation have important training implications and there is a need for training in the policy and social context of legislation, as well as in judicial techniques. It is a welcome development that judges in many jurisdictions increasingly see training and development as an essential part of their duties, regarding it as an entitlement rather than an obligation.

6.130   We considered whether training should be part of the function of a Judicial Appointments Commission and have no doubt that those responsible for the appointments process should maintain close contact with those who are involved in training. However, we were impressed by the strength of the case for training being "judge-driven", both as a means of ensuring independence from influence by the executive or other interest groups and because in that way the commitment of incumbents to the process is more likely to be secured. The points being expressed to us by the Director of the Judicial Studies Board in England and Wales and by the Federal Judicial Centre in the United States on this matter were compelling.

6.131   We were impressed by what we heard of the Judicial Studies Board in Northern Ireland and **we think that the membership of the Board, drawing representation from each judicial tier, is about right, although an academic input might bring benefits.** However, it is apparent that there is little understanding of its work outside the judiciary and those who are close to the judicial process. **We believe that the Board should produce an annual report on its activities and on its training plans for the judiciary. It should continue to be supported by an administrative secretariat.**

6.132   As for the nature of the training to be delivered, a number of suggestions were made in the course of the consultation process and the Board itself gave us some examples of its activities. Given the importance of training which goes beyond traditional judicial issues, **we think that the Judicial Studies Board should develop a prioritised training plan, with members of the judiciary making the major contribution but also taking account of the views of the professions and other stake-holders.** Such a plan, with regular updating, would be the basis on which to secure funding to ensure high quality training. Thought might be given to issues where joint training with the professions would be appropriate and to the potential value of externally run conferences.

6.133   We are conscious that judicial training in such a small jurisdiction is not easy to run in a way that is cost effective, proportionate to the available resources and at the same time comprehensive. Co-operation with other jurisdictions is therefore important and we note that this is already happening; **we recommend that the Judicial Studies Board pay particular attention to maximising the benefits to be secured from co-operation with England and Wales, Scotland and the Republic of Ireland** in this field. The co-operation between Australia, New Zealand and the Pacific Islands is an example that may be worth examining further.

6.134   As is already the case in England and Wales in relation to some appointments, and in other jurisdictions, **we believe that induction training should be mandatory.** We note that, with only a handful of new appointments to the judiciary each year, it makes sense to utilise induction training opportunities in England and Wales, rather than running bespoke programmes in Northern Ireland; but we are aware that in Northern Ireland it has proved possible to develop such practices as mentoring, sitting in with experienced judges and visits and briefings from other criminal justice agencies. The advantage of such methods for a small jurisdiction is that they can be tailored to individual needs and costs can be kept within bounds. Otherwise, **we think that training is more likely to have a beneficial effect and secure the necessary commitment if it is developed by the judiciary for the judiciary on a voluntary basis**. **The Judicial Studies Board should monitor closely the progress of voluntary training and the degree of participation in it.** The head of the judiciary and the chairman of the Judicial Studies Board can of course give a strong lead in encouraging attendance at training events.

CONDITIONS OF SERVICE AND COMPLAINTS MECHANISMS

6.135 Tenure, remuneration and other aspects of conditions of service are of considerable importance in the context of judicial independence. If judges are not confident that their positions are secure and that pay will be determined on a fair basis according to objective considerations, then there is the danger of their being open to influence by the executive. On the other hand, there must be procedures for dealing with complaints and with cases of incapacity or misconduct.

6.136 Consistent with the exhortations of human rights instruments about security of tenure, **we endorse the current arrangements that give full-time judges and magistrates tenure during good behaviour until a statutory retirement age**. Currently Supreme Court judges may be removed by Her Majesty The Queen on an address by both Houses of Parliament, while other appointees may be removed by the Lord Chancellor on grounds of incapacity or misbehaviour. Under devolution however, we would not envisage a political authority having the power to remove judges on the basis of an address from the Assembly; this would have serious implications for their independence. Rather, we suggest the adoption of a procedure more akin to the Scottish model. **We recommend that removal from office of a judge or lay magistrate should only be possible on the basis of the finding of a judicial tribunal constituted under statutory authority and convened by the First Minister and Deputy First Minister or the Lord Chief Justice, that a magistrate or judge was unfit for office by reason of incapacity or misbehaviour.** It would be necessary for such a tribunal to have been established specifically to consider the possibility of removal. This recommendation applies in respect of all judicial posts.

6.137 A clear and publicly known complaints procedure is an essential element of accountability and can be devised in a way which does not put at risk judicial independence. **We recommend that a complaints procedure be devised and published. This would make clear that complaints about the exercise of judicial discretion could only be addressed through the judicial (i.e. the appeal) process, essential if judicial independence is to** be maintained. **Complaints about conduct or behaviour would be the ultimate responsibility of the judiciary, although, as now, officials in the Court Service could be tasked with dealing with the administration of such matters**. Minor issues would continue to be handled by Court Service officials seeking comments from the judge whose behaviour was the cause of complaint and replying to the complainant accordingly. There would be a commitment to a prompt response. At a more serious level the Lord Chief Justice would be involved personally in seeking to resolve the matter. **We recommend that for the most serious complaints which appear to have substance, including those which might merit some form of public rebuke or even instigation of the procedure for removal from office, the Lord Chief Justice should have the option of establishing a judicial tribunal to inquire into the circumstances and make recommendations.** Removal from office would not occur as a direct result of the findings of such a tribunal; that would only be possible on the strength of the outcome of a tribunal constituted in accordance with the recommendation in the previous paragraph.

6.138 We gave some thought to whether there should be a published statement of ethics for the judiciary in Northern Ireland. We approached this, not out of any doubts over the integrity of Northern Ireland's judges, but because there might be advantage in the public having access to material on the standards required of the judiciary, as a confidence booster. This is especially so in areas such as conflict of interest where there is already in existence carefully drawn up guidance. It would also be an opportunity to raise awareness about the nature of judicial responsibilities. **We recommend that consideration be given to drawing up a statement of ethics which might be annexed to the annual report of the Judicial Appointments Commission.**

6.139 **On remuneration we recommend that judges' salaries continue to be fixed by reference to their equivalents in England and Wales, which are within the remit of the Senior Salaries Review Body.** This will remove any need for the local administration to become involved in setting pay rates for the judiciary here, an important consideration in terms of independence.

JUDICIAL STRUCTURE

6.140 The Lord Chancellor currently holds the pivotal position at the head of all tiers of the judiciary and magistracy in Northern Ireland, although he does not have line management responsibilities in the way that this term would be understood in other organisations. He does have a clear role in relation to disciplinary matters. However, devolution would throw into sharp relief the need for a clearly defined and understood structure for the courts and the judiciary in Northern Ireland. A feature of most other jurisdictions is the existence not only of a hierarchy of courts, but also some degree of hierarchy involving members of the judiciary.

6.141   While judicial decisions are subject to appeal, they are not made the subject of criticism or supervision by other judges. However, there are a number of functions in which the existence of a President or Chief Judge at each tier of the courts might be beneficial. These include the facilitation of disciplinary and complaints mechanisms, the co-ordination and management of court business, representational work in relation to other agencies and the desirability of having a figurehead who can guide, mentor or proffer advice when it is requested. **We recommend that the Lord Chief Justice should have a clearly defined position as head of the whole judiciary (including the lay magistracy[25]) in Northern Ireland.** The Lord Chief Justice might find it helpful to appoint a head or representative of each tier to assist in co-ordination and representational matters.

6.142   We have a further recommendation to make which is intended to demonstrate publicly that the magistracy is an integral part of the judiciary. In looking at the titles of the various tiers of judiciary we gave some thought to the nomenclature of resident magistrates. As we note in the next chapter, the term "resident" has its origins in the nineteenth century when there were particular reasons for wanting office holders to live in the district where they held office. It has no meaning or relevance in the modern context. Moreover we think that there is an opportunity, through a name change, to demonstrate publicly that the magistracy is an integral part of the judiciary. **We recommend that legislation be passed to redesignate resident magistrates as district judges (magistrates' courts).** We favour retention of the term magistrates' court as it is commonly understood and reflected in a very large number of legislative provisions.

JUDICIAL INDEPENDENCE

6.143   In concluding this chapter we come back to one overriding theme, that of judicial independence. It is in our terms of reference and has informed us throughout. It was emphasised in the Guiding Principles and Values published with our consultation paper (see also Chapter 3 of this report) and in the human rights principles underlying our work (paragraphs 6.11 to 6.14). Many of the recommendations in this chapter are framed in such a way as to safeguard or bolster judicial independence. We suggest that it be given legislative backing and our approach on appointments matters is intended to insulate the judiciary from influence, whether political or from sectional interests. It was this consideration which lay behind our recommendations for "judge-driven" training and behind our recommendations on such matters as tenure, complaints and salaries. In the consultation process which will follow this report we hope that consideration of matters relating to the judiciary will focus on quality and maintaining the essential independence of our judges.

---

25   See Chapter 7.

7 Lay Involvement in Adjudication

Introduction

7.1 One of the four aims of the criminal justice system identified in paragraph 4 of the *Policing and Justice* section of the Belfast Agreement was to "be responsive to the community's concerns, and encouraging community involvement where appropriate". Included in our terms of reference is a requirement to consider "measures to improve the responsiveness and accountability of and any lay participation in the criminal justice system".

7.2 These pointers are concerned with the criminal justice system as a whole and do not specifically refer to the process of adjudication. The non-adjudicatory role of lay people in criminal justice is addressed in several other parts of this report, including chapters dealing with the courts, community safety, juvenile justice and restorative justice. However, so far as adjudication is concerned, in these islands and many other jurisdictions juries have for generations had the responsibility of determining guilt or innocence, usually in more serious cases. Also, in a number of jurisdictions, lay people have judicial roles of various types in the trial of less serious or summary cases and of juveniles, or in pre-trial procedures. They may have such roles in their own right or sitting alongside professional magistrates or judges.

7.3 It was apparent throughout our work that the principle of jury trial in Northern Ireland was not at issue; and many people positively looked forward to the time when it would no longer be necessary to have guilt or innocence in scheduled cases determined by a single judge in trials conducted under the provisions of emergency legislation. It is not for us to comment on when that position might be reached or on the issue of so-called Diplock courts. However we wish to say at the outset that **we fully endorse the principle of jury trial in cases tried on indictment at the Crown Court**, which brings lay people to the very heart of the criminal justice process and, particularly in the circumstances of Northern Ireland, constitutes a symbol of normality with all that means for public confidence.

7.4 In the circumstances we see no need to go into detail about the theory lying behind the jury trial or experience in other jurisdictions. We do recognise that there are some issues surrounding the use of juries and while they do not in our view call the principle into question, some particular features of the jury trial in Northern Ireland are addressed at the end of this chapter. However, we now go on to look at other aspects of lay involvement in adjudication, in particular the position of justices of the peace (JPs) and the lay panellists who sit alongside resident magistrates in the youth courts in Northern Ireland. In considering this chapter, and the associated research carried out for the Review,[1] we invite readers to have in mind the three possible models identified in the research:

(i) *professional*, where only paid professionals or stipendiaries preside, as in adult magistrates' courts in Northern Ireland and as is the case in the Republic of Ireland;

(ii) *lay*, where the court is presided over by a bench made up entirely of lay people, as is the case with most magistrates' courts in England and Wales;

(iii) *hybrid*, where a mix of professionals and lay people make up the bench, for example in the youth court in Northern Ireland and the lower courts in a number of European jurisdictions.

Human Rights Background

7.5   To the extent that lay people carry out judicial functions in the criminal justice system, it is important to emphasise that human rights considerations have as much relevance as is the case with the professional judiciary. The references in the European Convention and the ICCPR to the right to be heard by a competent, independent and impartial tribunal apply to the magistrates' court in England, with three lay justices on the bench, as they do to Crown Court hearings presided over by a High Court judge. The *UN Basic Principles on the Independence of the Judiciary* are explicitly applied to "all judges including, as appropriate, lay judges".[2]

7.6   This has implications for the selection procedures and management processes, which must be based on considerations of merit, with no discrimination on grounds of race, colour, sex or political opinion and which must be consistent with the requirements of independence. Those selected should be "individuals of integrity and ability with appropriate training or qualification in law".[3] That does not rule out any lay involvement and is not interpreted as requiring legal expertise to a high standard, but it does place a premium on training and competence. Independence runs through all of the relevant instruments, meaning independence from the executive but also from any improper influence that might interfere

---

1   Doran and Glenn, Research Report 11.

2   *Procedures for the effective implementation of the Basic Principles on the Independence of the Judiciary.* Procedure 3. See Livingstone and Doak, Research Report 14, Appendix 8.

3   Article 10 of *UN Basic Principles on the Independence of the Judiciary.*

with impartial adjudication. We should stress our view that these human rights norms apply to all circumstances where judicial discretion is being exercised, including pre-trial procedures. We note Article 5(3) of the European Convention, which provides that "everyone arrested or detained ... shall be brought promptly before a Judge or other officer authorised by law to exercise judicial power...".

Current Position in Northern Ireland

7.7 In assessing the current and possible future role of lay justices in Northern Ireland, the cultural and historical background is particularly significant. It explains why, despite having a criminal justice system with the same roots, the tradition of a lay magistracy playing a central role in summary justice has not been sustained in Ireland, North or South, as it has in England and Wales.

7.8 The historical context is addressed in the research report prepared for the review.[4] In short, by the 19th century it was increasingly apparent that the development of the role of JPs to the point where they had jurisdiction over summary cases was hampered by a combination of factors, including a climate of civil unrest and the effective exclusion of the Catholic gentry from service in the office. There were concerns about partiality and inconsistency of approach and in some areas it proved difficult to make appointments. The response to this was to appoint full-time resident magistrates, at that time not necessarily qualified lawyers, whose role was initially to assist the justices in their work but which increasingly involved their sitting alone and dispensing justice in their own right. In the early days the resident magistrates were required to live in the area to which they were appointed, hence the term "resident" magistrate.

7.9 After partition, judicial functions in the Republic became the preserve of full-time judges while in Northern Ireland JPs initially retained the ability to hear summary cases in petty sessions. However the Summary Jurisdiction and Criminal Justice Act (Northern Ireland) 1935 confirmed the trend away from lay adjudication. It provided that courts of summary jurisdiction would in future be presided over by resident magistrates sitting alone and stipulated that those appointed to such positions would be practising barristers or solicitors of at least six years standing. From the debates leading up to the passage of this legislation, it is apparent that the motivating factors behind this change included concerns that some lay justices were inconsistent in approach and had a tendency to allow personal opinions to override impartial adjudication on the basis of the law.[5] It must also be pointed out that substantial numbers of lay magistrates were said to carry out their duties impartially and

---

4   Doran and Glenn, Research Report 11, Chapter 3.

5   Second Reading Debate at 17 HC Debates (NI), Cols 467 to 580 (11-12 December 1934).

courageously, while there was a body of opinion that the legislation was contrary to democracy and that unpaid justices had "brought in humanity... experience... knowledge of local conditions and the circumstances of our people". While this Act removed the ability of lay justices to sit at the scheduled summary courts where the vast majority of business was dealt with, it left them with some important judicial functions, many of which they continue to carry out today.

7.10   As of 1 November 1999 there were 901 JPs in Northern Ireland, whose functions are largely prescribed in the Magistrates' Courts (Northern Ireland) Order 1981. Some of their functions are concerned with matters outside the criminal law field, including administering oaths and statutory declarations and signing official forms such as passport applications. We confine ourselves here to their judicial functions within a criminal law setting, both in and out of court.

7.11   The most common "in court" function performed by JPs is presiding at special courts for remand purposes. If a person is charged with an offence and kept in custody, he or she must be brought before such a court as soon as practicable and in any event not later than the day following that on which the charge is laid (unless the following day is a Sunday, Christmas Day or Good Friday, in which case the court appearance can be the next following day). The JPs (or resident magistrates) sitting at such a court will exercise judicial discretion in determining whether to grant bail or remand a defendant in custody. In 1998 a total of 65 JPs presided at 264 of the 417 remand courts, with resident magistrates presiding at the remaining 153.

7.12   A JP may also sit in a special court to:

- extend the period of time that a suspect may be held in custody without charge beyond 36 hours;

- determine whether there is sufficient evidence to justify committing a defendant for trial at the Crown Court;

- adjudicate on a range of complaints against adults where the adult consents to have the case heard in this way (the list of such complaints is to say the least anachronistic and includes such activities as pretending to tell fortunes, wandering abroad and begging in a public place, leaving a cart unattended etc).

In the first two of these categories, the complexity of evidence and issues to be determined are liable to be such that it is very rare for JPs to preside and they are normally brought before resident magistrates; it is usually possible for these cases to be heard at the scheduled sittings of fixed petty sessions courts. It is extremely rare for a JP to be required to hear and determine an offence in the third category of case outlined above. Many of these offences are extinct and, in others that are to be prosecuted, the police will normally bring such cases before fixed courts of summary jurisdiction as part of their normal prosecution process.

7.13   Out of court, JPs and clerks of petty sessions have an important role in considering complaints that a person has or is suspected of having committed an offence and determining whether to issue a summons requiring that person to appear in court. About 40,000 summonses are issued each year in respect of criminal offences, of which some 25,000 relate to complaints by the police, the remainder being divided between motor tax, TV licence and other regulatory cases brought by government departments and public authorities. Where the police are involved, they currently take summonses prepared by the Central Process Office to JPs at their workplace or homes or have them dealt with by JPs attending police stations on a rota basis. Similar procedures apply in respect of witness summonses.

7.14   A JP may also issue a warrant of arrest on the strength of a complaint made in writing and substantiated on oath. In doing so, the JP must be satisfied that the warrant is lawful and must take account of all the circumstances including the fact that the liberty of the individual is at issue. Similarly, a considerable number of statutes empower a JP, if satisfied by a complaint in writing and on oath, to issue a search warrant authorising entry of premises and the seizure of goods found.

7.15   While JPs do not hear and determine cases in the magistrates' courts, we wish to register our view that many of the functions outlined above are extremely important. They affect the liberty, privacy and other human rights of the individual, require the exercise of judicial discretion and involve a degree of oversight of the processes employed by the police and other investigating agencies. At present JPs receive no formal structured training, although some local groups have arranged for resident magistrates and clerks of petty sessions to give them talks and seminars on relevant topics. JPs appearing in special courts receive training on an individual basis and build up a degree of knowledge and experience over time. In 1997, a *Procedural Guide for Justices of the Peace* was issued to all JPs. This detailed handbook replaced an earlier production dating from 1987 and comprehensively set out the jurisdiction, powers and procedures to be followed by JPs in Northern Ireland in the performance of their duties in and out of court.

7.16   The one area where there is significant lay involvement in adjudication at trials is in cases involving juveniles. A youth court is normally made up of a resident magistrate sitting with two lay panellists of whom one is a woman. Decisions of the court on guilt or innocence and on sentence are made by a majority of its members, although the resident magistrate's view prevails on a point of law. The jurisdiction of the youth courts is extensive in that they can deal with any offence other than homicide and have the ability to make any disposal that might otherwise have been available to the Crown Court if it had been hearing the case. Lay panellists also sit with resident magistrates in family proceedings courts, established by the Children (Northern Ireland) Order 1995 to deal with civil issues relating to the welfare, custody, care and protection of children, matters which are outside our remit. In 1998 there were 409 sittings of juvenile courts, as they were then known, dealing with criminal matters, and 518 sittings of family proceedings courts. Lay panellists also sit as assessors with county court judges in appeals from juvenile courts, although in these circumstances they are acting in an advisory capacity only, with decisions being taken by the judge.

7.17 There are 145 lay panellists of whom 93 are JPs. Lay panellists may be considered for appointment as JP after four years of satisfactory service. The rationale behind the involvement of lay panellists is that where children are involved they can bring a breadth of experience and knowledge to the court and help keep proceedings relatively informal. Appointees as lay panellists are required by statute to undertake training during their first year of appointment and further training is provided as part of an ongoing programme. The training programmes are co-ordinated through a lay panel training committee. They consist of:

■ a two-day induction programme covering procedures and disposals of the youth court, followed by observations at court and visits to juvenile establishments;

■ in-service training covering topics associated with offending behaviour and new legislation; and

■ locally arranged training and regular visits to children's homes and establishments and community based programmes.

APPOINTMENTS PROCEDURES

7.18 The Lord Chancellor appoints justices of the peace. He has appointed eight advisory committees in Northern Ireland, each chaired by a Lord Lieutenant, to recommend suitable candidates for appointment, to keep under review the level of cover in their respective areas and to make recommendations on the need for further appointments. The committees are encouraged actively to go out into the community, talking to employers and other organisations, in order to secure nominations from all parts of the community. The guiding principles for selection are:

■ merit, regardless of ethnic origin, gender, marital status, sexual orientation, political affiliation and religion;

■ personal qualities, such as integrity and the ability to command confidence; and

■ the need to include men and women from all walks of life in order to preserve a balanced representation.

Candidates for appointment are normally between the ages of 40 and 64. Appointments are for life, although the Lord Chancellor has decided that JPs aged 70 or over should be restricted to "out of court" work and placed on a reserve list, leaving the remaining 542 justices to focus on "in court" activities.

7.19   Appointments to the Juvenile Lay Panel in Northern Ireland are also made by the Lord Chancellor, on the basis of recommendations by an advisory committee chaired by a senior resident magistrate. The guiding principles for appointment and appointment procedures are similar to those that apply in relation to JPs but lay panel members must retire at 70. On 1 November 1999 there were 145 lay panellists.

7.20   These appointments procedures are similar to those which apply in England and Wales in relation to the appointment of lay magistrates there.

7.21   We record below some profile information on JPs and lay panellists (some of whom are, as we have indicated, also JPs) as of 1 November 1999, recorded by religious background, age and gender.

	JPs	Lay Panellists*
Religion		
Protestant	687 (74%)	95 (66%)
Catholic	218 (24%)	49 (34%)
Other	18 (2%)	1 (-)
Age		
20-29	-	1 (1%)
30-39	15 (2%)	4 (3%)
40-49	70 (9%)	38 (26%)
50-59	183 (20%)	61 (42%)
60-69	265 (29%)	41 (28%)
70+	381 (41%)	-
Gender		
Male	732 (79%)	64 (44%)
Female	191 (21%)	81 (56%)

*The figures for age ranges of lay panellists are recorded slightly differently from JPs in that they cover age groups 31-40, 41-50 etc rather than 30-39 and 40-49.

Views Expressed During the Consultation Process

7.22   Outside of the professionals and lay people actually involved in the criminal justice system, the question of whether there should be greater lay involvement in adjudication was not an issue upon which there were firm views. In general, when asked, most people tended to favour the introduction of lay magistrates able to deal with less serious cases on their own or sitting alongside professionally qualified resident magistrates. But there was no overriding common theme or argument behind such sentiments.

7.23   Some of those in favour saw a strong lay magistracy as establishing a link between the courts and the communities which they served, helping to enhance public confidence and understanding of the system. Others saw it as a means of redressing a gender and class imbalance on the part of the professional judiciary and magistracy. Such views came through in some of the focus groups and seminars. There was a feeling that lay people could bring humanity and a knowledge of the community to court business. The introduction of lay assessors in South Africa was quoted as a positive example of how lay involvement could enhance perceptions of the justice system in parts of the community that had formerly been alienated from it. They were seen as counteracting any tendency towards case-hardening on the part of full-time professional magistrates.

7.24   The more sceptical view came from those who were concerned that efficiency and speed might be compromised if lay people were appointed to the bench. Also, in a reflection of some of the concerns that led to the supplanting of the lay magistracy with professional resident magistrates, there was mention of the possibility of intimidation, undue local influence being brought to bear and inconsistency in decision making. There were one or two expressions of concern about the possibility of ex-paramilitaries being appointed to the bench.

7.25   During our consultations, resident magistrates and others in the judiciary supported the widespread view that lay panellists added considerable value to the deliberations of youth courts. However, they did not feel that a case had been made for introducing lay magistrates to hear adult cases and some were strongly opposed to the idea. Concerns were expressed about the implications for efficiency and delay, both in terms of organising sittings and the length of time which might be taken to deliberate over individual cases. They pointed to the growing complexity of legislation which made lay involvement more difficult and expressed doubts about whether it would be possible to find suitable lay people to deal with or sit alongside professional magistrates in hearing the more lengthy contested cases. Such views were also expressed by those representing practitioners and by some political parties.

7.26   Some lay panellists and JPs who spoke to us could on the other hand envisage a gradual move towards panels of lay magistrates adjudicating on minor matters.

7.27   As for the workings of the present system, lay panellists spoke favourably about their training regime, which they felt should be extended to JPs, whose training and guidance some felt to be inadequate. There were doubts, some of them expressed by JPs themselves, about whether the current selection arrangements secured appointments from a sufficiently broad cross-section in terms of class, gender and community background. There was a desire to get away from what was still felt to be a predominantly male middle-class image, associated with JPs. Open and transparent appointments procedures were favoured, with vacancies being advertised. We heard one suggestion that advisory committees tended to be made up of existing JPs who might be inclined to recommend appointments in their own image and that thought should be given to including representatives of trade unions, community groups and other organisations on such committees. We should record one expression of concern that the independence of the judicial function was open to compromise if the police were able to choose which JP held a special court or signed a summons or warrant.

7.28   It was clear to us that many JPs whom we met were strongly committed to serving their communities but, at the same time, some were seeking a more focused and clearly defined role. Lay panellists too were clearly committed to their work and, from observation and discussion, we doubt whether one comment - that they were subservient to the resident magistrates - reflects the general position.

Research and Experience in Other Jurisdictions

7.29   Lay involvement in the adjudication process is not a universal feature of the jurisdictions which we have examined and indeed in some there has been a move away from a lay magistracy over the years to greater reliance on professionals. In the Republic of Ireland, while after partition some minor judicial functions were retained by commissioners of the peace, it has since been determined that the exercise of such functions is the preserve of professional judges appointed under the Constitution. However, lay adjudication is sufficiently widespread to provide a variety of models which may have some lessons for us to draw on in the Northern Ireland context. As in many other areas, we have to make the point that arrangements suited to one criminal justice system and cultural and political environment do not necessarily transplant into another.

7.30   England and Wales provide perhaps the clearest example of a jurisdiction where the hearing of summary cases by a lay bench is the norm, although the stipendiary (full-time legally qualified) magistrate has become increasingly significant in recent years. The lay bench there has developed over the centuries as an integral part of the criminal justice system. There are currently around 30,000 lay magistrates in England and Wales and about 100 stipendiaries, who tend to be appointed in the larger conurbations with high volumes of court business.

7.31   Stipendiaries, sitting alone, usually take the more complex and lengthy cases, but the Lord Chancellor has made it clear that he sees them as complementary to, and not supplanting, their lay colleagues. At the time of our visit to Brighton Magistrates' Court, there were 175 lay magistrates and one stipendiary serving 250,000 people and manning up to eight full courts each day. A bench of three lay magistrates may hear all classes of summary cases as well as dealing with committals. A key feature of the system is the presence of a legally qualified clerk who is able to advise the magistrates on points of law and procedure and sentencing issues. Lay magistrates are expected to sit between 26 and 35 half days per year, although the pressure of court business can result in a significantly heavier workload.

7.32   With the increasing complexity of the law relating to all types of case, and the future incorporation of the *European Convention on Human Rights*, training is regarded as of central importance in England and Wales. A core programme for newly appointed magistrates is prescribed by the Lord Chancellor, providing a basic grounding in the rules of evidence, law and procedure and the principles behind sentencing. A minimum of 12 hours training is provided every three years. During our visit to Brighton we learned that from 1 September 1999 there was to be a more practical element for new appointees, with mentors being assigned to individual magistrates and records of competencies kept.

7.33   The appointments procedure in England and Wales is similar to that in Northern Ireland for JPs, with the central role being played by local advisory committees, chaired by Lords Lieutenant. Criteria for selection are set by the Lord Chancellor and include: character and integrity; listening and communication skills; social awareness; judgement; and commitment and reliability. In recent years particular emphasis has been placed on trying to secure a bench representative of the community in terms of class, gender and racial background. Also, the Lord Chancellor has responded to concerns that the advisory committees are dominated by magistrates, with the attendant danger that the focus of selection might be narrowed, by requiring that at least one third of their membership should consist of other local representatives not serving on the bench. We did hear concerns that in some areas there were difficulties in recruiting new and younger magistrates, able to give up the time to sit on the bench.

7.34   If part of the rationale behind the lay magistracy is to bring community awareness and a broad understanding of social issues into the courts, then the importance of a diverse and broadly representative bench is self-evident. Recent initiatives in England and Wales have been developed with this in mind. From the Scottish perspective we should draw attention to the experiment in Perth recorded in the research report prepared for the Review[6] where a proactive effort was made to secure nomination for lay appointees to the district court through approaching community councils, churches, voluntary organisations, trade unions, the private sector and others. In Scotland district courts, administered by local authorities, hear summary cases at the lower end of the spectrum.

7.35   It is worth recording that it was the lay magistracy in England and Wales that provided the stimulus for a significant innovation in New Zealand. There, at the time of a visit made by two of our members, a new paid judicial office of community magistrate was being created on a pilot basis to sit in the district courts and handle minor criminal matters. Community magistrates need not be legally qualified and it is not intended that they should be assisted by legally trained staff. It is expected that they will sit for two days a week and will take over

---

6   Doran and Glenn, Research Report 11.

what little remains of the jurisdiction of unpaid JPs as well as a more extensive jurisdiction covering non-defended criminal cases where the penalty is up to three months imprisonment or a fine of $5,000. They are not able to imprison. The rationale behind the move is to increase community involvement in the criminal justice system, relieve pressure on the district courts and enable full-time professionally qualified district judges to concentrate on more serious and complex cases. Six weeks of initial training is provided, divided between theory in judicial skills, observation at court and mentoring by a professional judge.

7.36   A number of European jurisdictions have lay judges sitting alongside professionals in court, on a similar basis to the lay panellists in Northern Ireland. During our visit to Germany, where juries were abolished in 1924, lay judges were seen as a significant link between the criminal justice system and the community. They are selected by city councils and serve for periods of four years, attending court on 12 days per year. Their role is seen as of most significance in local courts where they can exert considerable influence in keeping proceedings and language straightforward and comprehensible; they also bring a community perspective to sentencing which might sway the court in the direction of leniency or more severe penalties depending on the nature of the offence and public opinion.

7.37   Other countries where professional judges sit alongside lay people are Sweden, Denmark and Finland. Selection tends to be in the hands of local government or sometimes by election. In most of these jurisdictions, the professional judge takes the lead role in matters of law and procedure, while lay participation would tend to be on an equal basis when it comes to matters of fact and sentencing.

7.38   When we visited South Africa, lay assessors had just been introduced in magistrates' courts and consideration was being given to extending their role into the High Court. There the change was largely driven by a desire to transform the racial composition of the bench, formed of professional magistrates who were civil servants often drawn from the ranks of prosecutors and, in doing so, to enhance public confidence in the formal system of justice. Lay assessors receive formal training in the Justice College alongside prosecutors and court staff.

7.39   From our brief overview of other jurisdictions, it is apparent that a range of factors lie behind the involvement of lay people in the judicial process, including:

- tradition;

- establishing an institutional link between the courts and the community;

- public confidence;

- helping to keep language and procedure comprehensible to court users; and

- relieving pressure on the professional judiciary.

Training receives a high priority in some jurisdictions, although it is recognised that its purpose is not to convert lay people into qualified lawyers. Securing a representative lay bench is often an issue but, given the commitment involved, it is not always easy to recruit a cross-section of people in full-time work. We should also point out that there are many jurisdictions where adjudication is regarded as entirely a matter for professional judges or magistrates.

Evaluation and Recommendations

A LAY MAGISTRACY

7.40   We now consider the case for introducing a lay element on the bench in magistrates' courts hearing adult cases in Northern Ireland and go on to make recommendations about the work of JPs. We remind readers that the basic options under consideration are: no change, i.e. cases heard by professional magistrates sitting alone; the lay model, where cases are heard by a bench made up entirely of lay people; and hybrid, where lay people sit alongside professional judges or magistrates.

7.41   The case for introducing a strong lay magistracy in Northern Ireland seems quite compelling in the context of the Belfast Agreement which talks of a criminal justice system that is responsive, encourages community involvement and promotes public confidence. It is argued that the representativeness of the bench, in terms of class, gender and community background, could be enhanced and community values brought into the heart of the administration of justice. Enhancing the role of lay justices would also provide an opportunity to harness the strong commitment to community and voluntary work that exists in Northern Ireland. Some have suggested that a lay element would moderate any case-hardening tendencies that might be associated with professional resident magistrates, who hear cases on a daily basis; and there is a view that lay involvement might help provide an impetus towards the use in court of language and procedures which are understandable and take account of the interests of other court users. Overall, this is seen as a means of binding the community into the justice system after many difficult years.

7.42   It is also observed that one of our neighbouring jurisdictions, England and Wales, which has a very similar legal system, provides the ultimate demonstration that a lay magistracy works. However we are conscious of the words of the previous Lord Chancellor, Lord Mackay, who observed: "although similar systems were put into operation in other countries following the English pattern, I do not know of any in which it has survived with anything like the strength that obtains in England and Wales ... I do not believe that it is easy to replicate this system anywhere else".[7] The experience of the lay magistracy in Ireland over the centuries demonstrates that what works in one cultural and political context is not necessarily suited to another.

---

7   Lord Mackay in his Hamlyn lectures on the Administration of Justice in 1993, quoted by Doran and Glenn, Research Report 11, paragraph 5.11.

7.43   The argument about representativeness and being in a position to take account of community concerns is, on the face of it, a strong pointer in favour of lay involvement in adjudication. However, it must be viewed with some caution against the background of Northern Ireland. It would be inimical to human rights standards requiring a fair, impartial and independent tribunal, if there were any suggestion that lay adjudicators were on the bench to represent particular groups or to bring personal or sectional perspectives to bear in dealing with individual cases. There is a fine dividing line between bringing the experience and wisdom of everyday life to the bench and allowing extraneous factors to interfere with objectivity of judgement. Of course, representativeness can be taken as relating to the bench as a whole being reflective of society, and careful selection, training and ongoing support should help reinforce objectivity and independence, together with consistency of decision making. However, we should not underestimate the challenge that this would represent in a society emerging from a period of civil unrest and division, if Northern Ireland were to move to a predominantly lay bench.

7.44   If Northern Ireland were to have a lay bench for a significant proportion of adult summary trials or a hybrid model, there would be a requirement for large numbers of people to be recruited and trained and for them to commit themselves to a significant workload. We note that of the 923 JPs, only 65 sat in first remand courts during 1998. We think that it is open to question whether it would be possible to secure the necessary commitment from a sufficient number of people with the right qualities, representative of society in terms of such factors as gender, age, community background and employment status. Also, we wonder how comfortable such people would feel if they were adjudicating in high profile cases, perhaps involving public order or which aroused very strong public emotions. It would be a serious setback to public confidence if a decision to introduce more widespread lay adjudication had to be reversed because of difficulties over recruitment or because the system was unable to withstand pressures exerted on it.

7.45   Dispensing justice expeditiously is a key objective with human rights implications. We are conscious of and take account of a number of representations made to us to the effect that organising sittings around the availability of lay magistrates would be a major undertaking in itself, liable to result in some delay. Also it is possible that hearings of individual cases would take longer, given the need for lay justices to take advice from a legally trained clerk or, in the hybrid model, for them to discuss legal issues with a professional magistrate.

7.46   The current arrangements for adjudicating in adult summary trials have some significant attractions. With a small complement of 17 resident magistrates, managing cases and securing consistency in approach should be relatively straightforward, provided that the necessary structures are in place for training and regular contact between them. Moreover the professional model, employed also in the Republic of Ireland, has taken Northern Ireland through the last 30 years with all the difficulties and pressures which that entailed.

7.47 We note that the Community Attitudes Survey of 1997/98 recorded 77% of respondents as being confident or very confident in the fairness of judges and magistrates, a higher figure than for any of the other subjects of the survey (the figure for Protestant respondents was 82% and Catholics 67%). However, when asked in the omnibus survey of 1999 whether people felt judges and resident magistrates to be in or out of touch with what ordinary people think, only 34% found resident magistrates to be a bit in touch or very in touch. These findings point to the need for such measures as greater outreach into the community and enhanced training, rather than wholesale structural change.

7.48 The arguments for and against introducing either model of lay involvement in adjudication in adult cases (lay or hybrid) are finely balanced. On the one hand such an initiative might help bind the community into the criminal justice system and thus enhance public confidence; but there are some doubts about whether in the present circumstances of Northern Ireland this would be the outcome and it would be a major managerial and organisational undertaking. We are conscious that recommendations elsewhere in this report, if accepted, will bring about major change in the criminal justice system. Bearing that in mind and the importance of not putting the process under too much strain, **we do not believe that a sufficiently strong case has been made at present to warrant change from the current system whereby a professional magistrate sitting alone adjudicates at summary adult trials.** We considered the possibility of a pilot but that would not test out the fundamental issues associated with large-scale lay involvement. Nor do we see any point in asking lay people to try uncontentious cases such as guilty pleas in respect of minor offences.

7.49 That is not to say that we are recommending that the system should continue as before. We are conscious of the findings noted above that a substantial proportion of respondents believed magistrates and judges to be "out of touch" and we believe that present circumstances offer the opportunity for more interaction with the community. Accordingly, **we strongly endorse the view that efforts should be made to make the system more responsive to community concerns and to encourage lay involvement in an informal capacity. We make recommendations elsewhere about opening up the courts to the public and we believe that the judiciary could make a significant contribution to this. Participating in various types of discussion fora, facilitating court visits and seeking out the views of the public on the way in which the system works should significantly reduce the likelihood of their being "out of touch" and should enhance confidence generally.** Good communications skills in a variety of settings will of course be an important element of this.

JUSTICES OF THE PEACE AND LAY PANELLISTS

7.50 In one respect, our recommendations do involve a significant enhancement of lay involvement in adjudication. **We strongly endorse the continued involvement of lay**

panellists in youth courts and, by recommending that the age range covered by that court be extended to include 17-year-olds (Chapter 10) we envisage that the workload of lay panellists will be increased by some 50%. This is likely to require a significant number of additional people to be recruited to the panel. There is a particular value in having a lay input in cases involving children where a whole range of considerations, requiring different types of expertise, come into play. Moreover this expansion of the role of lay panellists would not impact upon the system as a whole in the way that might be the case with the introduction of lay magistrates in the adult courts.

7.51   The question arises of the future of JPs in the criminal justice system. We do not think that the current position is satisfactory. It is apparent that many of the 923 JPs play little or no part in the criminal justice system, while others, though willing and committed, are uncertain of the contribution that is expected of them. Some carry out significant judicial functions, but work is not allocated to them in a coherent way and nor does there seem to be any focus or structure in their training. We believe that it would be an enhancement of lay involvement and public understanding and confidence if lay people fulfilling these functions were recruited, trained and organised in a structured way that met the needs of the criminal justice system.

7.52   The functions of JPs are various and sometimes anachronistic, and we can see a case for removing those which they hardly, if ever, perform. This is in part so that they are clear about what it is that they are required to do but also in order to safeguard the interests of justice; for example we do not believe that it should be possible for a lay person to be approached with a case for extension of detention unless properly trained and with an understanding of what to expect. **We do not think that lay people should any longer have the power to extend the period during which a suspect might be held in custody by the police, hear committal proceedings or adjudicate on a range of complaints against adults. There should however continue to be a role for suitably trained lay justices in presiding over special courts for first remand hearings**, since this is a significant function which, if they were not performing it, would impose an additional burden on resident magistrates.

7.53   **We recommend that lay people should continue to have a role in hearing complaints with a view to issuing summonses and warrants.**

7.54   This leaves three distinct categories of work of a judicial nature for lay people in the criminal justice system:

- first remand hearings in special courts;

- hearing complaints with a view to issuing warrants and summonses; and

- sitting as lay panellists in youth courts and as assessors at the hearing of appeals to the county court from youth courts.

7.55   **We recommend that all lay appointees empowered to fulfil these judicial functions should be designated as lay magistrates.** This should not cause any confusion with resident magistrates if our recommendation is accepted on renaming them as district judges (magistrates' courts). If these arrangements are introduced, we envisage no further role for JPs in the criminal justice system.

7.56   It will be for the Lord Chancellor or the responsible appointing body to determine how many lay magistrates are required to fulfil the functions outlined above and to make the necessary appointments. Existing JPs, along with others in the community, would of course be able to apply to become lay magistrates. There is no reason why one individual should not fulfil all three functions, and there may be some advantage in that but **we recommend that a system be devised whereby lay magistrates would be formally authorised to perform each of the three functions only following appropriate training. We would envisage training being the responsibility of a sub-committee of the Judicial Studies Board. Current members of the Juvenile Lay Panel will already have received structured training and we envisage that they would therefore be eligible for re-appointment as lay magistrates without the need for a selection process in their case; it will of course be necessary to appoint significant numbers of additional lay panellists to provide for the expanded jurisdiction of the youth courts.**

7.57   **We envisage appointments to the position of lay magistrate being made using the same mechanism as used for other members of the judiciary. The selection procedure should, however, draw upon the advice of local committees, as now, which should include a mix of existing magistrates and representatives of outside interests, including people with a community focus. The objective should be to secure the appointment of magistrates on the basis of publicly available criteria through advertisement and a proactive effort to secure nominations from organisations in the community including, for example: the private sector, voluntary and community organisations, churches and other local groups. There should be a retirement age of 70 for lay magistrates.**

7.58   **It should be for the body responsible for courts' administration to organise the attendance of lay magistrates at court to enable them to fulfil their functions and stand-by rotas in case they are needed out of hours.** We regard this as a particularly important recommendation if the independence of the lay magistracy is to be safeguarded and public confidence in it sustained.

7.59   In making these recommendations we have been conscious of the resource implications. If resident magistrates were to assume responsibility for all first remand hearings at special courts, it is likely that there would be a requirement for an additional resident magistrate to provide the necessary flexibility for out of hours cover, at a cost of around £100,000 per annum. Even then there would be concerns over whether the resident magistrates would be sufficiently accessible at short notice in all districts. The Court Service advise that specially trained lay magistrates (perhaps 150), supplementing the work of resident magistrates, would provide the necessary resource as well as enabling the lay magistrates to sit sufficiently frequently to build up their knowledge and experience. As for "out of court" functions, resident magistrates would not be able to provide sufficiently comprehensive out of hours cover, especially to meet tight time-scales for hearing complaints before issuing warrants of arrest and entry/search. Ideally some 500-600 lay magistrates would be required for this purpose, many of whom would, of course, also be authorised to sit in special courts or in the youth courts. The cost implications of these changes will require careful consideration.

7.60   We estimate that the costs of training lay magistrates, recruited on this scale, would be in the region of £150,000 per annum, to include administrative staff, training events and materials. There would also be a relatively small additional cost to provide for a proactive approach to recruitment. However these costs should be offset against the cost of recruiting an additional resident magistrate.

7.61   We are conscious that, apart from the expansion of the youth court, our recommendations do not entail any increase in the formal role of lay people in adjudication. However, we believe that they will enhance the quality of lay input. Also, in addition to the greater role which we see for the professional magistrate (or district judge (magistrates' courts)) at the interface with the community, there are many other areas in which our recommendations in subsequent chapters should increase community involvement in the criminal justice system, for example in community safety partnerships, the development of community based diversionary programmes, youth conferences and in our proposals to improve public understanding of the criminal justice system. **We recommend that the quality and impact of lay involvement, especially in the youth court and in the county court, be monitored and evaluated as a possible basis for extending the work of lay magistrates.**

JURIES

7.62   In common with many other common law countries, jury trial has by tradition been recognised as the ideal mode of trying serious criminal cases in Northern Ireland. Although international human rights instruments do not expressly guarantee a right to jury trial in criminal cases, Northern Ireland has a strong adversarial tradition which is bolstered by a lay jury able to give a wholly independent assessment of the merits of the prosecution case.[8] However, the use of trial by judge alone - so-called "Diplock" trials - in cases connected with the Northern Ireland emergency over the last 27 years has meant that jury trial has not operated in as extensive a manner in Northern Ireland as in other common law jurisdictions. Although emergency legislation is outside the scope of our review, a large number of submissions were made to us calling for a restoration of jury trial as soon as possible. We also

---

8   Jackson and Doran, *Judge without Jury: Diplock Trials in the Adversary System* (1995), pages 287-304.

note from the attitudes survey commissioned by the review that there appears to be strong support for the principle of jury trial, with most people (77%) expressing the view that juries were better placed than judges sitting alone to decide questions of guilt.

7.63   Since 1996 there has been a considerable drop in the number of people tried in Diplock courts and a corresponding increase in the number of persons committed for trial by jury. We also noted the Home Secretary's announcement[9] that the Secretary of State for Northern Ireland is reviewing the arrangements for non-jury trials in Northern Ireland. That review is considering and will report on what changes could be made to the present system and, when ministers judge the time right, what arrangements might be put in place to facilitate the transition to a system of trial by jury and to safeguard the proper administration of justice in that event. The review is expected to be complete by Easter 2000.

7.64   As more cases are sent for jury trial, it will be essential to maintain confidence in the jury system. We are conscious that, while there has rightly been considerable attention given of late to the experiences of intimidated or vulnerable witnesses, much less attention has been given to the experiences of jurors. So long as section 8 of the Contempt of Court Act 1981 remains intact, jurors cannot be asked about their experiences in the jury room. However there is a range of other matters that they may be asked about, including the facilities available to them at court and the treatment they receive.[10]

7.65   It is important to insulate jurors as far as possible from the threat of any intimidation. A number of recent legislative measures have been taken in England and Wales and Northern Ireland to prevent intimidation, including the creation of new offences of intimidating jurors and harming or threatening harm to jurors and provision for the retrial of defendants who have been acquitted by juries which have been intimidated.[11] But there is also scope for considering a range of practical ways in which jury intimidation may be countered. A number of suggestions for reducing intimidation have been made in the context of endeavouring to return as many cases as possible to jury trial, including measures to protect the anonymity and privacy of jurors and the idea that juries be selected on a province-wide basis in certain classes of case.[12] We are also aware of the trauma that can be caused by the experience of acting as a juror in certain classes of case and of what is expected of jurors in long and complex cases such as some of those involving fraud or organised crime.

---

9   Terrorism Bill, Second Reading debate, 14 December 1999, Hansard Col 166.

10   A small survey of Belfast jurors conducted in 1989 asked many of these questions: see J Jackson, R Kilpatrick and C Harvey, *Called to Court: A Public View of Criminal Justice in Northern Ireland* (1991). For a summary of the findings, see Jackson, Quinn and O'Malley, *The Jury System in Contemporary Ireland* (1999) 62 Law and Contemporary Problems pages 203, 226-227.

11   See section 51(1)(2) of the Criminal Justice and Public Order Act 1994 (Article 47(1) of the Criminal Justice (Northern Ireland) Order 1996; sections 54-57 of the Criminal Procedure and Investigations Act 1996 brought into force in Northern Ireland by Northern Ireland Order 1504.

12   See S Greer, *Abolishing Diplock Courts* (1996), Gearty and Kimball, *Terrorism and the Rule of Law* (1995), pages 56-57, Lord Lloyd, *Inquiry into Legislation Against Terrorism (1996)*, Cm 3420, paragraph 16.18.

7.66   In the light of the considerations outlined above, in recognition of the role of juries in the criminal justice system and in order to sustain and enhance confidence, **we think that there are aspects of jury trials that should be reviewed including, inter alia, measures to prevent intimidation of jurors, and the role of juries in particular classes of case.**

8 Courts

Introduction

8.1 The courts are a focal point of the criminal justice system. The aims set out in the Belfast Agreement note the need for fairness, responsiveness to the community, ensuring confidence, and efficiency and effectiveness throughout the criminal justice system. It is with these aims in mind, and against the human rights background, that we examine particular aspects of the courts in Northern Ireland. Our terms of reference specifically point us to an examination of the structure, management and resourcing of the criminal justice system including measures to improve its responsiveness and accountability.

8.2 In this chapter we consider some of the principles behind the way the courts conduct their business. We examine the means by which information on the courts is supplied to the community and the ways in which the courts can relate to their local communities. In doing this we look at who uses the court and examine structures such as court user groups to enable court users to express their views.

8.3 We also consider the court environment and court buildings, in the context of work already being carried out by the Northern Ireland Court Service, to see what more might be done in the interests of court users and to ensure public confidence. We look at court-related aspects of the accessibility of justice and at whether court structures and procedures might be intimidating or confusing to some, together with the impact of symbols displayed, language used and the dress worn in courts. All of these issues are important in public confidence terms. We address the balance that has to be achieved in developing accessible modern procedures and practices with which members of the community can feel comfortable, while preserving the sense of dignity and respect that in our view should be associated with the courts.

8.4 The issue of ministerial responsibility for the Northern Ireland Court Service will be examined in Chapter 15. Whilst this chapter deals with aspects of the courts affecting all users, Chapter 13 covers in more detail the support that should be available to victims and witnesses.

Human Rights Background

8.5   There are some internationally accepted human rights principles which need to be taken into account when considering the way courts operate in Northern Ireland. These rights should be protected by government, not only through the enactment of laws but also through the management, structure and funding of the criminal justice system.

8.6   While human rights instruments have traditionally been most concerned in the criminal justice context with suspects and defendants, this is now changing with emphasis also being given to obligations towards all to whom the state may be said to owe protection.[1] Put simply, the state must ensure that those attending court can do so without risk of harm.

8.7   The right to a fair trial, a cornerstone of the criminal justice system, is articulated in Article 6 of the *European Convention on Human Rights* (ECHR) as follows: "In the determination of his civil rights and obligations or of any criminal charge against him, everyone is entitled to a fair and public hearing within a reasonable time by an independent and impartial tribunal established by law." We have already discussed the role of the judiciary in protecting this right, but there is also a responsibility on government to ensure that the courts are structured and resourced in a way that helps secure a fair trial. The ECHR also guarantees the right to the free assistance of an interpreter if a defendant cannot understand or speak the language used in court.

8.8   The United Nations *Declaration of Basic Principles of Justice for Victims of Crime and Abuse of Power*, dealt with in more detail in Chapter 13, is directly concerned with the needs of victims. As an unincorporated instrument it urges governments to ensure that the needs of victims are facilitated. For the courts and other agencies this includes taking measures to minimise inconvenience to victims, protect their privacy when necessary, and ensure their safety from intimidation and retaliation, as well as that of their families and witnesses. It also requires the avoidance of unnecessary delay in the disposal of cases.

Current Arrangements

COURT USERS

8.9   In looking at the criminal courts in Northern Ireland we need to have an idea of who is using the courts. A range of different groups can be identified including:

- witnesses;

---

1   Livingstone and Doak, Research Report 14. See also *Osman v UK* (1998) 28 October 1998 where the European Court recognised that states have an obligation to protect an individual whose life is known to them to be at risk from the criminal acts of another.

- victims of crime;

- jurors;

- the accused in a criminal case;

- relatives and friends of those involved in a case;

- interested members of the public;

- the legal profession;

- the prosecution;

- the police;

- other professional users such as the Probation Service, Victim Support and social services; and

- journalists.

8.10 The business of the courts is facilitated by the Northern Ireland Court Service. The Courts' Charter for Northern Ireland,[2] first produced in 1993 and being revised for publication in early 2000, identifies the court facilities which the Court Service aims to provide:

"In the programme of rebuilding and refurbishing courthouses continuing consideration is given to your convenience and comfort. As court buildings vary in age and layout it is not always possible to provide every facility that might be desirable. However, where resources permit, and it is physically possible to do so, better facilities will be provided:

- improved waiting and consultation areas;

- more reception or information points; and

- better access for the disabled."

8.11 The Court Service, within the resources available to it, is working to implement the commitments contained in the Charter. Steps have been taken to provide facilities for Victim Support, separate waiting rooms for witnesses and victims and information desks which also act as referral points for solicitors, probation and other agencies.[3] Another feature of this process has been an audit of 10 courthouses carried out by the William Keown Trust to assess the needs for disabled people in gaining access to buildings, facilities and services.

8.12 As well as setting out standards for court facilities, the Courts' Charter also sets standards which members of the public can expect when attending court. The Court Service aspires to ensuring that those attending court do not feel ill at ease or intimidated. Wherever possible

2   *Courts' Charter for Northern Ireland*, Northern Ireland Court Service, page 7. This document can be obtained by writing to the Northern Ireland Court Service, Windsor House, 9-15 Bedford Street, Belfast BT2 7LT. It is also available on the internet at www.nics.gov.uk/pubsec/courts/crtchart.htm.

3   One such information desk has been established at Belfast Magistrates' Court staffed by the Citizens' Advice Bureau.

witnesses should be provided with a place to wait away from the other side involved in the case. Also victims called to court as witnesses should, as far as possible, be able to familiarise themselves with the courtroom surroundings before they appear in court. In an effort to inform the public of these standards the Court Service has produced a range of leaflets explaining what happens in court.[4] As an additional assistance to witnesses, Victim Support Northern Ireland runs the Crown Court Witness Service at Belfast Crown Court which provides assistance to witnesses, victims of crime, their families and friends who may be attending court to provide support.

8.13   The Northern Ireland Court Service is currently involved in some innovative programmes to engage with the local community and promote greater public awareness and understanding of how the courts and the legal system work. Initiatives include:

- visits to courthouses by local schools at which the judiciary and court staff explain the function of courts and the roles of the participants (in the past 18 months 811 students have taken part, although coverage across Northern Ireland is not uniform);

- helping facilitate an annual mock-trial competition (twelve schools in Northern Ireland have been involved in this and two have won the national final in recent years);[5]

- all local schools and community groups in Dungannon are being invited to become involved in the design of a new courthouse for the town;

- courthouses at Armagh and Downpatrick were open to the public as part of the European Heritage Day on 11 September 1999.

8.14   It is important that the different groups involved in court business work together. At the Northern Ireland wide level, this is achieved through Court Service membership of inter-agency groups such as the Criminal Justice Board and Criminal Justice Issues Group, which enable cross-cutting issues affecting the criminal justice system as a whole to be addressed.[6]

8.15   Court user fora have been established at some court venues. One of the most recent examples is the Londonderry Court User Committee, chaired by the Recorder of Londonderry, which comprises representatives from a wide range of organisations and agencies, including the voluntary sector, involved in supporting the administration of justice. The committee provides a forum for discussion on a range of operational issues across all tiers of courts. There are also other types of fora such as statutory Family Business Committees.

---

4   Leaflets published include *Witnesses in Court, Small Claims Courts in Northern Ireland, Jury Service and You,* and *The Work of the Coroner in Northern Ireland.* These leaflets are available at all court offices or can be obtained by writing to the Northern Ireland Court Service, Windsor House, 9-15 Bedford Street, Belfast BT2 7LT.

5   Facilitated by the Northern Ireland Court Service in conjunction with the Citizenship Foundation.

6   See Chapter 15 for details of inter-agency and inter-departmental machinery.

Views Expressed During the Consultation Process

8.16   During the consultation process members of the Review Group undertook visits to Antrim courthouse, Belfast Youth and Magistrates' Courts, and Brighton Magistrates' Court. Through these visits we were able to form a view on how far the courts in Northern Ireland were able to meet the standards to which the Courts' Charter aspires and on ways in which improvements might be made.

8.17   In our meetings with a variety of groups, and in written submissions, court issues were raised in different contexts, both from a court user perspective and from the point of view of wider society. The attendance of many Court Service staff at our consultation seminars helped stimulate a useful exchange of views.

INFORMATION

8.18   Whilst depictions of courtroom scenes in television dramas are commonplace, only a minority of people have direct experience of being in a court in any capacity.[7] This lack of direct experience may help explain the lack of knowledge and understanding of courts, together with a feeling that they are somehow distant from the community, which was apparent amongst a range of people met by the group during the consultation process. There was a desire for more effort to be made to inform both the general public and court users about what goes on in the courtroom and it was argued that widespread public confidence in the system was dependent on a greater degree of understanding.

8.19   There was some criticism of the lack of accessible information. Suggestions made included a court information pack and school visits to courts. At a consultation seminar in Craigavon the practice of inviting local schools to visit the courthouse on a regular basis was welcomed, but there was often a lack of knowledge of initiatives which were already in place. A small minority expressed the view that, by the very nature of the court function, knowledge of courts would be confined to a small group in society and it should not be expected to be otherwise.

COURT GROUPS

8.20   The need for the criminal justice system to involve the community was a clear message during the consultation process. So far as the courts were concerned, initiatives which had been established, such as the court user and inter-agency groups, were broadly welcomed and there was a desire to see such good practice replicated across Northern Ireland. It was hoped

---

7   The November 1998 omnibus survey indicated that just over one third (34%) of respondents said that they had experienced contact with a court in Northern Ireland. See Chapter 2.

that improving court links with the community would demystify the courts and also provide users with a mechanism to hold the courts to account and allow for the discussion of ideas about the way courts operate.

8.21   Amongst those working in the courts, there was also a desire for structures to bring together the court professionals with user representatives to improve court efficiency, accessibility and facilities and address issues such as outreach.

COURT ENVIRONMENT

8.22   In addition to increased awareness about courts there was a desire for a more user friendly court environment. There were several aspects to this.

8.23   We heard from groups representing court users who wished to see improvements in the physical environment and the facilities available. For example, victims of crime needing to attend court wanted to be able to wait in comfort and safety, away from the defendant and his or her supporters, but this was not always possible. Within the courthouse separate waiting rooms and child-care facilities were suggested and there were calls for the specific needs of young people to be addressed. In particular instances the conditions in which people were required to wait, whether defendant, witness or member of the public, were criticised. The point was also made that courtrooms needed to be designed to ensure that those attending could see and hear what was happening. In the courtrooms which we visited in Northern Ireland we found instances where it was very difficult for defendants, witnesses or observers to hear what was going on.

8.24   As well as the physical environment, there were comments about the impression created at courthouses. There was a view that there was excessive formality, demonstrated by the dress worn in court, the procedures and the language used. Some argued that this created a barrier to some groups in society, particularly those from working class areas, and to victims of crime. A number of different groups and individuals called for the removal of wigs and gowns on the basis that they created undue formality and were off-putting to those attending court. We heard that resident magistrates had ended the practice of wearing gowns in the youth court. There were also those who did not feel that the dress worn by judges and lawyers at court was a problem and some argued that wigs and gowns contributed to an appropriate atmosphere of solemnity.

8.25   The need for more easily understood language in court was raised on a number of occasions, with one group we met saying "law language should be simplified removing Latin phrases from usage". It was suggested that particular problems in relation to courtroom language and "jargon" were created for children and young people and those with learning difficulties.

8.26 A demand was made by some groups for the right to conduct court business in Irish when desired. Some requested this specifically for defendants whilst others argued more generally for the use of Irish in court business.

8.27 There was concern about delays during attendance at court. Some felt that the length of time members of the public were kept waiting at courts displayed a lack of concern on the part of the professions. There were also complaints that the hours of court were inconvenient. However the main area of concern about delay was the time taken in actually getting cases to court, especially where defendants were being held on remand in custody. We address this aspect of delay in greater detail in Chapter 15.

8.28 We heard that the prominence of police at courthouses could create the erroneous impression that the courts were being run by the police. In our visit to Antrim Courthouse we noticed that the police were involved in a range of activities unconnected with their security role, such as giving directions to those attending the court and acting as jury keepers.

8.29 There were comments about the impression created at courthouses and the ethos that was reflected. The argument, largely articulated by political parties and groups representing the Nationalist community, was that the courts needed to create an environment in which all sections of the community could feel comfortable. There needed to be a real sense of parity of esteem, as expressed in the Belfast Agreement. This pointed to a neutral environment in which references to the monarchy and British State were removed, or to equal prominence for Irish and British symbols. An argument put forward by others was that removing symbols and references to the Crown might alienate another section of society.

8.30 Mixed views were expressed about the flying of flags, the proclamation of "God Save The Queen" as the judiciary enter some courts and about symbols and emblems. In one group it was felt that flags and proclamations were alienating but that the presence of a Royal Coat of Arms often went unnoticed and was not an issue. Views at seminars were not entirely polarised and there was often agreement that while flags and emblems could be provocative, removing symbols could be just as provocative. We heard the plea that any recommendation in this area should be guided by the need for sensible modernisation, making the system more transparent and intelligible.

8.31 The research and focus group discussions which we commissioned gave some insights into people's contact with, knowledge of and attitudes towards the courts. In short, this work demonstrated that few people had regular contact with the courts in any capacity. There was worry about the prospect of having to give evidence in court, fuelled by concerns about possible intimidation or retaliation and by unease about waiting and having to stand up and give evidence. Issues such as the wearing of wigs and gowns, oaths and Crown symbols gave rise to some concern, but for fewer people. However views expressed during focus group discussion[8] confirmed that for many the court system was seen as overwhelming.

---

8 Dunn, Morgan and Dawson, Research Report 12, Annex A.

8.32   Apart from the overwhelming nature of the court system a number of other issues relating to the way in which the courts operate were identified as leading to a feeling of frustration with the process and isolation from it. Delay in the system through postponements, long waits and broken appointments was viewed by people as a sign of a general lack of respect for the individual and at worst it was seen as a sign of contempt or incompetence. People wanted to understand what being in court meant. They wanted the language used in court to be clear and simple and clear information on how the courts system worked.

8.33   The large majority of people felt that the courts could help reduce the anxiety of those having to appear as witnesses by offering a range of support facilities. Opportunities for familiarisation with court layout and structure were seen as potentially helpful, as well as facilities designed to make witnesses feel more comfortable. [9]

COURT STRUCTURE

8.34   We set out the current court structure for Northern Ireland in Chapter 5. The structure of the courts did not arouse a great deal of comment during the consultation process. There were some suggestions that the creation of a constitutional court should be considered, perhaps dedicated to interpreting a Bill of Rights for Northern Ireland. Alternatively, we heard a view that the right of appeal to the House of Lords should be abolished and that a new court might operate on an all-Ireland basis as the Supreme Court for Ireland.

INQUESTS

8.35   An inquest is carried out to establish the identity of a deceased person and how, when and where that person died. A number of groups raised the issue of the inquest system and coroners' courts in Northern Ireland. Human rights groups were concerned that in Northern Ireland inquests, persons suspected of causing a death, or charged or likely to be charged with an offence relating to a death, could not be compelled to give evidence. There was also criticism that verdicts had effectively been abolished and replaced by findings which included only factual statements about the circumstances in which death occurred.

8.36   We recognise those serious concerns about the way the system is operating and the depth of feeling on this issue. We are also aware that the operation of the coroners' courts has not been reviewed since the Broderick Report in 1971.[10] This Review does not have sufficient

---

9   Amelin, Willis and Donnelly, Research Report 2, Annex A.

10   November 1971 (Cmnd 4810).

time or expertise available to undertake the major review of the coroners' courts we feel is now due. **We recommend an independent review into the law and practice of inquests in Northern Ireland.**

Experience in Other Jurisdictions

8.37   The Group found in most jurisdictions an increasing focus on the needs and demands of court users and the goal of a transparent and publicly understood system for the administration of justice. For example, the Department of Justice in South Africa has published a report, *Justice: Vision 2000,* which emphasises the role of the courts in ensuring access to justice.[11] They aim to review the language used in all court documents and establish citizens' advice desks and public information systems using modern technology in all courts. A need for more courts dispersed widely throughout the community was also identified.

8.38   We noted with interest the growing awareness internationally of the opportunities for bringing courts and the justice system generally closer to the community. *Les Maisons de Justice et du Droit*[12] in France provide a sort of one stop shop, with probation, social services, juvenile justice workers, legal aid, victim support, prosecutors and, in some instances, judges under one roof. Such institutions can provide easier access to the law, mediate disputes and engage in local outreach and crime prevention activities.

8.39   An example of this approach in a common law environment was the development of community-based courts about which we learnt during our visit to the United States. One such project, well evaluated, is Midtown Community Court, which opened in 1993 with the aim of responding to crime problems affecting the community on the West Side of Manhattan. The court is the focus, but the courthouse is home for a range of services including probation, police, social workers and counsellors. The judge can consult the professionals on individual cases and monitor the success or otherwise of treatment programmes being carried out from the premises, while the police can use the facilities there to provide immediate cautions and advice to defendants who might benefit from a diversionary outcome. Partnerships are formed with local schools, businesses and churches in order to develop community-based programmes, often based on restorative principles. Community links, familiarisation visits and outreach are seen as essential to the success of such ventures.

8.40   In establishing community courts such as Midtown, the American authorities have faced the challenge of persuading a sceptical public, who tend to be concerned about initiatives focused

---

11   Available on the internet at www.gov.za/reports/1996/justice.htm.

12   See Wyvekens, A. 1996 *Justice Proximité et Proximité de la Justice, Les Maisons de Justice et du Droit,* Droit et Société, pages 33, 363-388.

on placing offenders back in the community. Early signs point to some positive results. As well as achieving improved compliance rates for community sentences,[13] the projects can produce greater public confidence in the courts and the criminal justice system.[14]

Evaluation and Recommendations

PRINCIPLES

8.41   **We believe that the courts in Northern Ireland should operate efficiently but also effectively and in a way that promotes confidence in the criminal justice system.**

8.42   This principle needs to inform the activities of all the various agencies involved in court and requires their co-operation. It points to the following:

   ■ It is important that court hearings are conducted in a way that enables jurors, witnesses, defendants and other members of the public present to understand what is happening.

   ■ The Court Service is accountable to court users and the general public. This requires communication with the community of a kind designed to inform the public of the court system and its workings. It requires a proactive strategy of public education and outreach.

   ■ As with all areas of public administration, there needs to be continuous effort to improve levels of service. This involves ensuring that courts are organised and conduct their business in a way which facilitates the delivery of a fair system of justice and minimises any unnecessary fears of court users. Effectiveness means the proper administration of justice in the public interest of the state, the citizen and in particular of those who attend the courts in whatever capacity.

8.43   The rest of this chapter is about how to live up to those principles. The overarching purpose and vision of the courts is about providing the best possible environment and context in which the adjudication of criminal and civil cases can take place. From all that we have seen and heard, we believe firmly that if this is to be achieved then the courts should be regarded as an integral part of the community and as places where a range of agencies can contribute to the cause of justice. The French Maison de Justice et du Droit and the American community court experience are examples of this sort of approach and such models have much to commend them. In Northern Ireland, the Probation Service, Victim Support and other agencies are already to be found in our courts and our recommendations on such issues

---

13   Nearly 75% of offenders processed through Midtown complete their community service sentence as mandated, *BJA Bulletin,* NCJ 166821 p 3.

14   Bureau of Justice Assistance, *Overcoming Obstacles to Community Courts: A summary of workshop proceedings,* 1998, NCJ 73400, p.6. Available on the internet at www.ncjrs.org/txtfiles1/173400.txt.

as restorative and juvenile justice will place a premium on effective inter-agency working being closely related to court outcomes. How this is reflected in arrangements for the accommodation of local services, and the interaction between them, will depend very much on local circumstances.

8.44   We have stated throughout this report the need for a satisfactory complaints mechanism to underpin accountability and ensure that the needs of the public are addressed. This principle applies to the courts just as it does to other parts of the criminal justice system. As the Courts' Charter says, if mistakes are made the Court Service needs to be told so that steps can be taken to ensure the same mistakes do not happen again. An information leaflet explaining how verbal or written complaints may be made is available at all court offices.

INFORMATION/OUTREACH

8.45   While there has to be an element of formality and dignity about court proceedings, this does not mean that courts should be intimidating places. We believe it necessary to tackle unwarranted fears about courts as a means of improving access to justice and the responsiveness of the criminal justice system to the community. The level of worry about giving evidence in court indicated in research demonstrates the need to address this issue. The provision of information and education to potential court users has an important role to play. **The courts' administration should contribute to and be fully involved in the co-ordinated strategy of public education and information about the criminal justice system** in line with our recommendations in Chapter 3.

8.46   The Northern Ireland Court Service produces an annual report and corporate plan and is already active in producing information for court users. Particular instances of courts actively engaging with their local communities through, for example, school visits have been brought to our attention. **We endorse the current efforts of the Northern Ireland Court Service to provide information to the public and recommend that this work is developed further. Information points in courthouse reception areas should include a range of leaflets explaining what goes on in courts, while the internet and video might be used to disseminate information. Visits to courts should continue to be encouraged as a way of increasing community awareness and understanding.**

COURT GROUPS

8.47   We have noted that some groups have already been established in Northern Ireland bringing together various court users including the judiciary, victims groups and criminal justice agencies. Such groups can provide feedback from the users of the service to those managing the courts and allow discussion of a range of issues such as improving efficiency, court facilities and dealing with the needs of vulnerable groups. **We recommend the establishment of court user groups across Northern Ireland inclusive of the judiciary, the professions, criminal justice agencies, and voluntary organisations representing victims and witnesses. We also suggest that consideration be given to means of sharing best practice between such groups. We see the Criminal Justice Issues Group as a body bringing together the judiciary, the heads of the main criminal justice agencies, the legal profession and the voluntary sector to promote good practice throughout the system** (see Chapter 15).

COURT ENVIRONMENT

8.48   Suggestions were put to us concerning the physical environment of the court. We recognise that most courts will continue to sit in courthouses constructed decades, or even centuries, ago. The Court Service has made significant progress in developing its estate of 24 buildings and there is an ongoing programme of new building and refurbishment. It keeps its accommodation strategy under review. Despite the improvements, some courthouses do not meet standards required for the delivery of modern public services. The Court Service is committed to improving its estate to provide accommodation and facilities that meet the needs of court users and are reasonably accessible. It is projected that some £50 million will be spent on maintenance, refurbishment and capital projects at courthouses over the next three years, including a new 15 courtroom facility in Belfast.

8.49   In working to develop and improve the court estate we note and welcome the commitments given by the Court Service in the Courts' Charter. We think it is important that the way the courts are built and furnished should conform to the principles of the criminal justice system which we have set out in this report. Court design has to pay due regard to the needs of the court users, and those administering the courts have a duty to ensure that they are aware of what those needs are. Specific attention should be paid to the needs of victims and witnesses who should be dealt with sensitively and may require segregated waiting areas. **We recommend that it should be an objective for all court buildings to have appropriate reception, waiting and consultation areas for those attending court, with adequate refreshment facilities and proper access for the disabled. Consideration should also be given to the need to accommodate and staff information points, witness support facilities and other community services as considered appropriate in the local area.**

8.50   All those attending court need to be able to see and hear the proceedings in a safe and secure environment. This is not only about the design and acoustic facilities in court but also about the manner of proceedings, ensuring for example that the defendant is present in the courtroom when the proceedings begin and that speech is directed towards all those in court. Preventing the intimidation of witnesses and victims should be a high priority when addressing layout and procedures. Flexible courtroom facilities, which allow modifications according to the type of case being heard, can be useful. For example, while there is a strong case for a non-intimidating environment in youth courts, a key requirement for certain vulnerable witnesses may be special screening in the courtroom. With these considerations in mind, **we recommend that the layout of courtrooms should take account of the needs of the judge and those attending court to have good lines of sight and be able to hear the proceedings. Courtrooms should have the appropriate degree of formality, and be designed to minimise the risk of jury or witness intimidation. We also recommend research into audibility, layout and procedure in the courts throughout Northern Ireland to highlight any simple improvements that might be made. We note the importance of those participating in court speaking clearly.**

8.51   We endorse the approach to continued improvement in facilities at courthouses and recognise that this will be an incremental process. **Local court user groups will have a role in making suggestions for and monitoring improvements in facilities with reference to agreed standards.**

LANGUAGE AND DRESS

8.52   We have considered the dress worn and language used in court in view of the need to ensure that the environment is not overly intimidating and that the court ethos is reflective of modern society. We consider that there is merit in being able to identify the judiciary, lawyers and court officials within a court but that this purpose could be served by wearing white bands ("tabs") and a simple black gown to reflect the wearer's position within the system, i.e. judge, Queen's Counsel, junior barrister and solicitor. In our view the wearing of wigs is archaic, serves no useful purpose and can contribute to the discomfort that some members of the public feel about attending court. Whilst traditional robes may be appropriate on ceremonial occasions, **we recommend the simplification of dress worn in court and an end to the wearing of wigs except on ceremonial occasions.**

8.53   The Woolf Report on the civil justice system in England and Wales[15] identified a number of ways in which the civil justice system could help to ensure access to justice. One of these was that the system should "be understandable to those who use it". The report indicated that the system of justice and the rules which govern it should be broadly comprehensible not only to an inner circle of initiates but to non-professional advisers and, so far as possible, to ordinary people of average ability who are unlikely to have more than a single encounter with the system. It also advocated the removal from the language used in courts of words and expressions that were meaningless or confusing to non-lawyers. We agree with the thrust of

15   *Access to Justice* (1998), final report to the Lord Chancellor on the civil justice system in England and Wales, London: HMSO.

the recommendations of the Woolf report, that the proceedings in court should be comprehensible to non-lawyers. **We recommend that steps be taken to ensure the language used in the criminal courts is easily understood by lay people.**

8.54 We note the human right of everyone charged with a criminal offence to have the free assistance of an interpreter if he or she cannot understand or speak the language used in court. This right is upheld by the courts in Northern Ireland. If a judge believes that a defendant cannot understand or speak English an interpreter must be made available. The Northern Ireland inter-agency group on vulnerable or intimidated witnesses has found that there can be some difficulty in obtaining translators for different parts of the criminal justice system. Court Service data, however, indicate that there is rarely demand for the services of an interpreter in court.[16] Nevertheless it is in the interests of justice that interpreters should be readily available and **we endorse the work that is currently under way in drawing up a common list of interpreters to be used for victims, witnesses and suspects.**

8.55 The demand for the right to conduct court business in Irish was made during the consultation process. The Administration of Justice (Language) Act (Ireland) 1737 provides that the official language of the courts is English. As noted above, interpreters are only provided if a defendant cannot understand English; an individual appearing in court does not have a right to choose to use Irish. The position is similar in England where a translator is only provided when a person with insufficient command of English is on trial. However in Wales the Welsh language may be spoken by any party, witness or other person who desires to use it, subject to rules of court to give prior notice.[17]

8.56 In the Belfast Agreement the Government gave a commitment to promote the use of Irish in public life. Since the Agreement the Government has announced its intention to sign the *Council of Europe Charter for Regional or Minority Languages*. In specifying Irish under the Charter the Government has undertaken to eliminate any unjustified distinction, exclusion, restriction or preference relating to the use of a regional or minority language and intended to discourage or endanger the maintenance of it.[18] Under Part III of the Charter specific measures are proposed to promote the use of Irish in public life. **We recommend that consideration of the use of the Irish language in courts be taken forward in the wider context of the development of policy on the use of Irish in public life generally.**

---

16 In the period between January 1998 and June 1999 there were only two instances when the services of an interpreter were required in court.

17 Welsh Language Act 1993 section 22.

18 *Council of Europe Charter for Regional or Minority Languages* Part II.

SECURITY AND POLICE PRESENCE

8.57 The need to secure the courts and the safety of those attending is of paramount importance. We recognise the difficult conditions in which the courts have operated in Northern Ireland in the past. It is clear to us that there has been a requirement for police attendance at court entrances for security and public order reasons. We understand this need and believe that appropriate security measures must continue in line with the assessment of the security risk.

8.58 We have heard some disquiet about the impression created by the numbers of uniformed police inside courthouses. Some people felt this to be overbearing, although it is worth mentioning that one focus group was agreed that the police on duty were the most friendly people at the courts.[19] On our visits to courts there was a relatively high visibility of police, who on occasion were responsible for directing people entering the court building. Increasing normalisation of society will enable the police presence at court to be reduced on a phased basis. **In line with the assessment of security risk, the Court Service should assume full responsibility for security at its courthouses, for jury keeping and for the reception and provision of information for court users.** While this will reduce the burden on the police, the Court Service will require additional resources to enable it to take on these tasks.

8.59 As we have noted, research we carried out found that fear of intimidation was a significant factor in deterring attendance at court. This is a serious problem that must be addressed by the Court Service, in conjunction with the police, who will remain responsible for dealing with any incidents. **We recommend that the Court Service should have the responsibility, in consultation with the police, for drawing up policy in relation to countering intimidation of jurors, witnesses, victims and other members of the public on court premises and for ensuring that the policy is implemented.**

ETHOS OF THE COURTS

8.60 The courts in England and Wales and Northern Ireland have traditionally been identified with the symbols of the head of state. The traditional conceptualisation has been of the monarch as the source and fountain of justice, with the Sovereign's Majesty deemed always to be present in court. It was perhaps in recognition of this that the practice of displaying a Royal Coat of Arms behind the judge's chair evolved. In Northern Ireland, as in England and Wales, practice varies on displaying the Royal Coat of Arms on the outside of courthouses. In Northern Ireland some 50% of courthouses do not display the Royal Coat of Arms on the outside of the building. It is also practice for the Union flag to be flown at courthouses on days when the flag is flown on Government properties that are the responsibility of the

---

19   Dunn, Morgan and Dawson, Research Report 12.

Secretary of State for Northern Ireland.[20]

8.61   The Belfast Agreement makes a firm commitment to partnership, equality and mutual respect and makes securing the confidence of all parts of the community an aim of the criminal justice system. All parties to the Agreement acknowledged the sensitivity of the use of symbols and emblems for public purposes and the need to ensure that they are used in a manner that promotes mutual respect. One possibility would be to match the Royal Coat of Arms with an Irish symbol; but this would, in our view, risk introducing a political element into the court environment. We also considered the removal of all symbols, but felt that this could be misinterpreted as being inconsistent with Northern Ireland's constitutional position. On the other hand, we are conscious that the presence of the Royal Coat of Arms in a prominent position in the courtroom could be regarded by some as off-putting and inconsistent with the need for court proceedings to take place in a neutral environment.

8.62   It is with these considerations in mind that we make the following recommendations. **We recommend that there should be no change in the arrangements for displaying the Royal Coat of Arms on the exterior of existing courthouses. However, in order to create an environment in which all those attending court can feel comfortable we recommend that the interior of courtrooms should be free of any symbols. We recommend that the flying of the Union flag at courthouses should continue to be in line with flag flying practice at other government buildings which are the responsibility of the Secretary of State for Northern Ireland. These practices would become subject to any decision of the Assembly on devolution of responsibility for courts administration.** We look to a future when these issues can be addressed on an agreed basis to the satisfaction of all parts of the community. In time it may be more fitting to move towards symbols that emphasise the separation of the courts from the executive.

8.63   We do not recommend any change to the names of the Royal Courts of Justice or the Crown Court. We note that the form of the jurors' oath in Northern Ireland was brought into line with that in the rest of the United Kingdom in 1996 and makes no reference to the Monarch. The declaration of "God Save The Queen" on entry and exit of judiciary to some of the Crown Court venues and county courts in Northern Ireland occurs at the discretion of the judge and has no statutory basis. We note that in Scotland a shout of the word "Court" only is made on the opening and closing of courts. In England and Wales the practice varies. **We believe that the declaration of "God Save The Queen" on entry of the judiciary to the court is unnecessary and we recommend that this practice should end.**

---

20   Other public buildings in Northern Ireland are responsible for their own arrangements.

COURT STRUCTURE AND JURISDICTION

8.64   Under the current system most of the business handled by county courts is civil, their criminal jurisdiction being limited to appeals from magistrates' and youth courts. The courts at the tier below, the magistrates' court, and the tier above, the Crown Court, deal with criminal cases at first instance. Combining the jurisdiction of the county court with the Crown Court might on the face of it have merit. It could allow a more flexible use of court sittings and judiciary, facilitating the exchange of innovative ideas between civil courts and criminal courts in integrated court settings and perhaps facilitating career progression for resident magistrates (who we propose elsewhere should be re-titled district judges (magistrates' courts)). However, given that the county courts have a mixed civil and criminal jurisdiction, an arrangement which works and which was not raised with us during the consultation process, we do not feel that it is appropriate for us to make any recommendation on this issue. Nevertheless, it has been a number of years since the court structure in Northern Ireland was last examined and there may be a case for a review of the court structure and the jurisdiction of the various courts.

8.65   Some respondents to our consultation process suggested that there should be a Northern Ireland or all-island Supreme Court. Such ideas came from two distinct perspectives. The first was that there should be a constitutional court to interpret a Bill of Rights, while the second was concerned with the establishment of a final court of appeal. Both suggestions would involve removing cases from the jurisdiction of the House of Lords by reconstituting supreme judicial authority in a new court. Clearly the questions raised by such proposals go beyond our terms of reference and we make no recommendation on them.

Restorative
and
Reparative
Justice

9 Restorative and Reparative Justice

Introduction

9.1 Our terms of reference require us to consider "… measures to improve the responsiveness and accountability of, and any lay participation in the criminal justice system". This chapter considers the concept of restorative justice and how it is being applied, describes how it has been developed and applied in other countries, and examines its applicability in Northern Ireland.

9.2 We were not invited specifically to address restorative justice, or its application in Northern Ireland. We were, however, aware that the issue had been discussed by the participants in the multi-party Talks, and that there were some concerns about how the concept was being applied in Northern Ireland. The paper *Restorative Justice*, which was published at Annex D of our consultation paper,[1] was based on a government paper tabled during those talks. The paper outlined the concept and set out what action was being taken to develop the idea within the criminal justice system in Northern Ireland. We sought views on the Government's approach, as set out in *Restorative Justice*.

9.3 As part of our work on this issue we commissioned a report[2] to inform us on relevant research relating to restorative justice, and to advise us on its applicability in Northern Ireland. We draw upon the research report's findings extensively throughout this chapter.

---

1 Review of the Criminal Justice System in Northern Ireland: A Consultation Paper (1998) Criminal Justice Review Group, page 39, Belfast: HMSO.

2 Dignan and Lowey, Research Report 10.

What is Restorative Justice?

9.4   The term "restorative justice" has come to mean different things to different people in Northern Ireland. With this in mind and to set the context for the rest of the chapter, we believe it right to set out in some detail what we mean by restorative justice and how the term is defined internationally.

9.5   Much of the modern thinking about restorative justice developed out of the victim-offender mediation or reconciliation movement that began in Canada and the United States in the early 1970s. The term has been used as an expression that covers a variety of practices that seek to respond to crime in what is seen to be a more constructive way than through the use of conventional criminal justice approaches. It is a concept which is not easy to define, but one definition was put forward by Marshall[3] when he defined restorative justice as "a process whereby all the parties with a stake in a particular offence come together to resolve collectively how to deal with the aftermath of the offence and its implications for the future". It is a more inclusive approach to dealing with the effects of the crime, which concentrates on restoring and repairing the relationship between the offender, the victim, and the community at large, and which typically includes reparative elements towards the victim and/or the community.

9.6   As the research report notes, "even within a criminal justice setting, restorative justice initiatives display considerable variations, which is why it is difficult to formulate a precise definition that would apply to all of them".[4] The research report identifies a number of key attributes which underpin criminal justice-based restorative justice and which tend to be absent from more conventional approaches. These are:

- the principle of "inclusivity";

- the balance of interests;

- non-coercive practice; and

- a problem-solving orientation.

9.7   Restorative approaches can be described as "inclusive" in three main respects: they take account of the interests of victims, offenders and, sometimes, the wider community, in addition to the public interest in deciding how best to deal with a case; they extend the range of those who are entitled to participate in the process of dealing with the offence, and bring the victim and the offender more fully into the process; and they extend the range of potential outcomes of the process to include restoration for the victim and reintegration of the offender back into the community.

---

3   Marshall (1999), *Restorative Justice: An Overview.* London: HMSO

4   Dignan and Lowey, Research Report 10.

9.8   Restorative approaches are more sensitive to the need to strike an appropriate balance between the various interests at stake, including those of the victim and the offender, as well as the public interest. A key requirement is voluntary participation: neither the victim nor the offender should be forced to take part in a restorative justice process, or to participate in the outcome of that process. The restorative justice process is not itself a tribunal of fact: if guilt is disputed, then it is for the courts to decide. The final attribute often involves a problem-solving orientation that is forward looking and which aims to prevent future offending, and which goes beyond dealing with the aftermath of the particular crime. This is reflected most clearly in the aim of reintegrating offenders back into the community.

9.9   Restorative justice approaches in other jurisdictions are described at length in the research report[5] and are set out briefly later in this chapter. Approaches differ, but are often based upon the following elements:

- engaging with offenders to try to bring home the consequences of their actions and an appreciation of the impact they have had on the victims of their offence;

- encouraging and facilitating the provision of appropriate forms of reparation by offenders, towards either their direct victims (provided they are agreeable) or the wider community; and

- seeking reconciliation between the victim and offender where this can be achieved and striving to reintegrate offenders within the community.

Human Rights Background

9.10   Restorative justice processes in the criminal justice setting are subject to many of the rights and protections afforded by international instruments to offenders and victims. Both the *United Nations Standard Minimum Rules for the Administration of Juvenile Justice* (the Beijing Rules) and the *United Nations Convention on the Rights of the Child* encourage states to promote diversion from judicial proceedings for juveniles, providing that human rights and legal safeguards are respected. Rule 25.1 of the Beijing Rules also calls for "volunteers, voluntary organisations, local institutions and other community resources... to contribute effectively to the rehabilitation of the juvenile in a community setting and, as far as possible, within the family unit".

9.11   The *United Nations Declaration of Basic Principles of Justice for Victims of Crime and Abuse of Power 1985* includes provisions relating to fair treatment, restitution and assistance for victims, and describes mechanisms for improving the responsiveness of judicial and administrative processes. It focuses primarily on compensation issues.

---

5   Dignan and Lowey, Research Report 10.

9.12   Most relevant of all to the issue of restorative justice, because restorative justice tends to be a community-based process, are the *United Nations Standard Minimum Rules for Non-Custodial Measures 1990* (The Tokyo Rules). The Tokyo Rules are intended to provide a set of basic principles to promote the use of non-custodial measures, as well as minimum safeguards for persons subject to alternatives to imprisonment. They also promote greater community involvement in the management of criminal justice, specifically in the treatment of offenders, as well as encouraging among offenders a sense of responsibility towards society. They cover such issues as legal safeguards for offenders (such as Rule 3.4, which requires that "non-custodial measures imposing an obligation on the offender, applied before or instead of formal proceedings or trial, shall require the offender's consent", and Rule 3.6 which requires that "the offender shall be entitled to make a request or complaint to a judicial or other competent independent authority on matters affecting his or her individual rights in the implementation of non-custodial measures"), the powers of prosecutors to dispose of cases at the pre-trial stage, and the range of non-custodial sentencing dispositions which should be available to the courts. They also cover supervision of offenders in the community; the duration of non-custodial measures; the conditions that may be applied; treatment programmes; breach procedures; and public participation.

9.13   The Council of Europe issued *Recommendation R (99) 19 of the Committee of Ministers of Member States Concerning Mediation in Penal Matters* on 15 September 1999. The Recommendation notes developments in Member States in the use of mediation in penal matters. It recognises mediation in penal matters as a flexible, comprehensive, problem-solving and participatory option that enhances active participation in criminal proceedings of the victim, the offender, others who may be affected, and the community. The Recommendation sets out general principles for mediation in penal matters and suggests a legal basis, operational standards and qualifications/training which governments of Member States should consider when developing mediation in penal matters. Many of the issues that it covers apply equally to the use of mediation in a more general criminal justice context. In considering the issues that have been raised with us concerning restorative justice we have reflected upon all of the above instruments. We have also sought to apply the standards that they set in developing our recommendations.

Current Position in Northern Ireland

9.14   Restorative justice is a recent development in most countries, but its application in Northern Ireland is at a particularly early stage. It has become an issue of public debate in Northern Ireland in recent years, primarily because of the emergence of community restorative justice schemes in some Republican and Loyalist areas. Also, there are occasions on which restorative principles are applied to individual cases that arise in the normal course of the criminal justice process.

SCHEMES WITHIN THE CRIMINAL JUSTICE PROCESS

9.15   Two pilot schemes established by statutory agencies operate as part of the formal criminal justice process. They are both at an early stage of implementation, have dealt with only a small number of offenders, and have not yet been fully evaluated. They involve offenders who have admitted their offences and are a means of diversion away from prosecution and court appearance. Juvenile Liaison Bureaux participate in, and are responsible for, referring offenders to the schemes. Both are aimed at juvenile offenders, and they involve a restorative conference in which the offender and his or her family and the victim and his or her supporters will participate, if they so choose (the participation of both the victim and the offender is entirely voluntary). The conference gives the offender the opportunity to learn how his or her behaviour has affected the life or business of the victim, and the victim an opportunity to confront the offender.

9.16   The first is the restorative justice scheme in Mountpottinger, which is a police led "caution plus" model dealing with a variety of minor offences. The scheme uses a mix of trained facilitators from the police and from the other agencies involved. Where the victim agrees to participate a restorative conference will be held. Where the victim does not, the police will deliver a "restorative" caution. Early indications are that most of those who have participated have reacted positively to the experience, although the scheme is still at a very early stage and has yet to be formally evaluated.

9.17   The second scheme, in Ballymena, targets retail theft and is operated by the police in co-operation with retailers in the town. In this scheme the offender and the "victim", who is a local retailer drawn from a panel to represent the victims of this type of offence, will be brought together in a restorative conference convened by a trained police facilitator. We understand that consideration is being given to replicating the scheme in Belfast city centre and Lurgan. There are also some other approaches being developed within the formal criminal justice system with restorative elements. Some sentencers are using the power to defer sentences to allow victims and offenders to meet, and the Probation Service's Watershed Programme has a restorative aspect.

SCHEMES OUTSIDE THE CRIMINAL JUSTICE PROCESS

9.18   A number of community restorative justice schemes have developed in some Republican and Loyalist areas. These operate outside the formal criminal justice process, and would aspire to be based on restorative justice principles. The Northern Ireland Office, the RUC and the Probation Service have devised a joint protocol[6] based on the published document *Restorative Justice*,[7] setting out the principles and safeguards to be incorporated in community based schemes if the criminal justice agencies are to work with them. Those running the schemes in Loyalist areas have generally made efforts to involve the police and operate in a way that is (sometimes loosely) complementary to the normal criminal justice process. Those in Republican areas have no contact with the police, although they have developed links with other statutory agencies, and have no links with the formal criminal justice process at all.

9.19   Dignan and Lowey[8] set out the origins of these schemes and the contextual factors that led to their development.[9] They also draw attention to the dangers of such approaches - a theme we explore further in considering the way forward.

Views Expressed during the Consultation Process

9.20   We heard a wide range of views about restorative justice in the course of the consultation process, in the written submissions we received and in the course of the meetings and seminars that we held. Most of those who commented on this issue were broadly supportive of the concept of restorative justice although understanding of what it meant in practice varied widely. Opinions were divided, however, on how restorative justice should be delivered and fell broadly into two camps: those who supported the delivery of restorative justice processes within and by the community, with few or no links with the formal criminal justice system; and those who favoured restorative justice being integrated into and delivered as part of the formal criminal justice process and who opposed community restorative justice delivered without links to and accreditation by the formal criminal justice process. Opinions were strongly and sincerely expressed. We also heard a range of views between these extremes.

9.21   Restorative justice was seen as a valuable tool for dealing with young offenders in particular, and as a means of involving victims more fully in the process of dealing with offenders. Many felt that restorative justice would provide a useful additional tool for dealing with crime and criminality and that it was a more positive means of dealing with juvenile offenders, since it encouraged them to take responsibility for their actions. It did not preclude the use of

---

6   The *Community Response to Crime* protocol confirms the Government's commitment to restorative justice but sets out guidelines within which local schemes should operate. It also states that local schemes should be complementary to the criminal justice system, not an alternative, and that they should work with elements of the formal system, including the police.

7   *Review of the Criminal Justice System in Northern Ireland: A Consultation Paper* (1998) Criminal Justice Review Group, page 41, Belfast: HMSO.

8   Dignan and Lowey, Research Report 10, chapter 3.

9   See also Auld, Gormally, McEvoy and Ritchie, *Designing a System of Restorative Community Justice in Northern Ireland: A Discussion Document* (1997), published by the authors.

traditional sanctions, including imprisonment, but it opened up the potential for victims to seek explanation from offenders, express their feelings and to receive apology and/or reparation for their losses. By comparison the formal system did little to engage offenders and address the underlying causes of their offending behaviour.

9.22 Opinions differed on the types of offences for which restorative processes should be used, and the circumstances in which they should be used. Many felt that restorative processes were suitable only for minor crimes or for first time offenders, suggesting that some offences were too serious or sensitive to be dealt with by other than the traditional criminal justice process, or that persistent offenders should be excluded. Sexual crimes and domestic violence cases were often cited as unsuitable or fraught with danger for the victim, because of the risk of unequal power relationships and possible revictimisation. Others believed that they were particularly suitable for a restorative approach, arguing that the victims of such crimes should not be denied the opportunity to engage directly with the offender. Indeed in their submission the NSPCC argued that "the current adversarial system... rarely resolves the problem, repairs the damage or addresses the harm to relationships... a restorative justice process might operate as a model in some [child sexual abuse] cases to address these issues particularly where there may be reintegration of the offender into the family at a later point in time". Some felt that restorative processes were capable of being used for all crimes, even the most serious, and that they could be used at any stage of the criminal justice process.

9.23 Some argued that persistent offenders were those most in need of a restorative approach, in that the criminal justice system had obviously failed to address the underlying cause of their offending behaviour, or to challenge it in any meaningful way. A few argued that adults might benefit even more than juveniles from a restorative approach, since they were more likely to understand and empathise with the views and concerns expressed by their victims.

9.24 There was general support for the proposition that those involved in delivering restorative justice programmes, whether as part of a community-driven or a criminal justice agency approach, should receive substantial human rights training as well as specialist training in mediation and dispute resolution, through accredited and specifically designed training programmes. In addition, some suggested that all restorative justice schemes should be subject to explicit codes of conduct, to ensure that they operated in a lawful and fair way, respecting the rights of all participants. They argued that such codes should be based on domestic law and international human rights standards. One group argued that they should also be subject to an explicit child protection policy. Some also suggested that all restorative justice schemes should be subject to regular, rigorous and independent inspection to ensure that standards were being met, that schemes should be evaluated, and that inspection and evaluation reports should be published.

9.25 Supporters of community restorative justice schemes argued that the pace at which such schemes developed links with criminal justice agencies, and in particular the police, should be determined by the community, not the criminal justice system. This argument hinged on the perceived lack of legitimacy of the RUC and other criminal justice agencies in the areas that most needed the development of a restorative approach. Those communities, whether Nationalist or Unionist, which most needed a community-driven restorative justice approach were precisely those where the criminal justice agencies and the criminal justice process were distrusted most. Community restorative justice was seen as a way of harnessing the energy of local communities and enabling them to deal in a legitimate way with crime-related problems, where often it was felt that the criminal justice system had failed. Government insistence that such schemes should work in co-operation with the RUC was rejected by some. One party commented: "if the RUC were to be involved [in restorative justice schemes] this would immediately take away any legitimacy which such programmes had built up in many Nationalist areas. To insist on RUC involvement is to emasculate the community participation which is precisely the strength of such schemes." However, the involvement of the police and other criminal justice agencies was not ruled out for the future: "the establishment of new institutions for policing and criminal justice may allow more organic links to develop."

9.26   Another submission suggested a "sensitive and pragmatic approach from government towards such programmes. Such an approach would recognise that statutory involvement from different criminal justice agencies... may occur in different ways and over differing timeframes in the context of evolving projects". The same submission went on to say that, "provided that activists are suitably trained, and acting within the law, the relationship between restorative justice projects and the various elements of the criminal justice system should be permitted to evolve at the chosen pace of local communities", a view which was echoed by at least one other submission.

9.27   A majority of those who put forward views on restorative justice were extremely wary of or, in some cases, absolutely opposed to the development of community restorative justice schemes. They believed that restorative justice should be developed as an integral part of the criminal justice process, and delivered by or with the explicit sanction of criminal justice agencies. We heard a wide range of concerns expressed about community restorative justice schemes and their relationship to paramilitary punishment beatings, including:

■ The motivation for the development of community restorative justice schemes. Many believed that community restorative justice schemes were being developed by paramilitaries because of the growing unacceptability of punishment attacks within the community, and the need to replace such attacks with other methods of controlling their communities.

■ The risk that those involved in meting out sanctions arising from such schemes would resort to or threaten punishment beatings.

- The perceived or potential involvement of those with paramilitary links in such schemes, and the risk of schemes being driven by people who did not represent the community as a whole, for reasons which had little or nothing to do with concerns about crime.

- The risk that the rights of offenders would be abused, that such schemes would use unlawful means for dealing with alleged offenders, or that offenders and victims would be coerced into participating.

- The risk of such schemes acting as community courts, determining not only what should happen to the offender, but also guilt.

- However human rights-proof the schemes were internally, they operated within and were sustained by an environment of coercion and threat, including the threat of punishment attack.

9.28　　Some favoured particular models of restorative justice. The New Zealand family group conferencing model was cited by many as an example of a proven approach that was fully integrated into the criminal justice process for juvenile offenders, and as an approach that bound in a wide range of stakeholders. This model was particularly attractive to some sentencers. Others favoured police-led models, such as that being piloted in Mountpottinger, or in some of the Australian states. Others suggested a partnership approach, in which the statutory agencies, the voluntary sector and local communities worked together to deliver restorative justice processes, within an overall statutory framework.

9.29　　A number of issues concerning the operation of restorative justice were also raised with us in the course of the consultation process, including:

- the need for participation of victims and offenders to be truly voluntary, and for the victim and offender to have the right to opt out of the process at any stage;

- the possibility of a dedicated agency or group of staff in a statutory agency being responsible for the operation of restorative justice schemes, and in particular, fulfilling the role of co-ordinator/facilitator in a conferencing model;

- the need for broadly based community support and the development of sufficiently varied local programmes to allow restorative "packages" to be developed; and

- the avoidance of piecemeal development of restorative justice schemes, and the need for schemes to be universally available across Northern Ireland.

Research and International Comparisons

9.30   The research report[10] reviews the available research on restorative justice and provides a detailed description and analysis of the development and operation of restorative justice in a number of other countries, including England and Wales, Canada, the USA, Australia, New Zealand, South Africa, and Scotland. We had the opportunity to hear a great deal about the application of restorative justice in New Zealand and Australia during our visit to New Zealand (which coincided with an Australasian conference on youth justice[11]). We also learned much from our visits to Canada, the Netherlands, South Africa and England and Wales.

9.31   We do not intend to repeat much of the material in the research report, but we do wish to emphasise that we concur with many of its conclusions, and agree with its analysis of the dangers inherent in a communitarian approach to restorative justice. There are, however, a number of lessons that we wish to draw out from the report and from our study visits. We also wish to describe briefly the New Zealand and Australian models, since they are central to our considerations.

9.32   Various restorative justice approaches have been developed, but the main variants include, victim-offender mediation, family group (or community) conferencing, and sentencing circles.

VICTIM-OFFENDER MEDIATION

9.33   Victim-offender mediation originated in Canada in 1974, and is heavily influenced by the Mennonite movement. It involves the quest for reconciliation between victim and offender, and a process of dialogue between victims and offenders relating to the offence in the presence of a trained mediator. It can occur face-to-face, or by shuttle mediation, where the mediator acts as a go-between. It offers victims the chance to tell offenders about the physical, emotional and financial impact that their offence may have caused, and gives them an opportunity to put unanswered questions to the offender.

9.34   Outcomes can include: an apology to the victim for the harm caused, reparation of various forms, including financial recompense, work for or on behalf of the victim, specific undertakings in relation to their behaviour (for example to undertake counselling or treatment), or a mix of all of these.

9.35   Schemes operate in a number of countries, including North America and England and Wales. In England and Wales they have tended to operate at the pre-court and court stages of the criminal justice process. Pre-court schemes offer mediation with a view to securing an agreed package of reparation in conjunction with a police warning or caution. This is known as a

---

10   Dignan and Lowey, Research Report 10.

11   "Youth Justice in Focus", conference held in Wellington, New Zealand, 27-30 October 1998.

"caution-plus" programme. Court-based schemes operate on adjournment between conviction and sanction, or following deferment of sentence and, if successful, will lead to a reduction in the sentence, or to some form of reparation being included in the disposal of the court.

FAMILY GROUP (OR COMMUNITY) CONFERENCING

9.36   Family group (or community) conferencing emerged in New Zealand and Australia in the late 1980s and early 1990s. It differs from victim-offender mediation in a number of ways. Firstly, in victim-offender mediation participation is normally limited to the victim and offender, whereas conferencing can encourage the participation of a much wider group, including those who are concerned for the well-being of either the victim or the offender, those who have concerns about the offence and its consequences, and those who may be able to contribute to a solution to the problem presented by the offence. There are two principal variants of the conferencing model.

THE NEW ZEALAND VARIANT

9.37   The first variant is the family group conferencing approach which originated in New Zealand, and which is an integral part of the youth justice system (applying to 14-17 year olds inclusive). It has a variety of goals, a number of which accord with a restorative approach. These include: an emphasis on young offenders paying for their wrongdoing in an appropriate way; the involvement of families and offenders in decision making arising from the offending; the participation of victims in finding solutions; and consensus decision making. There are both pre-prosecution and court level systems, with the family group conference having a central role in both systems.

9.38   In the pre-prosecution process, once the police have established an intention to charge, they are able to direct a youth justice co-ordinator to convene a family group conference without reference to the court. If the conference achieves agreement about what should be done and the young offender completes the plan, then the matter will not proceed to court. Where agreement is not reached, or when the members of the family group conference agree that the young offender should appear in court, the police are able to refer the case to the court.

9.39   If a young offender is arrested and charged the formal youth justice process operates. The young offender will appear in court without entering a plea. If the charge is not denied, the judge will direct a youth justice co-ordinator to convene a family group conference. Otherwise, the case will proceed to a defended court hearing at which if the charge is proved, the court must order a family group conference and consider the outcome prior to imposing an order on the young offender.

9.40 A family group conference involves the victim (or the victim's representative), the offender and members of the offender's family. It is attended by the police and facilitated by a youth justice co-ordinator who is employed by the Department of Social Welfare. Others, such as a social worker and a legal advocate for the young offender, may attend the conference at the request of the co-ordinator or the offender.

9.41 The legislation allows for considerable variation in practice at family group conferences, with the family of the offender applying the procedures they wish. In practice, youth justice co-ordinators have played a key role in advising families about how to proceed. They inform those entitled to attend of the conference details, discuss the process with the family and invite other interested parties, such as social workers, sports coaches or teachers.

9.42 A family group conference may proceed even if some participants who are entitled to be there decline to attend. It is not dependent on the attendance of victims. Offenders do not have to attend either, although conferences rarely proceed without them.

9.43 The objective is that those who attend the family group conference should agree a plan or recommendation. The conference has to designate a named person to be responsible for ensuring that the plan is carried out. If there is no agreement, the matter must be referred back to the youth court. The proceedings of family group conferences are confidential. Neither the enforcement agency (usually the police) nor the court may use information from the conference, even if there is no agreement and the matter goes on to a contested trial.

9.44 Similar models have been introduced in other jurisdictions, notably Australia, and there are small-scale pilot projects in South Africa and England and Wales.

THE AUSTRALIAN VARIANT

9.45 The second main conferencing model originated in a police district in Wagga Wagga, New South Wales. This variant was originally police-led, in that the police decided which cases were appropriate for conferencing and convened and facilitated the conferences. The conference itself was carefully scripted (the New Zealand model is not), partly to ensure consistency and partly to ensure that the restorative nature of the conference was maintained, even though those delivering it might have been unfamiliar with it, and relatively untrained. It was sometimes referred to as restorative policing, and had been seen by some as a method for transforming police attitudes, role, perceptions and organisational culture.

9.46 Police-based restorative conferencing techniques have been introduced in a number of other Australian jurisdictions, to a number of police departments in the USA, to parts of Canada, and to three police forces in England and Wales, including Thames Valley (on which the

Mountpottinger scheme is modelled). Ironically, responsibility for conferencing in New South Wales has been moved from the police to the Office of Juvenile Justice because the police were not seen to be the most appropriate agency to have responsibility for conferencing.

SENTENCING CIRCLES

9.47   The third restorative justice variant is known as sentencing circles. These were developed in Canada. They bring together victims and their supporters, offenders and their supporters, judge and court personnel, prosecutor, defence lawyer, police and all community members who have an interest. The aim is to work consensually to devise an appropriate sentencing plan to meet the needs of all the interested parties. Sentencing circles have been used in some of the Canadian provinces, and in some US states, such as Minnesota.

OUTCOMES

9.48   The research report[12] assesses the extent to which each of the two main restorative justice models - victim-offender mediation and family group conferencing - are successful in achieving their objectives. They stress that while both models have been reasonably intensely evaluated, including the process itself, implementation and reconvictions so far, the evaluations have not yet addressed the cost effectiveness of the models in comparison with conventional criminal justice processes, nor their preventive potential.

9.49   In general, however, the research report draws the following broad conclusions:

- The majority of victims are willing to meet with their offenders, provided they are adequately informed of the arrangements, and these are convenient.

- A high proportion of cases result in an agreement being reached, and high levels of compliance are reported for agreements that involve the payment of compensation or other types of reparation.

- For many victims, material reparation is less important than symbolic forms of reparation, such as an apology.

- The majority of victims are satisfied with the process, and the outcomes secured, although victim satisfaction rates vary across the different types of schemes.

- The majority of offenders report both the process and the outcome to be fair. At the same time, offenders frequently report that the experience of meeting their victim is likely to be emotionally challenging, and many say that it is harder than going to court.

---

12   Dignan and Lowey, Research Report 10, chapter 5.

- It is too soon to draw conclusions on the effect of restorative processes on re-offending rates, although some studies have shown slight reductions in re-offending and reductions in the seriousness of offences subsequently committed.

- There is little to choose between victim-offender mediation and family group conferencing as regards the extent to which they achieve their goals, but the conferencing model provides a forum in which a much broader range of interests can be represented, and the plan of action can also reflect this wider set of interests. A police-based model can only be suitable for more minor offences as it operates pre-prosecution.

- There is some evidence that involvement in restorative justice approaches can help change police attitudes and culture.

IMPLEMENTATIONAL STRATEGIES

9.50   The research report[13] also considered the relationship between restorative justice and the rest of the criminal justice system. The report noted four principal options:

(i)   the "subsidiary" model, which leaves in place the main features of the conventional retributive criminal justice system, subject to the development of reparative outcomes, such as court-ordered compensation by the offender to the victim, and community service orders;

(ii)   the "stand-alone" model, where restorative schemes that are locally based or designed to deal with specific problems are encouraged to develop in a way that is complementary to, but not an alternative to, the formal criminal justice process;

(iii)   the "partially integrated" model, in which approaches incorporating restorative justice principles are partially integrated into the criminal justice system including the "Halt" scheme in the Netherlands and the new "reparation order" in England and Wales (descriptions of which are set out in Chapter 10 on juvenile justice);

(iv)   the "fully integrated" model, in which a restorative justice approach is fully integrated into and underpins the philosophy of the criminal justice system, of which New Zealand and some of the Australian conferencing approaches are examples, at least in relation to juvenile justice.

9.51   The report concludes that "the most effective way of securing restorative justice's undoubted potential is to adopt a fully integrated approach. By establishing restorative justice as a mainstream response that operates at the heart of the criminal justice system it is much more likely that the problems of marginalisation and subordination which are associated with stand-alone programmes or a partially integrated compromise approach will be avoided".

---

13   Dignan and Lowey, Research Report 10.

Evaluation and Recommendations

9.52   We were struck by the widespread support for the concept of restorative justice put forward in the consultation process, not only across a wide spectrum of political opinion, but also amongst the voluntary and community groups whose views we heard. We were taken also by the sharp differences of opinion on how restorative justice should be delivered. On the basis of what we have heard during the consultation process, what we have seen in the course of our study visits, and what we have learned from the research we commissioned, we believe that the application of restorative justice has much to offer in Northern Ireland.

9.53   We believe that restorative justice might be particularly useful in dealing with juvenile offenders without a long history of criminality but whose offending is a matter of real concern to local communities. It is no accident that many of the restorative justice approaches developed in other jurisdictions have focused upon juvenile offending, and no coincidence that those countries who have integrated a restorative justice approach into their criminal justice systems have done so primarily for juveniles. As a result, **we recommend the development of restorative justice approaches for juvenile offenders.** The discussion in this chapter focuses primarily on the application of restorative justice to that age group.

9.54   That is not to say, however, that its application to older offenders should be neglected or ignored; indeed, those schemes in other jurisdictions that have targeted adults have shown some very promising results. There is less experience in other countries upon which to draw, however, and we believe that while the underlying principles of restorative justice apply equally to all age groups, the application of restorative justice to adults and young adults may demand different processes, bring in a different range of interests and deal with different offending behaviour. **We recommend that restorative justice schemes for young adults (i.e. those between 18 and 21 years of age inclusive) and adults be piloted and evaluated carefully before final decisions are made on whether and how they might be applied across Northern Ireland as a whole.**

9.55   In the remainder of this section we focus on the broad parameters that need to be addressed in designing a court-based restorative justice process for juveniles, and on the potential for pre-court restorative justice processes for juveniles. However, the detail of precisely how restorative justice should be delivered will need to be considered more fully in discussing, developing and implementing our recommendations. We consider the following questions:

- where restorative justice should stand in relation to the criminal justice system;

- the choice of aims and guiding principles which should underpin restorative justice in Northern Ireland;

- how restorative justice might be delivered, and at what levels;

- the potential outcomes of restorative justice;

- who should participate, and who should co-ordinate; and

- who should be involved in developing and delivering options and programmes?

CHOICE OF IMPLEMENTATIONAL STRATEGY

9.56   We considered at length the options available for implementing restorative justice for juveniles, including:

- encouraging the development of community-driven schemes with few or no formal links to the criminal justice system;

- encouraging the development and spread of stand-alone schemes, such as the Ballymena Retail Theft Initiative and the Mountpottinger Restorative Justice Scheme;

- developing a partially integrated approach, along the lines of the Dutch "Halt" scheme or the English youth panel and reparation order approach; and

- developing a fully integrated approach, along the lines of the conferencing approaches in New Zealand.

9.57   Community-based schemes, which have no or only tenuous links with the formal criminal justice system, will by definition not lie at the heart of mainstream approaches for dealing with offending behaviour on the part of juveniles. We do not therefore see these as central to our approach, but, in view of the interest in them and their existence in parts of Northern Ireland, we address the issues that they raise at the end of this chapter.

9.58   We have also seen evidence that most stand-alone mediation and reparation schemes in other countries have only had a limited impact in their locality. Because they have only received a small number of referrals, have been seen as separate from criminal justice, and have often been treated as an add-on or by-way to mainstream criminal justice. Some have also tended to ignore victims, focusing on solely rehabilitative principles. Often they have been restricted to "minor" offences or the types of offences which the criminal justice system finds it difficult to deal with, such as those arising from neighbour disputes and disputes between people who know each other. While, they can have a role to play, we do not see stand-alone or partially integrated schemes in themselves enabling the full potential of restorative justice to be realised in Northern Ireland.

9.59   The New Zealand scheme, in contrast, aims to be the mainstream option for youth justice. No case can reach sentence at court except through a family group conference. Conferencing can result in custody as part of the plan. In Australia, however, family group conferences are restricted to minor offences. The result has been that they only account for some 10% of youth justice resolutions, with many cases going straight to court. In both countries, the police are still able to deal with minor cases through informal warnings or formal cautions. **We recommend that in Northern Ireland the police continue to have the option of issuing informal warnings or cautions to juveniles.**

9.60   We note the research report's conclusion[14] that "the research evidence… is overwhelmingly supportive of an integrated approach in which restorative justice is fully incorporated within the criminal justice system as a "mainstream" response. This does not imply, however, that restorative justice measures will be used in all cases, or to the exclusion of all other responses". We support that view. **We recommend that restorative justice should be integrated into the juvenile justice system and its philosophy in Northern Ireland, using a conference model (which we term a "youth conference") based in statute, available for all juveniles (including 17 year olds, once they come within the remit of the youth court as we recommend in the next chapter), subject to the full range of human rights safeguards.**

CHOICE OF AIMS AND GUIDING PRINCIPLES

9.61   Since the parameters of any restorative justice system and its implementation must stem from its principles, deciding which of the several philosophies a future Northern Ireland system might adopt for juvenile justice is crucial. Some principles we have identified in other jurisdictions are:

- *Meeting the needs of victims*, emphasising victim as well as offender needs, and stressing such outcomes as practical reparation, financial compensation, or an apology. This involves giving victims a real place in the process, not just regarding them as a means to reform the offender.

- *Devolving responsibility for determining restorative outcomes* to a conference, so that traditional criminal justice participants (judges, police, prosecution) neither dominate the process, nor become involved to an unnecessary extent with the development of an agreed plan. The youth court would need to *approve* plans for any case where the conference has been ordered by the court, but would not amend the plan unless it was deficient.

- Focusing on *families*, and giving families a measure of responsibility for deciding plans and monitoring them, so devolving power to the family (of the offender) and also putting in mechanisms to strengthen the family to work with the offender in addressing his or her offending behaviour.

- Focusing on *the community*, by developing mechanisms to listen to the concerns of the local community, and by the community supporting youth conferencing in their area by developing facilities and programmes.

---

14   Dignan and Lowey, Research Report 10, chapter 7.

- *Rehabilitative justice*, where what is important is the prevention of offending by the young person. The youth conference focuses on the offending behaviour and what can be done creatively to produce a plan and programme for the offender that will reduce his or her offending.

- *Retributive justice*, where the aim is for plans to reflect the seriousness of the offence, but insisting on *proportionality*, in the sense that a plan should fall within the range of what a youth court would give as a sentence for that offence (this principle is included in the Australian legislation).

- *Reintegrative shaming*, where the offender acknowledges the harm that the offence has done, but where the youth conference subsequently clearly separates the offender from the offence, indicates the worth of the offender as a person, and focuses on the potential of the offender in the plan. It is noteworthy that where conferences in the New Zealand research have been reintegrative, rather than just shaming the offender, offenders both find them fairer and also are less likely subsequently to reoffend.

- *Repairing relationships*, which is a fundamental aspect of restorative justice. Crime represents a ruptured relationship between the victim and the offender. Even if they had no previous relationship, the crime creates one. Where possible and appropriate, an aim should be to repair the relationship between the victim and the offender, or at least to reduce the possibility of future hostility and conflict.

9.62   Differing approaches to restorative justice will give differing emphases to these principles, and it is unlikely that such principles will all be applicable in any one case. **We recommend that a Northern Ireland system should focus on:**

- **reparative justice and meeting the needs of victims, so giving them a real place in the youth conference, rather than just regarding it as a means to reform the offender;**

- **rehabilitative justice, where what is important is the prevention of re-offending by the young person, so that the youth conference focuses on offending behaviour;**

- **proportionality, rather than pure retributive justice;**

- **reintegrative shaming, where the offender acknowledges the harm done, but where the youth conference clearly separates the offender from the offence and focuses on the potential for reintegrating the offender into the community in the plan and on the prevention of re-offending;**

- **repairing relationships which have been damaged or broken by crime;**

- **devolving power to youth conference participants (see below for discussion of who those participants might be) to create the youth conference and the plan, but requiring subsequent approval for the plan from the court for cases which have gone to court (see below in relation to police/prosecution referrals);**

- encouraging victims to bring one or more supporters (who might be, but need not necessarily be, a member of Victim Support);

- encouraging offenders to bring significant others (especially their families, but also particular members of the community important to them) to the youth conference, but not placing such a strong emphasis on the responsibility of the family to deal with offending as is done in New Zealand.

9.63   A youth conference would be particularly suitable where there are family, school, mental health, drug, alcohol or substance abuse problems, and where there is agency involvement already. Such issues, and their impact on the offender's criminality, can be addressed in the conference. A youth conference will provide an opportunity to develop creative plans to meet the needs of victims and the needs of juvenile offenders. **Even where there is a need for custody or a traditional criminal justice community sanction (such as probation, community service or a compensation order), we recommend that these should be capable of being combined with other elements within a youth conference order (allowing a number of elements to be incorporated into a plan, not all of which can be combined at present).** Youth conference orders should also be able to include an apology (where there is an identifiable victim) and reparation (where necessary using a compensation order or the new reparation order we propose in the next chapter, on juvenile justice).

REFERRALS TO A YOUTH CONFERENCE

9.64   In all that follows, we are assuming that a youth conference is only used where the offender admits the offence, or where a court has established guilt, and that formal admission of the offence (whether or not there has been any previous admission to the police or in court) takes place at the beginning of the youth conference. Such an admission would have no legal standing in any subsequent court proceedings. We consider first the court-based model, before moving on to schemes that are driven by prosecutors or the police.

COURT-BASED CONFERENCING

9.65   **We recommend that a court-based youth conferencing scheme should operate on the basis of court referrals, with the youth conference resulting in a report to the court which contains a draft plan. If approved by the court, the plan will form the basis for the court disposal** (which might, depending on the plan, contain one or more traditional disposals, for example probation or custody). **Court-ordered referrals should be required after guilt has been admitted or determined, but before disposal. They should be discretionary for offences that are triable only on indictment.**

9.66 **Where the court orders a youth conference, we recommend that there should be no requirement to request a pre-sentence report, so as to avoid introducing a further cause of delay.** We envisage that preparation for the conference and the conference plan will often incorporate the type of information presented in a typical pre-sentence report and will involve input from the Probation Service where it would be relevant or helpful. The youth conference will, therefore act as a source of advice to the sentencer which includes the views of relevant statutory agencies, the victim, the offender, and the offender's "significant others". There may, of course, be confidential matters for a report to the sentencer that could not be shared with all conference participants. The relationship between the conference, pre-sentence reports and the information needed by the court will have to be examined in developing detailed proposals.

9.67 Determining the disposal would be a matter of the youth court receiving and checking the plan, amending it where necessary, and the plan becoming the basis for the youth conference order or another disposal determined by the court.

THE ROLE OF VICTIMS

9.68 The position of victims is central to our philosophy of restorative justice. It follows that they should have the opportunity, if they wish to attend youth conferences and contribute to the discussions that will result in a plan to be recommended to the court. We believe that **every effort should be made by the conference co-ordinators to contact victims, to encourage them to attend and to organise conferences in such a way as to facilitate the attendance of victims.** In this context, we should stress that the term "victim" relates to all those people who may have suffered directly as a result of any offence being considered by the conference.

9.69 However, there can be no question of compelling or pressurising victims to attend against their will. Nor should they be expected to take responsibility for what happens to the offender or the outcome of the conference; these are rightly matters for criminal justice personnel and the courts. Great care must be taken not to allow restorative justice to result in victims feeling intimidated or put upon.

9.70 The question arises of whether the victim should be able to send a representative to a conference in his or her place, an arrangement that is possible in New Zealand. In the Northern Ireland context we do not think that this is a good idea; we see the youth conference as focusing on those who are directly involved in the circumstances of the case and on the relationship between those people. That is the factor that will govern attendance. However, particularly given that this could be a difficult experience for them, **victims should**

be able to be accompanied at the conference by a supporter (or, at the discretion of the co-ordinator, more than one supporter – a restriction on numbers would be inappropriate, especially in the case of child victims).

9.71 **If the victim does not wish to attend the conference, then he or she should be offered the alternative of submitting a written statement (describing the effect of the offence and indicating whether an apology, reparation or compensation would be received positively).** If there is no input at all from the victim, should the conference proceed? The New Zealand and Australian models do not require the attendance of victims; indeed in New Zealand there was concern in the early years that victims attended only about half the conferences, apparently in some cases because not enough effort was made to take account of the convenience of victims in organising conferences. Provided that every effort is made to encourage and facilitate their attendance, **if victims do not wish to attend a youth conference that should not prevent it from going ahead. Victims should not have a veto on conferences taking place.**

THE OFFENDER, THE FAMILY AND SIGNIFICANT OTHERS

9.72 The involvement of an offender's family in contributing to a youth conference is likely to be an important factor affecting the success of the outcome. We would envisage the offender's parents or guardian attending a conference in almost all circumstances. In New Zealand and Australia, the term "family" is seen as a very broad concept and, especially (but not only) if the offender is estranged from blood relations or has no family, co-ordinators will seek to include "significant others" in the process. These might be teachers, youth club leaders, church leaders or people in the community who know the young person well. **We recommend that in Northern Ireland, for purposes of attendance at youth conferences, "family" should be viewed in its broad context to include those, such as church or youth leaders, who play a significant role in the offender's life.**

9.73 We think that there are many circumstances where the attendance of "significant others" from the offender's extended family or the community could have a positive impact on a youth conference. However, we do not believe that the concept of the extended family is such that people from this group should be able to attend youth conferences as of right, especially if that were to be against the wishes of the young person. While the offender should have no veto on the attendance of parents or guardians, it will be for the co-ordinator, in the preliminary contacts, to try to persuade the young person that any "significant other" who might contribute to the production of a conference plan, should attend.

9.74 The offender should have no veto over the attendance of the victim and his or her supporter(s), or over that of representatives of agencies who provide information and advice to the youth conference. Nor should the victim have a veto over the attendance of anyone (though it will be important to ensure that the victim is not intimidated or threatened during the conference and active steps may be necessary to adjourn the conference if this is occurs).

9.75 In exercising discretion over whether a "significant other" should participate in a conference, the co-ordinator will take account of whether the person's position and relationship with the offender are such that he or she will have a positive contribution to make. That does of course mean that the co-ordinator will have the discretion to decide that people from the community should <u>not</u> attend.

WHO WOULD PARTICIPATE IN THE YOUTH CONFERENCE?

9.76 **We recommend that the following should always take part in a youth conference:**

- **the co-ordinator;**

- **the juvenile and the juvenile's parents or guardians; and**

- **either a police officer or prosecutor.**

9.77 **We recommend that the following *may* participate in the youth conference:**

- **the victim (if he or she agrees) and the victim's supporters;**

- **significant others relevant to the offender (at the co-ordinator's discretion);**

- **a defence solicitor or barrister (where this is wished by the offender or his or her guardian); and**

- **where appropriate, professionals such as probation and social services, who can provide information to the conference about possible options for the plan and about the offender's background (but only as information providers and at the co-ordinator's discretion).**

THE ROLE OF THE YOUTH CONFERENCE CO-ORDINATOR

9.78 We see the role of the youth conference co-ordinator as being to:

- contact the offender, the offender's family, the victim, the defence solicitor or barrister and any others who should attend, to explain the purpose of the youth conference and to arrange a time and venue;

- identify, with the offender, his or her family and other agencies, the possible range of outcomes, drawing from available programmes in the offender's locality as well as traditional disposals;

- identify the victim's needs and wishes;

- run the youth conference;

- present the agreed plan to the court or, if no plan is agreed, report to the court why that was so; and

- monitor the implementation of the plan and, where necessary, initiate breach proceedings.

9.79 **We recommend that the youth conference co-ordinator should have the same type of monitoring and breach powers as probation officers in relation to monitoring probation orders and their requirements. If offenders do not complete their plans in their entirety or, in the judgement of the co-ordinator, sufficiently, then breach proceedings would start.** For court referrals this would mean the case being brought back before the court. In all instances, the youth court should review the case at a predetermined point.

WITHIN WHICH AGENCY SHOULD CO-ORDINATORS BE BASED?

9.80 New Zealand conference co-ordinators are based nationally within the government department that deals with social work and social welfare, though within a separate agency (the Children, Young Persons and their Families Service). Some, including senior members of the judiciary, believe that this is not the ideal model, because the priorities for the department have been child protection and residential accommodation for young people, rather than family group conferencing.

9.81 We think it is very important to indicate firmly, in the Northern Ireland context, that the youth conference is a youth justice matter, not a welfare option or community alternative justice. We therefore think that the youth conference and the youth conference co-ordinators need to be located within a department or agency which is seen publicly as epitomising justice values. It should not be located within the prosecution service since there could be conflicts of interest between trying to mediate a youth conference plan and prosecuting. We see similar difficulties in locating responsibility for conferencing within the police.

9.82 **We recommend that the youth conference and youth conference co-ordinators should be housed within a separate arm of the Department of Justice** (which we discuss at Chapter 15 of this report) **or one of its agencies.**

9.83 Co-ordinators would be employed by the organisation within which they were based. They should be specially trained for their task. We would not wish to specify any particular previous experience for co-ordinators, but we recognise that they may be drawn from a number of backgrounds, including former or seconded police officers, prosecutors, probation officers, social workers etc, or have no previous criminal justice experience.

INTER-AGENCY STRUCTURES

9.84   The most difficult issues for the New Zealand model have been the development of options and programmes that can be used for young people in conference plans. We heard concerns in New Zealand that there was a lack of suitable options, particularly for more serious offending. We think attention needs to be given to this well in advance of starting the youth conference programme in Northern Ireland.

9.85   **We recommend that the development of restorative justice, and in particular the development of the menu of national and local programmes and projects which the youth conference can draw upon, should be driven at both national and local level.** It will need a great deal of careful inter-agency planning to develop the detailed arrangements and to deal with accreditation, evaluation and training. To achieve this, new inter-agency arrangements at both central and local levels will be necessary. **We recommend that a national level inter-agency body responsible for youth conferencing should be established; it might be a sub-group of the Criminal Justice Board** (which is described in Chapters 3 and 15). **It could have responsibility for ensuring the availability of programmes across Northern Ireland to support community sanctions, restorative justice generally, and youth conferences in particular. It should deal with the accreditation and setting of standards for restorative justice, including those that apply to community restorative justice schemes, and encourage the spreading of good practice.**

9.86   The Community Safety and Policing Partnerships, which we recommend in Chapter 11, might also have a role in assisting in the development of local programmes and options that might form part of youth conference plans. By doing so they would contribute to community safety within their local area. They might also help to publicise the youth conference system locally. **We recommend that youth conference co-ordinators should take the lead in developing networks and inter-agency arrangements in local areas, and should co-ordinate the development of a local menu of programmes and options that might form part of a youth conference order. They should develop close links with a variety of organisations and groups with an interest in youth conferences in local areas, including funders, programme providers, community groups, sentencers, the police, probation, social services and education authorities.**

FUNDING AND RESOURCE ISSUES

9.87 In implementing the youth conference model, **we recommend that priority be given to establishing facilities for court-referred youth conferences, and that the system be expanded to provide for police and prosecutor referrals more slowly.**

9.88 Around 2,000 juveniles appear before the youth court annually. This may increase to around 3,000 once 17 year olds are brought within the jurisdiction of the youth court. On the assumption that youth conference co-ordinators would deal with an average of four youth conferences each week, and on the assumption that most cases appearing before the youth court would require a youth conference, then we estimate that around 20 full-time co-ordinators would be required at around staff officer level to cover the workload, together with leave and sick absence, led by a chief conference co-ordinator, and with a small support staff. Staffing might, therefore, cost in the region of £750,000 per annum. Accommodation costs for the staff are excluded from this estimate, as are the costs of providing facilities for holding youth conferences (although we would expect that existing court or agency facilities might be used). Nor are the costs of providing programmes included (although we would expect these to be offset, to some extent, by a reduction in the use of traditional disposals, including custody). We do not believe that the work of conferences would add substantially to the workload of other agencies involved. In particular the Probation Service is unlikely to incur additional costs related to youth conferencing per se. Resources devoted to youth conferences will to some extent be offset by a reduction in the effort devoted to the preparation of pre-sentence reports for juveniles.

YOUTH CONFERENCE OUTCOME

9.89 We noted that the youth conference co-ordinator would submit a conference plan to the court for consideration before sentencing. Such a plan would contain a variety of information about the circumstances of the offender, the nature of the offence, a brief description of who attended the conference and how it went, and the elements of the plan that emerged from the conference. We envisage that a plan might include a combination of any or all of the following elements:

- an apology to the victim;

- financial compensation;

- reparation in kind;

- service to the community;

- participation in programmes to address offending behaviour and/or related social problems, e.g. substance, alcohol or drug abuse, gambling, employment related training, etc;

■ other traditional disposals, including probation orders, community service and custody; and

■ a youth conference order, which might combine any of the above elements (including traditional sentencing options that cannot currently be combined).

PRE-PROSECUTION RESTORATIVE JUSTICE SCHEMES

9.90   We have focused in this section on the arrangements for a court-based restorative justice system for juvenile offenders. We recognise, however, that it is important to develop pre-prosecution restorative justice diversionary schemes, in appropriate cases building upon the initiatives already being developed. We also believe that many aspects of the court-based model we have proposed are equally applicable pre-prosecution. Whilst the energies of youth conference co-ordinators must, initially, be directed towards developing the court-based scheme and providing a service to the courts, **we believe that in the longer term, as resources permit, youth conference co-ordinators should assist with pre-court conferences as part of a diversionary strategy.**

9.91   We envisage the development of two principal forms of pre-court restorative justice diversion, the first of which would be driven by the police as part of their discretionary power to issue informal advice and warnings, and formal cautions, and the second of which would be driven by prosecutors. The two models would comprise:

■ referral by the police (at the discretion of the police), prior to a decision to prosecute, with the youth conference resulting in no official record of the offence (informal warning level) or resulting in the equivalent of a formal caution;

■ referral by the prosecutor (at the discretion of the prosecutor), with the youth conference resulting in no official record of the offence (informal warning) or the equivalent for official record purposes of a formal caution.

9.92   Other types of restorative schemes should also be available for police and prosecutor driven pre-trial diversion, such as those that are currently being developed in Northern Ireland, or processes akin to the "Halt"[15] scheme in the Netherlands. The Milton Keynes caution plus scheme has, however, demonstrated the difficulty of losing potential offenders to schemes because they have been arrested and then rapidly charged, rather than referred for consideration for a caution. New Zealand experience is similar. Given the pressure for speedy processing of juvenile offenders and the possible future introduction of strict time limits, we think it possible that many offenders who might otherwise benefit from a diversionary approach, will be referred by the police to prosecutors for prosecution. Any need for

---

15   See the next chapter on juvenile justice for a description of the "Halt" scheme.

prosecutors to refer back to the police for caution in order to permit a youth conference would introduce more complication and delay than if they had the option to refer directly to youth conferences. **We think it is important that, when resources permit, youth conferences, as with other forms of diversion, should be available through prosecutor referral as well as police referral.**

9.93   **For prosecutor referrals, the right to prosecute should remain until the plan has been completed.** If there is a breach of the elements of the plan, this should be reported by the co-ordinator to the prosecution. We see this as important in public confidence terms, given the likelihood that more serious cases will be reported to the prosecutor, and to reassure people that offenders are not being given the opportunity to "get away with it". **In the case of police referrals the co-ordinator should monitor the implementation of any agreed plan and report back to the police, but the police should not have the option of proceeding further.** This is consistent with the current position in relation to police cautions.

DEFERRED SENTENCES AND COMPENSATION ORDERS

9.94   We note in passing that it is not possible at present for a sentencer to make a compensation order at the same time as deferring sentence. That means that in using deferral of sentence as part of a restorative or reparative approach for adults and young adults any agreement entered into by the offender involving direct financial compensation must be entirely voluntary, and there are no established mechanisms for monitoring the payment of the compensation nor for receiving the money from the offender and passing it onto the victim. **We recommend that the courts' sentencing powers be reviewed to facilitate the possibility of restorative interventions, including the formal payment of compensation before sentence is finally passed.**

COMMUNITY-BASED RESTORATIVE JUSTICE

9.95   In considering our approach to community restorative justice, we took account of the existence of such schemes in Northern Ireland but also concerns expressed by a wide range of people, organisations and political parties. The research report[16] points in very clear terms to the dangers inherent in the sort of model advocated by Auld and others.[17] In Northern Ireland in particular, coercion or threat, real or implied, are ever-present dangers which cannot be ignored, even with well-intentioned schemes which on the face of it include safeguards for the rights of offenders and victims. There are concerns about double jeopardy,

---

16   Dignan and Lowey, Research Report 10, chapter 3.

17   Auld, Gormally, McEvoy and Ritchie, *Designing a System of Restorative Community Justice in Northern Ireland: A Discussion Document* (1997), published by the authors.

if a juvenile finds himself or herself involved in a community-based scheme and also faces action through the formal criminal justice system; and in a community-based scheme, it may be difficult to ensure that the alleged offender is able to receive professional advice about his or her rights.

9.96   We are also aware there can be a thin line between voluntarily agreed measures where an offence is committed on the one hand, and community-based schemes that effectively determine guilt and impose sanctions. These concerns do not mean that the state should ignore, or worse still, seek to stifle the undoubted energy and commitment of those in the community who wish to make a real contribution to dealing with crime in their locality. Nor is it for us to comment on those schemes that are directed at dealing with non-criminal behaviour, such as the mediation of civil disputes. It does, however, mean that those within the community who wish to contribute to the way in which criminal activity is dealt with should work in partnership with, take referrals from, and be subject to accreditation and monitoring by the criminal justice system if the rights of individuals, both offenders and victims, are to be protected and upheld. We note the requirement in Rule 3 of the Tokyo Rules that non-custodial measures imposed on the offender before or instead of formal proceedings shall require the offender's consent. We believe that individuals who are referred to schemes which are able to impose non-custodial measures on offenders should have the right to be able to refer to a solicitor or another appropriate adult before agreeing to consent to such measures.

9.97   We think it important that only statutory criminal justice agencies should be able to refer offenders to community-based schemes, so that the state retains ultimate responsibility for criminal justice. This will mean that individuals who claim that their human rights have been denied may be able to seek a direct remedy against a public authority under the Human Rights Act 1998. We cannot, therefore, endorse schemes that act outside the criminal justice system, which are without links to the criminal justice system, and yet which purport to deal with criminal activity.

9.98   In the light of the above considerations, however, **we believe that community restorative justice schemes can have a role to play in dealing with the types of low-level crime that most commonly concerns local communities. However, we recommend that community restorative justice schemes should:**

(i)   **receive referrals from a statutory criminal justice agency, rather than from within the community, with the police being informed of all such referrals;**

(ii)   **be accredited by, and subject to standards laid down by the Government in respect of how they deal with criminal activity, covering such issues as training of staff, human rights protections, other due process and proportionality issues, and complaints mechanisms for both victims and offenders;**

(iii)   be subject to regular inspection by the independent Criminal Justice Inspectorate which we recommend in Chapter 15; and

(iv)   have no role in determining the guilt or innocence of alleged offenders, and deal only with those individuals referred by a criminal justice agency who have indicated that they do not wish to deny guilt and where there is prima facie evidence of guilt.

10 Juvenile Justice

INTRODUCTION

10.1   Our terms of reference invite us to "... address the structure, management and resourcing of the publicly funded elements of the criminal justice system and... bring forward proposals for future criminal justice arrangements...". Juvenile justice is an important and integral part of the criminal justice system. Early in our consultation process it became clear that a number of organisations were anxious that we should examine the ways of dealing with juvenile crime and the arrangements for managing and delivering juvenile justice. What we say in this chapter must be read in conjunction with our proposals for youth conferencing in Chapter 9. Those proposals form the heart of a new approach, and our thinking on other aspects of juvenile justice is, to an extent, built around them.

10.2   This chapter addresses the issues which have been raised with us in the course of our consultation process, including:

- the aims and human rights standards to which the Government should adhere in developing and delivering juvenile justice arrangements;

- the arrangements for the management of the juvenile justice system;

- the range of disposals which are available to the courts in respect of juvenile offenders;

- the way in which the prosecution process and the courts operate in respect of juvenile offenders;

- the arrangements for the provision of custodial facilities for juveniles; and

- the age range that the juvenile justice system should cover.

10.3   Juvenile offending is a concern in almost every country, and Northern Ireland is no exception. People are most likely to offend when they are young, and for many young people involvement in crime is something that occurs as they make the transition from childhood to adulthood, and which then tails off. A minority of young people appear to start their offending at a very early age and continue to offend more frequently and persistently into adulthood. Juvenile offenders account for much of the petty criminality in society, and for a significant proportion of more serious crimes. It is the responsibility of society as a whole to provide the opportunities and mechanisms that minimise the likelihood of young people committing offences, and to provide an effective and helpful means to deal with offending that does occur. That is why most countries have developed criminal justice systems and processes which take account of the special needs of juveniles and which emphasise and uphold their fundamental rights.

Human Rights Background

10.4   A range of international instruments bear upon juvenile justice arrangements in Northern Ireland, most notably:

- the *European Convention on Human Rights 1950* (ECHR);

- the *International Covenant on Civil and Political Rights 1966* (ICCPR);

- the *United Nations Convention on the Rights of the Child 1989* (UNCRC);

- the *United Nations Guidelines for the Prevention of Juvenile Delinquency 1990* (the Riyadh guidelines);

- the *United Nations Standard Minimum Rules for the Administration of Juvenile Justice 1985* (the Beijing Rules); and

- the *United Nations Rules for the Protection of Juveniles Deprived of their Liberty 1990* (RDL).

10.5   Not all of these instruments have the same nature and status. The ECHR is one of very few instruments to be formally incorporated into the domestic law of the United Kingdom. The other instruments can be divided into two types: those that are considered internationally binding, and those that are not. We consider the nature and status of each of these instruments briefly, noting that they are examined in more detail in the research report on juvenile justice[1], which is published along with this report, and that the meaning of the terms "binding" and "non-binding" were considered in Chapter 3.

THE EUROPEAN CONVENTION ON HUMAN RIGHTS

10.6   The Human Rights Act 1998 formally incorporates the ECHR into domestic law by making it unlawful for a public authority to act in a way that is incompatible with a Convention right. The Convention and the jurisprudence around it, as they relate to juvenile justice, are

---

1   O'Mahony and Deazley, Research Report 17.

regarded as somewhat less advanced than subsequent human rights instruments on the rights of children. The Convention continues, however, to be used to address juvenile justice issues, such as the issues surrounding the trial and detention of T and V in the Bulger case.[2]

THE INTERNATIONAL COVENANT ON CIVIL AND POLITICAL RIGHTS (ICCPR) AND THE UNITED NATIONS CONVENTION ON THE RIGHTS OF THE CHILD (UNCRC)

10.7   Juveniles are entitled to benefit from all the rights contained in the ICCPR. It was the first global document to contain specific provisions relating to the administration of youth justice including:

■ the separation of accused juveniles from adults, and speedy adjudication (Article 10(2)(b));

■ the incarceration of juvenile offenders separately from adults (Article 10(3));

■ provisions relating to public adjudications where the offender is a juvenile (Article 14(1)); and

■ a requirement that criminal procedures shall take account of the age of juvenile offenders and the desirability of promoting their rehabilitation (Article 14(4)).

10.8   The UNCRC is more recent and important in relation to juvenile justice. It spans the spectrum of civil, political, economic, social and cultural rights. It focuses specifically on the rights of children up to the age of majority. Articles 37 (torture, capital punishment, and deprivation of liberty) and 40 (juvenile justice) create international standards in relation to juvenile justice.

10.9   Although the ICCPR and the UNCRC are not directly applicable in the domestic law of the UK, the courts may use them as persuasive authority in their interpretation of the law. They may also have an impact on the operation of the juvenile justice system and wider criminal justice system in other ways. Although the United Nations does not have the power to enforce binding international instruments directly, it has established a number of international institutions to monitor their implementation and make reports on member countries. Examples include the Human Rights Committee of the United Nations (established under the First Optional Protocol to the ICCPR) and the UN Committee on the Rights of the Child (established under the UNCRC). In addition, the Belfast Agreement specifically invites the Northern Ireland Human Rights Commission to draw on such instruments in defining the scope of additional rights to be constituted in a specific Bill of Rights for Northern Ireland.

---

2   Cases of *T & V v United Kingdom*, at the European Court of Human Rights (App. Nos. 24724/94 and 24888/94), judgments, 16 December 1999.

NON-BINDING INTERNATIONAL LAW

10.10 There are three non-binding international instruments concerning the operation of the juvenile justice system: the *United Nations Guidelines for the Prevention of Juvenile Delinquency 1990* (the Riyadh Guidelines); the *United Nations Standard Minimum Rules for the Administration of Juvenile Justice 1985* (the Beijing Rules); and the *United Nations Rules for the Protection of Juveniles Deprived of their Liberty 1990* (RDL). Together these instruments address the full range of juvenile justice issues. They set standards covering the prevention of crime, the child's involvement in the criminal justice process, and the conditions under which children may be deprived of their liberty.

10.11 These instruments are non-binding in that they have no direct legal impact upon either international or national legislative bodies, and they are purely recommendatory. They serve, however, to identify current international thinking on human rights for juveniles and to inform national and international debate on juvenile justice issues. They represent the minimum recommended standards.

10.12 In considering the issues that have been raised with us in the course of the consultation process, and the options for change, we have reflected upon all of the above instruments and sought to develop recommendations that meet and build upon the standards that they set.

Operation of the Juvenile Justice System in Northern Ireland

10.13 There have been very recent changes in juvenile justice legislation, which have led to significant changes in the way in which juvenile justice operates in Northern Ireland. Some of these have only been in operation for a matter of months. This section of the report sets out in brief how the juvenile justice system currently operates. A more detailed description of the history and operation of the system is set out in sections 5 and 6 of the research report.[3]

10.14 The juvenile justice system in Northern Ireland deals with those aged 10 years or over and under 17. Because the law presumes children under ten to be *doli incapax* (incapable of crime) they cannot be prosecuted for criminal offences. If they come to the notice of the police in connection with a criminal act they are drawn to the attention of social services and dealt with under child welfare legislation. Those aged 17 or over are deemed to be adults, and are dealt with in the adult courts.

---

3   O'Mahony and Deazley, Research Report 17.

10.15 The first point of contact with the juvenile justice system is the police, who have considerable discretion in how they deal with juvenile offenders. Specialist officers deal with juveniles as part of the Juvenile Liaison Scheme. The officers have four broad options open to them:

(i) To take no further action.

(ii) To issue an "informal warning and advice", in which case the juvenile is warned about the consequences of the behaviour and is given advice about staying out of trouble. This does not form part of the juvenile's criminal record, but the police do keep a record of the warning for their own purposes.

(iii) To administer a "formal caution" which does not form part of the juvenile's criminal record but which can be cited in court at a later date.

(iv) To prosecute the case through the courts, usually where the offence is particularly serious or the juvenile has a history of previous offending behaviour, and where a formal caution is considered inappropriate.

10.16 In 1997 just under 13,000 cases were dealt with through the Juvenile Liaison Scheme. No further action was taken in 22% of cases, 56% resulted in informal warning or advice, 12% resulted in a formal caution, and 10% were prosecuted. Trends over the period from 1987 to 1997, and the nature of juvenile offending in Northern Ireland, are set out in the research report.[4]

10.17 A recent innovation has been the introduction of Juvenile Liaison Bureaux, which built on the Juvenile Liaison Scheme and involve representatives from the police, social services, probation and education. The Bureaux consider cases where the juvenile has admitted the offence and advise on whether he or she should be prosecuted or diverted, for example by way of a formal caution. The final decision remains with the police. Until recently only seven Bureaux were in operation in Northern Ireland. A full-time co-ordinator was appointed in 1998 to extend the number of Bureaux to cover the whole of Northern Ireland and to standardise their operation. Twenty-one Bureaux have now been established across Northern Ireland and there are plans to establish the remaining seven necessary to complete coverage of Northern Ireland in coming months. There are also some plans to extend the role of the Bureaux into "children's panels", which would consider cases referred by any of the agencies involved, and which would aim to identify children who are "at risk" of offending, and offer them and their families help before problems arise.

10.18 A Diversionary Working Group was established in 1997. It is chaired by a Northern Ireland Office official and comprises representatives from the Department of Health and Social Services, Department of Education, the RUC, Health and Social Services Boards, Probation Service, the Youth Service, and Whitefield. Two major voluntary organisations - the Extern Organisation and the Northern Ireland Association for the Care and Resettlement of

---

4   O'Mahony and Deazley, Research Report 17, section 5.

Offenders - are also represented on the Group. The aim of the Group is to encourage the development of diversionary approaches for juveniles across Northern Ireland. Whitefield plays a major role in diversionary activity. It operates under the aegis of the Juvenile Justice Board (see below) and is funded by grant from the Northern Ireland Office. It works in partnership with other statutory and voluntary agencies and has developed 12 community-based projects across Northern Ireland. It works with and supports young people who are at risk of involvement in crime, and receives almost two thirds of its referrals from Social Services, the remainder coming from the education sector, Juvenile Liaison Bureaux, the courts and a number of other sources. It can also deal with adjudicated referrals from the Probation Service. It provides programmes tailored to the needs of individuals and their families, with an emphasis on developing life skills, education, training and work opportunities, and individual support to sustain young people in the community.

10.19   Juveniles are normally dealt with in the youth court, unless they are charged with adults or, in the case of certain serious offences, they are tried in the Crown Court. The youth court has jurisdiction to hear and determine cases brought against children under 17 for offences other than homicide. It is normally constituted by a resident magistrate and two lay panel members drawn from the Divisional Juvenile Court Panel, one of whom must be a woman. The youth court is less formal than the adult magistrates' court, and the public is excluded from the proceedings. There is no dock, there are no wigs and gowns worn in court, and most of the participants sit on the same level. The bench at which the resident magistrate and the two lay panel members sit is normally raised a little above floor level, but not so much as in the adult courts. The prosecution process, however, can be lengthy, and the average time juveniles spend on remand is around 4.5 months.

10.20   In 1997, 1,814 criminal cases were disposed of in what was then termed the juvenile court and only 22 juveniles appeared in the Crown Court as defendants. Most juveniles appearing before the youth court pleaded guilty and of those who plead not guilty most were acquitted. The nature of juvenile offending is different from that of adults. As the research report notes:

> "... the majority of juveniles are proceeded against for property related offences. Proportionately, more juveniles are proceeded against for theft, criminal damage and burglary than adults. Adults are more involved in serious crimes such as violent and sexual offences. It is also clear that the vast majority of juveniles dealt with are male and at the older end of the age spectrum, mostly 14 to 16 years of age, and that the vast majority plead guilty and are simply sentenced by the courts after considering the facts and relevant reports."[5]

10.21   The range of disposals available to the courts in Northern Ireland for juveniles includes:

■ an absolute or conditional discharge;

---

5   O'Mahony and Deazley, Research Report 17.

- a monetary penalty such as a fine, recognizance or compensation order;

- a community order, such as probation, community service (which is only available for those 16 years or over) or an attendance centre order (which is not available in every area in Northern Ireland); and

- a custodial order, such as a juvenile justice centre order (which is available for 10-16 year olds inclusive), detention in a young offenders centre (which is available for 16-21 year olds, inclusive), or for grave crimes, detention at the Secretary of State's pleasure (which is available for 10-16 year olds inclusive) or detention under Article 45(2) of the Criminal Justice (Children) (Northern Ireland) Order 1998(which is available for 10-16 year olds inclusive). In the case of the latter two orders, it is for the Secretary of State to determine where the juvenile should be held.

10.22   In 1997 probation accounted for 33% of all disposals, conditional discharges 25%, while custody accounted for 19%. The least used were fines (6%), recognizances and absolute discharges (5%) and suspended custodial sentences (3%).

10.23   The Criminal Justice (Children) (Northern Ireland) Order 1998, which came into force in January 1999, introduced a number of significant changes into the juvenile justice system. The principal aims of the Order were to reduce the number of juveniles remanded in custody and reduce the time sentenced children spend in a custodial setting. The changes that the Order made included:

- the introduction of criteria for remands in custody and a presumption of bail other than in exceptional circumstances;

- the introduction of seriousness and persistent offending as criteria for custody;

- the renaming of the juvenile court as the youth court and training schools as juvenile justice centres;

- the creation of a new determinate juvenile justice centre order of between six months and two years duration, the second half of which is served under close supervision by the Probation Service in the community, to replace the old semi-determinate training school order; and

- allowing time served on remand in custody to count as part of a custodial sentence.

10.24   Responsibility for the provision of custodial facilities for juvenile offenders rests between the Northern Ireland Office, through the Juvenile Justice Board, which is responsible for the provision of juvenile justice centres, and the Northern Ireland Prison Service. The latter provides young offenders centre facilities and adult prisons. Juvenile justice centres fall into two types: those which are funded by the Northern Ireland Office, but managed by voluntary boards; and those which are managed and funded directly by the Northern Ireland Office. St

Joseph's in Middletown (which provides a very small number of places for female offenders) and St Patrick's in Belfast fall into the former category, while Rathgael in Bangor and Lisnevin in Millisle fall into the latter. Rathgael and Lisnevin are managed by a "Juvenile Justice Board", which is comprised of Northern Ireland Office officials (although it must be said that this arrangement was intended to be temporary, and that it had been decided by the Northern Ireland Office that changes in this area would be delayed pending our report). All juveniles sentenced to or remanded in custody by the courts are sent first to Lisnevin, which is a closed institution, with the possibility of being moved to another centre after their case is considered at a case conference. Case conferences are held weekly.

Views Expressed During the Consultation Process

10.25   From a very early stage of the consultation process it became apparent that despite the recent legislative reforms, which were generally welcomed, there were still concerns about the operation and management of the juvenile justice system and the way in which juvenile offenders were treated in Northern Ireland. Around 25% of the written submissions received in the course of the consultation process referred, amongst other issues, to juvenile justice. Issues concerning the treatment of juvenile offenders also generated a great deal of constructive debate in the consultation seminars. Restorative justice emerged as a theme throughout the discussions relating to juveniles, as it does in international comparisons, but comments on the potential application of restorative justice to juveniles, young adults and adults were addressed in the previous chapter.

10.26   A wide range of issues was raised in the course of the review, including:

- the principles underlying the juvenile justice system;

- the age of criminal responsibility and the age at which young people make the transition from the juvenile justice system to the adult system;

- the need for development and use of diversion at all stages of the juvenile justice process;

- the impact on juveniles of the laws of evidence and in particular those on the right of silence;

- the use of bail and remands in custody for juveniles;

- the way in which the youth court operates;

- the range and nature of disposals available to the courts for juveniles, including the use of indeterminate sentences for grave crimes (Secretary of State's pleasure cases);

- restorative justice;

- the way in which the juvenile justice system, particularly the custodial elements of that system, is operated and managed;

- where political responsibility for juvenile justice should lie, and whether there should be a Minister or Commissioner for children;

- the development of partnership approaches to dealing with juvenile offending;

- the training needs of all juvenile justice personnel, including the legal profession;

- the needs of ethnic minority children and those with learning or other disabilities;

- the need for research into the effectiveness of juvenile justice disposals and diversionary techniques;

- the need to focus resources on dealing with juvenile offenders in the community;

- finding ways in which the views of young people can be taken into account in developing juvenile justice; and

- the extent to which the staff within the juvenile justice system are reflective of the general population.

10.27   A number of organisations commented upon the need for principles to underpin and inform the operation and development of the juvenile justice system. Some advocated that the principles that might formally be established for the criminal justice system in respect of children and young people should be closely and explicitly based on those underpinning the Children (Northern Ireland) Order 1995. Some argued that the principles underlying the juvenile justice system should be based upon and informed by the Human Rights Act 1998 and international rights instruments as they relate to juvenile justice. Others argued that the welfare of the child should be *the* paramount concern of the juvenile justice system. One consortium of organisations with an interest in children's rights argued, "an agreed set of principles and values for the criminal justice system as a whole... is to be commended provided they represent legally enforceable standards". The same group went on to suggest that any statement of principles and values should include statements relating specifically to children to the effect that "... the best interests of the child shall be the primary consideration in all matters affecting him or her... the rehabilitation and reintegration of the child shall be assisted as far as possible... the promotion of the development of the child to full and responsible citizenship shall be supported". Others expressed similar comments, but argued that the need to protect the public should be the primary concern in the case of serious, persistent and violent crime.

10.28   Some of those who commented on juvenile justice issues called for the age of criminal responsibility to be reviewed. Some argued that the age should be raised to 14, others that it should be kept under regular review. One noted that "... one of the specific recommendations of the United Nations Committee on the Rights of the Child [in its response to the first

United Kingdom report] was that consideration should be given to raising the age of criminal responsibility", and that the former Standing Advisory Commission on Human Rights had recommended an inquiry and research into the issue. Others argued that children aged 10-13 years old inclusive must be held accountable for their actions and pointed to the fact that the rebuttable presumption of *doli incapax* had been abolished both in England and Wales and Northern Ireland.

10.29   Some organisations recommended that 17 year olds should be brought within the juvenile justice system, rather than being dealt with as adults, suggesting that the current situation was in contravention of the provisions of the *United Nations Convention on the Rights of the Child*. Others agreed but pointed out that there were both practical and welfare problems in housing 10 year olds and 17 year olds together in a custodial environment.

10.30   Several of those who commented supported the development of diversion. One commented that "... any criminal justice system which relates to children and young people should have at its core the aim of reducing the number of children who are caught in the system... this is best served by investing in the community and developing projects to divert children from offending". Another suggested that the opportunities for diversion should be maximised and to this end that the partnership model of youth offending teams introduced in England and Wales should be developed in Northern Ireland. Some also recommended that the resources that the Government expected to save as the use of juvenile custody declined should be ploughed back into diversionary, community-based schemes.

10.31   There were calls from some for a review of the law of evidence as it relates to juveniles. Many called for juveniles to exempted from the provisions of the Criminal Evidence (Northern Ireland) Order 1988 and from the provisions of the Prevention of Terrorism (Temporary Provisions) Act 1989, the Northern Ireland (Emergency Provisions) Act 1996, and the Criminal Justice (Terrorism and Conspiracy) Act 1998. Two groups called for those representing juveniles in criminal cases to undergo specific training in relation to obtaining information from a child and advising a child, and for training about the *United Nations Convention on the Rights of the Child* and other international instruments.

10.32   Some groups raised concerns about the use of remands in custody by the courts, believing that too many juveniles continued to be remanded in custody for long periods, despite recent legislation. Some recommended that research should be conducted into the reasons for remands. Others suggested that a lack of bail support and bail hostel facilities might contribute to the perceived over-use of remands in custody by the courts.

10.33   There were concerns about the disposals available to the courts for juveniles. Some believed that while prison accommodation is rarely used for children under 17, the use of custody should be restricted further, in that it should not be possible to hold 15, 16 and 17 year olds, whether girls or boys, in prison or young offenders centre accommodation. They wanted the power to transfer those 15 years or over to a young offenders centre to be severely restricted or removed altogether. Others argued that the courts should have the power to commit 17 year olds to a period of custody in a juvenile justice centre. Some felt that the range of community disposals available to the courts for juveniles was limited, and that some form of community service should be made available for those under 16. Others argued for the abolition of, or at least the review of, the use of indeterminate sentences for juveniles, arguing that their use contravened international instruments.

10.34   Many of those who commented on the operation of the juvenile justice system recommended a review of the way in which the youth court operates, advocating the development of a more "child-friendly" court. Issues commonly cited were the design and layout of the court, the use of plain English, the need for all those participating in the proceedings to make themselves heard, with procedures which cater for the needs of ethnic minorities and children with learning or other disabilities.

10.35   We heard a range of views and proposals about the way in which the juvenile justice system should be operated and managed, particularly the custodial elements of that system, and where political responsibility for the system should lie. Many called for a coherent and co-operative approach across agencies to developing and delivering juvenile justice, suggesting ideas such as a Minister with overarching responsibility for children, a Children's Commission, a Children's Ombudsman, a Juvenile Justice Board drawing together all those agencies and actors with an interest in juvenile justice, and the creation of a Department for Children. Others called for the management of juvenile facilities to be separated from the development of policy, criticising the current management arrangements, or for responsibility for the provision of care and justice services to be combined within a single organisation. Some were concerned about the centralisation of custodial provision for juveniles, and recommended small, local units to provide custodial facilities. Others took the opposite view, and recommended centralisation to ensure that the scale of the centre was sufficient to enable appropriate education and rehabilitative programmes to be provided for all those in custody or on remand. Some also drew attention to the perceived deficiencies of the complaints mechanisms for juveniles, particularly in custodial institutions, noting the absence of an independent element.

10.36   We also heard of the need to ensure that staff in the juvenile justice system were reflective of the population of juveniles for which they were responsible, and the need to ensure that staff and sentencers were adequately trained to deal with the particular needs of juvenile offenders.

10.37   A strong case was made for research into the effectiveness of juvenile justice disposals and diversionary techniques. Most of those who commented on these issues advocated the development of a programme of research into "what works" in Northern Ireland. Some also suggested that the Government should develop innovative new mechanisms for involving young people in the development of policies and services for juveniles, citing a number of participative and consultative models emerging in other fields.

10.38   This section does not aspire to be comprehensive. A rich variety of issues was raised with us in the course of our consultation process and it is impossible to record all of the views expressed.

Research and International Comparisons

10.39   We commissioned a review of relevant research information in respect of juvenile justice, to look at models and systems of juvenile justice in other jurisdictions, to consider accountability mechanisms, to consider the international instruments which bear upon the issues of juvenile justice, and to consider what options existed for juvenile justice in Northern Ireland. As mentioned above, the research report is published along with this report.[6]

10.40   We do not intend to reproduce the bulk of the material that is included in the report in this chapter. We do, however, think that it is important to draw upon the report and the information we gathered in the course of our study visits to set out a number of themes that are emerging in approaches to juvenile justice in other jurisdictions.

10.41   The arrangements for juvenile justice were particularly interesting in a number of the jurisdictions we visited. We found Canada, England and Wales, the Netherlands, New Zealand, Scotland and South Africa particularly instructive, for a number of reasons. New Zealand had possibly the most comprehensive care and justice legislation of any of the jurisdictions we visited, and was particularly notable for the development of a comprehensive statutory statement of principles relating to juvenile justice and the development of an integrated mainstream approach to restorative justice for juveniles. Canada had just introduced new juvenile justice legislation which was rights-based, and which also incorporated a statement of guiding principles. Approaches to juvenile justice in England and Wales have been developing apace in recent years. Scotland has long had a very different approach to juvenile justice, based more on a welfare model, while the Netherlands has developed an innovative, simple, and quick approach to dealing with petty juvenile crime that we felt was worthy of consideration. South Africa did not have a recognisable juvenile justice system as such, but is fast developing a comprehensive, rights-based approach as a result of a Law Reform Commission project. We also consider the juvenile justice developments that are likely to flow from the Children's Bill currently before the Oireachtas in the Republic of Ireland.

CANADA

10.42   New legislation is being introduced in Canada designed to build upon the arrangements set out in the Young Offenders Act 1984. Important principles of the new Act are:

---

6   O'Mahony and Deazley, Research Report 17.

- proportionate sanctions;

- clear differentiation in the approach to be taken between violent and non-violent offenders; and

- non-court processes for all non-violent first time offenders.

10.43   The intention is that the law should be clear and that custody should be a last resort and used only for violent offenders. To achieve this the Act sets out explicit sentencing principles. It will also introduce a mix of rehabilitative and restorative measures and a number of more punitive measures. The Act contains a preamble and declaration of principles that make clear the purpose of the youth justice system. The preamble and principles underscore that protection of society is the primary objective of the youth justice system. The preamble also recognises the UNCRC to which Canada is a signatory. The core principles of the Act state that:

- the protection of society is the paramount objective of the youth justice system, which is best achieved through prevention, meaningful consequences for youth crime and rehabilitation;

- young people should be treated separately from adults under criminal law and in a separate youth justice system that emphasises fair and proportionate accountability, keeping in mind the dependency and level of development and maturity of youth. A separate youth justice system also includes special due process protections for youth as well as rehabilitation and reintegration;

- measures to address youth crime must: hold the offender accountable; address the offending behaviour of the youth; reinforce respect for social values; encourage repair of the harm done to victims; respect gender, ethnic, cultural and linguistic differences; involve the family, community and other agencies; and be responsive to the circumstances of youth with special requirements; and

- parents and victims have a constructive role to play in the youth justice system, and should be kept informed and encouraged to participate.

ENGLAND AND WALES

10.44   The Crime and Disorder Act 1998 and the Youth Justice and Criminal Evidence Act 1999 have introduced a range of new arrangements and disposals relating to juvenile justice. Under the Crime and Disorder Act all the agencies involved in dealing with juvenile justice at the local level are brought together into youth offending teams. The Act establishes a duty on local authorities to establish such teams and requires chief officers of police, probation committees and health authorities to co-operate. It also sets out the aims of the youth justice system and provides the courts with a number of new sentences for juveniles, including action plan orders, which require the offender to comply with a three month action plan, supervised by a probation officer, social worker or other member of a youth offending team, and a final warning scheme to replace juvenile cautions.

10.45   The Act also established the Youth Justice Board, a non-departmental public body, with a monitoring and advisory role. This includes a role in disseminating best practice, providing training, and commissioning and purchasing secure juvenile accommodation.

10.46   The Youth Justice and Criminal Evidence Act 1999 creates a new sentence of referral to a youth offender panel, available for juveniles convicted for the first time, lasting for a period of between three and 12 months, depending on the seriousness of the offence. The youth offender panel will work with the juvenile to agree and implement a programme for the juvenile to follow. The panel comprises a member of the youth offending team and at least two other members who will be directly recruited from the community by the youth offending team. The parents or guardians of the juvenile can be ordered by the court to attend meetings with the panel.

10.47   The programme, which takes the form of a contract agreed between the panel and the juvenile, will be guided by the following three principles:

    (i)   making reparation to the victim;

    (ii)   achieving reintegration into the law-abiding community; and

    (iii)   taking responsibility for the consequences of offending behaviour.

10.48   Contracts should always include an element of reparation to those affected by the offence, if those individuals consent, and this could involve a direct apology or financial or other reparation. Where there is no identifiable victim, reparation can be made to the community. Any additional elements of the contract will depend on the factors that appear to have led to the offending behaviour.

THE NETHERLANDS

10.49   A major role in the juvenile justice system in the Netherlands is played by the "Halt" system, whereby petty offenders (vandalism, petty property crime up to a value of £500 and shoplifting up to a value of £80) are diverted, primarily by the police, but also by prosecutors, to one of 63 local Halt schemes.

10.50   In general the scheme operates within tightly defined legislation and regulations as follows:

    ■ When a juvenile is arrested for a petty crime, the nature of the crime and the circumstances of the crime are considered by the police. If they match the criteria laid down in regulations for referral to a Halt scheme, and the juvenile and juvenile's parents or guardians consent, the case is referred to a Halt office. If the police are in any doubt, they consult the Halt staff or the local prosecutor.

- The case is normally referred to a Halt scheme on the day of arrest, and the first interview with Halt staff would take place within one week of the arrest. In the meantime the Halt staff contact the victim, if one exists, and find out the nature and cost of any damage caused.

- Within two weeks of arrest the Halt staff will have negotiated a package with the offender and his or her parents, which may include up to 20 hours of community service, payment for the damage caused, and could include an educational assignment. The entire process is completed within seven weeks of arrest.

10.51   The Halt scheme is respected by the police, the prosecutors, Parliament and the public. It is believed to work well, and offers the advantage of being a quick and effective response to petty juvenile crime. A reparative element is central to the scheme, and the community service often brings the offender face to face with the victim. It is common, for example, for shoplifters to work for the shop from which they have stolen, and for property damage to be repaired by the offender. Victims are generally happy with the Halt process. It is not, however, used for more serious cases, or for very minor cases for which a police warning is more appropriate.

NEW ZEALAND

10.52   The Children, Young Persons and their Families Act 1989 underpins the operation of both the child welfare and justice system in New Zealand. The Act contains two separate processes: one concerned with care and protection and one focusing on youth justice. The aims and principles, which underlie the Act in respect of youth justice, are clearly set out in it.

10.53   The family group conference is the mainstream response by the juvenile justice system to juvenile offending in New Zealand. The way in which the family group conference works, and the philosophy which underlies it, are set out more fully in the last chapter, but at this point we should note that the family group conference can be and is used as both a police diversionary measure and a tool of the court. The family group conference produces a plan that normally includes:

- a punitive element, such as community work, a condition not to drive a motor vehicle, or to abide by a curfew or a non-association clause;

- a restorative element, such as an apology, either face to face or in writing, community service, or the payment of reparation by money or in kind; and

■ a rehabilitative element for the offender, such as drug and alcohol counselling, change of residence and lifestyle, or psychological counselling and treatment.

SOUTH AFRICA

10.54   The juvenile justice system in South Africa is not separate from that for adults. In December 1996 the South African Law Commission established a project committee to investigate the development of a separate juvenile justice system. The project committee published an issue paper in 1999,[7] which identified a wide range of issues to be considered, including those surrounding the operation of a juvenile justice system and the incorporation of international principles on juvenile justice in legislation.

10.55   The issue paper made it clear that any legislation should aim to promote the well being of the child and to deal with each child in an individualised way. The central focus of the system that the Law Commission subsequently recommended was on the diversion of cases away from the criminal justice system, either to the welfare system or to suitable diversion programmes. The involvement of the family and the community was seen as of vital importance, as was sensitivity to culture, tradition and the empowerment of victims.

10.56   The Law Commission also advocated that where a child did go through the criminal justice system, he or she should be tried by a competent authority, with legal representation and parental assistance, in an atmosphere of understanding. It strongly recommended that the child should participate in decision making and that all proceedings should take place within the shortest appropriate period of time, with no unnecessary delays.

SCOTLAND

10.57   The Kilbrandon Committee Report in 1964 led to the passing of the Social Work (Scotland) Act 1968, which replaced the juvenile jurisdiction of the Scottish courts in respect of care cases, and all but the most serious criminal cases, with a more specialised welfare orientated children's hearing system. This was implemented in 1971, and operated without fundamental change until 1997 when the 1968 Act was replaced by the Children (Scotland) Act 1995.

10.58   The 1995 Act incorporates principles within specific provisions, and conforms to the provisions of the UNCRC. The children's hearing system considers cases involving juveniles under 16 referred to it by the "Reporter",[8] who in turn will receive referrals from the police

---

7   South African Law Commission, *Discussion Paper 79: Project 106: Juvenile Justice.*

8   The Kilbrandon Report envisaged that the decision to refer children to a children's hearing should be that of a single individual, namely the Reporter. The Reporter is involved in all aspects of the hearing procedure - the referral of cases, the hearing of cases and the recording and transmitting of decisions.

and, in more serious cases, the prosecutor. The hearing is conducted by a panel of lay people. It decides on the measures that should be taken to help the individual child. If the facts of the case are in dispute, the case will be considered by a court to determine innocence or guilt, and referred back to the children's hearing.

10.59 A number of outcomes are possible from a children's hearing, including: a decision to take no further action; the imposition of a supervision requirement; the imposition of a residential requirement (including secure detention); or the imposition of conditions restricting contact with other children. The courts consider appeals against the decision of a children's panel. The 1995 Act also introduced the concept of a "Safeguarder", appointed by the panel or the court where they consider it necessary, to represent the child's best interest in children's proceedings. Reparative and restorative interventions are rarely used.

THE REPUBLIC OF IRELAND

10.60 The juvenile justice system in Ireland is in the process of significant change. A comprehensive Bill to modernise and improve the law relating to children is currently before the Oireachtas. The Bill includes a range of provisions relating to juvenile justice, with the aim of diverting children away from court and custody. The Bill's provisions include:

- raising the age of criminal responsibility from 7 to 12 years;

- putting in place a system of police-led "family conferences", which will include parents and victims, and will produce action plans which could include curfews, school attendance, and compensation for the victim; and

- a power for the courts to require parents to get treatment for addictions, to attend a parenting course, to compensate victims or to control their children.

EMERGING THEMES

10.61 A number of themes emerged from our examination of juvenile justice arrangements in other jurisdictions. These included:

- the inclusion in statute of clear statements of principles, firmly based upon international instruments, for the juvenile justice system which set out the purpose it serves and what it hopes to achieve;

- the increasing use of diversion as a means of dealing with juvenile offenders;

- the development of approaches which aim to address offending behaviour and so reduce the propensity of juveniles to commit crime, and which build restorative elements into the operation of the juvenile justice process;

- a move away from court-based retributive approaches to juvenile justice, except for serious and persistent offenders;

- a move away from welfare-based models towards models which focus more on justice outcomes, and which are evidence-based and subject to rigorous evaluation;

- the development of open and transparent processes at all levels which enhance the accountability of the juvenile justice system and, ultimately, its credibility;

- the trend towards conferencing, panels and other means of determining programmes for offenders in settings other than formal courts; and

- the trend in many other jurisdictions to place juvenile justice policy and practice centre-stage in the response to the problems created by crime and criminality, and to devote considerable resources to tackling youth crime.

Evaluation and Recommendations

10.62   We were struck by the range and complexity of the issues raised with us in relation to juvenile justice in the course of our work. The juvenile justice system is a microcosm of the wider criminal justice system, and many of the issues that bear upon the system for adults are thrown into even sharper relief where juveniles are concerned. Given the limited time and resources available to us to carry out this review, it has not been possible to examine many of the issues raised with us with the rigour they deserve. We do, however, have a number of recommendations to make in several areas.

THE AIMS AND PRINCIPLES OF THE JUVENILE JUSTICE SYSTEM

10.63   Other countries, such as New Zealand, Canada and South Africa, have drawn upon all the international instruments to which we have referred in this chapter to develop the aims and principles of the juvenile justice system that are enshrined in their legislation. We considered what those principles and aims might be, and whether they might be incorporated into future legislation on juvenile justice in Northern Ireland.

10.64   We believe that there would be value in drawing up and agreeing the aims and principles of the juvenile justice system, drawing in particular upon the *United Nations Convention on the Rights of the Child*, the *International Covenant on Civil and Political Rights*, the

United Nations Guidelines for the Prevention of Juvenile Delinquency, the *United Nations Standard Minimum Rules for the Administration of Juvenile Justice*, and the *United Nations Guidelines for the Protection of Juveniles Deprived of their Liberty*. We believe that such a set of aims and principles would inform the development of juvenile justice policy, providing a yardstick against which policy and practice can be measured, and that it would inform the work of all those involved in the administration of the juvenile justice system. We note that the Northern Ireland Office published a set of aims for the juvenile justice system in 1999,[9] and we suggest that these should be reconsidered and, if necessary, revised in the light of the international instruments.

10.65   We believe that the focus of the juvenile justice system in Northern Ireland should be the prevention of offending. It should embrace the rehabilitation of the offender and diversion. It should provide meaningful consequences for those juveniles who commit crime. It should pay particular regard to the provisions of the *United Nations Guidelines for the Prevention of Juvenile Delinquency*, and the duty to regard the best interests of the child as a primary consideration under Article 3 of the *United Nations Convention on the Rights of the Child*. We also believe that there is considerable merit in enshrining such a statement of aims and principles in future juvenile justice legislation.

10.66   **We recommend that in drawing up legislation flowing from this Review, the Government should develop, agree and incorporate a clear statement of the aims of the juvenile justice system in Northern Ireland and a statement of the principles which should guide those who exercise the powers conferred by the legislation with due regard to the international human rights standards to which the United Kingdom has given commitment.**

THE AGE OF CRIMINAL RESPONSIBILITY

10.67   International instruments and practice in other jurisdictions provide only limited guidance in respect of the age of criminal responsibility. International practice varies widely. England and Wales, Northern Ireland and most Australian states set the age at 10. Canada sets the age at 12, and Germany and many other countries at 14.

10.68   Article 40(3)(a) of the *United Nations Convention on the Rights of the Child* requires states to "promote the establishment of a minimum age below which children shall not have the capacity to infringe the penal law". Rule 4.1 of the Beijing Rules also states that the age of criminal responsibility "shall not be fixed at too low an age level, bearing in mind the facts of emotional, mental and intellectual maturity". Whilst providing no precise guidance, the UN Committee on the Rights of the Child constantly refers in its Concluding Observations on

---

9   *Aims of the Juvenile Justice System* (1999), Northern Ireland Office, available from Juvenile Justice Branch, Criminal Justice Services Division, Massey House, Stoney Road, Belfast, BT4 3SX.

State Party Reports to the desirability of setting the highest possible minimum age. Countries where the minimum age of criminal responsibility has been set at 10 or below have been criticised.

10.69   We have heard persuasive arguments for the raising of the age of criminal responsibility, but we are also aware of broader societal concerns about youth offending. We do not share the views of some that the criminality of 10-13 year olds is rapidly rising; there is little evidence to support this. We do, however, believe that 10-13 year olds should be held accountable for their actions, but that the means of doing so need not necessarily be the same as for older children. We believe that, where appropriate, 10-13 year old children should continue to be criminally responsible for their actions, but that they should not be drawn into the juvenile custodial system and that the presumption should be that they will be diverted away from prosecution unless they are persistent, serious or violent offenders. Where there is a need for accommodation outside the family home for children in this age group, we believe that it should be provided by the care authorities, rather than the juvenile justice system. **We recommend that children aged 10-13 inclusive who are found guilty of criminal offences should not be held in juvenile justice centres, and that their accommodation needs should be provided by the care system.** This will require discussion with the social service authorities about practicalities and funding.

THE DEFINITION OF A CHILD

10.70   The international view on the age at which a young person should be separated from the adult criminal justice system is clear. Article 1 of the UNCRC defines a child as a person below the age of 18 years "… unless, under the law applicable to the child, majority is attained earlier". Those below the age of 18 attract, therefore, the protections of the Convention. The Beijing Rules (Rule 2(2)(a)) define a "juvenile" as a "child or young person who under the respective legal system may be dealt with for an offence in a manner which is different from an adult". The age of majority in Northern Ireland is 18, and it is clear that the current exclusion of 17 year olds from the juvenile justice system is contrary to the UNCRC. **We recommend that 17 year olds be brought within the ambit of the youth court.**

10.71   We noted that in England and Wales 17 year olds come within the remit of the juvenile justice system and are dealt with by the youth courts. Some we spoke to in England and Wales suggested that the inclusion of 17 year olds had changed the character of the court in that many more motoring offences and offences of violence were being dealt with by the court than had been the case previously, and that it had also increased disproportionately the volume of cases before the youth court. Others, including the Magistrates' Association for England and Wales, believed that the experience of bringing 17 year olds into the juvenile justice system had been positive. The experience of England and Wales will need to be taken account of in preparing for the inclusion of 17 year olds within the youth court in Northern

Ireland. Resource issues for the relevant agencies will also have to be considered. The Northern Ireland Court Service, for example, has indicated that business in the youth court will increase by 50% and that it will require funding in the region of £150,000 per annum for additional judicial and staff support.

THE AVAILABILITY OF DISPOSALS TO THE COURTS

10.72   We considered what disposals should be available for juveniles at the various stages of their development. We first of all considered whether the juvenile justice centre order should be available for 17 year olds (which it is not at present). If the option of sending 17 year olds to the juvenile justice centres were available to the courts, it would open up the possibility of almost doubling the size of the population at the centres. This would in our view change the nature and ethos of the centres to an extent that would make it more difficult to provide properly for the younger age group of 14-16 year olds. Moreover we believe that 17 year olds should benefit from the sort of regime that is available at the young offenders centre for young people up to the age of 21. **In the particular circumstances of Northern Ireland we recommend that it should continue to be the practice for 17 year olds to be remanded and sentenced to the young offenders centre.** We gave some thought to the position of 17 year olds who might be vulnerable by reason of lack of maturity or for other reasons; we recognise that this could equally apply to some in the 18 to 21 year old age bracket. **We recommend that the staff at the young offenders centre pay particularly close attention to the 17 year olds in their care and be prepared to take special measures, including the provision of separate accommodation, for any who are assessed as being vulnerable or immature.**

10.73   Rule 18.1 of the Beijing Rules sets out a number of community-based disposals which should be made available to the courts so as to avoid institutionalisation to the greatest extent possible (and should be read together with Rule 19.1, which advocates the least possible use of institutionalisation and for the minimum necessary period). Article 40(4) of the *United Nations Convention on the Rights of the Child* also encourages states to provide "a variety of dispositions... and other alternatives to institutional care".

10.74   We believed that it was necessary to consider how the range of community based disposals for juveniles might be expanded, particularly given the proposal we put forward in Chapter 9 to introduce youth conferencing and youth conference orders. The courts already have some community-based disposals available to them, but not necessarily of a sufficient variety for all age groups and to deal with offences of varying degrees of seriousness. For example, community service orders are only available for 16 year olds and above. We do not believe that traditional community service orders are best suited to the needs of those under 16, both because of the hours involved (which might interfere with the education of the young person) and the nature of the activities undertaken. We believe, however, that there is scope for providing a form of community service order for those under 16, with a reduced maximum number of hours to be served and with the activities tailored to the needs of the age group. **We recommend that a form of community service should be developed for those under 16 years of age, with a maximum period of service of 40 hours. The service to be undertaken should be tailored to the needs of juveniles of that age group and be of a nature most likely to maintain and promote the development of the juvenile in responsible, beneficial and socially acceptable ways. The arrangements should be piloted and evaluated rigorously.**

10.75   We also considered whether there was a need for "reparation orders" introduced by the Crime and Disorder Act 1998 in England and Wales. Such orders are available where a child or young person is convicted of any offence other than one for which the sentence is fixed by law. By allowing the offender to undertake some form of practical reparative activity that will benefit the victim (if the victim so wishes), it is hoped that the victim will gain a greater insight into the reasons for the offence, and will therefore be able more easily to come to terms with it. Reparation to the victim will also help the offender to realise the distress and inconvenience that his or her actions have caused, to accept responsibility for those actions, and to have the opportunity to make some amends either directly to the victim, or to the community as a whole. We believe that reparation orders would provide the courts with an additional community-based disposal while addressing the needs of victims. **We recommend the introduction of reparation orders in Northern Ireland.** We believe that the introduction of reparation orders and the new form of community service for those under 16 years of age will provide useful additions to youth conference co-ordinators and sentencers in creating imaginative, appropriate and proportionate youth conference plans. We considered whether there was a need to introduce "action plan" or "referral to a youth offender panel" orders but concluded that the types of activities that are envisaged as part of those orders would be encompassed within our proposals for youth conferencing and youth conference orders in Chapter 9.

10.76   We were asked to consider the use of the sentence of detention at the Secretary of State's pleasure for grave crimes. We have considered the international instruments which bear upon the issue and can find no reason why the courts should not have the ability to commit a juvenile to custody for an indeterminate period where that is a proportionate response to the nature and circumstances of the crime. There are mechanisms for review and release for those detained at the Secretary of State's pleasure, as there are for adults detained under mandatory or discretionary life sentences. As a result the current arrangements do not appear to contravene Article 37 of the UNCRC which requires that "neither capital punishment nor life imprisonment *without possibility of release* shall be imposed for offences committed by persons", or Rule 19.1 of the Beijing Rules. We do, however, consider the adequacy of current release mechanisms for such sentences at Chapter 12.

BAIL AND REMANDS

10.77 We note the concerns about the use of bail and remands in Northern Ireland. In considering the issues raised, we were mindful of international instruments, most notably Rules 13.1 to 13.5 of the Beijing Rules, particularly Rule 13.1, which states that "detention pending trial shall be used only as a measure of last resort and for the shortest possible period of time". Rule 13.2 states that "whenever possible, detention pending trial shall be replaced by alternative measures, such as close supervision, intensive care or placement with a family or in an educational setting or home". However, we are also aware of concerns that some juveniles who should be remanded in custody are being freed, and that they continue to commit offences while on bail. In addition we are aware of the risk, and the perception, that the juvenile justice system may be used by other agencies to "offload" their difficult cases. These are difficult and complex issues which merit close attention.

10.78 **We recommend:**

(i) **the piloting and evaluation of bail information and support schemes to provide the courts with information and advice to assist them with making bail and remand decisions in respect of individual juveniles;**

(ii) **the development of bail hostel accommodation specifically for juveniles, particularly within Belfast;**

(iii) **that those remanded in custody should be assessed as quickly as possible to determine the nature of the regime required, including the degree of supervision; and**

(iv) **that remands in custody should be for the shortest period of time possible.**

JUVENILE CUSTODY

10.79 We visited Lisnevin Juvenile Justice Centre to see for ourselves what it was like and to hear of the facilities and programmes that it provides. We agree with the views expressed by some that it is unsuitable as a facility for holding juveniles, and we feel that its remote location makes it very difficult for families to maintain contact with those held there. However, we were impressed by some of the programmes which it offers to those on remand and those held under a juvenile justice centre order, and by the dedication and professionalism of the staff we met. We would not wish to see these positive features lost. We believe that the retention of the current arrangements is neither feasible nor desirable. Lisnevin is not suitable for holding juveniles; there are no secure facilities for girls (which has necessitated the holding of a young girl in Maghaberry young offenders centre in recent times); and the falling population of the centres has made the provision of the full range of facilities difficult. That is not to say that each of the current centres is not doing good work at present; rather their work is hampered by the fractured nature of custodial provision. **We recommend that Lisnevin Juvenile Justice Centre be closed.**

10.80   We have considered a number of options for the future of juvenile custodial facilities, including:

■ the creation of a single juvenile justice centre, providing both secure and open facilities for girls and boys of all denominations;

■ the creation of a number of small, locally-based custodial units across Northern Ireland; and

■ the retention of the current arrangements.

10.81   The creation of a number of small custodial units across Northern Ireland, each providing five or six places, would enable juveniles to be placed closer to their families than is currently the case. But it would create difficulties in a number of respects, such as providing the necessary individual assistance which Rule 13.5 of the Beijing Rules calls for, including social, educational, vocational, psychological and medical, and physical facilities. It would also be difficult to provide secure facilities with such an arrangement, and it might necessitate in addition the creation of a single secure unit for Northern Ireland.

10.82   The creation of a custodial complex on a single site, with a mix of both secure and open facilities, might not ease the difficulties of maintaining ties between juveniles and their families: no single site will be readily accessible for all of the families of juvenile offenders. A site in the Greater Belfast area would be most likely to ease the difficulties of family visits, since the majority of the population of juvenile justice centres come from the Greater Belfast area; but it would also be necessary to take account of accessibility of transport links from other parts of Northern Ireland. In addition, and bearing in mind that the custodial population is likely to settle to a total of less than 40 remand and committed juveniles, the development of a single centre would enable the full range of facilities to be provided, and for secure and open facilities to be provided for both girls and boys on a single site. We note, however, that there are likely to be difficulties in finding a suitable green-field site in the Greater Belfast area and that it might be necessary to develop the new centre on an existing site.

10.83   We understand that work is currently being undertaken by the Government on the future of the juvenile justice custodial estate. This will, of course, require detailed consultation before final decisions are made. From our consideration of the issues we think that the balance of argument points towards a single site solution. We wish to stress the importance of the diversity of needs of juvenile offenders being met by juvenile justice centre staff whose competence and expertise is based on professional education and training, in-service training and on the job instruction and development. Whatever the outcome of the review of the juvenile justice centre estate, it would make sense to draw on suitably qualified staff from, and the expertise developed at, existing juvenile justice centres.

10.84   We wish to stress the importance of ensuring that there is good liaison between the juvenile justice centres and community-based agencies. Co-operation and co-ordination are necessary if programmes are to be planned in order to secure an effective transition from the custodial to the community setting, which is a feature of the juvenile justice centre order. Such an approach is also required if the educational, care, welfare and housing needs of the juveniles are to be properly catered for when they are released back into the community. Accordingly, we wish to emphasise the importance of the Probation and Social Services ensuring good liaison arrangements with the juvenile justice centres, for example, by way of allocation of staff to the centres to help prepare for release and ensure that the care needs of those held on remand or on foot of a juvenile justice centre order are met.

DIVERSION AND PARTNERSHIP APPROACHES

10.85   Rules 11.1 to 11.4 of the Beijing Rules and Article 40(3)(b) of the *United Nations Convention on the Rights of the Child* encourage states to promote diversion from judicial proceedings, providing that human rights and legal safeguards are respected. Rule 25.1 of the Beijing Rules also calls for "volunteers, voluntary organisations, local institutions and other community resources... to contribute effectively to the rehabilitation of the juvenile in a community setting and, as far as possible, within the family unit".

10.86   We note that there is already a range of diversionary and partnership activity. Police diversion by informal advice and warning and formal cautions is already well established. "Caution-plus", Juvenile Liaison Bureaux, children's panels, and other inter-agency approaches are also developing. Whitefield House provides a number of community-based projects, developed in partnership with other statutory, voluntary and community organisations. A wide range of voluntary and community resources already contributes to dealing with juvenile offenders in the community. All of this is to be welcomed and endorsed.

10.87   We agree, however, that there are opportunities to further develop diversion at all stages of the process. Other changes that we recommend in this report in respect of the role of prosecutors (who will have a significant role to play in inter-agency work on juveniles, including Juvenile Liaison Bureaux in future), the application of restorative justice, and community safety will help in that context. We agree also that more resources will be necessary to develop these approaches. **We endorse the development of further diversionary mechanisms based on a partnership approach and recommend that any savings arising from the rationalisation of the juvenile justice estate should be reallocated to diversionary programmes and other community-based sanctions for juveniles. We recommend also the development of prosecutor-driven diversionary schemes for juveniles, including the power to refer back for a police caution and the development of agreed guidelines on good practice in diversion at police and prosecutor level.**

THE RIGHT OF SILENCE AND EMERGENCY LEGISLATION

10.88   Concerns about the application of emergency legislation to juveniles were drawn to our attention. Our terms of reference explicitly excluded us from considering emergency legislation, which was the subject of a parallel review. We felt that it was right, however, for us to draw to the attention of those reviewing the law on terrorism the concerns that have been raised with us, and we have done so.

10.89   As for the law on the right of silence, we note that there has been little research into the effects of the Criminal Evidence (Northern Ireland) Order 1988, and none on its specific effects on juveniles. The law on silence is considered in more detail in Chapter 3. **In respect of juveniles, we recommend that the Government should commission independent research into the effects of the Criminal Evidence (Northern Ireland) Order 1988 on juvenile defendants as a matter of urgency, and that the findings of that research should be published.**

10.90   We have also considered the training needs of "appropriate adults", who play an important part in facilitating communication and ensuring fair procedure whilst a juvenile is in police detention. **We recommend that those who volunteer to act as appropriate adults should receive training by a wide range of agencies, to include training on the needs of those who have learning or other disabilities, or who are suffering from a mental disorder, and children's rights and broad human rights awareness.**

COURTS ISSUES, CHILDREN'S EVIDENCE AND DELAY

10.91   Article 40(2)(b)(iii) of the *United Nations Convention on the Rights of the Child* guarantees the right "to have the matter determined without delay by a competent, independent and impartial authority and judicial body in a fair hearing according to law". Article 12(2) also guarantees the right of the child to be heard in any judicial or administrative proceedings affecting him or her. Rule 14.1 of the Beijing Rules provides a similar guarantee, and Rule 14.2 adds that "the proceedings shall be conducive to the best interests of the juvenile and shall be conducted in an atmosphere of understanding, which shall allow the juvenile to participate therein and to express herself or himself freely".

10.92   No-one has argued that the youth court is not an "independent and impartial judicial body", but concerns have been raised about the way in which the youth court operates, and about the length of time it takes for cases to be disposed of (we recognise, however, that delays are not caused solely by the youth court: other agencies and procedural requirements contribute to the time taken to deal with criminal cases involving juveniles). It is possible that in some locations relatively infrequent sittings of youth courts might contribute to delay. We have heard some suggestions put forward for developing the court as a more child-friendly venue, whilst retaining a measure of dignity and authority to bring home the gravity of the proceedings.

10.93   We have also visited a youth court while it was in session, and have observed the proceedings. We were impressed by the way in which the court operated, and by the professional and understanding way in which the panel handled the cases before them. We also noted that the court itself was much less formal than its adult equivalent, and that the magistrates and advocates wore no wigs or gowns. We were less impressed by the way in which the prosecution and defence advocates handled the cases, and noted the limited opportunities afforded to the defendant to participate and for his or her parents to participate and express themselves freely. We also noted that there were audibility problems in court, and that it was apparent that the defendant and his or her parents could not always hear what was being said. We are conscious of the development of the Child Witness Service in Belfast and the Child Witness Pack by the NSPCC, which we welcome and endorse. We have a number of recommendations to make that we believe will enhance the effectiveness of the youth court and make it a more user-friendly venue.

10.94   **In respect of the operation of the youth court we recommend that:**

   (i)   **Guidelines should be developed for the layout and operation of the youth court, emphasising the need for all the participants in court to sit at the same level, the need for all participants to be able to hear what is being said in court, the need for simple and plain language to be used during the proceedings, and the need for the defendant and his or her parents to be given opportunities to participate and express themselves freely.**

   (ii)   **Defence and prosecution advocates should be encouraged, through professional education and development, to enhance their expertise in respect of handling juvenile cases and their awareness of the human rights instruments and jurisprudence as they relate to juveniles. This should not interfere with the juvenile's right to the lawyer of his or her choice. Professional and lay members of the bench should receive similar training under the auspices of the Judicial Studies Board.**

   (iii) **In the light of the outcome of evaluation, the child witness scheme should be made available at all criminal court venues in Northern Ireland, including youth courts.**

   (iv)   **Efforts to deal with delays in cases being brought before the youth court should continue.**

(v)   **Given the need to tackle delay and the impact of extending the jurisdiction of youth courts to include 17 year olds, there should be an examination of youth court sittings and consequential implications for magistrates' courts.**

10.95   The judgments of the European Court in the cases of *T & V v United Kingdom*[10] emerged as we were finalising this report. They raise important issues in relation to juvenile justice. We have not had an opportunity to consider fully the implications of the judgments for juvenile justice in Northern Ireland. Therefore, **we recommend that the Government should consider carefully the implications of judgments of *T & V v United Kingdom* for the operation of the juvenile justice system in Northern Ireland.**

COMPLAINTS AND INSPECTION ISSUES

10.96   The main international instrument that deals with the administration of juvenile facilities is the *United Nations Rules for the Protection of Juveniles Deprived of their Liberty*. Rules 24-25 and 72-78 relate to the information that should be provided to juveniles when they arrive in custodial facilities, inspection arrangements for juvenile custodial facilities, and the nature of complaints mechanisms that should be made available to the juvenile.

10.97   Concerns were raised with us about the adequacy of the complaints and inspection arrangements for the juvenile justice system, particularly within juvenile justice centres. We discuss in Chapter 3 the principles that should apply to complaints mechanisms throughout the criminal justice system. Mechanisms for inspecting the elements of the criminal justice system are considered in Chapter 15. These apply equally to the juvenile justice system.

10.98   **We make the following recommendations in respect of the complaints mechanisms and inspection arrangements:**

(i)   **Complaints mechanisms should be reviewed as a matter of urgency to ensure that they conform to the *United Nations Rules for the Protection of Juveniles Deprived of their Liberty*, and to ensure that they include an independent element.**

(ii)   **On admission to a juvenile justice centre, all juveniles should, as now, be given a copy of the rules governing the juvenile justice centre and a written description of their rights and obligations in a language they can understand, together with a description of the ways in which they can make complaints, as well as the address of public or private agencies and organisations which provide legal assistance.**

---

10   *Cases of T & V v United Kingdom*, at the European Court of Human Rights (App. Nos. 24724/94 and 24888/94), judgments 16 December 1999.

(iii) For those juveniles who have difficulty in understanding the written guidance, the guidance should, as now, be explained to them.

(iv) All agencies providing facilities and services for juvenile offenders, including juvenile justice centres, should come within the remit of the Criminal Justice Inspectorate, in respect of those services or facilities.

(v) Each juvenile justice centre should have a local advisory committee that brings in local professional and community representatives, including representatives of nearby residents.

THE MANAGEMENT OF THE JUVENILE JUSTICE SYSTEM

10.99 We have considered how the juvenile justice system should be managed at the operational level, and where policy responsibility for juvenile justice issues should lie. We note that the current arrangements for managing the juvenile justice system are intended to be temporary and do not believe that they represent a satisfactory long-term solution, given the mix of policy and direct management responsibility associated with the Juvenile Justice Board as constituted at the time of writing. In considering how best to structure and manage responsibility for juvenile justice services, we considered the following issues:

- whether and how operational management responsibility for juvenile justice custodial and community services could be brought together;

- how policy responsibility for juvenile justice could be separated from service delivery, and where political responsibility for the juvenile justice system should lie, both before devolution of criminal justice issues and after;

- how co-operation and co-ordination between the agencies responsible for children's services, including juvenile justice services, could be encouraged;

- whether there was a case for combining responsibility for the delivery of juvenile justice and probation services; and

- whether there should be a Minister responsible for the co-ordination of all policy on children.

10.100 We considered a number of options for the delivery of juvenile justice services, including: the creation of a non-departmental public body; a government department purchasing services from statutory agencies and the voluntary sector; the incorporation of juvenile justice in the Probation Service; and the creation of a next steps agency within a government department. On balance, we are not convinced that non-departmental bodies are the ideal vehicles for securing effective management, accountability and co-operative working between agencies in this environment. The purchaser/provider model has its attractions, but does not necessarily make for co-operative working between service providers. As for incorporation in the Probation Service, we have some reservations about whether it would be appropriate for juvenile justice to be located within an organisation that has as its primary focus adult offenders, although we should stress that we see a continuing role for Probation in working with juveniles.

10.101   On balance we favour the next steps agency option. This would facilitate the development of a strong professional management team responsible for the provision of juvenile justice services in the custodial and community settings. They would act in accordance with a framework document that would make the clear distinction between their responsibility for services and the sponsor department's responsibility for policy development. We should stress that this would still allow for purchaser/provider arrangements. The agency would have responsibility for direct service provision but would also be required to consider buying in services from the voluntary sector. It would be subject to the full range of accountability mechanisms that apply to next steps agencies, and to the accountability mechanisms that we set out in Chapters 3 and 15 of this report. Accordingly, **we recommend the creation of a next steps agency which would take on responsibility for the range of responsibilities which fall to the current Juvenile Justice Board as are set out in Article 56(5) of the Criminal Justice (Children) (Northern Ireland) Order 1998.** These responsibilities include:

(i)   making and giving effect to schemes for children who are subject to attendance centre orders or juvenile justice centre orders and schemes for the prevention of crime by children; and

(ii)   entering into arrangements with voluntary organisations or any other persons (including government departments and public bodies), or providing voluntary organisations or any other persons with facilities for the purposes of, and to give effect to, the schemes at (i) above.

In effect this would mean that the agency would be responsible for the provision of custodial and community facilities for juvenile justice orders, attendance centre orders, and schemes of the type provided by Whitefield. Other agencies would continue to provide services for juveniles. For example, the Probation Service would be responsible for securing compliance with probation orders and community service orders.

10.102   **We recommend that the development of juvenile justice policy should be separate from the functions of the juvenile justice agency and should be a matter for a separate unit in the department within which the agency is placed. That unit should be responsible for advising the Minister in relation to policy and legislative proposals. The unit should also be responsible for developing a strategy for the delivery of juvenile justice services, and should develop and publish aims, standards and**

performance indicators. In doing so it would work in partnership with the Juvenile Justice Agency we propose at paragraph 10.101 and the advisory board we propose at paragraph 10.103 below.

10.103   We do see value in having a broader input into the work of the agency and juvenile justice matters generally through drawing on expertise from outside the sponsor department. This could be achieved through the establishment of an advisory board bringing together senior professional and administrative representatives from the other agencies and departments with a stake in providing services for children, such as probation, education, health and social services, together with representatives of some of the major community and voluntary organisations with an interest in juvenile justice issues. The head of the Juvenile Justice Agency would attend the board, together with his or her senior managers and representation from the sponsor department. The board would have a consultative and advisory role in relation to the Minister on matters relating to policy and service delivery. However, we believe that additional benefits would be secured, in terms of encouraging co-operative working and consideration of best practice across agency boundaries, if this juvenile justice advisory function were combined with that proposed for probation and prisons in Chapter 12. Accordingly, **we recommend that an overarching Probation, Prisons and Juvenile Justice Advisory Board be adopted.** It would of course always be possible for specific juvenile justice issues to be addressed by a sub-committee of such a board.

10.104   We also considered where political responsibility for the juvenile justice system should lie, and whether there should be a Minister for all services relating to children (as there is for women's issues, for example). **We recommend that, pending devolution, political responsibility for the juvenile justice system should remain with the Secretary of State for Northern Ireland and that policy and legislative advice should continue to be provided by the Northern Ireland Office. After devolution, we believe that ministerial responsibility should lie with whichever Minister is responsible for prisons and probation.** We make no recommendation in respect of whether there should be a Minister responsible for all children's issues, and suggest that the Northern Ireland Executive Committee might consider this after devolution of responsibility for criminal justice issues.

THE ROLE OF RESEARCH, CONSULTATION AND COMMUNICATION IN POLICY FORMULATION AND EVALUATION

10.105   We endorse Rules 30.1 to 31.4 of the Beijing Rules, and **we recommend the use of research as a basis for developing an informed juvenile justice policy. We recommend that all new initiatives and legislation should be routinely monitored and subject to rigorous and independent evaluation.**

10.106   We found in the course of our consultation process that there was considerable ignorance of juvenile justice policy and practice in Northern Ireland, and that much effort was required to tease out people's views on current juvenile justice institutions. That people knew very little about juvenile justice practice was not surprising, since juvenile justice policy has received little attention in the media in Northern Ireland, and because the Government has not sought to raise the awareness of the public about juvenile justice issues. We believe this has contributed to the widespread belief that the juvenile justice system doesn't work, a belief that has, in part, led to support for and acceptance of so-called "alternative justice". As a result, **we recommend that in developing policy and practice the views of the public and of young people in particular should be taken into account. To achieve this, innovative approaches to consultation should be developed, and consideration should be given to how best to seek out the views of young people. We also recommend that, to enhance public confidence in the juvenile justice system, a communication strategy be developed to advertise successes, develop public awareness of existing practice and new initiatives, and to provide information to sentencers on the availability of programmes and other community disposals.**

Community
Safety

11 Community Safety

Introduction

11.1　This chapter considers the development of partnership approaches to reducing the level of crime, reducing the fear of crime, and enhancing community safety both locally and nationally.

11.2　The Policing and Justice section of the Belfast Agreement set out what the participants to the multi-party negotiations believed were the aims of the criminal justice system. These included the need to "... be responsive to the community's concerns, and encouraging community involvement, where appropriate...". The terms of reference of the review also required us to consider "... measures to improve the responsiveness and accountability of... the criminal justice system". As a result we believed that it was right to consult on and consider the arrangements for community safety in Northern Ireland, and ways in which the criminal justice system can target its resources more effectively in preventing crime.

What is Community Safety?

11.3　No one would deny that crime constitutes a significant social and political issue, in Northern Ireland and in many other countries. Rising crime rates have fuelled public concern in most countries, and whilst Northern Ireland has enjoyed a relatively low rate of "ordinary" crime, it is nonetheless a cause for concern amongst the public here. The growing awareness of drugs, so-called "joy-riding", domestic violence and general anti-social behaviour are but a few examples of crime-related issues which the people of Northern Ireland are worried about. People are not necessarily most concerned about "big" crime issues: they often focus more on the types of crime of which they have experience and which are problems in their own area. In parallel there is a growing realisation that the formal criminal justice processes - through the detection, apprehension, prosecution, sentencing and punishment of offenders - have only a limited effect on controlling crime. This was a message that came across to us very clearly in the course of our work, from the literature reviews we commissioned, from our study visits to other jurisdictions, and through our consultation process. That is why the approach to preventing crime has changed in recent decades in Northern Ireland and in many other countries, and why it continues to change.

11.4   Until relatively recently the term "crime prevention" was perceived as a by-product of the formal criminal justice process. For most people it meant a visit from the local police crime prevention officer to explain how they could make their home more secure. Crime prevention is much more than this. Jan van Dijk defined it as "the total of all policies, measures and techniques, outside the boundaries of the criminal justice system, aiming at the reduction of the various kinds of damage caused by acts defined as criminal by the state".[1] As the research report on the literature on community safety notes: "More recently it has become acknowledged that preventing crime requires the combination of approaches which seek to address the development of criminality among young people, reduce criminal opportunities and act upon the social conditions that sustain crime." [2]

11.5   The term "community safety" is wider again and addresses not only criminal behaviour as such but also anti-social behaviour and other factors that affect people's perceptions of safety. It is now understood as an approach which is local, in that local problems require local solutions. It is delivered through a partnership approach, drawing together a variety of organisations in the public, voluntary, community and business sectors. In the United Kingdom the Morgan Report[3] came to the view that the term "crime prevention" was often narrowly interpreted, and reinforced the view that it was solely the responsibility of the police. The report advocated the use of the term "community safety" as it was open to wider interpretation that would encourage greater community participation from all sections of the community in the fight against crime. Other countries have followed a similar path, as our research and study visits have shown, and many of those we have studied have developed mechanisms both within central government and at local level for developing and delivering community safety policy and practice.

Current Arrangements in Northern Ireland

11.6   A wide range of organisations and sectors are involved in crime prevention and community safety in Northern Ireland. Their activities in this area include situational crime prevention aimed at reducing opportunities for crimes to be committed, diverting people who are most likely to commit crimes away from offending behaviour and addressing broader policy and

1   van Dijk (1990) "Crime Prevention: Current State and Prospects", in Kaiser and Albrecht, (eds) *Crime and Criminal Policy in Europe,* Freiburg: Max Planck Institute, 205.

2   Crawford and Matassa, Research Report 8.

3   Morgan, *Safer Communities: The Local Delivery of Crime Prevention Through the Partnership Approach, Standing Conference on Crime Prevention* (1991), London: Home Office.

service provision issues which can impact on the level of criminal behaviour. There is already a considerable amount of activity in this field in Northern Ireland, with the RUC, Police Authority, Probation Service and the Northern Ireland Office having taken initiatives, as have a range of other statutory agencies in the field of social provision, including those responsible for housing, social services, local government and education. Voluntary and community organisations are also playing an important role in delivering services across Northern Ireland, working in partnership with public agencies, and the business sector is increasingly involved in community safety initiatives.[4]

11.7   Community safety activity is not, however, a core activity of any of the above organisations and agencies. It can therefore be difficult for agencies to find resources for community safety initiatives from their current budget structure. In addition, no agency has been given or has taken overall responsibility for setting crime prevention and community safety policy, or for funding, monitoring or evaluating community safety initiatives, either at local level or across Northern Ireland as a whole. A recent innovation, in the form of the development of the Community Safety Centre, has sought to encourage and advise those who wish to develop community safety initiatives, and to spread good practice in community safety to all those organisations and groups with an interest in making communities safer for those who work and live within them. The Centre is funded by the Northern Ireland Office, and is managed by an inter-agency board, but does not itself have a budget for funding initiatives. We were impressed by the work of the Centre and its growing track record and knowledge base, but we were also concerned that it was being asked to do a difficult job in the absence of a clearly defined and articulated community safety strategy, a point which was drawn out in a review of the Centre which is published as a research report along with this report.[5]

11.8   At present there are several mechanisms for funding community safety initiatives. Those who wish to develop a community safety project in their area can look to a variety of sources of funding, including the European Special Fund for Peace and Reconciliation or charitable sources. They must also contend - as do many other projects in the social and economic spheres - with the short-term nature of funding arrangements and the uncertainty, which such funding engenders. Short-term funding makes it difficult to mount long-term community safety initiatives, such as those aimed at preventing criminality, and to retain skilled and experienced staff.

11.9   A number of local councils have set up community safety partnerships and projects, several of which are funded from the European Special Fund for Peace and Reconciliation. In some cases these are being taken forward, under contract, by voluntary organisations. In others the projects are being delivered directly by council staff. None of the projects are at an advanced stage. CCTV schemes are being introduced in many towns across Northern Ireland funded by the Police Authority.

---

4   See Feenan, Research Report 13, section 2, for a fuller description of community safety partnership activity.

5   Crawford and Blair, Research Report 7.

11.10   The Crime Prevention Panel, led initially by the RUC, was established in 1977. The Panel comprises representatives of government departments, voluntary organisations, the Community Safety Centre, the RUC, the business sector and employers' organisations. A representative of an organisation other than the RUC chairs the panel. Its aim is to identify concerns about crime and, where possible, to co-ordinate partnership approaches to reducing crime and the fear of crime. At present the Panel's work is focused on property crime.

11.11   Despite the existence of a range of activities that are community safety related, the concept is still in its infancy in Northern Ireland. This is partly because of the understandable focus on terrorist crime by the Government, local politicians and the public over the past 30 years, and partly because of the relatively lower rate of "ordinary" crime, which Northern Ireland has experienced both before and during that period. If, as we all hope, peace is sustained in Northern Ireland, the focus will shift and "ordinary" crime will assume the importance in local political debate that it has in many other countries. We are also conscious of concerns that ordinary crime may be increasing. That is why we believe it is important to consider the structures for delivering community safety policy and initiatives, the funding mechanisms, and the arrangements for ensuring that those involved in delivering community safety services are held properly accountable to political structures and the public. These are, therefore, the issues on which we concentrate in this chapter. We commissioned a number of research projects to inform our consideration of these issues. We also examined the arrangements in other jurisdictions at first hand, in the course of our study visits. Most importantly of all, we listened to what people had to say to us in the course of our consultation process.

Research and International Comparisons

11.12   We recognise the dangers of comparing arrangements in different jurisdictions, and acknowledge that what works in one country may not work in another country with a very different institutional, social and economic context. There are no universal approaches to preventing crime. We believed, however, that we should consider the lessons learned elsewhere, both good and bad, in considering what, if any, changes we should recommend for the delivery of community safety in Northern Ireland.

11.13   We commissioned a literature review of community safety structures in a number of other jurisdictions as part of our research programme. The review is published along with this report.[6] Much of the material used in this chapter, particularly in the descriptive sections, draws directly upon that review, which considered the recent experience of community safety in France, the Netherlands, Canada, New Zealand, Scotland, the Republic of Ireland, and

---

6   Crawford and Matassa, Research Report 8.

England and Wales. It looked in particular at the structure of central and local institutions for community safety. It also considered different models of inter-organisational relationships within and between central and local arrangements, and set out a number of the key issues to be considered in the context of Northern Ireland. Another research report also considered community safety partnership models in Scotland and the Republic of Ireland.[7]

11.14   As part of our research into community safety issues we also commissioned a literature review of research on crime reduction and reducing criminality. The review, which is published along with this report, drew together a summary of the research literature.[8] The review reinforced the point that many governments were beginning to require proof of effectiveness from those programmes that claimed to reduce crime or criminality. A number of tentative lessons emerged from the review, the most important of which is that it is important to build in rigorous monitoring and evaluation of all new initiatives at the design stage, and to fund the evaluation of the initiatives properly to ensure that the evaluation is both rigorous and relevant. Only by doing so can a government determine the worth of a new initiative and whether it should be extended, subjected to further evaluation, or discontinued.

11.15   In addition we had the opportunity to study the arrangements for community safety at first hand in some of the jurisdictions considered by the literature review, most notably England and Wales, the Netherlands, New Zealand, Scotland, and the Republic of Ireland.

FRANCE

11.16   The French approach to crime prevention flowed from the Bonnemaison Committee Report (1983) that had been commissioned as a result of widespread urban disorder in the summer of 1981. It led to the creation of a three-tiered structure in 1983 involving:[9]

- a national council for the prevention of crime, which was chaired by the Prime Minister, with a total membership of over 80;

- departmental councils, which are chaired by the chief administrator for the region, with the chief judicial officer as vice-chair; and

- local crime prevention councils (CCPDs), which co-ordinate preventative action at the local level, define local aims with particular reference to victims, and monitor implementation (over 850 have been established in almost all the large and medium sized French cities).

---

7   Feenan, Research Report 13.

8   Blair, Research Report 4.

9   The administrative structure in France below national level consists of three tiers:
    - 22 regions - for which there is no crime prevention structure;
    - departments; and
    - towns or cities.
    It is these last administrative levels which have been used to co-ordinate the delivery of crime prevention.

This structure was reorganised in the late 1980s and early 1990s and the focus moved to structures concerned with urban regeneration, ensuring that concerns about social exclusion and community safety were taken account of in the policies and services of a wide range of agencies.

11.17   Contracts negotiated between central government and most local CCPDs were developed as a way of funding and integrating local initiatives. Some were focused on urban regeneration with a crime prevention element, and others were specifically directed towards crime prevention. These contracts set out commitments for a period of three years to facilitate medium and longer term planning, and have recently been based upon a local crime data analysis to identify the nature and scale of local crime problems, an assessment of the fear of crime in local populations, and an analysis of the existing responses to crime and insecurity by public authorities.

THE NETHERLANDS

11.18   The approach to crime prevention in the Netherlands was set out in the Dutch Government report *Society and Crime* in 1985. It argued that crime prevention should be the focus of action against petty crime, and that the formal criminal justice process should be used as a last resort in relation to such crime. It set out three guiding principles for preventive policies:

(i)   the strengthening of surveillance of, and control over, potential offenders, by those who are well placed to do so;

(ii)   the development of urban and environmental planning, to limit the opportunities to commit crime; and

(iii)   the reinforcement of social integration (through family, school, work and recreation).

11.19   National crime prevention policy is primarily the responsibility of a Directorate of the Ministry of Justice (the Prevention, Youth and Sanction Department) co-ordinated through an inter-ministerial committee. The Directorate has a substantial budget and is on a level with the other Directorates in the Department. It has four main responsibilities:

(i)   promoting crime prevention among municipalities and businesses;

(ii)   supporting police-based crime prevention;

(iii)   co-ordinating victim policies; and

(iv)   regulating the private security industry.

11.20   Co-operation between the government and corporate sectors has been an important feature of crime prevention. A consultative body, the National Platform on Crime Control, comprises representatives from the public and private sectors. It has a number of steering groups which focus on particular issues, such as IT-related crime and organised crime. Wider crime prevention policy is delivered as part of the "Major Cities Policy", which was introduced in 1993 and covers four main policy areas: education; employment; health and welfare; and public safety. The policy now covers 19 major cities. It aims to strengthen the social and economic base and quality of life, and relies on a neighbourhood-based approach to social problems, delivered through a partnership between central and municipal government, criminal justice and social agencies, businesses, neighbourhood groups and individuals. The Government set aside £100 million over the period 1995-1999 and £40 million per year thereafter to combat juvenile crime, and an additional £8 million to tackle drug-related crime. Prime responsibility for designing and delivering initiatives occurs at the municipal, district and neighbourhood level, in partnership with other agencies, including police and prosecutors. Each of the municipalities has crime prevention co-ordinators and local crime prevention committees.

11.21   The Netherlands have also developed a pragmatic, evidence-based approach to developing policy and to the initiation, planning and implementation of projects. This places considerable emphasis on the role of evaluation and research, which is a requirement of any crime prevention funding. Around 10% of funding is devoted to evaluation.

NEW ZEALAND

11.22   New Zealand provides an interesting model, because of the similar size of its population (3.7 million), its mix of different communities, and because of the relationship between, and respective powers of, central and local government, which are similar in many respects to those in Northern Ireland. New Zealand's interest in crime prevention and community safety policy began in the mid-1980s. The Roper Report[10] recognised that the responsibility for crime prevention did not lie solely with the police, but with the community as a whole. The Government proceeded to develop a model based on the French system, setting up four pilot Safer Community Councils in 1990, overseen by a Prime Ministerial Safer Communities Council, and managed by the Crime Prevention Administration Unit.

11.23   In 1992 the Government created an inter-departmental working party, the Crime Prevention Action Group, to develop a coherent crime prevention strategy. It developed a strategy for crime prevention that co-ordinated policy, research and service delivery from government agencies, local government and the wider community within one strategic crime prevention framework. In 1993 the Crime Prevention Unit was established within the Department of the Prime Minister and Cabinet to advise the Government on crime prevention, develop a crime prevention plan based on a knowledge of "what works", and ensure co-operation between concerned groups. Seven key areas were given to the Unit by Ministers:

(i)   Supporting "at risk" families.

---

10   *Report of the Ministerial Committee of Inquiry into Violence* (1987).

(ii)   Reducing family violence.

(iii) Targeting youth "at risk" of offending.

(iv)   Minimising formal involvement of casual offenders within the criminal justice system through diversion schemes.

(v)   Developing an approach for the management of programmes that address the misuse and abuse of both alcohol and drugs.

(vi)   Addressing the incidence of "white collar crime".

(vii) Addressing the concerns of victims and potential victims.

11.24   The Unit supports the development of Safer Community Councils (SCCs), which are usually formed under the sponsorship of a local authority, or the Maori equivalent of a local authority, the *iwi*. (It is worth noting that local authorities in New Zealand have very limited powers and responsibilities, and are closer to local authorities in Northern Ireland than those in many other jurisdictions.) The SCCs are responsible for preparing a community safety profile of their area, and for developing crime prevention strategies based on that profile. Sixty-one SCCs had been formed, representing around two-thirds of local authorities. Local authorities were given a small amount of funding to support the establishment and maintenance of the SCC, and a small amount of seed-corn money to fund small-scale local crime prevention projects. SCCs engage in both situational and social crime prevention, working closely with the police and business community.

ENGLAND AND WALES

11.25   Crime prevention and community safety policy and practice in Northern Ireland has tended to follow developments in England and Wales, at least until recent years. There has been some divergence in practice more recently because of the very different institutions of government, particularly at the local level, which exist in the two jurisdictions.

11.26   In England and Wales the approach to crime prevention and community safety has been heavily influenced by two circulars and a major report. The first document, an interdepartmental circular in 1984, recognised that:

> "A primary objective of the police has always been the prevention of crime. However, since some of the factors affecting crime lie outside the control or direct influence of the police, crime prevention cannot be left to them alone. Every individual citizen and all those agencies whose policies and practices can influence the extent of crime should make their contribution. Preventing crime is a task for the whole community."

11.27   The 1980s and early 1990s saw the development of a number of central government initiatives to promote crime prevention, most notably the Safer Cities Programme launched in 1988. The second document, a follow-up circular in 1990,[11] reinforced the concept of a partnership approach to combating crime, and was accompanied by a good practice booklet which provided advice on what constituted good practice in designing and implementing crime prevention policy.

11.28   The Morgan Report[12] in 1991 provided the philosophy and structure which underpin community safety policy in England and Wales today. The report elaborated on the term "community safety" and advocated specific institutional structures and arrangements, including a three-tiered structure of responsibility. It also recommended additional funding from central government to support the proposed new duty on local authorities. Its principal recommendations included:

- giving local authorities statutory authority, working with the police, to develop and stimulate community safety and crime prevention;

- appointing a co-ordinator with administrative support to the local authority structure;

- the nomination by chief constables for each local authority area of the "most senior local operational police officer" in order to promote coterminous boundaries;

- paying particular attention to young people and crime in local partnerships;

- making best use of the voluntary sector;

- involving business as a partner instead of regarding it solely as a source of funds;

- consideration by the Government of how a strong focus at the centre could be provided;

- the need for a clear statement of crime prevention training needs and an action plan to address those needs; and

- the provision by central government of a community safety impact statement for all new legislation and policy initiatives.

11.29   The Morgan Report's principal recommendations were taken forward, albeit with some important changes, by the Crime and Disorder Act 1998. The Act:

- places a new statutory duty on local authorities and the police, requiring them *together* to co-ordinate and promote local community safety partnerships (the guidance on which requires the police and local authority to produce a joint crime audit, consult and involve a wide range of other agencies, including the voluntary and community sectors, and produce and publish a "community safety strategy");

---

11   *Crime Prevention - The Success of the Partnership Approach*, 11/90.

12   Morgan, *Safer Communities: The Local Delivery of Crime Prevention Through the Partnership Approach, Standing Conference on Crime Prevention* (1991), London: Home Office.

- requires local authorities, in exercising their various functions, to consider the crime and disorder implications and the need to do all that they can do to prevent crime and disorder in their area;

- requires local authorities to establish one or more multi-disciplinary "youth offending teams" to bring together " the experience and skills of relevant local agencies to address the causes of a young person's offending and so reduce the risk of re-offending", and to encourage children and young persons not to commit offences; and

- creates a number of new orders, including the anti-social behaviour order, the curfew order, the child safety order, and the parenting order.

11.30   In addition, as a result of the Comprehensive Spending Review, a "Crime Reduction Programme" was announced by the Government in July 1998, together with the publication of a research review of national and international evidence of "what works" to reduce crime.[13] Under the programme £250 million is to be invested in crime reduction over a three-year period from April 1999, overseen by an inter-departmental committee, and with up to 10% of the budget devoted to the evaluation of initiatives.

11.31   Both the Crime Reduction Programme and the new arrangements under the Crime and Disorder Act 1998 are in their infancy, and it is too early as yet to make a judgement as to their effect. The arrangements for implementing the latter are still being developed, and there is evidence of local authorities adopting a variety of structures to meet the requirements of the Act. No new resources have been made available to enable local authorities or the police to fulfil their new responsibilities under the Act.

SCOTLAND

11.32   The police in Scotland have played, and continue to play, a central role in crime prevention. Recent government initiatives have, as in other countries, sought to develop an awareness that crime cannot be tackled by the police alone, and that responsibility for tackling crime needs to be shared amongst the statutory, voluntary and community sectors.

---

13   Goldblatt and Lewis, *Reducing Offending: An Assessment of Research Evidence on Ways of Dealing with Offending Behaviour* (1998), Home Office Research Study 187, London: Home Office

11.33   In 1992 the Scottish Office launched a new strategy document[14] which led to the creation of the Scottish Crime Prevention Council to carry the strategy forward. Following a review of the Council in March 1999, Ministers agreed to wind up the Council and replace it with a less formal body with an extended membership to reflect the growing prominence of community safety and community planning. A new body, the Scottish Community Safety Forum, will shortly be formed. Its remit will be to advise the First Minister of the Scottish Executive on crime prevention and community safety policy; create wider partnerships in community safety and crime prevention; stimulate innovative approaches to crime reduction and community safety. It will also promote the joint Scottish Executive, Association of Chief Police Officers in Scotland (ACPOS) and the Convention of Scottish Local Authorities (CoSLA) Strategy, which is designed to improve community safety in Scotland through partnership between public, private and voluntary bodies.

11.34   The Community Safety Strategy *Safer Communities Through Partnership*[15] promotes the idea that local authorities and the police should lead local partnerships involving public, private and voluntary bodies to tackle community safety issues at local level. Out of 32 local authorities in Scotland, 29 have community safety partnerships. Guidance in the form of *Safer Communities in Scotland*[16] has been issued to the police, local authorities and other community safety partners and will be enhanced with training for community safety practitioners. The Scottish Executive Crime Prevention Unit and CoSLA will review the partnerships' action planning process to ensure initiatives are being monitored and evaluated to improve the delivery of "safer communities". The Scottish Executive Crime Prevention Unit has a budget of £3m to fund community safety projects. Half will go to projects identified by partnerships as addressing wider community safety issues and the other half will fund CCTV projects.

THE REPUBLIC OF IRELAND

11.35   Crime prevention policy in Ireland is developed by the Department of Justice, Equality and Law Reform in conjunction with the Garda Síochána. Crime prevention was, and still is, one of the core functions of the Garda. Since 1992 and the publication of the report *Urban Crime and Disorder,*[17] there has been a growing consensus, in line with international trends, that crime prevention is delivered most effectively through inter-agency co-ordination at a local level. This, together with the Strategic Management Initiative (SMI),[18] led to a shift in

---

14   *Preventing Crime Together in Scotland: A Strategy for the 90s* (1992), The Scottish Office, Edinburgh: HMSO.

15   *Safer Communities Through Partnerships: A strategy for Action,* (1999), The Scottish Office, Edinburgh: HMSO.

16   *Safer Communities in Scotland,* (1999), Scottish Executive, Edinburgh.

17   Report of the Interdepartmental Working Group (1992) *Urban Crime and Disorder*, Dublin: Stationery Office.

18   The SMI was launched in 1994 with the purpose of improving the service of government departments to the public. The first stage of the initiative was a requirement that departments produce a strategy statement.

government policy. The Department of Justice, Equality and Law Reform published its developing crime prevention policy as part of its strategy document *Community Security – Challenge and Change*.[19] The report emphasised the need for the Department to adapt its management structures in line with international views on how to plan and implement policy on crime.

11.36   The discussion paper *Tackling Crime* followed in 1997.[20] This highlighted the need "to secure community involvement and support for anti-crime measures, so that effective partnerships are forged between the general public and the relevant statutory and voluntary agencies in the fight against crime." The debate stimulated by the 1997 discussion paper led to the formation of the National Crime Forum, which reported in 1998.[21] The report recommended a more coherent and co-ordinated strategy at central government level aimed at reducing poverty and social exclusion. It recommended the creation of a National Crime Council (which was established in July 1999 and which comprises 16 representatives from the judiciary, the Garda Síochána, the Department of Justice, Equality and Law Reform, and a range of statutory, voluntary and community organisations and individuals with an interest in crime and the effects of crime). At local level, the report commended the use of partnership models, citing the 13 local drugs task forces as good examples, and recommended the creation of local crime councils, organised at local government level, to complement the National Council. Both tiers would involve representatives of the relevant statutory agencies, together with a range of voluntary and community groups.

SOUTH AFRICA

11.37   Although not covered by the literature review, we had the opportunity to hear of the arrangements for crime prevention in South Africa in the course of our study visit. The concept of crime prevention was relatively new, but had become an issue of central importance to the government as a direct result of escalating crime levels post-apartheid, and a crisis of confidence in the effectiveness of the formal criminal justice process and the agencies of the criminal justice system. Crime was seen as the single most important issue facing the Government. It was seen to constrain development, undermine the process of reconciliation and undermine public confidence in the Government. It also threatened the building of a human rights culture and compromised the process of transformation to democracy. As a result the Government had initiated the development of a National Crime Prevention Strategy in 1995, driven by an inter-departmental committee consisting of the Ministers for Safety and Security, Justice, Correctional Services and Defence.

---

19   *Community Security - Challenge and Change* (1996), Department of Justice, Dublin: Stationery Office.

20   *Tackling Crime - Discussion Paper* (1997), Department of Justice Dublin: Stationery Office.

21   *Report of the National Crime Forum* (1998), Institute of Public Administration, Dublin: IPA.

11.38 The strategy consisted of four elements, which set the framework for the development of crime prevention programmes at all levels of government (national, regional and local). The four elements were:

(i) reform of the criminal justice system, to reduce delay and improve efficiency and effectiveness;

(ii) environmental design of communities to make it harder for criminals to operate, and to strengthen social networks and cohesiveness;

(iii) changing public values and attitudes to crime, by educating the public as to the costs of crime and the role they can play in preventing crime; and

(iv) measures to combat transnational crime.

11.39 We were briefed on the scale and nature of reforms to the criminal justice system, and on the way in which the three tiers of government were bound into the process. Of particular interest was the development of "Community Safety Forums", which had originated in 1994 as a means of building relations between the new South African Police Service and the community and developing the legitimacy of that service. These were in the process of being transformed into local authority-led institutions, and their remit was being broadened to include community safety and crime prevention at the local level.

Views Expressed during the Consultation Process

11.40 Crime prevention and community safety issues generated a good deal of comment during the consultation process, both in the formal written and oral submissions to the Review, and in the consultative seminars. There was a good deal of agreement across all shades of the political and social spectrum as to how effort on crime prevention and community safety might best be co-ordinated and delivered, and what arrangements were necessary to ensure that the most effective use was made of available funds in reducing crime.

11.41 It was widely recognised that it was not for the police or the formal criminal justice process alone to deal with crime and criminality, and that many of the underlying causes of crime could only be addressed by well co-ordinated social, economic and criminal justice policies. No one dissented from this view. A small minority believed, however, that it was the function of government to deliver community safety, through the co-ordination of policies at the macro level, and that the Government should not seek to foist its responsibilities upon the community. The majority view was that the statutory, voluntary and community sectors, and individuals all had a role in developing and delivering community safety. One viewpoint put forward strongly at a seminar in Omagh was that "the widest involvement possible of the community is desirable in developing policy and services in this area". This was echoed in

Belfast, where the comment was made that "deprivation cannot be tackled by throwing money around. There needs to be empowerment of communities to help them help themselves." However, money, or more explicitly the lack of long-term funding, was identified as a particular problem: communities did not have the resources to devote to community safety activity, and if the Government was serious about empowering communities then it needed to provide the necessary resources. Some also suggested that the balance of government spending was wrong, and that resources should be shifted away from the prosecution and punishment of offences to the prevention of crime.

11.42 Others were mindful of the pervasive paramilitary presence in some communities, and the danger of paramilitary elements being involved in delivering community safety initiatives. They did not dissent from the view that community involvement was important, particularly in respect of dealing with minor crimes, but they counselled that those representing communities in such activity must be truly representative, to avoid influence from paramilitary or organised crime creeping in. One group envisaged "...community co-operation by way of existing state agencies or recognised private sector bodies e.g. Chambers of Commerce, local churches, local government or police liaison committees, etc, in order to protect against possible abuse". Another group noted that there might be limitations to community involvement where issues of specific sensitivity were being dealt with, such as the issue of how sex offenders are dealt with in the community on release from prison.

11.43 The concept of a partnership approach to dealing with community safety and crime prevention received considerable support. Many respondents favoured an inclusive approach in which partnerships were developed amongst the statutory, voluntary and community sectors to address local problems identified in local areas. Some recommended that the structures and institutions which develop and implement a community safety strategy should themselves embody the principles of partnership, in that all sectors of society should be involved in the development of policy at the strategic and local level, as well as in the delivery of services and programmes in the community.

11.44 As to who should be involved in such partnerships, a number of those who commented suggested that, within the statutory sector, the police, probation, education and housing authorities, health and social services, and local councils all had a role to play. There was a wide range of potential partners suggested in the voluntary sector, including Extern, the Northern Ireland Association for the Care and Resettlement of Offenders, Victim Support, Women's Aid, Mediation Network and the National Society for the Prevention of Cruelty to Children, to name but a few. There was also a wide range of community organisations and individuals that could contribute, depending on the nature of the local problems to be addressed. These might include the churches, young people's organisations, local politicians, women's groups, and parent-youth support groups.

11.45 A minority of those who commented recognised that there would be difficulties in involving statutory sector partners, and in particular the police, in some areas where they were mistrusted by the community. This view was expressed by a number of groups and individuals, from both the Nationalist and Loyalist traditions. However, they all acknowledged that under a new political dispensation, when the agencies of the state were under the control of and accountable to local political structures, and in a situation where the police service had been reformed, the difficulties of involving such partners would lessen considerably.

11.46 Most individuals and organisations agreed that effective co-operation and information sharing between statutory agencies was vital, and that mechanisms were necessary within central government to ensure that departments and agencies worked co-operatively to achieve agreed objectives. This was of particular importance in the area of community safety, where the causes of crime and criminality were seen as a complex mix of social and economic deprivation and the breakdown of local communities, demanding complex, multi-faceted, well co-ordinated responses. As a precursor to this, however, it was argued that central government should develop and articulate a clear and overarching strategy for community safety, which set out the roles and responsibilities of the agencies and groups involved. One group suggested that the Community Safety Centre should establish a strategic overview and planning system for the field of crime prevention. Others suggested that responsibility for community safety issues should be brought together under a single governing body, department, or Minister, to ensure co-ordination of policy development and service delivery. One group suggested that there should be a department devoted to youth justice with responsibility for crime prevention. Another counselled against a "corrective or punitive" agency leading the development of community safety strategy. Many also commented that it was difficult for some statutory agencies to participate without a statutory duty to prevent crime in their remit.

11.47 At local level, many pointed out that there was no single body or structure which took responsibility for community safety. However, there was no consensus on what, if any, body should be responsible for leading or facilitating community safety efforts at the local level. Indeed many argued that that it would be counterproductive to have one (or even two) lead bodies for community safety as in England and Wales, because different local areas had different problems, which would require different bodies to come together to create solutions. Some argued, however, that local authorities should take the lead in encouraging the development of community safety initiatives in their areas, since councillors were elected representatives of the community they served. Others suggested that the social partnership model, which had been used successfully to bring together political, business and community interests in disbursing European funding, should be used in each council area. Some suggested that community police liaison committees would serve as a useful forum for discussing community safety issues. Yet others suggested that no fixed model should be adopted, and that arrangements should develop organically and in response to local needs, and that no one agency or organisation should have a predetermined leadership role.

11.48   Many saw funding for community safety initiatives as an important issue. Some believed that funding for community safety should be ring-fenced and not siphoned off into other areas of an agency's work. Others recommended that clear funding mechanisms should be developed to facilitate those coming forward with proposals. All too often it was difficult to secure a funding package to enable projects to proceed, irrespective of the merits of the proposal, and even where funding was secured, it was short-term. Linking funding to monitoring and evaluation was recommended, but those delivering projects would need to have access to specialist advice in relation to monitoring and evaluation techniques.

11.49   A number of issues were identified as being essential targets of any community safety strategy, although it was recognised that not all would be priorities in any given area. These included:

- drug prevention work, where an effective, properly resourced anti-drugs strategy was called for;

- alcohol and substance abuse;

- domestic violence, which was regarded by many as endemic in Northern Ireland;

- youth crime and anti-social behaviour, which was seen as a growing feature of many parts of Northern Ireland;

- fostering community cohesion;

- the availability of mediation services to local communities to assist in resolving neighbourhood disputes; and

- educational work with young people, covering crime issues and civic responsibilities.

Evaluation and Recommendations

11.50   The literature reviews, our visits to other jurisdictions and the consultation process have given us much food for thought. The research report reviewing the literature on community safety initiatives in other jurisdictions in particular has set out a number of issues to be considered in developing arrangements for community safety policymaking and service delivery to suit the needs of Northern Ireland.[22] These take account of the nature of the crime and disorder problems in Northern Ireland, the social and cultural context, and the political and institutional landscape. From looking at what happens elsewhere and bearing in mind local needs, we believe that key priorities for community safety in Northern Ireland should include:

---

22   Crawford and Matassa, Research Report 8.

- a local partnership approach involving all relevant agencies and bodies in the statutory, voluntary, community and private sectors;

- local strategies based on local crime profiles and people's worries and concerns about crime;

- a Northern Ireland-wide community safety strategy to provide drive and leadership;

- allocating responsibility for community safety to a central high-profile part of government;

- empowering and encouraging statutory agencies to participate in community safety activity through the provision of statutory remits;

- community safety featuring in inter-agency and inter-departmental funding and policy initiatives, such as those concerned with urban regeneration (Making Belfast Work is an example of this working in practice);

- the funding of national and local level projects, based on good practice guidelines;

- the centrality of evaluation and research into "what works";

- the monitoring and evaluation of projects to learn lessons; and

- the creation of a database of best practice so that information can be shared.

A COMMUNITY SAFETY STRATEGY FOR NORTHERN IRELAND

11.51   We considered first what the aims of a community safety strategy should be in Northern Ireland. Our consultation process has demonstrated a strong desire for developing community safety through an inclusive partnership approach, in which communities, elected representatives, statutory agencies, and the voluntary and private sectors work together co-operatively to tackle crime. **We recommend that the aim of a community safety strategy in Northern Ireland should be to create the conditions which promote an inclusive partnership-based approach in developing community safety initiatives between relevant agencies, voluntary groups, the private sector and local communities, with a view to reducing crime, the fear of crime and enhancing community safety.** No fully articulated community safety strategy exists in Northern Ireland at present, and **we recommend the development of a Northern Ireland community safety strategy based upon extensive consultation with relevant agencies, political structures, and the voluntary, private and community sectors.**

11.52   We considered whether there were any specific issues of concern in Northern Ireland generally upon which a community safety strategy for Northern Ireland should focus. A number of such issues were raised with us in the course of the consultation process. Others we have observed in the media and in our discussions with key players within the criminal justice system. **We recommend that in developing a community safety strategy for Northern Ireland specific consideration be given to:**

- **offences against women, particularly domestic violence;**

- **child abuse;**

- **interventions in relation to youth offending;**

- **the needs of ethnic minority communities;**

- **drug, substance and alcohol abuse;**

- **street violence, low-level neighbourhood disorder and anti-social behaviour;**

- **car crime; and**

- **reducing criminality (i.e. addressing the factors which lie behind criminal behaviour).**

This should not seek to duplicate or take over the work of partnerships already in place, such as the Domestic Violence Forum and the anti-drugs co-ordinating machinery, but should rather place them in the context of an overarching strategy.

COMMUNITY SAFETY STRUCTURES

11.53   In developing our thinking on community safety structures, we took full account of the approaches adopted in other jurisdictions such as France, New Zealand, the Netherlands and England and Wales. However we were also mindful of specific Northern Ireland considerations. For example we have a small jurisdiction, which allows for short lines of communication but militates against over complex multi-layered structures; and we did not want to make recommendations that would result in an environment overcrowded with overlapping consultative and executive bodies. Nor did we wish to interfere with crime prevention work currently undertaken by the police or the community-based approach of the Probation Service. We also took account of Northern Ireland's vibrant community sector, which was apparent to us during our consultations.

11.54   The recommendations of the Independent Commission on Policing also had to be taken into account. We welcome the Commission's recognition of the need for co-ordination between policing and other agencies and non-governmental organisations for public safety purposes. We considered whether to recommend that the proposed Policing Board might take on lead responsibility for co-ordinating community safety activity and the development of a community safety strategy. We decided against such an approach. The lessons from other jurisdictions and comments made during the consultation process militate against the police or a police focused body (or any other single agency) being in the lead on community safety matters; partnership is the key. Moreover, we believe that in order to ensure that community safety receives proper attention throughout the system, responsibility for its promotion and co-ordination needs to be located centrally within government. However partnership with and involvement of the police and policing bodies will be of critical importance.

11.55　At the local level we considered which agencies and groups should be involved in local community safety partnerships, recognising that their precise composition should be tailored to local needs. We concluded that local partnerships might include representatives from some or all of the following groups:

- statutory agencies, such as police, probation, social services, education and health;

- voluntary agencies and groups;

- local government;

- community groups; and

- the private sector.

11.56　We considered whether the leadership of local partnership structures should be given to any particular organisation, whether leadership should be shared amongst one or more organisations, or whether one organisation should adopt a sponsorship or responsible authority role. We looked at the option of placing lead responsibility for creating and maintaining community safety partnerships in the hands of local authorities, as had been suggested by some in the consultation process. We noted, however, (as did one of the research reports[23]) that their functions related only slightly to the achievement of community safety objectives and that they had no statutory authority to spend money on community safety activities as such. On the positive side they had a local focus, which no other organisation could match, and their members were local people, directly accountable to the local electorate.

11.57　For purposes of delivering, promoting and encouraging community safety at the local level, we strongly endorse the philosophy of partnership between local service providers, the community and the police, as envisaged in the Crime and Disorder Act 1998 and as practised in many jurisdictions which we have looked at. In particular we want to enable the energy that exists at community level to contribute. We note that the Independent Commission on Policing came to similar conclusions and made proposals "for a different style of policing, with the police working... in partnership with the community to solve public safety problems together". The challenge is how to translate this into viable local structures, bearing in mind our concern not to see a proliferation of consultative bodies or complicated inter-agency relationships.

23　Feenan, Research Report 13.

11.58   Our initial thinking on how best to deliver community safety at the local level was that local authorities in Northern Ireland should be encouraged to lead community safety activity in their council area, funding local projects and using whatever partnership and consultative model they saw fit. They would be eligible to receive seed-corn funding from the centre to provide for the employment of development workers or to put towards the funding of local initiatives. This would allow local authorities the flexibility to develop approaches which they judged best met the needs of their local communities. Individual community safety initiatives might, depending on the problem being tackled, be led by statutory or voluntary agencies, or community bodies. **We recommend that there should be no presumption that any particular body should always take the lead in individual community safety projects.**

11.59   The Independent Policing Commission's proposals for District Policing Partnership Boards, and the role the Commission envisaged for such Boards in relation to community safety activity, required us to consider how what we had in mind would mesh, if at all, with their recommendations. In particular we considered whether one local body could fulfil both our community safety remit and the role envisaged by the Policing Commission in relation to policing.

11.60   We also took account of the Secretary of State for Northern Ireland's statement to the House of Commons on 19 January 2000 in respect of the Government's decisions in relation to the report of the Independent Commission on Policing in Northern Ireland, in which he said:

> "Patten proposed the creation of district policing partnership boards to provide an element of local accountability. He envisaged that they should have a primarily consultative role, with an ability to monitor police delivery against an agreed local plan, and I endorse that. He also proposed an additional community safety role, with powers to purchase services on top of normal policing. The latter activity is currently a subject being considered by the criminal justice review. Until decisions are taken on the review, which will be published shortly, I do not intend to extend their function in that way. It will be better, in any case, to concentrate on building up relationships at the local level, in what I propose to call district policing partnerships. I also intend to consider further the arrangements proposed for Belfast, where I am not satisfied that it would be right to have four separate partnerships."[24]

11.61   We believe that there are good reasons for combining the functions of community safety and policing within one local body. To do so would avoid putting too great a burden on local councils (and we were aware of the plethora of existing bodies to which local authorities are expected to contribute) and would enable a single body to consider the community safety and policing needs of local communities. Policing is an important aspect of community safety, but

---

24   Hansard, 19 January 2000, Col 846.

not the only aspect, and community safety can in turn contribute to effective policing. We wish to recommend a broader role for these bodies, which would focus on community safety. **Rather than District Policing Partnerships we recommend that:**

- **Community Safety and Policing Partnerships (CSPPs), chaired by local authority elected members, should be established.**

- **The role and remit of the CSPP should be set out in statute, supplemented by good practice guidelines.**

- **The membership of the CSPP should be as recommended by the Policing Commission for District Policing Partnership Boards, with a majority of elected members, and with independent members selected to represent business and trade union interests and to provide expertise in matters relating to community safety. We suggest that consideration be given to inviting councils to seek nominations through bodies such as Chambers of Commerce, Business in the Community, the Northern Ireland Committee of the Irish Congress of Trade Unions and the Northern Ireland Council for Voluntary Action. The District Partnership Boards, currently in place to administer European funding, provide a useful model.**

- **The CSPP should prepare a local community safety strategy based on local crime profiles, people's worries about crime locally, and the availability of local services.**

- **When carrying out this wider community safety role, the CSPP should consult widely in the community and work in partnership with community, statutory, and voluntary agencies; on the statutory side, the police should be involved along with others such as the Probation Service, the Public Prosecution Service, social services, education, health and the Northern Ireland Housing Executive.**

- **It should be open to the CSPP to invite other relevant agencies to the monthly public meetings envisaged in recommendation 36 of the Policing Commission Report.**

- **The CSPP should submit an annual report of its activities in relation to community safety to the district council or councils to which it relates, and then to the Policing Board and the central Community Safety Unit (which is referred to below) for their information.**

11.62   We endorse the spirit of paragraph 6.29 of the Independent Policing Commission's report. The functions of the CSPPs should be advisory, explanatory and consultative. But they should also be proactive in developing a local community safety strategy and in developing links with the statutory and voluntary agencies with a role to play in delivering community safety. They should foster and develop partnerships within the district, working closely with the central Community Safety Unit, to deliver the services necessary to achieve the aims of the local community safety strategy.

11.63   We envisage a central community safety body concerned with the development of a community safety strategy for Northern Ireland, with the co-ordination and promotion of the concept of community safety throughout the government, voluntary and private sectors, and with encouraging initiatives by providing financial and other resources.

11.64   **We recommend that there should be a central Community Safety Unit responsible for:**

- **developing a community safety strategy for Northern Ireland;**

- **providing a focus for the promotion and co-ordination of community safety throughout government, the voluntary and the private sectors;**

- **developing effective and innovative public consultation mechanisms in developing community safety policy, including the development of mechanisms to engage the Civic Forum;**

- **encouraging initiatives, by funding and evaluating pilot projects, at the local level, and by making crime mapping information available to local partnership bodies;**

- **setting the monitoring and funding requirements for centrally-funded projects;**

- **spreading good practice and mainstreaming successful demonstration projects;**

- **advising Ministers on community safety policy; and**

- **publishing an annual report setting out progress against strategic objectives, funding activity and the contributions of departments and agencies towards community safety objectives.**

11.65   An important role of the central unit will be to ensure that good practice guidelines are made available to those involved in community safety initiatives at the local level. **We recommend that the Community Safety Unit should develop guidance packs, covering such issues as:**

- **advice for developing local schemes;**

- **training manuals;**

- **publicity and "how to consult" guides;**

- **crime audit guides and assistance;**

- **help and guidance in relation to monitoring and evaluation; and**

- **advice on preparing bids for funding.**

11.66   In pursuing its remit we would expect the central unit to develop links with its counterparts in Scotland, England and Wales and the Republic of Ireland and with European and international crime prevention institutions to keep up to date with best practice elsewhere. While much of its focus will be on the development of partnerships to address community safety issues that concern local communities, it should also include in its remit such matters as workplace and corporate security. As in other fields, the unit would not necessarily lead on such matters but, through links with the police and Health and Safety Executive for example, would be in a position to demonstrate that they were being fully addressed. A central community safety unit would also, if necessary, take an interest in the development of policy on the private security industry. In respect of organised crime, we would see it as contributing to the work of wider inter-agency machinery of the type we recommend at Chapter 15.

11.67 The organisation, staffing and location within government of the central unit will be of pivotal importance in developing and delivering a community safety strategy, as we noted from our research and study visits. We believe that there is much to commend the arrangements within central government in France and, in particular, New Zealand. We believe that central government should take a strong lead on community safety issues and spell out that community safety is a central priority in Northern Ireland. The creation of a properly funded and staffed central unit would do much to underline the importance that the Government attaches to community safety in the minds of the public in Northern Ireland.

11.68 Staffing will be an important issue. **We recommend that a central Community Safety Unit be staffed by a team of people who bring a range of knowledge and experience to bear, including knowledge of community safety, wider government social and economic policy, finance, research and evaluation, and training issues. There would be merit in some staff working in the team on a secondment basis, from the police and probation for example, and at least one research officer should be included. It should be headed by someone of sufficient stature to command respect and confidence within and beyond government in Northern Ireland. In addition, given the acknowledged expertise developed within the Community Safety Centre, we recommend that it and its staff be integrated into the team.**

11.69 In considering where the unit should be located within government, we were mindful that responsibility for economic and social matters would be devolved to a Northern Ireland Assembly in advance of criminal justice. One option would be to devolve responsibility for the Community Safety Unit, along with the economic and social portfolios, in recognition of the role to be played by departments and agencies outside the criminal justice system. However, on balance, given the importance of co-ordination with the criminal justice agencies and possible accountability difficulties in relation to reserved matters, **we recommend that, until such time as responsibility for criminal justice issues is devolved to the Northern Ireland Assembly, the Community Safety Unit should be located within the Northern Ireland Office.**

11.70 Once criminal justice issues are devolved the issue arises of whether the Unit should remain within a Northern Ireland department responsible for justice matters. In a number of jurisdictions community safety at the national level is a major responsibility in a high profile part of the machinery of government. We were particularly attracted to the New Zealand model where a Crime Prevention Unit operates within the Department of the Prime Minister and Cabinet, thus helping secure the commitment of all departments. **On devolution, we recommend that the Community Safety Unit be located within the Office of the First Minister and Deputy First Minister. If that proves impracticable then it should be located within a justice department; but steps should be taken through central machinery to ensure that community safety is addressed on a co-ordinated, inter-departmental basis. Committing departments and agencies to contributing to an annual report on community safety would be one way of encouraging such an approach.**

11.71   The partnership model might operate at the central government level. There would be merit in the Community Safety Unit having access to an advisory body that brings together representatives from local partnership bodies together with representatives of the relevant departments and statutory agencies. The role of the body would be to act as a sounding board in relation to the Community Safety Unit's work, as an independent source of advice and expertise to the Unit, and, together with the Unit, to develop funding criteria. **We recommend the creation of a non-statutory and advisory Community Safety Council, which should comprise representatives from local partnership bodies together with representatives of the relevant departments and statutory agencies, and should be supported by the Community Safety Unit.**

11.72   **We also recommend that relevant agencies should have a clear statutory responsibility for helping to prevent crime and reduce the fear of crime and to contribute to community safety. Relevant agencies might include the Probation Service, social services, education and health authorities, and the Public Prosecution Service.**

FUNDING OF COMMUNITY SAFETY ACTIVITY

11.73   We considered whether the Community Safety Unit should have a programme budget to resource and evaluate Northern Ireland-wide demonstration projects and particularly promising local projects, and to spread good practice through the development of a readily accessible central database of project activity. We do not think that the current position, where funding is often short-term and comes from diverse sources, is sufficiently robust to support a coherent community safety strategy. **Based on what we have seen elsewhere, we recommend that the Community Safety Unit should have a budget to fund demonstration projects, to fund projects which are of a scale or geographic extent beyond the capabilities of local partnership arrangements, for the production and dissemination of good practice guides, and to provide seed-corn funding for the administration and implementation of local partnership projects and arrangements. We further recommend that the arrangements for funding new initiatives should include a requirement that a percentage of the funds allocated be devoted to evaluation of the project.**

11.74   The detailed consultation we suggest should include consideration of the number and kinds of projects that should be resourced. We do not make a detailed recommendation as to the size of the budget, but note that £250 million has been allocated to a three year crime reduction programme in England and Wales, which would equate to £7.5 million in Northern Ireland, or a budget of around £2.5 million per annum. Any funding provided by the Unit should be in addition to, not instead of, the funds which statutory agencies already devote to community safety and crime prevention, although it is important that their expenditure is consistent with the overall strategy.

11.75   On funding, recommendation 32 of the Policing Commission - district councils to have the power to contribute an amount initially up to the equivalent of a rate of 3p in the pound towards the improved policing of the district - gave us food for thought. From the examples given by the Commission of projects which might be funded in this way (security cameras, youth club schemes) it is clear to us that community safety activity was what they had in mind. **We make the following recommendations:**

- **That district councils be given the power to contribute an amount initially up to the equivalent of a rate of 3p in the pound, for the purpose of funding community safety initiatives.**

- **The legislation containing the power to raise such funds and authorising expenditure on community safety matters should on its face, or through regulations, contain clear guidelines about the raising of such funds and the use to which they might be put. For example, expenditure should be based on a clearly established analysis of local crime as defined in the local community safety strategy.**

- **CSPPs should be encouraged to seek funds from other sources, including the private sector.**

- **CSPPs should be able to seek a limited amount of funding from the central Community Safety Unit. Such funding might be provided on a matching basis, thus providing the CSPPs with an incentive to seek alternative sources of funds, whether from district council funds, the private sector or elsewhere.**

11.76   Finally, we wish to make several general comments in relation to the funding conditions which the central Community Safety Unit and CSPPs might apply to both Northern Ireland-wide and local projects. **We recommend that the Community Safety Unit should draw up funding guidelines as a matter of priority.** Any or all of the following funding conditions might be applied:

- that there is evidence based on an analysis of local crime of problems to be addressed, in accordance with the local community safety strategy;

- that pilot projects should be rigorously evaluated (on a basis agreed by the Community Safety Unit) and that an element of funding should be set aside for evaluation;

- that all projects should include monitoring by reference to guidelines prepared by the Community Safety Unit;

- that there should be transparency, with the identity of those involved in the project, and the purpose of the project, being made public;

- that community involvement in designing and implementing the project should be an expectation; and

- that there should be clear accountability mechanisms, including financial accountability to local or national structures, and the publication of research findings, evaluation reports, monitoring reports, and annual reports.

Sentences, Prisons and Probation

12 Sentences, Prisons and Probation

Introduction

12.1   In this chapter we examine the arrangements for dealing with adult offenders after their conviction in the courts; and we touch upon the position of those who are remanded in custody before trial. We look at sentencing options available to the courts including the administration of indeterminate sentences, and at some issues surrounding the custodial arrangements for prisoners; and we consider the structural arrangements for ensuring that sentences of the court are carried out, that is the organisation of the Northern Ireland Prison Service and the Probation Board for Northern Ireland. However, we should stress that this chapter does not purport to be a comprehensive review of correctional policy: such an exercise would be an enormous undertaking in its own right.

12.2   In looking at these issues we are conscious of the very great difficulties experienced by the Prison Service and the Probation Board in providing services within a divided society at a time of civil strife. In the circumstances it was inevitable that much of the focus of the Prison Service should have been on the challenge of controlling large numbers of paramilitary prisoners against a backcloth of associated campaigns inside and outside prison. This has had a profound effect not only within prison but also on the lives of prison staff and their families outside. It is to the credit of the staff that the Prison Service was not only sustained throughout the past 30 years but that there has been a positive record of improvement in the delivery of services to prisoners and their families.

12.3   Staff of the Probation Board have worked with individuals and communities in circumstances where tensions and strife have created a most difficult climate in which to operate. Yet they have a reputation for commitment and innovation which has engendered confidence in them and their work from within all sections of the community. With the changing environment in Northern Ireland, both the prison and probation services are entering upon a new period of challenge and opportunity.

Human Rights Background

12.4   When offenders are entrusted by the courts to the prison or probation services, there is inevitably an element of coercion in the process. In such circumstances the protection of human rights assumes particular importance, especially where a custodial sentence is involved. A number of human rights instruments deal with the position of people following conviction and are relevant in relation to issues of prisons, probation and sentence. Among the instruments are non-binding conventions (such as the *Standard Minimum Rules for the Treatment of Prisoners* and the *European Prison Rules*) which deal with prisons issues in considerable detail. The purpose of this section is not to rehearse all the instruments which impact on prisons, probation and sentence, but instead to draw attention to those instruments whose provisions are particularly relevant for the evaluation and recommendations that follow.

12.5   A number of conventions deal directly or indirectly with the impact of prison sentences and the regime inside prison. The starting point is that the *European Convention on Human Rights* requires that "no one shall be subjected to torture or to inhuman or degrading treatment or punishment" (Article 3) and the *International Covenant on Civil and Political Rights* requires that "all persons deprived of their liberty shall be treated with humanity and with respect for the inherent dignity of the human person" (Article 10(1)). In general prisoners retain their rights while in prison except those which they explicitly forfeit by virtue of the fact that they are serving a custodial sentence. As set out in *European Prison Rules,*[1] "imprisonment is by the deprivation of liberty a punishment in itself. The conditions of imprisonment and prison regimes shall not, therefore, except as incidental to justifiable segregation or the maintenance of discipline, aggravate the suffering inherent in this" (Rule 64). Instruments such as the *European Prison Rules* not only require prison regimes to be organised to ensure that conditions are compatible with human dignity and so as to minimise the detrimental effect of imprisonment, but set standards to be met, for example in relation to such detailed matters as heating, lighting, ventilation and hygiene.

12.6   The separation of certain classes of prisoners within prisons is dealt with by the various instruments. There is variation, however, in the descriptions of the separation required. The separation of children from adults is dealt with in the *International Covenant on Civil and Political Rights* which says, "accused juvenile persons shall be separated from adults" and "juvenile offenders shall be segregated from adults" (Article 10). However, the *Convention on the Rights of the Child* says, "every child deprived of his liberty shall be separated from adults unless it is considered to be in the child's best interests not to do so" (Article 37). The separation of remand prisoners from sentenced prisoners is dealt with in the *International Covenant on Civil and Political Rights* which says, "accused persons shall, save in exceptional circumstances, be segregated from convicted persons and shall be subject to

---

1   *The European Prison Rules* (1987), Council of Europe.

separate treatment appropriate to their status as unconvicted persons" (Article 10). The separation of male and female prisoners is dealt with in the *European Prison Rules* which say, "males and females shall in principle be detained separately, although they may participate together in organised activities as part of an established treatment programme" (Rule 2).

12.7 Internal prison disciplinary arrangements are also covered by human rights instruments. The requirements of due process (*European Convention on Human Rights*, Article 6) apply to any determination of civil rights and obligations and criminal charges against prisoners, although the extent to which prison disciplinary proceedings are subject to Article 6 safeguards would appear to depend on whether they meet certain criteria set out in the European Court of Human Rights' judgment in the case of *Engel*.[2] As for punishment, the *Standard Minimum Rules for the Treatment of Prisoners* require that "discipline and order should be maintained with no more restriction than is necessary for safe custody and well-ordered community life" (Rule 27); that prisoners are not punished twice for the same offence; and that corporal punishment, punishment by placing in a dark cell, and all cruel, inhuman or degrading treatment should be prohibited (Rule 31).

12.8 Under the *European Convention on Human Rights* persons deprived of their liberty are entitled to have the lawfulness of their detention decided by a court (Article 5(4)). European case law suggests that in certain circumstances prisoners who are serving indeterminate sentences should be able to test their continued detention and that decisions should be taken by a judicial body.[3]

12.9 The overarching requirement of Article 3 of the *European Convention on Human Rights* ("No one shall be subjected to torture or to inhuman or degrading treatment or punishment"), applies to non-custodial disposals as much as to imprisonment. More detailed guidance is contained in the *United Nations Standard Minimum Rules for Non-custodial Measures* (The Tokyo Rules). Among its principles are: the protection of the offender's dignity (Rule 3.9); the protection of the offender's rights against unauthorised restrictions (Rule 3.10); and respect for the privacy of the offender and the offender's family (Rule 3.11). As for the non-custodial measures themselves, they should be "used in accordance with the principle of minimum interventions" (Rule 2.6) and "should be part of the movement towards depenalisation and decriminalisation instead of interfering with or delaying efforts in that direction" (Rule 2.7).

2   *Engel and Others v Netherlands,* 8 June 1976, Series A, No 22 1 EHRR 647.

3   For example *Thynne, Gunnell and Wilson v United Kingdom* 25 October 1990, Series A No 190, 13 EHRR 666.

Current Arrangements – Sentences

12.10   The main options available to the courts following conviction of adult offenders (that is those aged 17 or older) and the numbers sentenced by the courts in 1997 are set out in the table.

Sentencing of Adult Offenders by the Courts in Northern Ireland in 1997	
Court Disposal	Numbers Sentenced
Immediate Custody	
Prison	1464
YOC	508
Training School Order	5
Total Immediate Custody	**1977**
Suspended Custody	
Prison (Suspended)	1,726
YOC (suspended)	496
Total Suspended Custody	**2,222**
Supervision in the Community	
Attendance Centre Order	4
Community Service Order	576
Probation Order	898
Total Supervision in the Community	**1,478**
Fine	**21,274**
Conditional Discharge	**1392**
Other	
Recognizance	1,235
Absolute Discharge	420
Disqualified	2
Other	9
Total Other	**1,666**
TOTAL	**30,009**

Notes: 1. Custody probation orders were not available to sentencers in 1997.
2. Sentencing data is based on the most severe penalty imposed by the court for the principal offence.
3. Training school orders and attendance centre orders are juvenile disposals. Adults given these disposals would have been juveniles when proceedings commenced.

Receptions to prisons and the young offenders centre by sentence length are set out in the table.

Receptions to Prisons and the Young Offenders Centre April 1998 to March 1999	
Imprisonment	**Receptions**
Fine default	1950
Up to 3 months	242
3 to 6 months	297
6 to 12 months	309
12 months to 2 years	198
2 to 5 years	196
Over 10 years	18
Life and Secretary of State's pleasure	24

Note: Fine defaulters will normally serve a small number of days in prison.

Judges and magistrates have the option of deferring sentence by up to six months to enable them to have regard to conduct after conviction and to any change in circumstances.

12.11   A probation order may be made for between six months and three years. It may be freestanding, requiring the offender to report to the probation officer on a regular basis; or the court can attach conditions, for example participation in programmes designed to address offending behaviour. A community service order may be imposed, requiring the offender to undertake supervised work in the community for 40-120 hours if the offender is 16 and 40-240 hours for 17 year olds and over. The combination order is a relatively new sentence, introduced by the Criminal Justice (Northern Ireland) Order 1996 and enables the court to combine a probation order with a community service order. The Probation Service also produces pre-sentence reports on offenders, to assist the court in the sentencing process.

12.12   So far as custodial sentences are concerned, the key issue we considered was release mechanisms. We describe here the arrangements for prisoners with fixed, determinate sentences and go on to look at the position in relation to indeterminate sentences.

FIXED SENTENCES

12.13   There is no parole board in Northern Ireland to consider the release of fixed (determinate) sentence prisoners. Instead all such prisoners serve the period determined by the court, less remission. In practical terms prisoners will be released having served half the sentence as pronounced unless they have lost remission as a result of disciplinary infractions while in prison. Release is unconditional, although prisoners who are convicted of further offences while on remission may, and in some cases must, be required to serve the unexpired portion of their previous sentence before serving their subsequent sentence. (There are slightly different arrangements for scheduled offenders serving five or more years for offences after

March 1989.[4] They are automatically released but are on licence until the two-thirds point of their sentence.) Determinate sentence prisoners are not subject to statutory supervision on release, except as described in the following paragraph. These arrangements contrast with England and Wales where, for prisoners with sentences of over four years, there is discretion to release between the half and two-thirds point of the sentence; and once released, there is a period spent under supervision by the Probation Service in the community, during which time the offender may be required to meet certain conditions and is at risk of recall. For sentences of under four years release takes place once half the sentence is served, as in Northern Ireland.

12.14   There are two other types of sentence which should be mentioned. Under the Criminal Justice (Northern Ireland) Order 1996 judges may sentence offenders who consent to community supervision to a mixed custodial/probation sentence, a custody probation order. This would normally be instead of a longer custodial sentence. The custodial element of the sentence is treated in the same way as other determinate sentences, that is to say prisoners will benefit from remission in the normal way. The probation element is subject to conditions set at the point of sentence. There is also provision under the 1996 Order allowing the court to provide for the supervision under licence of persons convicted and imprisoned for sexual offences. The licensed supervision begins at the point of release and lasts until the end of the sentence period.

INDETERMINATE SENTENCES

12.15   Indeterminate (or life) sentences are where there is no fixed date for release from prison. Release from these sentences, should it happen, is currently a decision of the executive rather than the courts.

12.16   An indeterminate sentence is mandatory where an offender is found guilty of murder but may be given (and therefore is discretionary) for other serious offences, for example attempted murder or rape. A person convicted of a very serious offence while under the age of 18 may be sentenced to a period of detention at the pleasure of the Secretary of State and must be so sentenced if the offence is murder. Although there is no fixed date for release, in practice most offenders will be released at some point from their indeterminate sentences, although they remain on licence and are subject to recall to prison if they are a risk to the public.

12.17   In Northern Ireland the mechanisms for considering the release of all indeterminate sentence offenders, including those held at the pleasure of the Secretary of State, are broadly the same.

---

4   Scheduled offenders are those convicted in Diplock courts of offences scheduled in the Northern Ireland (Emergency Provisions) Act 1996.

Release on life licence is the responsibility of the Secretary of State who is advised by the Life Sentence Review Board. In cases of murder the Secretary of State must also consult the Lord Chief Justice and trial judge if available before deciding on release.

12.18   The Life Sentence Review Board comprises senior officials of the Northern Ireland Office and the Prison Service and has available to it the advice of probation, psychiatry and psychology professionals. The Board reviews cases on a regular basis and will either recommend release or will set a date for further review. The Board may also make recommendations about case management. Although decisions to release are taken by Ministers, in practice the Board has a major role in that it decides, albeit within policy set by Ministers, when cases should be reviewed and more importantly, when they should be referred for ministerial decision.

12.19   In Northern Ireland, unlike England and Wales, there is no separate tariff for retribution and deterrence after which risk of re-offending becomes the major factor in determining whether or not the individual should be released. Instead issues of retribution, deterrence, risk of re-offending and the public interest are matters which are relevant, albeit to varying degrees, at all points of sentence. One implication of this is that there is a standard timetable for the consideration of cases. Thus, unless there are significant aggravating circumstances, an adult murderer will have his or her case considered by the Board for the first time no later than the 10 year point in sentence. Pleasure cases will be considered no later than the eight year point.

12.20   In Northern Ireland there is a system of phased release from life and pleasure sentences. Offenders will spend a period of three months during which they attend work from prison during the week and have home leave at weekends. They then spend a period of six months in the community reporting fortnightly to prison before they receive their licence. Following release, non-scheduled licensees are supervised in the community by probation; scheduled licensees are normally not supervised.

NORTHERN IRELAND (SENTENCES) ACT 1998

12.21   As a consequence of the Belfast Agreement, a statutory scheme has been put in place for the accelerated release of scheduled offenders, provided that they are not affiliated to an organisation that is not maintaining a ceasefire. It is not for us to address the workings of this scheme that derives from the Belfast Agreement. However, it is of interest to note that the Sentence Review Commissioners, appointed by the Secretary of State to take decisions under the scheme, are independent and include people with a background in criminal justice and penal matters. Panels of Commissioners considering life sentence cases must include at least one person with expertise in psychiatry or psychology. The rules under which the Commissioners operate are very similar to those of the Parole Board in England and Wales. However, the Northern Ireland Sentence Review Commissioners do not include a judicial element.

Current Arrangements –
The Prison and Probation Services

NORTHERN IRELAND PRISON SERVICE

12.22   The Northern Ireland Prison Service is a separate prison service within the United Kingdom. Its main statutory duties are set out in the Prison Act (Northern Ireland) 1953 (and prison rules made under that Act) and in the Treatment of Offenders Act (Northern Ireland) 1983. The Secretary of State is accountable to Parliament for its operation.

12.23   Since April 1995 the Prison Service has been a next steps agency within the Northern Ireland Office. This means that Ministers set the policy framework within which the agency operates, allocate resources and approve its corporate and business plans. Ministers may also issue directions on matters of concern. The Director General is responsible for the day to day management of the Prison Service, except for those areas that the Minister does not delegate to him in relation to the freedom of certain offenders (for example the permanent release of life sentence prisoners). The Director General is also the Minister's principal adviser on policy matters relating to prisons.

12.24   The mission, aims and objectives of the Northern Ireland Prison Service were set out in the strategy document *Serving the Community*, published in 1991.[5] It defined the aim of the Northern Ireland Prison Service as being "to hold in secure and humane confinement persons who have been given in to custody by the courts and to reduce the risk of re-offending by encouraging them to take full advantage of the opportunities offered during their confinement". Within that aim its specific objectives are to keep prisoners in custody and to produce them at court or release them as required; to provide prisoners with all the necessities of life, including the opportunity to engage in constructive activity; to enable prisoners to retain family ties and to assist sentenced prisoners in their preparation for release; to treat prisoners as individuals regardless of beliefs and political opinions and to allow them the opportunity to serve their sentences free of paramilitary influence; and to manage resources efficiently and effectively and to enhance the morale and abilities of staff.

12.25   The Northern Ireland Prison Service has four custodial institutions: HM Prisons Maghaberry, Magilligan and Maze and HM Young Offenders Centre, Hydebank. Magilligan and Maze house exclusively adult males. Maghaberry is primarily an adult male prison. However, there is within its walls separate purpose built accommodation, Mourne House, which houses all Northern Ireland's female prisoners including remands, convicted prisoners and young female offenders. The prison population and staffing levels in 1998-99 were as follows:

---

5   *Serving the Community: the Northern Ireland Prison Service in the 1990's* (1991), Northern Ireland Prison Service.

Establishment	Staff in Post	Average Prison Population 1998-99	
		Male	Female
Magilligan	452	340	-
Maghaberry	860	477	25
Maze	909.5	387	-
Young Offenders Centre	289	173	-
Court Escort Group	98	-	-
Prison Service Headquarters	255.5	-	-
Prison Service College	52.5	-	-
Total	2955.5	1377	25

12.26   The management of individual prisons is the responsibility of the governor. Under Northern Ireland prison rules, the governor is "in command of the prison" and "responsible for prisoners' treatment according to the law".[6] However the governor must operate within prison rules and standing orders and the overall policies set by Prison Service headquarters. Services within prisons are provided by Prison Service staff and other specialists including chaplains, medical practitioners, nurses, probation officers and psychologists.

12.27   Each adult prison has a Board of Visitors; each young offenders centre a Visiting Committee. These bodies, comprising members of the public, are required to satisfy themselves as to the treatment of prisoners including their health and welfare, the facilities available, and the cleanliness and adequacy of prison premises.[7]

12.28   Arrangements for prison discipline and control are set out in prison rules that give governors powers both before and after adjudication.[8] Following adjudication by a governor, a number of punishments are available. The most severe of these is loss of remission of up to 28 days. More serious offences can be referred to the Secretary of State (in effect Prison Service headquarters) who can delegate his powers to the Boards of Visitors (or Visiting Committees). More severe sanctions are available to a Board: it can, for example, impose a loss of remission of up to 90 days.

12.29   Criminal offences in prison are investigated by the police. A protocol is being developed between the police, DPP and Prison Service defining offences that fall outside the system of prison disciplinary arrangements, and are therefore subject to police investigation.

12.30   We note that in 1997 there was a series of incidents in the Maze prison culminating in the murder of the loyalist prisoner, Billy Wright. These were investigated by a team led by Mr Martin Narey, from the Home Office. Subsequently Maze was subject to an inspection by Sir

---

6   *The Prison and Young Offenders Centre Rules (Northern Ireland) 1995,* Rule 116.

7   *The Prison and Young Offenders Centre Rules (Northern Ireland) 1995,* Rule 124.

8   *The Prison and Young Offenders Centre Rules (Northern Ireland) 1995,* Rules 31-50.

David Ramsbotham, Her Majesty's Chief Inspector of Prisons. Both reports focused on the management of paramilitary prisoners and we do not consider it necessary to go into these matters further for purposes of this review.

12.31   We should emphasise that the Prison Service is in the throes of major change. As a result of releases already made the number of prisoners eligible for release under the accelerated release arrangements flowing from the Belfast Agreement has rapidly diminished. All but a handful should be released by the end of July 2000, the second anniversary of the enabling legislation coming into effect. This has big implications for the focus and ethos of the Service; for its size, with staff numbers expected to reduce by about 1100; and for its estate, with the Maze prison expected to close around July 2000. The Service's forecast budget for 1999/2000 is £160.7 million of which £20 million represents the costs of the staff reduction programme.

PROBATION BOARD FOR NORTHERN IRELAND

12.32   Until 1982 the Probation Service was an integral part of the Northern Ireland Office, having previously been part of the Ministry of Home Affairs. In 1979 the Black Report noted:

> "The service (probation) is currently administered directly by the Northern Ireland Office and from an administrative point of view this may well be satisfactory. However, if the service is to enjoy fully the confidence of the community, which will be essential if it is to carry out its work successfully, we consider that this can be best achieved if the community participates directly in the management of the service. We recommend therefore that the probation service be administered by a Board drawn from a wide spectrum of the community in Northern Ireland." [9]

There was a desire to ensure community involvement in the development of policy as well as to distance the Probation Service from central government (and from what was perceived to be the security-oriented Northern Ireland Office). Following on from this the Probation Board was established.

12.33   The Probation Board for Northern Ireland is a non-departmental public body established under the Probation Board (Northern Ireland) Order 1982. It is appointed by and is accountable to the Secretary of State. The 1982 Order gives the Probation Board both mandatory and discretionary functions. Its mandatory functions are to provide an adequate and efficient probation service (this includes supervision in the community of offenders who are the subject of a probation or community service order and the provision of pre-sentence reports on offenders to assist the courts in determining the most suitable method of dealing with them); to make arrangements for offenders to perform work under community service

---

9   *Report of the Children and Young Persons Review Group - Legislation and Services for Children and Young Persons in Northern Ireland* (1979).

orders; to undertake such social welfare duties in prisons as the Secretary of State considers necessary; and to take on such other duties as may be prescribed. The Board's discretionary functions, which it may undertake with the Secretary of State's approval, are to provide probation hostels, bail hostels and other establishments for use in connection with the supervision and assistance of offenders; and to operate schemes for the supervision and assistance of offenders and the prevention of crime.

12.34   In practice the Board sees its main activities as: providing reports to the courts to help inform the sentencing process; supervising offenders subject to community orders; providing welfare services to prisoners and their families; and assisting prisoners with resettlement after release. It has carried out non-statutory supervision of some offenders on a voluntary basis, but this work has had to be curtailed to make way for an increasing statutory workload at a time of financial stringency. The Probation Board also funds services provided by the voluntary sector and community initiatives aimed at supporting the statutory supervision of offenders in the community and the prevention of offending. In 1998/99 it spent almost £1.9 million on grants to voluntary bodies, nearly half of which was on accommodation services and employment services.

12.35   As a non-departmental public body, the Probation Board operates at arm's length from government. However, it is accountable to the Secretary of State through the Northern Ireland Office which, on a basis approved by Ministers, sets out the policy framework within which the Board is expected to work; provides an annual strategic steer; provides the Board with its financial resources; and ensures that the Board operates within the set policy and resources framework. The Government's three primary aims for probation work are:

(i)   to protect the public by helping reduce crime through the prevention of re-offending by supervising offenders effectively;

(ii)   to provide high quality information, assessment and related services to the courts; and

(iii)   to provide value for money whilst maintaining fairness and high standards of service delivery.

12.36   The development of probation policy is the responsibility of the Northern Ireland Office. It is advised on probation matters by the criminal justice unit of the Social Services Inspectorate which also, as the name suggests, is responsible for the inspection of probation work.

12.37   The Probation Board consists of a Chairman, a Deputy Chairman and no less than 10 nor more than 18 other members. The Chairman is paid a salary, based on one day's work a week, whilst the other members, who attend monthly Board meetings and sit on various sub-committees, receive an attendance allowance plus expenses.

12.38   During the year 1998/99 the Probation Board employed 287 people, of whom 196 were in probation grades. Its statutory case load, as at March 1999, was as follows:

Probation Orders	1925
Community Service Orders	767
Custody Probation Orders	263
Combination Orders	143
Juvenile Justice Centre Orders	18
Total	**3116**

In addition there were a number of clients being supervised on a voluntary basis. In 1998/99 the Probation Service received 7239 requests for pre-sentence reports from the courts. Its total budget for 1999/2000 is £11,875,000, which includes £11,578,000 received from the Northern Ireland Office.

12.39 The Probation Service operates out of 37 offices, 10 of which are in Belfast, four in prisons, and the remainder in the main urban centres of Northern Ireland.

Views Expressed during the Consultation Process

12.40 During our consultation seminars there was some discussion of issues relating to sentences, prisons and probation. They tended to be considered alongside issues to do with crime prevention and the treatment of victims.

12.41 A number of themes emerged. There was recognition that certain offenders, particularly serious ones, required punishment, for purposes of retribution, deterrence and protecting the public. But there was also a strong emphasis on the need for rehabilitation and the need for systems to focus on the individual needs of offenders. Offenders should be encouraged to change their behaviour, for example through programmes designed to address offending behaviour (although there was no consensus whether these should be compulsory or otherwise). Although post-release supervision of prisoners on its own had advocates, others felt that offenders upon release form prison required support in the community that should amount to more than supervision. Accommodation difficulties, especially for people released from prison, were mentioned.

12.42 A number of those not familiar with the criminal justice system were surprised to learn that there was no parole board operating in Northern Ireland. There was speculation that the introduction of a parole system might provide a useful incentive to offenders and encourage them to make better use of their time in and out of prison.

12.43   Mixed views were expressed about sex offenders. There were concerns that the system was not dealing adequately with the risk that they posed. On the other hand there was a view that the pendulum had swung too far against them to the extent that their human rights were being threatened.

12.44   A number of important themes emerged in written and oral submissions. Many of those who wrote or spoke to us advocated closer working relationships between the authorities working with offenders. For example, there needed to be closer co-ordination of effort on the development of programmes, evaluation and setting targets, and better arrangements for joint working (including arrangements to ensure continuity between prisons and the community). An important aspect of better co-ordination would be in relation to the development of accredited offending behaviour programmes for delivery in prison and in the community. As to the possible amalgamation of the Prison and Probation Services, those who addressed the issue did not favour this option.

12.45   There was disquiet about the mechanisms for release from indeterminate sentences. The current system was regarded as lacking transparency and openness. Various models for a new system were suggested: for example, the Parole Board for England and Wales and the Northern Ireland Sentence Review Commissioners.

12.46   There were mixed views on whether there should be an element of discretionary release for determinate sentence prisoners. Some felt that the combination of a parole board and discretionary release would give offenders the incentive to make better use of their time in prison. On the other hand it was also suggested that the period of time to be served in prison should be set by the court at the time of sentence and that the management of prisoners might become more difficult if there were uncertainties about the timing of release.

12.47   We also take account of issues raised by the Northern Ireland Affairs Committee. In 1998 the Northern Ireland Affairs Committee conducted an inquiry into the efficiency and effectiveness of the Northern Ireland Prison Service.[10] It examined management issues, including those arising out of agency status, but also looked at the effects of the Belfast Agreement, including the effects of early releases and reduction in size of the Prison Service. The Committee's recommendations have been broadly endorsed by the Government. Some of the issues were examined further by us. These included the holding of juvenile females in Mourne House and the adjudication function of Boards of Visitors. The Committee also suggested that the Secretary of State for Northern Ireland should consider "how best to improve links between the Northern Ireland Prison Service and the Northern Ireland Probation Service", perhaps as part of our review.[11]

---

10   Northern Ireland Affairs Committee: *Fourth Report: Prison Service in Northern Ireland*, House of Commons, 1998.

11   *op cit* paragraph 71.

Research and International Experience

12.48   We commissioned research on the roles and functions of prisons and probation, including the international experience. The resulting research report[12] gives a description of the structures in Northern Ireland and, for comparative purposes, descriptions of the systems operating elsewhere in the British Isles and in some Commonwealth and western European jurisdictions. The report also looks at offending behaviour programmes and the implications, including for structures, of their further development.

12.49   During our visits to other jurisdictions we looked at prisons and probation issues. We spoke to staff working in the correctional field in Canada (at both federal and provincial level), Germany, the Netherlands, New Zealand and South Africa. Among the issues we addressed were: structural arrangements; inspections and complaints procedures; parole and conditional release; the arrangements for programmes to address offending behaviour; and the problems of dealing with small populations of female offenders. While we were in Alberta we had the privilege of visiting two provincial prisons (as well as a juvenile institution) where we were able to speak directly to practitioners and inmates, and to see at first hand mixed facilities for males and females.

12.50   We have drawn on the lessons learned in these jurisdictions in the evaluation that follows. We would like to draw particular attention to the work done by the Correctional Service of Canada in the development of programmes to address offending behaviour. It has developed cognitive-based offending behaviour programmes and, against a background of rigorous research, assessment and evaluation, has been expanding their use in custodial and community settings.

Evaluation and Recommendations

SENTENCES AND THE TREATMENT OF OFFENDERS

Sentencing Options

12.51   We received few representations concerning the adequacy or otherwise of the sentencing options available to the courts in respect of adult offenders. The adequacy of sentencing powers is not a matter that we have examined in any depth and accordingly we do not wish to make recommendations in this area, save in one respect.

---

12   Blair, Research Report 5.

12.52   We have focused on restorative justice in the context of juveniles (see Chapter 9 above) but believe that it can also be applicable in suitable cases involving adults, especially young adults. A comprehensive court-based scheme for adults, involving conferencing and court orders based on conference outcomes, is unlikely to be viable in the short term. However, the option of a restorative intervention should be available, especially as confidence in restorative justice increases, as we believe it will once it becomes embedded in the juvenile justice system. Accordingly, **we recommend that the current sentencing framework for adults be reviewed to establish whether it could adequately accommodate restorative interventions where appropriate and, if not, to consider what changes might be made in order for it to do so.** One area of examination would be the possible use of deferred sentences in a way that enabled restorative options to be tried before final sentence.

CUSTODIAL SENTENCES AND RELEASE FROM CUSTODIAL SENTENCES

12.53   During consultation a number of concerns were expressed about the nature of custodial sentences available in Northern Ireland. We considered a number of possible changes in relation to both determinate and indeterminate sentences.

Determinate Sentences

12.54   We considered whether there should be a parole board for Northern Ireland, together with an element of discretionary release for certain categories of prisoner, and whether there was a case for introducing mandatory supervision in the community after release.

12.55   Although the evidence is limited, recent research would suggest that a period of parole in the community has a positive impact on reducing re-offending. We note, however, that the reasons behind this "parole effect" are not entirely clear, in particular, whether it is a result of the licence itself, supervision, treatment (through programmes delivered in the community) or deterrence, or some combination of all these factors. If the effect is primarily a result of treatment, we note that there is already a mixed custodial/probation sentence available in Northern Ireland under the Criminal Justice (Northern Ireland) Order 1996, the use of which is increasing (233 custody probation orders were made in 1998/99 and 263 clients were under supervision in March 1999). We are also aware that the introduction of discretionary release would require not only setting up a parole board, which has never operated in Northern Ireland, but also new mechanisms to collect the information necessary to feed into its decision making. The argument has been put to us that with determinate sentences there are benefits to be had from there being a clear, fixed release date to work towards. These benefits are from the perspective of the prisoner, the prison authorities and, sometimes, the victim. On balance we do not think that a sufficiently strong case has been made for the introduction of discretionary release for determinate sentence prisoners.

12.56   However, although research is not conclusive, we considered the separate question of whether there should be a period under supervision in the community following release. This is the norm for non-scheduled life sentence prisoners and it may be that supervision, and the active support from probation staff that goes with it, would benefit particularly those prisoners who have served longer sentences. We do not think that a sufficient case has been made to warrant introducing statutory supervision of all prisoners released after serving sentences of, perhaps, two years or more. However, we can see that certain types of prisoner might benefit from voluntary supervision or support on release, as has been the position in the past. **We recommend that it should be a recognised function of the Probation Service to provide aftercare and support, including supervision, to discharged prisoners and that the service should be adequately resourced to this end. Our expectation is that the Prison and Probation Services should work together to prepare release packages for prisoners. These arrangements should be evaluated with a view to considering whether compulsory supervision should be introduced.**

12.57   During consultation a number of people expressed concern at the public's confusion about sentencing and the bewildering disparity between the sentence as pronounced in court and the period of time a person actually serves in prison. There have been a number of cases where offenders found guilty of serious offences have, to the consternation of the public, been released shortly after conviction.

12.58   Part of the reason for the confusion is the fact that, quite properly, time spent in prison awaiting trial will count towards the period of imprisonment, a fact that is not always taken fully into account in press reports. But the other reason for confusion is that, as noted above, in most instances under Northern Ireland's remission arrangements an offender will serve only half the sentence as pronounced.

12.59   We considered whether to suggest changes in the level of remission. Some remission is clearly necessary: the main sanction in relation to offences in prison is the capacity to reduce the period of remission. However it is not clear that 50% remission is necessary for this purpose: other prison systems manage with less. On the other hand Northern Ireland's remission rate has been in operation for a long period of time and is well understood by those involved in the system. Any reduction in the remission rate might lead to an increase in prisoner numbers (judges do not take account of remission rates when sentencing) but it is not obvious that it would have a commensurate impact on levels of offending or that it would simplify matters. We concluded therefore that there was not a sufficient case to suggest a change in remission rates.

12.60   However, the degree of public confusion remains an issue and it can have a particular impact on victims. We consider that this can be better dealt with by means of greater transparency at the point of sentencing. **We recommend that judges when sentencing should explain in greater detail and in simple language the impact of the sentence, including the fact that, with remission, the offender may be eligible for release having served half the**

sentence and that time spent in prison awaiting trial may count towards the period served. In this context we note that in England and Wales there is already a practice direction in which Lord Chief Justice Bingham enjoined sentencers to give "clear and accurate" explanations of this kind.[13]

Indeterminate Sentences

12.61   Throughout the consultation period there were criticisms of the arrangements for the release of life sentence prisoners. The present system was thought to lack openness and transparency and there were concerns that it was subject to undue political involvement. The Life Sentence Review Board mechanism was compared unfavourably with the much more open system for certain prisoners that had been set up under the Northern Ireland (Sentences) Act 1998.

12.62   We consider that the present arrangements are unsatisfactory for a number of reasons:

- the Life Sentence Review Board arrangements apply equally to mandatory, discretionary and pleasure cases. This is despite European case law which suggests that there are aspects of discretionary and pleasure cases which require to be considered by a body with judicial input.

- the involvement of politicians in the decision making process leads to a perception that political considerations may affect decisions;

- the system does not sit easily with our desire to achieve transparency in the criminal justice system;

- the rights of individuals are better protected when courts decide on retribution rather than politicians or civil servants acting on their behalf;

- issues of retribution and deterrence are difficult for the Life Sentence Review Board to determine in non-Diplock cases. In Diplock cases, the Board has access to the detailed reasoning of the court and its findings of fact and will take these into account when making its decisions. These are not available where there has been a jury trial and it is often difficult to know what evidence has been accepted by the court in reaching its verdict;

- although it is possible to make good guesses about the period of time that life prisoners are likely to serve in prison, there can be no certainty. It is therefore difficult to manage the sentence and prepare for possible release without creating expectations that might not be met.

12.63   There is already a model in Northern Ireland for a different system. The Sentence Review Commissioners set up under the 1998 Sentences Act operate a system which is independent of Ministers and which is more open in its procedures, including allowing prisoners to make representations in person.

---

13   Custodial Sentences: Explanations 1998 1 WLR 278.

12.64 **We recommend that the current Life Sentence Review Board be replaced by an independent body that is not part of the Northern Ireland Prison Service or the proposed Department of Justice. Its membership should include individuals with an expertise in psychiatry or psychology and it should have a judicial input that would enable it to act as a tribunal for dealing with discretionary and Secretary of State's pleasure cases. Its membership might also include individuals with expertise in criminology.**

12.65 **In relation to all indeterminate sentence cases, including mandatory life sentence cases, we recommend that judges when sentencing should be required to set a period for retribution and deterrence (equivalent to the tariff set in England and Wales). In most cases the period would be a fixed term of years, although it must be envisaged that some offences might be so serious that a whole life period would be appropriate. The period would be announced in open court and would be appealable. Once this period had been served, it would be the responsibility of the independent body to determine, primarily on grounds of risk, when the prisoner should be released.** Based on the experience of the Sentence Review Commissioners, an independent body would cost about £354,000 per annum. It could in due course take over the remaining functions of the Sentence Review Commissioners.

PRISON REGIME ISSUES

12.66 During consultation our attention was drawn to a number of aspects of the prison regime where there were perceived to be issues affecting public confidence. These were matters concerning prison adjudication and the arrangements for female offenders.

Adjudication

12.67 Currently offences against prison discipline are dealt with either by prison governors or by a panel drawn from the prison's Board of Visitors (or young offenders centre Visiting Committee). Governors carry out the vast majority of adjudications. However, Boards of Visitors have more severe penalties available to them (they may award a loss of up to 90 days remission for each offence compared to prison governors whose maximum award is 28 days) and Boards will be used to adjudicate in more serious offences where it is felt that the sanctions available to governors are inadequate.

12.68 There are a number of concerns about the current system. First, there is the role of the Boards of Visitors. Given the infrequency with which they are called upon to adjudicate, there have been questions raised about the quality of the process. More pertinently a number of people, including members of Boards of Visitors, have argued that the adjudication function sits uneasily with the other aspects of the Boards' role that are to do with monitoring the treatment of prisoners, their facilities and the adequacy of prison premises.[14] The argument in favour of Boards of Visitors is that they constitute an independent tribunal (see the findings in *Campbell and Fell v United Kingdom*[15]). That may be necessary to satisfy Article 6 of the European Convention on Human Rights.

12.69 We think it is undesirable that members of Boards of Visitors should be perceived by prisoners, however wrongly, as having a punitive role. We also note the relative inexperience that can arise from infrequent adjudications. **We recommend that the practice of Board of Visitors adjudication should end.** This change might need to be supplemented by some increase in the sanctions available to prison governors. (In England and Wales when Boards of Visitors lost their adjudicatory function, governors there were given the authority to make awards equivalent to the loss of 42 days remission.)

12.70 The second, more significant, concern about the current system has to do with due process. There is the question whether the prosecution of offences within prison generally should attract the safeguards under Article 6 of the *European Convention on Human Rights*; in other words whether they should be treated as criminal offences rather than as offences against prison discipline. And, even if it is accepted that there is a need for a separate prison disciplinary system, there are two further questions: whether the penalties available within the disciplinary system are too onerous; and whether there are offences within the disciplinary system which should more properly be dealt with as criminal matters.

12.71 The European Court accepts that there are practical and policy reasons for establishing special disciplinary regimes within the prison context. It cites as examples "security considerations and the interests of public order, the need to deal with misconduct by inmates as expeditiously as possible, the availability of tailor-made sanctions which may not be at the disposal of the ordinary courts and the desire of the prison authorities to retain ultimate responsibility for discipline within their establishments".[16] However the Court has stated that, although states may make a distinction between criminal law and disciplinary law, this is subject to certain conditions[17] and states may not, through defining offences as disciplinary, deprive individuals of the safeguards inherent in Article 6.

12.72 In a number of cases, including the case of *Campbell and Fell v United Kingdom,* the Court has set out the factors to be taken into account in the prison setting in deciding whether or not a matter is criminal. These are the domestic classifications as criminal or disciplinary; the nature of the offence itself and whether it would normally appear in the criminal code; and

---

14 *The Prison and Young Offenders Centre Rules (Northern Ireland) 1995*, Rule 124.

15 *Campbell and Fell v United Kingdom* 28 June 1984 7 EHRR 165 Series A No 80.

16 *Campbell and Fell v United Kingdom* 28 June 1984 7 EHRR 165 Series A No 80, paragraph 69.

17 *Engel and Others v Netherlands* 8 June 1976, Series A, No 22 1 EHRR 647.

the nature and severity of the penalty faced.[18]

12.73   As to the application of these principles the Court concluded in relation to the applicant Campbell that the loss of a total of 570 days remission (and a range of other privileges) for the offences of mutiny or incitement to mutiny and doing gross personal violence to an officer was such as to constitute a criminal matter. By contrast, in the earlier case of *McFeeley v United Kingdom*[19] the Court had concluded that the harshness of accumulated disciplinary awards did not detract from the disciplinary nature of the offences. Although assaults on prison officers belonged to both the criminal and disciplinary sphere, they could be regard as disciplinary, provided the punishments imposed did not alter the characterisation of the offences. (McFeeley, held in the Maze prison, had been adjudicated upon at 14 and later 28 day intervals for refusing to wear prison uniform or to work, losing 14 and later 28 days remission at each adjudication. He was also adjudicated on twice for assault, losing four months and three months remission.)

12.74   It is difficult to extract from the Court's findings on the facts of relatively few cases, general principles which can form the basis of a practical system to ensure that future offences are dealt with in a manner that complies with the Convention. In saying this we are conscious that there are other United Kingdom cases currently before the European Court which fall between the boundaries set by *Campbell and Fell* and *McFeeley*.[20]

12.75   We draw two main conclusions. First, recognising the overlap between criminal and disciplinary offences, there is a need for practical guidance on where the line should be drawn in individual cases. **We understand that the Prison Service, RUC and DPP are currently considering a protocol that would guide the prison authorities on the circumstances in which the RUC and DPP should be brought in to deal with prison offences, and we recommend that this protocol be speedily completed and published.** Secondly, we are conscious that removing adjudications by Boards of Visitors will result in a very significant reduction in the sanctions available within the prison disciplinary system (a reduction from loss of 90 days remission to 28 days). We are conscious that the prison discipline system exists as a safeguard for staff and for other prisoners, and that the sanctions available must be adequate for the task. **We recommend some increase in the penalty available to governors, which would need to be consistent with European Court findings (including in relation to cases currently before the European Commission).**

---

18   *Campbell and Fell v United Kingdom* 28 June 1984 7 EHRR 165 Series A No 80 (see also *Engel and Others v Netherlands* 8 June 1976, Series A, No 22 1 EHRR 647).

19   *McFeeley v United Kingdom* 15 May 1981 3 EHRR 161.

20   For example, *Application No 39665/98 lodged by Okechukwiw Ezeh* (Ezeh, a prisoner in England, was given an award including 40 additional days for using threatening, abusive or insulting words or behaviour).

Female Prisoners

12.76　Our attention was drawn to the problems surrounding the holding of female prisoners in Northern Ireland. They are all held in Mourne House which forms part of HM Prison Maghaberry. There are very few such prisoners. In recent months the numbers imprisoned have averaged less than 20. However this small number may contain all classes of prisoner: high security, low security; long sentence, short sentence; convicted, unconvicted; adult, young offender and even on rare occasions juvenile. Clearly it may be difficult for the prison authorities to devise a regime which provides separation between certain types of prisoners (for example between young offenders and adults, or remand and sentenced prisoners) without running the risk that some females may be held in what amounts to solitary confinement. There is the added problem that the prison authorities must not discriminate in the treatment they give to male and female prisoners. Thus it is difficult for them to take specific measures designed to suit the regime for a small class of female prisoners unless they are prepared to extend equivalent treatment to a very much larger class of male prisoners whose needs may be very different.

12.77　It is difficult to know what remedial action could be taken. In this context we note with interest the discussion about issues of separation which appears in the explanatory memorandum attached to the European Prison Rules.[21] These Rules have been relaxed to allow contacts between classes of prisoners (see Rule 11). The explanatory memorandum notes that recent experience has modified views about the need for segregation and continues:

> "Thus there may be some value to younger prisoners, in certain circumstances, in the stability that can result from participation in regime activities with older prisoners. The same may apply in regard to participation by men and women in the same treatment programme. Similarly it may be helpful to untried prisoners, for whom work or other regime experience may be unavailable or limited, to have the opportunity to enjoy that which is available to sentenced categories of prisoners."[22]

12.78　There are no easy solutions to the problems that arise because of the small number of female prisoners at Mourne House. We conclude that the issue should be kept under review not only generally but more specifically in the light of the needs of the prisoners actually being held in Mourne House at any time. One possibility might be to enable female prisoners to share certain facilities and participate in programmes with male prisoners. We expect that the establishment of adequate secure accommodation for girls on the juvenile justice side will obviate the need to hold juveniles in Mourne House.

21　*The European Prison Rules* 1987, Council of Europe.

22　Explanatory Memorandum, *The European Prison Rules*, Council of Europe 1987.

OFFENDING BEHAVIOUR PROGRAMMES

12.79   During consultation there was support for the development of offending behaviour programmes, particularly those aimed at sexual offending. Although such programmes are not panaceas, research evidence suggests that they are effective with certain prisoners at certain times. The importance of these programmes was highlighted in our research[23] and in our visits to other jurisdictions.

12.80   In our view it is very important that offending behaviour programmes are widely available within Northern Ireland, in both community and custodial settings. We are aware that the Prison Service in co-operation with the Probation Board has already developed mechanisms for accrediting, monitoring and evaluating offending behaviour programmes in Northern Ireland prisons. **We recommend that a mechanism be set up to oversee programmes in both prisons and the community with a view to ensuring continuity and consistency, and also ensuring that evaluations are published and, where appropriate, form the basis for the roll-out of successful schemes. We discuss later in this chapter structures to facilitate this end.**

ELECTRONIC MONITORING

12.81   During consultation we heard some suggestions that electronic monitoring (electronic tagging) should be introduced in Northern Ireland. This technique, which typically involves an offender wearing a small electronic transmitter on wrist or ankle, is used in a number of European and North American jurisdictions to monitor the location of offenders within the community, for example to ensure that they are at home or at work within specified times.

12.82   Electronic monitoring will not in itself prevent offending. However the ability to know quickly whether a tagged person is abiding by conditions can act as a deterrent and may allow intervention by the authorities before misbehaviour gets out of hand. It follows that electronic monitoring may be a useful adjunct to other techniques and disposals. Electronic monitoring is currently used:

- as an alternative to a prison sentence (for example schemes in the Netherlands and Sweden);

- as a mechanism to allow the earlier release of sentenced prisoners (for example in the Netherlands and newly introduced in England and Wales);

- as a condition of bail allowing an alternative to remand in custody (attempted in England and Wales in 1989 and reintroduced there in pilot form in 1998); and

---

23   Blair, Research Report 5.

■ as an additional community sentence to be used alongside existing community sentences such as probation orders and community service orders (piloted in England and Wales since July 1995 and in Scotland from August 1998).

12.83 Electronic monitoring was not an issue that we were able to pursue in detail. We are conscious that there may be benefits in certain circumstances in using the technology, particularly where the alternative might be imprisonment. However, there are human rights implications that would need to be considered. It could be argued that the wearing of tagging devices amounts to a degrading form of punishment and that where its use imposes undue hardship on members of the tagged individual's household this might infringe the right to privacy and family life. Its use in certain circumstances in Northern Ireland might also have the effect of putting offenders at risk. We are also aware that private contractors in England and Wales have been used to run electronic monitoring schemes, an approach that would need careful consideration in the Northern Ireland context. **We conclude that electronic monitoring is a technique that should be kept under review in the light of developing experience elsewhere, including in England and Wales. It is an issue which could be remitted to the Criminal Justice Issues Group.**

THE PRISON AND PROBATION SERVICES

12.84 In this section of the chapter we examine the case for closer links between or amalgamation of the Prison and Probation Services; we address some issues concerning the structures and management of the Northern Ireland Prison Service; we go on to look at the organisation of the Probation Board and make some recommendations aimed at enhancing the co-operation and co-ordination between the two services.

Closer links between the Prison and Probation Services

12.85 The Northern Ireland Affairs Committee in its report on the Northern Ireland Prison Service suggested that we should "consider how best to improve links between the Northern Ireland Prison Service and the Northern Ireland Probation Service".[24] This we did when we took evidence from both organisations. The issue was also examined in the research report on prisons and probation that we commissioned.[25]

12.86 There are obvious distinctions between the roles of the Prison Service, which is about custody, and those of the Probation Service, which is community orientated. However, increasingly there is overlap in their areas of work. In addition to holding prisoners securely, the Prison Service mission requires it to prepare prisoners for release. It shares with the Probation Service this role of rehabilitating offenders and seeking to prevent further

---

24 Northern Ireland Affairs Committee: *Fourth Report: Prison Service in Northern Ireland*, 1998, House of Commons.

25 Blair, Research Report 5.

offending. Indeed probation staff are among those involved in the delivery of the programmes within prisons which seek to achieve these ends. Furthermore, some prisoners will come under the supervision of the Probation Service when discharged from prison. In the past this group was confined to certain life sentence prisoners who were supervised as part of their licence but the size of the group is growing with the introduction of combined sentences of imprisonment and probation supervision.

12.87   The reality is that some probation clients will become prisoners (and *vice versa*) in the course of their lives. All of this underlines the need for a common correctional policy in which the disposals available to sentencers and the services provided by prisons and probation are directed at the common ends of protecting the public, preventing offending and re-offending, and rehabilitating the offender. However, although co-operative working patently exists between the Prison Service and the Probation Service as evidenced by the joint protocol between the two organisations and the service level agreements within prisons, both organisations agree that there is room for further development.

12.88   We detect a number of factors that militate against the closer working of the two organisations:

  ■ the Prison Service and the Probation Service are different in the way that they relate to government. The Prison Service is a next steps agency and, although this status gives it a degree of independence in its day to day operation, it is under the direct responsibility of Ministers and acts with the authority of the Secretary of State. By contrast the Probation Service is a non-departmental public body whose relationship with Ministers, and with its Board, is governed by statute. Although the Director General of the Prison Service may have less autonomy, he is nevertheless the main adviser to Ministers on prisons issues. By contrast, advice to government on probation policy and standards is a matter for a policy division in the Northern Ireland Office, often drawing on assistance from the Social Services Inspectorate, rather than from the Probation Service;

  ■ under Northern Ireland Prison Rules,[26] the governor is "in command of the prison" and "responsible for prisoners' treatment according to the law". This arrangement, which is necessary for good order and discipline, is not always comfortable for staff operating within the prison environment, such as probation officers, whose organisational or professional accountability lies elsewhere;

  ■ under the Probation Board (Northern Ireland) Order 1982 the statutory involvement of probation staff in prison is the provision of welfare services to prisoners and their families. Although in practice a more comprehensive service is provided, other work in prison does not have the same statutory imperative. At the same time there is an acknowledged role for Prison Service staff in providing welfare services;

---

26   *The Prison and Young Offenders Centre Rules (Northern Ireland) 1995,* Rule 116.

- there is no consensus on which profession should take the lead in the development and delivery of offending behaviour programmes. The professions of probation, psychology, psychiatry and social work all have an interest, as indeed do custodial professionals.

But at the heart of the issue is the fact that there are two organisations, each with its own ethos, operating in an area where old boundaries are becoming increasingly blurred.

12.89　We considered whether to recommend unifying the two organisations. Such an arrangement would help to ensure the development of common policies and a more coherent direction in the correctional field generally. There are many precedents for such an arrangement, including in a number of the jurisdictions that we visited (for example there are combined correctional services in Canada at both federal and provincial level and in New Zealand).

12.90　However unification is not a panacea. Even in unified correctional services there remain organisational tensions between community and custodial staff. In the Northern Ireland context there is a very real danger that the Prison Service with its larger staff, larger budget and higher profile would tend to dominate the unified organisation to the detriment of community working. We would be concerned that the community ethos and credibility achieved by the Probation Service might be put at risk if such an amalgamation took place at this stage or within the foreseeable future. Also, we were concerned that the process of amalgamation would be difficult to manage, particularly in circumstances when the Prison Service was having to focus on staff reductions and restructuring. We considered that it was not necessary or desirable to combine the Prison and Probation Services in Northern Ireland at this time. However, many of the recommendations in the following paragraphs are aimed at developing new, parallel structures for the two services which would put them on an equal footing in organisational terms and facilitate close working between them.

Prisons

12.91　We are aware that the Northern Ireland Prison Service is currently undergoing its quinquennial review, a process that takes place with all next steps agencies. For our part, we consider that the Service is suited to agency status and would not wish to recommend any change. However, there may be a case for some outside ventilation in the management of the service. **We suggest that consideration be given to recruiting a small number of non-executive members to the management board of the Service. They might be selected on the basis of the particular managerial skills that they would bring to the board.**

12.92　We considered possible arrangements to bring about community input at local establishment level, for example local consultative committees, but concluded that no formal change should be recommended. The nature of the Northern Ireland prison system is such that there are no local prisons – all prisons draw their populations from Northern Ireland as a whole. Moreover the Boards of Visitors or Visiting Committees appointed to each establishment ensure the direct involvement of members of the public in the work of individual establishments. However, **we recommend that prison governors should be expected to consider programmes of outreach into nearby communities,** something which despite the efforts they have made in the past (for example initiatives taken by successive governors of HM Prison Magilligan), has been very difficult to do for security and related reasons.

12.93   Given the change process already affecting the Northern Ireland Prison Service, and in the light of the work already done on this by the Northern Ireland Affairs Committee, we did not think it appropriate for us to get involved in detailed considerations of internal staffing and management issues. However, for reasons which are understandable, it is noteworthy that there is a significant imbalance in community representation amongst prison service staff, by way of religious affiliation; moreover in a contracting service it will be difficult to bring about any significant short term change to this situation by way of recruitment strategies. In such circumstances, **we attach great importance to the training of prison staff in cultural awareness; furthermore, given the extent of change being experienced by the Service, we endorse the view that particular emphasis should to be given to training in new roles and skills to enhance the ability of prison officers to work effectively with prisoners.** It is important that resourcing, manning and rostering arrangements allow sufficient time for training and development.

12.94   Within prisons, the Prison Service should continue to sustain a neutral working environment and we believe that, on foot of this, attention should be paid to the uniform. More generally, **we consider that this would be an opportune time for the Northern Ireland Prison Service to look at its uniform requirements**. We are aware that in some prisons elsewhere in the United Kingdom different types of uniform are worn. We are also aware that the current uniform developed at a time when the focus of prison staff was on control and when interaction between prison officers and prisoners was not a major consideration. A different style of uniform might be more consistent with the role of the modern prison officer whose focus is on the development of positive and constructive relationships with prisoners.

Probation

12.95   In assessing whether the Probation Service should remain a non-departmental public body, we looked at the reasoning behind its establishment as one in 1982; considered whether the objectives behind its establishment had been achieved; asked whether these objectives would remain valid in a peaceful Northern Ireland with a devolved government; and looked at the pros and cons of any change in status. We also took account of two relatively recent developments: the quinquennial review of the Probation Board in 1996/97; and the outcome of the prison-probation review that began work in England and Wales in 1997.

12.96   In 1996-97 the Probation Board was subject to a comprehensive review as part of the normal review cycle for non-departmental public bodies. The review, undertaken by external consultants, comprised a prior options study of all the functions of the Probation Board and a review of its planning, financial and control framework. The consultants recommended that the Board remain a non-departmental public body, although they noted that, if probation services had still been integrated within the Northern Ireland Office, next step agency status would have been an attractive option. They did however speculate that given the unique democratic framework in Northern Ireland and the "complexities of the various communities", non-departmental public body status would probably still have been favoured. The consultants suggested some changes in the accountability framework, recommending that a management statement be prepared. This statement would provide a clear framework of responsibilities and accountabilities, a mechanism for strategic monitoring by the Northern Ireland Office and an aid to the development of more meaningful performance indicators for the Probation Board. The management statement was published in April 1999.[27]

12.97 In England and Wales a prison-probation review was set up in July 1997 to look at the better integration of probation and prison services and at ways to improve their efficiency and effectiveness. The review considered a number of options including the amalgamation of the two services. Following consultation the Home Office announced its conclusions in April 1999. The services were to remain separate but work more closely together. A unified Probation Service led by a National Director of Probation was to be created. Chief Probation Officers were to be transferred to the employ of the Home Office. There would be a reduction in the number of local probation committees, which would be restructured to form Probation Boards, with boundaries that facilitated effective working with the Prison Service.

12.98 We believe that the decision to establish a Probation Board in 1982 was taken for sound reasons and that it has been largely vindicated by subsequent experience. Probation has distanced itself from central government and the NIO, with its security associations; and we believe that it has benefited from the involvement of committed people from outside government in its management. This has proved particularly significant given the democratic deficit associated with direct rule and the importance of securing local input into a community based organisation. On the other hand, that distance from government has a number of disadvantages.

12.99 We recognise that it is difficult to secure membership of a board such as this that is truly representative in terms of background, judged by such measures as gender, religion, class and geography. Also it is not always easy to determine whether the key driver behind the Board is to provide community input into the running of probation services or to give a management and strategic lead; the management statement would suggest the latter. We are conscious that the current structure makes for lines of accountability that are at the very least open to interpretation and debate, given the respective roles and responsibilities of the Secretary of State, NIO, Board and professional staff; this has to a large extent been addressed by the publication of the management statement. In terms of the relationship with the Prison Service, it has not always been easy to resolve issues about the respective responsibilities of

27 *Probation Board for Northern Ireland Management Statement* (1999) Northern Ireland Office, Probation Board for Northern Ireland.

the two services. There are also the problems that arise from the original legislation having lists of mandatory and discretionary functions which do not necessarily align with the actual priorities of the Probation Board as they have evolved or been changed since 1982.

12.100   On balance we believe that non-departmental public body status was the best option for Probation while political responsibility for criminal justice matters remained with the Government at Westminster and the NIO, as its sponsoring department, remained closely associated with security policies. However, looking ahead to devolution, the balance of arguments begins to change. There will no longer be a democratic deficit and, given the involvement of locally elected representatives in government on an agreed basis across the community, the arguments about distancing the service from government become much less compelling. Moreover, the involvement of a board, with responsibility for delivering the service, a local sponsoring department, a Minister and an Assembly and scrutiny committee could make for complex accountability arrangements which could militate against efficient, effective and co-ordinated working.

12.101   We are also conscious of some potential benefits of establishing the Probation Service as a next steps agency, on the same basis as the Prison Service. It would facilitate co-operation between the two services and give probation equal status within the relevant department of a devolved administration, when it came to consideration of policy issues and priorities in the criminal justice sphere. Lines of accountability would be clearly delineated in the framework document that governs relationships between an agency, its sponsoring department and the Minister. There would be a clearly defined framework for standards, target setting and monitoring of performance.

12.102   This is a suitable point to stress our belief that the Probation Service has an important and developing role to play. In this chapter and elsewhere in our report we highlight functions in which it will have a significant role, for example in the development of offending behaviour programmes in the community, new arrangements for dealing with youth offending and new arrangements for community safety. The service must be allowed to evolve to meet these challenges. **The Probation Service must, on the basis of it being able to demonstrate value for money and efficient working, be properly resourced to reflect its workload and its continuing need to support voluntary organisations working alongside it.** In particular, it would be a false economy to bear down on the capacity of probation to the point where sentencers did not feel able to use community sanctions to the full, and to the point where the Probation Service lost the capacity to work on a voluntary basis with offenders and those at risk of offending.

12.103   **We recommend that, on devolution of criminal justice matters, the Probation Service be reconstituted as a next steps agency. This would mean that responsibility for probation services would lie directly with the relevant Minister, on the same basis as the Prison Service. Both agencies would be supported by small management boards comprising senior staff. A senior officer of the Probation Service should sit on the**

prisons management board and a senior prisons official should sit on the probation management board. We believe that this would improve the quality of decision making and assist co-operative and strategic working in the correctional field. As far as the Prison Service is concerned, it would also ensure that all the major professions operating within prisons could have representation on its management board.

12.104   We consider that, with a devolved administration in Northern Ireland, some of the reasons for having an independent Probation Board will disappear. However, we are conscious of the value of retaining a diverse input to the development of probation services and of retaining a "challenge" function from outside government and believe that there should be a formal structure to achieve this. We equally believe that it would be desirable to have such a wide-ranging input to the development of correctional policy more generally, reflecting the need for a more "joined up" approach. **We recommend that the responsible Minister be supported by an advisory board which would advise on all matters to do with probation, prisons and juvenile justice** (see also Chapter 10). **It would comprise the heads of the three organisations and members with an interest in correctional and related matters drawn from the voluntary and community sector, children's organisations and social and related services. The advisory board would assist the Minister in considering strategic and policy issues, determining priorities, setting standards and monitoring service delivery. The board would have a special interest in ensuring co-ordination and co-operation on the delivery of services where appropriate.**

12.105   We are aware that this arrangement would result in probation staff becoming civil servants and there may be fears that the new status would compromise their professional integrity. However, there are many precedents for professional staff working within the civil service in a manner which is entirely satisfactory. **The framework document determining the relationships between the Probation Agency and the core department should make clear that operational decisions in relation to individual cases are entirely a matter for the professional staff. It should also make clear that, although these decisions may be scrutinised in the course of inspection, neither administrative civil servants in the core department nor the Minister would play a part in them, unless consulted by the professionals.**

12.106   In order to foster closer links and more co-operative working between prisons and probation, **we recommend that particular consideration be given to the following:**

■ **staff exchanges between the organisations;**

■ **joint training programmes; and**

■ **joint approaches to the development of offending behaviour programmes that can be delivered in the custodial and community settings, together with arrangements for accrediting, monitoring and evaluating them (with evaluations being published).**

We believe that such an approach will be particularly beneficial given that the ethos and culture of the two organisations is likely in any event to become much closer in future years. If that process can be accelerated, then so much the better.

Victims
and
Witnesses

13 Victims and Witnesses

Introduction

13.1 Under our terms of reference we are required to consider "measures to improve the responsiveness and accountability of, and any lay participation in the criminal justice system". We interpret this as including the need to be responsive and accountable to the victims of crime and to witnesses.

13.2 In this report we have already dealt with issues relating to victims and witnesses. For example:

- we have looked at arrangements to improve the services provided by the courts, including the establishment of court user groups, and have shown how these new arrangements will be of benefit to victims and witnesses (see Chapter 8);

- we have identified the responsibility of the prosecution service for ensuring liaison with victims following the point of charge and we also discussed the position of victims in the context of giving reasons for decisions on whether or not to prosecute (see Chapter 4); and

- in our proposals for new juvenile justice arrangements we have pointed up the potential benefits to the victim of the restorative mechanisms that they embody (see Chapters 9 and 10).

13.3 Also, in looking at the guiding principles which underpin the criminal justice system, we have highlighted the responsibility which the system as a whole and its constituent parts have towards the victims of crime and to those who, like witnesses, are involved in the criminal justice system out of public duty. Both groups will benefit from the greater levels of accountability that we propose and from the new systems of audit and inspection that we will suggest in our consideration of structures.

13.4 The purpose of this chapter is to look more closely at victim and witness issues that are not adequately covered elsewhere in our report. It is also to set out the underlying principles on which the recommendations on victims issues in this chapter and elsewhere in our report have been made.

Human Rights Background

13.5   In November 1985 the United Nations adopted the *Declaration of Basic Principles of Justice for Victims of Crime and Abuse of Power.* In addition to issues of compensation (which have been considered by a team led by Sir Kenneth Bloomfield[1]), the Declaration defines what is meant by the term "victim" before going on to deal with issues of access to justice and fair treatment, restitution and assistance. In particular the Declaration underlines the requirement to treat victims with compassion and respect and describes mechanisms for improving the responsiveness of judicial and administrative processes. These include: the provision of information to victims about the progress of cases; allowing the views and concerns of victims to be made known; assistance during the legal process; avoiding delay; and measures to minimise inconvenience, protect privacy and prevent intimidation or retaliation.

13.6   There is no explicit reference to victims in the *European Convention on Human Rights.* However judgments of the European Court have drawn attention to the responsibility of a State to take appropriate steps to safeguard the lives of those within its jurisdiction. For example in the case of *Osman v United Kingdom* the Court implied that this went beyond the state's primary duty to put in place an effective system of criminal law and law enforcement and might, in certain cases, require the state to put in place operational measures to protect an individual whose life was at risk from the criminal acts of another individual. However, the Court recognised that "such an obligation must be interpreted in a way that does not impose an impossible or disproportionate burden on the authorities".[2]

13.7   Two Council of Europe recommendations deal with the position of victims. The first recommendation was on the position of the victim in the framework of criminal law and procedure.[3] It was aimed at ensuring that the needs of victims, including their physical, psychological, social and material needs, are properly catered for at all stages in the criminal justice process, including by means of compensation and restitution. The second was on assistance to victims and the prevention of victimisation.[4] Taken together, these recommendations are a wide-ranging and comprehensive summary of good practice.

13.8   The issue of witnesses is dealt with explicitly in the *European Convention on Human Rights* and the *International Covenant on Civil and Political Rights.* Both, however, focus on the right of the defendant to examine the witnesses against him and to have witnesses on his behalf. Although there is no explicit reference to the particular needs of witnesses, for example, for help or protection, recent judgments have drawn attention to the need to

---

1   *Report of the Review of Criminal Injuries Compensation in Northern Ireland* (1999) A Report to the Secretary of State for Northern Ireland.

2   *Osman v United Kingdom* 28 October 1998.

3   Recommendation No R (85)11 adopted by the Committee of Ministers on 28 June 1985.

4   Recommendation No R (87) 21 adopted by the Committee of Ministers on 17 September 1987.

balance the defendant's rights to examine witnesses against the rights of witnesses themselves. For example, in recent cases the Court has indicated that at stake may be concerns about their life, liberty and security of person as well as their rights to respect for private and family life: "Contracting states should organise their criminal proceedings in such a way that those interests are not unjustifiably imperilled."[5]

Current Position in Northern Ireland

13.9   In Northern Ireland, as elsewhere, there has been an increasing focus on victims' issues. In parallel the view that criminal justice is primarily a matter solely between the state and the offender has lost credibility. There has been a realisation that the operation of the criminal justice system can inadvertently add to the distress and suffering of victims. At the same time there has been growing awareness that an effective criminal justice system depends crucially on the willingness of victims and witnesses to report offences and to give evidence. In Northern Ireland in particular, victims' issues have been highlighted because of the special concerns about the victims of the civil unrest.

13.10   The development of thinking in Northern Ireland is consistent with developments in Western Europe, North America, Australia and New Zealand, where the needs of victims and witnesses are becoming better appreciated. There has been an increasing focus on issues such as information, explanation, consultation, support and protection. For example in the Netherlands, policy in respect of victims has developed steadily since 1981 as the result of the work of three government committees and legislative change. Initially the focus was on violent sexual crimes but policy was later extended to all felonies. Key elements of the Dutch approach are: the correct treatment of victims; provision of clear and relevant information (including explicit mechanisms to check what information victims wish to receive and to ensure that it is provided on a personal basis); and restitution.

13.11   In recent years in Northern Ireland there have been a number of significant developments in relation to victims and witnesses.

VICTIM SUPPORT

13.12   Victim Support (Northern Ireland) has expanded and developed its work to the point where it now offers a service to victims of crime throughout Northern Ireland. Its volunteers offer emotional support to victims in the immediate aftermath of crime and give practical help by advising on claims for insurance and compensation and providing information about where

---

5   *Van Mechelen v Netherlands* 1997 HRCD 431 (see also *Doorson v Netherlands* 1996 22 EHRR 330).

to go for assistance with specific problems. The organisation is increasing the range of crimes in respect of which it offers support and these now include assault, robbery, and other forms of violent and sexual crime in addition to property offences such as burglary and criminal damage. Projects have recently been established in two hospital Accident and Emergency Departments to offer support to victims who have suffered personal injury. The development of Victim Support in Northern Ireland has been encouraged and assisted by the Northern Ireland Office which, as principle funder, has increased the annual grant from £370,000 in 1996/97 to £747,000 in 1999/2000.

13.13   Victim Support operates a witness support service in the Crown Court at Belfast and Antrim. The scheme was established in 1996 and in 1998/99 supported 1,188 witnesses. Victim Support has recently formed a partnership with the National Society for Prevention of Cruelty to Children to provide a child witness service for children attending court. Both organisations work closely with the Department of the DPP in seeking to identify cases where such services could best be used.

13.14   Support for victims of particular types of crime is provided by a range of other voluntary organisations, including Women's Aid, NEXUS and Rape Crisis. These also receive help through public funding and work in partnership with statutory agencies. The Domestic Violence Forum is an example of inter-agency co-ordinating machinery involving the statutory and voluntary sectors working to reduce the harm caused by such activity and deal with its consequences.

WE WILL REMEMBER THEM

13.15   In 1997 the Secretary of State commissioned Sir Kenneth Bloomfield to consider ways of recognising and acknowledging the suffering of those who have become victims as a consequence of events in Northern Ireland during the last 30 years. The recommendations in his report, *We Will Remember Them*, are being taken forward by Adam Ingram, the Minister for Victims, and the Victims Liaison Unit within the Northern Ireland Office. They include a number of initiatives designed to provide financial and material support to victims and their families and to facilitate liaison between the Government on the one hand and victims and their representatives on the other. A team led by Sir Kenneth Bloomfield was also asked to take forward a review of the fitness for purpose of the Criminal Injuries Compensation Scheme and the report of this group was published in July 1999. [6] The Government is currently considering the recommendations it contains.

13.16   Both reports cover a range of issues, many of which go beyond our remit. However, in *We Will Remember Them*, Sir Kenneth Bloomfield considered specifically the position of victims within the formal criminal justice system. He described encountering a wide range of

---

6   *We Will Remember Them,* (1998) Report of the Northern Ireland Victims Commissioner, Sir Kenneth Bloomfield.

opinion that "too often the victim seemed to be 'out of the loop' when it came to dealing with the crime from which he or she had suffered". For example, he reported argument that victims should be alerted to the release of offenders from prison. There were frequent situations where malefactors remained at large in close proximity to their victims because of lack of evidence. There was also unwillingness of witnesses to give evidence and many victims were concerned about their treatment in court, including the robust approach of barristers in our adversarial system. In this context Sir Kenneth Bloomfield drew specific attention to the Northern Ireland Code of Practice for victims of crime and recommended that it be conscientiously observed and critically monitored.

THE STEPHEN LAWRENCE INQUIRY

13.17   The inquiry into matters arising from the death of Stephen Lawrence was completed in February 1999.[7] Although it was concerned with events in another jurisdiction, we considered what impact it might have on our deliberations. Four of the report's recommendations were about witnesses and victims. It was recommended that: there should be improved guidelines for the handling of victims and witnesses, particularly in the field of racist incidents and crimes; proactive use should be made of contacts within ethnic minority communities to assist with victim support and working with sensitive witnesses; trained victim/witness liaison officers should be available and used in racist incidents and where a sensitive approach to young and vulnerable witnesses and victims was required; and appropriate bail conditions should be used to prevent the intimidation of victims and vulnerable witnesses. These recommendations were accepted by the Home Office, which announced a number of initiatives to develop good practice and drew attention to relevant work already being carried out in relation to vulnerable or intimidated witnesses.

VICTIMS OF CRIME – A CODE OF PRACTICE

13.18   *Victims of Crime - a Code of Practice* was published in February 1998.[8] It was prepared by a steering group comprising representatives of the Director of Public Prosecutions, Northern Ireland Court Service, the Northern Ireland Office (including the Northern Ireland Prison Service), the RUC, the Probation Service and Victim Support. The Code of Practice sets out the level of service, for example in relation to investigation, information, and support, that agencies in the criminal justice sector are committed to delivering to victims. The emphasis is on the right of victims to be treated with respect and sensitivity, to be given emotional and practical support and to have their interests taken into account. The Code also deals with

---

7   *The Stephen Lawrence Inquiry*, Report of an Inquiry by Sir William Macpherson of Cluny, CM 4262.

8   *Victims of Crime - a Code of Practice*, Northern Ireland Office, February 1998.

special arrangements in respect of children and ethnic minorities and provides information about other support services. The Code of Practice is supplemented by commitments given to victims in the RUC charter[9] and to witnesses and victims in the Northern Ireland Court Service charter.[10]

VULNERABLE OR INTIMIDATED WITNESSES

13.19   In May 1998 a working group was set up in Northern Ireland to consider the implications for Northern Ireland of the recommendations in *Speaking up for Justice*, the report of the Home Office led inter-departmental working group on vulnerable or intimidated witnesses in the criminal justice system.[11] The Northern Ireland working group comprised representatives of the Northern Ireland Office, the Department of the DPP, the Northern Ireland Court Service, the RUC and Victim Support.

13.20   *Speaking up for Justice* arose out of concerns that, although measures were in place to assist child witnesses, many adult victims and witnesses found the criminal justice process daunting and stressful. This was particularly true of those who were vulnerable because of their personal circumstances, for example their relationship with the defendant, or because of the nature of the offence, for example rape. There was also concern that some witnesses, possibly because of age or disability or difficulties they had in communicating, were potentially denied justice as a result of being deemed incapable of giving evidence. And there was an underlying worry that some victims and witnesses feared intimidation and, in consequence, failed to report offences or refuse to give evidence in court. *Speaking up for Justice* contained 78 recommendations. Some of these addressed the need to change or improve inter-agency arrangements and administrative procedures, while others required changes in the law and were incorporated in the Youth Justice and Criminal Evidence Act 1999.

13.21   Although Northern Ireland was represented on the Home Office group by the Northern Ireland Office and the Department of the DPP, it was considered that there were sufficient differences in structures and existing arrangements to require separate consideration. For example, the RUC has a highly developed witness protection scheme as a result of past high levels of paramilitary crime. The Northern Ireland Vulnerable or Intimidated Witnesses Working Group undertook two consultation exercises. The first resulted in an agreement by Northern Ireland Ministers to extend the criminal evidence provisions in the Youth Justice and Criminal Evidence Act 1999 to Northern Ireland by means of an Order in Council (the Criminal Evidence (Northern Ireland) Order 1999). These provisions include physical measures to reduce the stress of giving evidence at trial (such as informal dress, screening of

---

9   *Royal Ulster Constabulary Charter,* Royal Ulster Constabulary.

10   *Courts' Charter for Northern Ireland,* Northern Ireland Courts Service.

11   *Speaking up for Justice*, (1998) Report of the Interdepartmental Working Group on the Treatment of Vulnerable or Intimidated Witnesses in the Criminal Justice System, Home Office.

witnesses from the accused, live link CCTV and the use of pre-recorded interviews); restrictions on the freedom of defendants to cross-examine their alleged victims personally; further restrictions on what evidence about an alleged victim's sexual behaviour can be considered relevant in a trial for a sexual offence; and further restrictions on publishing information that might reveal the identity of a witness. The second consultation exercise focused on changes that did not require legislation but could be achieved administratively within the existing law.

13.22   The final report of the working group was published in July 1999[12] during the period of this review. Ministerial agreement for legislative change having been given, it concentrated on administrative changes. In general it endorsed for Northern Ireland the spirit of the recommendations in *Speaking up for Justice.* The report drew special attention to the need for effective training mechanisms and the need to be able to access expert advice and specialist information for dealing with particular types of vulnerability. It also recommended a number of improvements such as the early identification of intimidated witnesses by the police, ensuring proceedings are initiated in respect of intimidation offences, providing courts with information about witness intimidation at bail hearings, providing witnesses with information on action to take if they are intimidated or if they are aware of bail conditions being breached, and holding police interviews in places which suit the witness.

DIRECTOR OF PUBLIC PROSECUTIONS

13.23   In parallel to these developments, the DPP has undertaken a number of related initiatives. These are within the context that there is already a considerable degree of contact between the investigative and prosecutorial agencies and victims and witnesses in Northern Ireland. The DPP has issued his staff with information and formal instructions designed to ensure the proper organisation of consultations with victims and witnesses and their conduct in a professional manner. He has also introduced a comprehensive training programme designed to equip all staff with the knowledge and skills required to help victims through the criminal justice process. The Home Office report *Speaking up for Justice* endorses the view that there are advantages in having contact between the prosecution and victims and witnesses at an early stage. These include better prospects of evaluating the likely performance of a witness; allowing the witness direct access to the prosecution team; increasing witness confidence in the criminal justice systems; reassuring a victim that all aspects of the case will be fully examined and that their interests will be properly taken into account; and, providing an opportunity for the victim or witness to raise concerns.

---

12   *Vulnerable or Intimidated Witnesses (NI) Working Group - Final Report*, (1999) Northern Ireland Office.

Research Findings

13.24   The work that we commissioned on attitudes to the criminal justice system sought views on victim and witness issues.[13] In summary, it demonstrated that there was considerable fear about becoming involved as a witness in the criminal justice system. This related not just to the intimidating nature of the court itself, but also to the possibility of being intimidated by parties to the proceedings or their supporters.

13.25   There was support for mechanisms to protect witnesses in court, for example screens. There was also agreement about the need for mechanisms to support and protect witnesses more generally. There was little detail but ideas included arrangements for explanations to witnesses and court visits in advance of trial. For many, the biggest fear of being in court related to the public nature of the occasion, the very personal nature of questions that might be asked and possible publicity.

13.26   This picture is confirmed by attitudinal surveys. For example the greatest worry of 96% of people who would be willing to appear in court was the fear of intimidation or retaliation; while 62% expressed concern about standing up and talking.[14]

Views Expressed During the Consultation Period

13.27   Both in written responses and in the consultation seminars there was comparatively little detailed discussion of victim and witness issues. However, this probably reflected the degree of unanimity that existed in relation to some of the issues being raised. There was an enormous amount of sympathy for the position of victims and a genuine desire to ensure that their legitimate concerns were met in a manner that did not result in their being re-victimised. There was recognition, too, of the important role of witnesses and the need to encourage them and protect them. But there were relatively few specific suggestions as to how these important ends might be achieved, and no complete consensus.

13.28   Some of the discussion of victims and witnesses was in the abstract. However, the Review Group benefited on several occasions from hearing directly the actual experience of victims and their relatives.

---

13   Dunn, Morgan and Dawson, Research Report 12.

14   Amelin, Willis and Donnelly, Research Report 3.

VICTIMS

13.29   There was general consensus that the criminal justice system did not give victims the level of support and assistance that they required, although only a few respondents considered how this problem might be addressed. There was also a widely held view that sentencing should take into account the requirements of victims, although apart from some positive comments about restorative justice, the practicalities of doing this were only touched on.

13.30   One of the messages that came across to us was the belief that there was little recognition by the criminal justice system of the centrality of victims to the criminal justice process. Although victims were intrinsic to the offence and often played a key role in reporting the offence and providing the evidence to prosecute, they felt alienated from the system. The perception was that the state took over the prosecution of "their" offence and was more concerned to secure a conviction (or otherwise dispose of the case) than to establish the truth about what had happened. At times victims felt that they were being re-victimised. When there were delays in dealing with cases, victims were left in a state of uncertainty. When cases came to court, victims sometimes felt as if they, not the offender, were in the dock. If a conviction was secured there was inadequate information about outcomes, including the release date of the offender. Throughout the criminal justice process there was an undercurrent of fear about possible retaliation by the offender and concerns that various aspects of the process, for example the lack of separate waiting areas in courthouses, might result in intimidation. There was an implication that the balance in the system was too much in favour of offenders at the expense of the victim. There was a suggestion that the guiding principles and values of the criminal justice system should ensure that the interests of the victim took precedence over those of the offender.

13.31   There was a widely held view that more and better information about their case should be available to victims but no very clear assessment of how it might be achieved. As to victims losing control over "their" offence, there were some suggestions that the victim might initiate prosecution or that someone, possibly the prosecutor, should take on board the role of representing the victim in court. On the other hand Victim Support argued that victims should not be given the burden of having to take decisions on what should happen to offenders; the state could not abrogate its responsibility in this area.[15]

13.32   There was also a suggestion that victims should have a right to make a statement to the court about the impact of the offence on them. But Victim Support argued for something rather different, the opportunity for the victim to make a statement in their own words to the prosecution or police that could then be deployed by them in court.[16]

---

15   *The Rights of Victims of Crime*, (1995) Victim Support.

16   *op cit.*

13.33   There was a widely held view that witnesses, too, required more support from the criminal justice system, notably in terms of protection and support at court, as well as improved facilities. Indeed, on many occasions during the consultation the needs and concerns of witnesses and victims were seen as virtually interchangeable. Clearly both victims and prosecution witnesses were seen as likely to benefit from protection outside court and from any steps taken inside court to make the process less intimidating.

13.34   Some respondents drew specific attention to the needs of defence witnesses. Their presence and their contribution were essential for a fair trial. However, they were equally likely to be intimidated by the criminal justice process and did not have the direct support of any of the statutory agencies.

Evaluation and Recommendations

DEFINITION

13.35   We accept the definition of "victim" in the UN *Declaration of Basic Principles of Justice for Victims of Crime and Abuse of Power*. Thus a victim is anyone who has suffered harm as a result of violation of criminal laws, regardless of whether a perpetrator has been identified or is being dealt with by the criminal justice system. Moreover "victim" may include, where appropriate, the immediate family or dependants of the direct victim and others who have suffered harm in intervening to help victims or prevent victimisation. We also accept that the provisions for victims should be applicable to all without distinction of any kind, for example on grounds of age, sex, religion, ethnic or social origin, nationality or political opinion. This does not mean that we believe that all victims must be treated identically regardless of circumstances. To the contrary, the definition is a reminder that victimhood can take a variety of forms and that the responses of the criminal justice system must be similarly varied. Moreover, as the Stephen Lawrence Inquiry has reminded us, the appropriate response in any individual case may depend critically on the background of the victim.[17]

VICTIMS' RESPONSIBILITIES

13.36   We are aware that victims have a great number of responsibilities within the criminal justice system. These include assisting investigation, making statements and giving evidence.

---

17   *The Stephen Lawrence Inquiry* (1999), Report of an Inquiry by Sir William Macpherson of Cluny, London: HMSO, Cm 4262 (The Macpherson Report).

However, we wish to highlight our view that this does not amount to a requirement that victims should have to take decisions about what should happen to offenders or about how cases should be progressed or, in particular, whether there should be a prosecution; nor should it do so in future. For reasons of fairness, consistency and public interest, those decisions are properly taken by the state. We note that we are supported in this view by the organisation JUSTICE, in its report on the role of the victim in criminal justice,[18] and by Victim Support.[19] This was also a conclusion of the Canadian House of Commons Standing Committee on Justice and Human Rights which entitled its report on the role of victims in the criminal justice system *Victims' Rights - A Voice, not a Veto.*[20] None of this is to imply that victims should not be consulted about aspects of their case but that such consultation cannot be a mechanism for the state passing on or evading its responsibilities. Nor does it mean that victims cannot, if they freely wish, become involved in restorative conference,s particularly where these are aimed at conciliation and redress for victims.

RESPONSIBILITY FOR VICTIMS ISSUES

13.37   The UN Declaration and Council of Europe recommendations remind us that victims have needs at all stages in the criminal justice process including long after conviction and sentence, the point at which the criminal justice system might regard an offence as having been adequately dealt with. And responsibilities in relation to the prevention of victimisation could be seen to exist even before an offence has been committed.

13.38   Within the criminal justice system and in developing the criminal justice plan that we recommend in Chapter 3, it will be important to reflect the high priority attached to victims issues. **The interests of victims should feature in the codes of practice and plans of all criminal justice organisations that interface with them, and in the criminal justice plan that we advocate for the system as a whole.** This would be consistent with the work already underway in relation to the existing Northern Ireland Code of Practice for Victims and in the charters of criminal justice organisations. For those organisations subject to formal inspection arrangements (see Chapter 15) and which have responsibilities to victims and witnesses, they should be subject to formal inspection to ensure that the necessary standards are being met. Such inspection should be against the background of more clearly delineated responsibilities for dealing with victims.

13.39   We considered whether there should be set up within the criminal justice system a new separate office with specific responsibility for victims. One option was that the person holding this office would maintain a general oversight of the services available to victims,

---

18   *Victims in Criminal Justice: report of the JUSTICE Committee on the role of the victim in criminal justice* (1998).

19   *The Rights of Victims of Crime*, (1995) Victim Support..

20   *Victims' Rights - A Voice, not a Veto: report of the Standing Committee on Justice and Human Rights,* (1998) Shaughnessy Cohen MP, Chair.

would act as an advocate for victims and would act as the central "one-stop-shop" for handling complaints raised by victims. However, we were concerned that in a relatively small jurisdiction like Northern Ireland this approach might merely serve to diminish the stature and effectiveness of the Criminal Justice Inspectorate while at the same time cutting across the responsibilities of the individual criminal justice organisations.

13.40   Nevertheless, we consider that the position of victims within the criminal justice system requires particular and continuing scrutiny. **We recommend that a sub-group of the Criminal Justice Issues Group should maintain a specific focus on victims issues, should monitor and evaluate the new arrangements and should report regularly** (see Chapter 15). **It should include both statutory and voluntary agencies that are concerned with the provision of criminal justice services to victims. The possibility of a victims' advocate should be considered again in the future if new arrangements on behalf of victims are seen not to be working effectively.**

13.41   Given the variety of criminal justice organisations with which victims may have dealings, there is a real danger of an inconsistent approach in the support given to victims by different agencies or, worse, that there might be gaps in coverage. To counter this, **we recommend that the agency which has lead responsibility for working with victims at particular points in the criminal justice process should be clearly delineated.**

13.42   **We recommend that the lead role in ensuring the provision of information and explanation to victims and seeking their views be taken by the police until such time as the case is passed to the prosecutor, that is until a suspect is charged or a summons issued (although as a matter of practicality it is recognised that the police will have a significant role until the file is received in the prosecutor's office). The lead role (including notifying the victim of the outcome of the case in the courts) would subsequently be taken by the prosecutor until the case is finished in the courts. The prosecutor would also lead on any issues arising out of an appeal. Where a custodial sentence was imposed, the Prison Service would then take the lead. Where a non-custodial sentence was imposed, and the victim had an interest in being kept informed, the Probation Service would take the lead. In the case of a diversionary measure which involves victims, the agency or body responsible for implementation would have responsibility for informing victims about the progress and, where contact between victim and offender is envisaged, for taking steps to ensure the safety of victims. Each lead agency should have a clearly advertised point of contact.** None of this is to suggest that the lead agency should have sole responsibility at any point. Who should take action must depend on the precise service or support needed. Instead the lead agency should be the first contact point for queries, requests and complaints: victims should not themselves be required to navigate the bureaucracy in order to gain the help they require.

We are conscious that significant resources may need to be deployed to facilitate these arrangements and that the mechanisms may need to be phased in over time. This process should be aided by improved information sharing between criminal justice organisations.

INFORMATION, EXPLANATION AND CONSULTATION

13.43   An important theme during our consultation was whether victims had sufficient access to information and explanations and whether they were adequately consulted about the decisions being taken in their case. Concerns expressed were consistent with earlier research findings that there was a strong feeling on the part of victims of crime that they were not well enough informed about their case, that they were not given enough details about court procedures before and at court and that the part they played in the court process was not acknowledged and consequently not appreciated enough.[21] We consider it essential to distinguish between the issues of information and explanation on the one hand, and consultation on the other. The provision of information and explanations should be relatively straightforward. Information, for example about trial dates, should be factual and explanations, although they will often require considerable sensitivity, should be similarly factually based. In contrast, consultation is explicitly a two-way process in which the views of victims are sought and may (in some cases should) be acted upon.

13.44   The criminal justice agencies in Northern Ireland already have commitments, set out in the Code of Practice for victims, in which they undertake to provide information at various stages in the criminal justice process. There is a lacuna, however, in the fact that the commitment of the police is limited to the provision of information in "serious" cases, although this restriction is, we understand, applied sensitively.

13.45   On the basis of the evidence we have seen, the comments we have been given and our own knowledge of the criminal justice system, we are very conscious of the importance of information to victims both as a means of building confidence in the system as a whole and as a means of securing accountability. **We recommend that the criminal justice agencies in Northern Ireland should build on their existing commitments in the Code of Practice for victims, in which they undertake to provide information at various stages in the criminal justice process (although not if it is against the wishes of the victim). The provision of information should not be limited to cases that the criminal justice system might classify as "serious".** What might appear to be a relatively minor offence could have a disproportionate impact on the victim and would need to be handled accordingly. On the other hand, proportionality requires that there cannot be a blanket requirement to provide identical information in all cases. **We recommend that it should be for the lead agency to ensure the necessary information is made available, although it may be**

---

21   See Jackson, Kilpatrick and Harvey, *Called to Court: A Public Review of Criminal Justice in Northern Ireland* (1991), Belfast, SLS.

appropriate for the information to be passed through or provided by a third party. We would stress the point that information must be in a form which is accessible to victims and given sensitively. Frequently it will be appropriate for information to be given in person.

13.46   Issues surrounding consultation are more problematic. Broadly there are a number of concerns. One is that it might result in victims being required to take decisions that are properly for the authorities. (We have already indicated above that victims generally should not be placed in the position of having to take key decisions about the handling of their case or the treatment of the offender.) Alternatively there is the danger that consultation might lead to unrealistic expectations on the part of the victim with the potential to increase the sense of frustration and dissatisfaction if the victim's views cannot be met. There is also a danger, depending on the form it takes, that consultation with a victim who is to be called as a witness might prejudice (or be said to prejudice) the legal process.

13.47   Despite these problems, account must be taken of the need to recognise the position of victims and the dependence of the criminal justice system on them. **We recommend that wherever possible victims should be informed and consulted about the development of their cases. But when and how to consult them, particularly those who are witnesses, must be a matter for the professional judgement of the prosecutor.** Set out below are a number of areas where we consider that better consultation and more explicit information are required.

DECISIONS WHETHER TO PROSECUTE

13.48   The Director of Public Prosecutions in Northern Ireland already undertakes to inform victims where there is a decision not to prosecute and is considering doing so in writing in cases involving death, serious violence, sexual abuse, domestic violence, road traffic accidents where serious injury was occasioned, or where it is considered that "the reported facts are likely to have had a significant adverse impact upon the victim".[22]

13.49   As discussed above in our consideration of prosecution issues (Chapter 4) there may be considerable sensitivities about giving reasons for not prosecuting a particular case. In particular, there is the danger that reasons might be given in such a way that inferences will be drawn about the guilt of someone, without that person having had the opportunity to defend themselves in the courts. However, we do believe that it is of great importance for public confidence that victims should understand what is happening in the processing of "their case". We therefore wish, in this part of our report, to draw attention to our recommendation in Chapter 4, that prosecutors should be prepared to provide victims and their families with as full an explanation of a decision not to prosecute as is possible without prejudicing the interests of justice or the public interest.

---

22   *Victims, Witnesses and the Prosecution,* The Department of the Director of Public Prosecutions for Northern Ireland.

DECISIONS ON WHETHER TO VARY CHARGES

13.50   The Director of Public Prosecutions already undertakes to "consider the proper interests of victims and witnesses in deciding whether or not the public interest requires prosecution".[23] We understand that the consultation(s) which prosecutors have with the victim are an important source of this information. In addition we note that the DPP will, if requested, explain why a charge is being reduced or a plea taken to a lesser offence and listen to anything the victim may have to say.

13.51   The question arises whether the prosecutor should be required to consult about such changes. On the one hand it would be consistent with the general undertaking to take the victim's proper interests into account. On the other hand there might be a risk that the case would be prejudiced through involving a victim in this way. **On balance and subject to our overriding recommendation that when and how to consult must be a matter for the professional judgement of the prosecutor, we recommend that the general rule, building on the Director of Public Prosecutions' current practice, should be for victims to be consulted about important changes in the way that "their" case is being handled. We also recommend that information about such changes should be actively offered rather than the victim having to request it, although we accept that it might not be possible to consult victims in certain circumstances, for example, if they are not at court when decisions have to be taken.** It would of course be open to the victim to decline the information (or the consultation) or to opt out of the process more generally.

VICTIM EFFECT STATEMENTS

13.52   We are aware that there is a growing expectation that the effects of a crime on the victim should be known to the court, particularly to help with sentencing. However, thoughts on how this should be achieved vary considerably. For example Victim Support argues that victims "who have information that they wish to convey, but which does not form part of the formal evidence, should have the opportunity to give a statement in their own words directly to the police and the prosecution service".[24] It suggests that this statement could have a number of uses in relation to the prosecution process, including in relation to sentencing. In contrast, in Canada, where victim impact statements have been authorised since 1988 and required to be considered by judges since 1995, the Government has agreed to amend the Canadian Criminal Code to clarify that judges may allow the oral presentation of a previously written statement.[25] It is also worth noting that the Council of Europe recommends that: "all relevant information concerning the injuries and losses suffered by the victim should be made

---

23   *op cit.*

24   *The Rights of Victims of Crime*, (1995) Victim Support.

25   *Response to the Fourteenth Report of the Standing Committee on Justice and Human Rights* (1998), Government of Canada.

available to the court".[26] However, this recommendation seems to be aimed primarily at ensuring that the victim's need for compensation is taken into account when determining sentence.

13.53   We note within Northern Ireland that courts, when sentencing, already take into account any information that is available about the seriousness of the offence. It is the responsibility of the prosecution to ensure that all relevant information is available to the judge. However, it is not clear how fully and explicitly the victim is involved in this process, or that information about the effects of the offence on the victim is routinely available to the sentencer in all courts, including youth courts.

13.54   There are potentially a number of risks if victims become more involved in the provision of information about the impact of crime. Not least is the fact that a statement, like any other matters considered at sentence, will form part of the evidence and so the victim may be questioned about it in court. Moreover, there would be issues of equity if it were perceived that victims who were punitive or victims who were forgiving were having a differential impact on sentences. As we have said previously victims should not be required to take decisions about what should happen to offenders nor be seen to have any form of veto over sentencing.

13.55   However, there is a good case for encouraging the victim of a crime to give factual information about that crime's effects. Not only is it consistent with what we have suggested earlier in relation to consultation, and necessary to ensure that the victim's legitimate interests are safeguarded (for example where the victim has continuing concerns about safety which the authorities, including the court, should take into account) but it may also, in itself, be helpful in allowing the victim to come to terms with the offence. In many cases knowledge of the crime's effects, not only on its immediate victim, but also upon the victim's family, is an important factor in enabling sentencers to assess the level of seriousness of defendants' wrongdoing. This is especially important where death has resulted or where violence has caused injury, including psychiatric damage. In this context the distress, often lingering, caused to families by domestic burglaries should not be forgotten. We acknowledge that considerable information on the effect of crime is already made available in Crown Court cases. **We recommend that practice be reviewed to ensure that the prosecutor, who will be responsible for a wider range of cases than hitherto, considers the effect of the crime on the victim and makes certain that those acting on behalf of the prosecution, including independent practitioners, bring all relevant information to the attention of the court and up-date it regularly. This would include not only information from the victim but also information from others, for example medical professionals, who would be able to advise on the effect on the victim or on similar cases. We consider it important that the responsibilities of the prosecutor in this regard be given due prominence in relevant publications of principles and codes of practice.**

26   Recommendation No R (85)11 adopted by the Committee of Ministers on 28 June 1985.

13.56 Unfounded allegations against victims of crime made by defending advocates in mitigation speeches can cause great distress, especially when reported in the media. **We draw attention to the importance of maintaining the duty of prosecuting advocates to challenge allegations about victims made by the defence in the absence of supporting evidence.**

INFORMATION ON THE RELEASE OF PRISONERS

13.57 In Northern Ireland, with the exception of arrangements in relation to prisoners released under the Sentences (Northern Ireland) Act 1998, there is no legal requirement for the Northern Ireland Prison Service to inform victims when an offender is to be released from prison. Despite the lack of legislation, there is a protocol under which child victims of sex offenders will be told about release (the limitations of which are among the issues being considered as part of the Government's consultation on the control and supervision of sex offenders) and we understand that the Prison Service currently deals sympathetically with requests for information. Moreover, although there is no formal mechanism for victim involvement, the Prison Service will take into account concerns about victims' safety when deciding on whether to allow temporary release and on the conditions that should be attached. However, providing information about release dates can be problematic, for example if there are concerns about the safety of the prisoner, and the Prison Service may be vulnerable, particularly in circumstances where there is no legal requirement for passing on information. For victims there may be difficulty knowing who to approach for information.

13.58 There are a number of issues related to the fact that prisoners may be released earlier than the victim had anticipated. Victims may not be aware that the time to be served will be reduced by any time in prison awaiting trial and may not know that most prisoners, because of remission, will serve in prison only half the sentence as pronounced. In the case of life sentence prisoners, victims may not be aware that prisoners do not necessarily serve a minimum period recommended by the judge. They may also be unaware that prisoners may be given temporary release, either for compassionate reasons or to assist with the transition from prison and that such temporary release may happen well before expiry of the sentence. Victims may not know that their concerns about safety can be taken into account by the prison authorities.

13.59 **We recommend three changes in practice relating to the giving of information about the release, or likely release date, of prisoners:**

  - **Where an offender is sentenced to custody and where the victim wishes, the Prison Service should be responsible for explaining the impact of the sentence including** the likely release date and the likely arrangements for temporary release. It should be the responsibility of the prosecutor to check whether the victim wishes to use this service and if so to put the victim in touch with the Prison Service.

■ Where information about release is requested by the victim, the Prison Service should be required to give it, provided the prisoner is not put at risk.

■ The Prison Service should put in place formal mechanisms to deal with concerns expressed by victims about safety, particularly in relation to temporary release.

31.60   These recommendations would be in addition to any special arrangements in respect of particular classes of prisoner such as sex offenders. They might require permissive legislation. However, the precise administrative arrangements should be determined by the Prison Service, who should consult those involved with the support of victims. In particular, it would need to consider how the victims of prisoners currently serving their sentence would be brought into the scheme.

SUPPORT FOR WITNESSES

13.61   The criminal justice authorities are already taking a number of steps to improve the services available to witnesses, particularly those who are vulnerable or intimidated. They include the important legislative changes in the Criminal Evidence (Northern Ireland) Order 1999 and the various administrative measures we have cited. However, we would like to draw special attention to certain measures that may require a special focus.

13.62   We are aware that Victim Support, with funding from the Northern Ireland Office, already operates a witness support scheme for prosecution witnesses in Belfast Crown Court (which is currently located in both Belfast and Antrim). Those operating the scheme provide essential help and support to witnesses in what can be a strange and challenging environment. We are also aware of the child witness scheme that is being piloted in Belfast Crown Court as a joint venture by Victim Support and the National Society for the Prevention of Cruelty to Children. In principle, and subject in the case of child witnesses to the evaluation of the pilot, we consider that such schemes should be more widely available, including in magistrates' courts. Based on the assumption that 180 to 200 additional volunteers would be required this could cost £245,000 to £300,000. **We recommend that publicly funded witness support schemes should be made available at all Crown Court and magistrates' courts venues. Children should be included in such arrangements on a basis determined in the light of the outcome of evaluation of the current pilot scheme.**

13.63   Defence witnesses, too, may be uncertain and fearful of the experience of going to court and giving evidence. Nevertheless, we accept that within our adversarial system there would be difficulties in providing a common service to both prosecution and defence witnesses. In the first instance it should be for defence solicitors to provide information about courts and their procedures. However we consider that Court Service staff should be available to facilitate defence witnesses in the same way that they are available to facilitate other members of the public who have to come to court. Support for defence witnesses is an issue which the Criminal Justice Issues Group may wish to consider in the future.

Law
Reform

14 Law Reform

Introduction

14.1   Our terms of reference invite us to consider "... mechanisms for addressing law reform". In this chapter we consider the existing mechanisms for reform of the civil and criminal law in Northern Ireland, law reform mechanisms in a number of other jurisdictions, and what arrangements for law reform might best meet the needs of the people of Northern Ireland. Though our terms of reference required us to focus on the criminal law, the nature of this topic is such that it cannot properly be examined without some reference to civil law matters.

Current Arrangements for Law Reform in Northern Ireland

14.2   Reform of criminal law and procedure is primarily a matter for the Northern Ireland Office, but some aspects of criminal procedure relating to the operation of the courts are the responsibility of the Northern Ireland Court Service. There is no independent mechanism to advise the Government on criminal law reform.

14.3   Reform of the civil law in Northern Ireland is the responsibility of the Office of Law Reform within the Department of Finance and Personnel. The non-statutory Law Reform Advisory Committee for Northern Ireland was created in 1989, with a remit to scrutinise the civil law of Northern Ireland, with limited exceptions, and to submit reform proposals to the Secretary of State for Northern Ireland. The Committee is composed of part-time members drawn from the legal profession, including barristers, solicitors and academic lawyers, with one member who is not legally qualified. A High Court judge chairs the Committee. An official of the Office of Law Reform acts as part-time secretary to the Committee. The Committee has no full-time dedicated support staff.

14.4   Further information on the current arrangements for law reform in Northern Ireland is set out in the research report on law reform in Northern Ireland, which is published along with this report. [1]

---

1   Dickson and Hamilton, Research Report 9, chapter 2.

Views Expressed During the Consultation Process

14.5 In our consultation paper we sought views on how law reform might be addressed in future and asked for views and comments on the following questions.

- Would an independent law commission be an appropriate way of taking forward the task of proposing law reform in Northern Ireland?

- How might the members of such a commission be selected, and would who appoint them?

- Are there other models that the review should consider?

14.6 We found almost universal support for the creation of an independent Law Commission to take forward the task of proposing law reform in Northern Ireland. However, few of those who commented on this issue put forward detailed proposals on how such a commission might operate, who might comprise its membership and to whom it should report. One or two respondents expressed reservations about whether there would be sufficient business to justify such a commission.

14.7 There was a broad sense that there needed to be political neutrality in the area of law reform. Consideration of law reform issues by an independent and politically impartial body was thought to be highly desirable in Northern Ireland.

14.8 We sought the views of the Office of Law Reform. It believed that there was a need for an independent body with responsibility for the systematic development and reform of civil and criminal law. The Office of Law Reform envisaged such a body working in a complementary arrangement with independent law reform agencies in other jurisdictions in the United Kingdom and working in partnership with those in government responsible for advising Ministers on law reform matters. Lay representation at commissioner level and provision for full-time and part-time commissioner appointments were proposed. Two full-time and three part-time commissioners were thought to reflect an appropriate complement, in the first instance. There was seen to be merit in the commission adopting similar practice to most other law commissions ,with the ability to prepare its own programme of law reform and have specific projects referred to it by government.

14.9 We heard a range of other views and submissions mostly in support of a government-funded, independent body, established on a statutory basis, to consider all aspects of the civil and criminal law. There were suggestions that it should have its own research capacity, that it should have a substantial support staff with access to a law library, and that it should be adequately funded.

14.10 There was general agreement that the law reform body should research and consider matters referred to it by the Government. Some believed that it should have the ability to set its own programme or, at the very least, initiate projects of its own volition.

14.11   We heard suggestions that a commission's functions should include thematic reviews of law, procedure and practice together with the regular examination of international developments in these areas. The need for broad legal, academic, and lay membership of the body attracted wide consensus. Another feature raised was the need for co-operation between the law reform body and other rights bodies in Northern Ireland, such as the Equality and Human Rights Commissions established under the Northern Ireland Act 1998.

14.12   We heard some views in favour of a law commission being established soon and that this should not be contingent upon devolution of responsibility for the criminal law. The need for adequate machinery within government to advise on and carry out proposals for legislative change was recognised. The Office of Law Reform suggested that, in the event of responsibility for criminal law and procedure being devolved to the Northern Ireland Executive, administrative responsibility for advising Ministers on civil and criminal law issues should be brought together within one department, most likely a Department of Justice.

14.13   Another body of opinion, presented in the context of proposals for an all-Ireland dimension to law reform, favoured exploration of options for a north/south arrangement in relation to civil and criminal law reform. This could be followed by Ministers establishing arrangements to review relevant law throughout the island of Ireland with a view to harmonisation. It was suggested that consideration be given to establishing an all-Ireland law commission, representing all stakeholders in both justice systems, and tasked with developing an all-Ireland legal framework.

14.14   Most, though not all, respondents believed that responsibility for advising on reform of civil and criminal law should be brought together within a commission. A strong message to emerge was the need for a more proactive body that would consult widely and obtain all relevant views and expert opinions and identify areas of law in need of reform and development. The need for objective research, clarification of the law and simplification of language were commonly advocated tasks for a commission. Many emphasised that a law commission should cover procedural aspects of criminal law as well as the substantive law and might have a strong practical emphasis.

Research and Experience in Other Jurisdictions

14.15   In this section we draw heavily upon the research report on law reform in Northern Ireland,[2] and on what we learned during our programme of study visits, to describe the arrangements for law reform in a range of other common law jurisdictions.

---

2   Dickson and Hamilton, Research Report 9.

14.16   In England and Wales, Scotland and the Republic of Ireland independent law commissions have responsibility for keeping all of the law, including the criminal law, under review with a view to its systematic development and reform.

14.17   The research report describes, under common headings, the law reform mechanisms employed in each of the jurisdictions closest to Northern Ireland. It includes reference to models employed elsewhere with focus on the community orientated approach to law reform in South Africa and Canada; difficulties associated with part-time membership of law reform bodies; novel accountability mechanisms employed in New Zealand; and the role played by the private sector in the United States.

ENGLAND AND WALES

14.18   The Law Commission for England and Wales was established by the Law Commissions Act 1965 as an independent body to review all the law in England and Wales with a view to its systematic development and reform. Specific types of law reform cited in the Act are codification; elimination of anomalies; repeal of obsolete and unnecessary enactments; consolidation; simplification; and modernisation of the law.

14.19   The Commission comprises four teams, each headed by a commissioner and responsible for a particular branch of the law.[3] Typically, each team comprises three lawyers and three research assistants and manages some five projects at a time. A team is selected to take charge of an approved programme item or reference from the Lord Chancellor. In addressing a particular area of the law the Commission will produce a consultation paper which describes the current law and its shortcomings, as well as setting out possible options for reform. After considering the responses to the paper, a final report is submitted to the Lord Chancellor and subsequently published.

14.20   The Commission has a staff of around 70 who are seconded from the Lord Chancellor's Department. In 1998 the Commission's budget was £3,818,500. Commissioners are appointed by the Lord Chancellor for up to five years at a time, after a public advertisement in the press. The Act provides that the Law Commission must submit programmes of law reform for approval by the Lord Chancellor, consider any proposals for law reform which are made or referred to it, and prepare programmes of consolidation and statute law revision.[4] Once a programme has been accepted by the Lord Chancellor, the Commission decides how to plan its work.

---

3   Common Law, Company and Commercial Law, Criminal Law and Evidence, and Property and Trust Law.

4   Section 3(1) of the 1965 Act.

14.21   In its thirty-second annual report the Commission explained its working methods as follows:

> "The Commission's work is based on thorough research and analysis of case law, legislation, academic and other writing, law reports and other relevant sources of information both in the United Kingdom and overseas. It takes full account both of the *European Convention on Human Rights* and of other European law. ... It normally publishes a consultation paper inviting views before it finalises its recommendations. The consultation paper describes the present law and its shortcomings and sets out possible options for reform. The views expressed in response by consultees are analysed and considered very carefully. ... The Commission's final recommendations are set out in a report which contains a draft Bill where the recommendations involve primary legislation". [5]

14.22   The Commission initiates or accepts a law reform project according to its assessment of the relevant considerations, the most significant of which are stated as: the importance of the issues; the availability of resources in terms of both expertise and funding; and the suitability of the issues to be dealt with by the Commission. The Commission aims to make the law simpler, fairer, more modern and accessible, primarily by means of statute law consolidation. The Commission now places considerable emphasis in its reports on the jurisprudence of the European Commission and the European Court of Human Rights. It engages assistance from legal and other consultants and acknowledges the importance of empirical research, which on occasion has been funded from outside the Commission.

14.23   There is a statutory requirement for the Law Commission and the Scottish Law Commission to work in consultation with each other. A formal agreement exists between the Commission and the main government departments under which the latter aim to provide an initial response to a Commission report within six months; a final response without unreasonable delay; and an opportunity to comment on any major obstacle they see to implementing the report. Periodic consultations take place with the Home Office as the Commission's criminal law team prepares its report. After the report is published the Home Office sets up an inter-departmental working group on which the Law Commission might be represented. This group makes recommendations to the relevant Ministers.

14.24   The Commission strives to have a media profile and it maintains an extensive web-site, where reports are accessible free of charge. The Commission publishes three magazines per year, detailing government or government-sponsored law reform projects in the United Kingdom and other countries and listing the Commission's reports that are awaiting implementation.

14.25   In terms of accountability, the Commission submits an annual report to the Lord Chancellor, which is then presented to Parliament. It is also subject to a quinquennial review carried out by the Cabinet Office, and its accounts are audited.

---

5   *Law Commission Thirty-Second Annual Report.* (1997) Law Com No 250, page 45.

SCOTLAND

14.26   The Scottish Law Commission was established by the same legislation as that in England and Wales, and many of the provisions of the legislation apply equally to both Commissions. [6] The Commission works in teams, though they operate differently and are not permanently constituted as in England and Wales. Otherwise the methodology employed by the Scottish Commission in considering issues is similar to that in England and Wales. By convention, only the chairman of the Commission is a judge of the Court of Session.

14.27   The Scotland Act 1998 confirms that the Scottish Law Commission's remit will continue to include all the law applying in Scotland, whether in relation to reserved or devolved matters. The Commission is accountable to the Minister for Justice and is required to make an annual report that is laid before Parliament.

THE REPUBLIC OF IRELAND

14.28   The Law Reform Commission was established by the Law Reform Commission Act 1975 as a statutory body corporate. Its remit includes criminal and civil law reform in accordance with programmes of law reform established under the 1975 Act and requests on specific topics addressed to it by the Attorney General under the Act. (Such programmes are drawn up by the Commission in consultation with the Attorney General and are submitted by the Taoiseach to the Government for its approval.) In addressing particular issues the Commission will normally publish a consultation paper to seek views from interested individuals and organisations. Responses are analysed and a seminar may be organised to discuss preliminary findings with interested bodies. All relevant views are taken into account by the Commission in preparing the final report. The text of the report is finalised by the Commission, publication arranged by the Secretary, and a copy forwarded by the President of the Commission to the Taoiseach and/or Attorney General, as appropriate.

14.29   After consultation with the Attorney General, the Government is responsible for appointing five persons (including a President) as members of the Commission for up to five years. The posts are not advertised. Currently, the Commissioners are all lawyers. The Act does not define or distinguish between the roles and responsibilities of the President and the Commissioners. Terms and conditions of appointment are determined by the Government.

14.30   To date the President has been a judge of the Superior Courts. This has aided communication between the Commission and the judiciary. Grant-in-aid to the Law Reform Commission in 1998 was IR£557,000.

14.31   Requests by the Attorney General form a substantial part of the Commission's work. In March 1998, a consultative committee, comprising representatives of a range of government

---

6   The Law Commission Act 1965.

departments, the Bar Council and the Incorporated Law Society, was established under the auspices of the Office of the Attorney General. The committee assists the Attorney General in the consultations about the programme, in selecting specific topics for examination by the Commission and in monitoring implementation of recommendations of the Commission.

14.32   The Commission is highly regarded by government departments. It takes very seriously its position as an independent body and is valued for the fact that its proposals are generated in a politically neutral and unpressurised environment with an emphasis on law reform in the general public interest.

14.33   An annual report by the Law Reform Commission is submitted through the Attorney General to the Taoiseach, and laid before both Houses of the Oireachtas.

CANADA

14.34   The Federal Law Commission of Canada was founded by the Law Commission of Canada Act 1996. The Commission offers Canadians a forum to present their views on issues of law and justice. Its programme of study is theme-based rather than related to particular areas of law.

14.35   Study panels, each headed by a Commissioner, consist of volunteer members and include representatives from federal government departments and the community. The Commission circulates discussion papers, draft studies and interim reports setting out its tentative recommendations, and organises formal consultation sessions to assist in the elaboration of specific research programmes. It uses a web-site to assist in the consultative process and to provide direct access to research papers as well as an opportunity for dialogue through on-line discussion groups.

14.36   The Commission engages in significant outreach through visiting schools, community groups and other organisations. It engages with the media in its efforts to increase understanding and awareness of the law as a feature of everyday life on the part of all Canadians from all parts of the community and all backgrounds. The Commission has also initiated joint activities with the legal professions, law faculties and other university departments, voluntary professional associations, the Uniform Law Conference, the Social Sciences and Humanities Research Council of Canada, and various non-profit making organisations and policy institutes. The strategy is complemented by contacts with several federal departments and agencies and with parliamentarians from all political parties.

14.37   The Canadian Commission has five part-time Commissioners, three of whom, including the President, are professors of law at different Canadian universities, the other two being the Commissioner of Ontario Provincial Police and the Director of Corporate Development for

Island Telecom Incorporated. It has five permanent staff comprising an Executive Director; a Director of Research; a Communications Manager; an Administration and Financial Services Officer; and an Executive Secretary.

14.38   One of the Commission's first tasks was to solicit nominations for a Standing Advisory Council to advise the Commission on its strategic direction and long-term programme of studies. In practice the Advisory Council has also assisted in planning the research, building networks and launching co-operative projects, adopting procedures and mechanisms for consultation with Canadians, and recruiting the Commission's full-time staff. The Advisory Council has 22 members drawn from across the country and reflecting its diversity.

SOUTH AFRICA

14.39   Established in 1973 and reconstituted in 1996, the South African Law Reform Commission has played a major role in developing the criminal justice system since 1994. It has focused on the development, improvement, modernisation and reform of South Africa law. The Commission is chaired by the Chief Justice, assisted by a judge of the Constitutional Court, a High Court judge, a barrister, two practising solicitors and an academic lawyer who, in contrast to other jurisdictions studied, is the only full-time member. Seventeen full-time researchers and a similarly sized administrative staff serve the Commission. The President can appoint additional members, if necessary.

14.40   The Commission is committed to developing relevant, accessible law. It has power to undertake investigations to modernise, improve, develop and reform particular aspects or even whole branches of criminal law and procedure. Its objective is to serve society by producing better law and it does so by recommending new laws to Parliament through the Minister of Justice. In making its recommendations, the Commission aims to make the law simpler, fairer, cheaper and more accessible.

14.41   The Commission is heavily focused on consultation throughout its work, and has developed close relationships with academics, the private sector and non-governmental organisations. There are a large number of project committees ranging over a wide subject matter including sentencing, security legislation, AIDS, domestic violence, childcare, juvenile justice etc. A committee, which brings in external expertise and members of the community, is assisted by a full-time researcher, and drives each project. The project committee typically works through the process, which involves publication of an issues paper, workshops at regional level, and a discussion paper (which has often included draft legislation). Consulting the public is central to the Commission's approach: it has in recent years adopted a policy of making itself more transparent, accessible and community oriented. The Commission has extended its consultative process by conducting workshops countrywide in urban and rural areas while approaching issues about the legal system from a multi-disciplinary perspective.

14.42 The Commission oversees the project committee's work and presents the final report to the Minister of Justice. Since 1996, the Minister has accepted 88% of the Commission's recommendations. The Commission's programme of work is for it alone to determine, but most of its projects come from the Minister. Others, including members of the public, can put forward topics for consideration. All of its projects are relevant to national priorities.

UNITED STATES OF AMERICA

14.43 In the United States of America law reform is a matter for politicians, the legal professions and academics. Many initiatives have been taken forward by groups of attorneys and teachers acting in consort. Since the 1870s law reform has been linked with the official organisation of the Bar.

14.44 The American Law Institute was established in 1923 "to promote the clarification and simplification of the law and its better adaptation to social needs, to secure the better administration of justice, and to encourage and carry on scholarly and scientific legal work". The Institute produces drafts for consideration by its Council and its membership and then publishes various restatements of the law, model codes, and other proposals for law reform. These publications are copiously referred to by attorneys and judges in court cases and are used in many law schools. The Institute has adopted a multi-media approach comprising a comprehensive range of educational materials and services.

NEW ZEALAND

14.45 Law reform in New Zealand is a matter for the Minister of Justice, but the Government is also advised by the statutory Law Commission, which is an independent, central advisory body established by the Law Commission Act 1985 to undertake the systematic review, reform and development of the law of New Zealand.

14.46 The Law Commission, funded by the Ministry of Justice, has a membership of five Commissioners (one full-time High Court judge as President and four part-time members). The part-time members bring experience of current practice from different parts of the legal profession. It is served by approximately 15 legal researchers and a director, together with a substantial and fully staffed law library. Its purpose is to help achieve law that is just, principled and accessible, and that reflects the heritage and aspirations of the peoples of New Zealand. It is assisted by a Maori committee, which helps the Commission identify projects to advance Maori culture and help achieve a reflection of that culture in the Commission's work. The committee is made up of six leading members of the Maori community, including three Maori judges.

14.47   The Commission may initiate projects or be given references by the Minister for Justice. It consults widely when developing its proposals for reform and generally publishes discussion papers inviting responses before formulating final recommendations. In all its work the Commission has regard to the desirability of simplifying the expression and content of the law. Its proposals have a strong practical bent and it assesses the practical and operational effects of proposed changes to criminal law, criminal justice and criminal procedure.

14.48   The Law Commission's reports are presented to the Minister of Justice, tabled in Parliament and published. Recent reports cover the law of succession, a review of the Official Information Act 1982, reform of the procedure for *habeas corpus*, and the use of anonymous witnesses in criminal proceedings. Other work during 1998 included an examination of the prosecution process, an examination of alternatives to formal prosecution, a review of the jury system, and a range of work in public and commercial law.

Evaluation and Recommendations

14.49   In our deliberations we took full account of views expressed to us during the consultative process, international practice, research and human rights instruments. We also gave careful consideration to the research, commissioned by us to examine this area, which supported the establishment of a new independent law reform body. There were features of models in other jurisdictions that we regard as having worked well. These included project working, together with a proactive and transparent approach to consultation in developing and reporting on proposals.

14.50   Much success in the area of law reform in other jurisdictions has been attributed to the functioning of their independent law commissions. Current arrangements for law reform in Northern Ireland are clearly not conducive to addressing law reform in a holistic and systematic way. We believe that a more systematic approach would be met by establishing an independent law reform body responsible for both civil and criminal law, procedure and practice in Northern Ireland. We were impressed by the practically oriented commissions in South Africa and New Zealand. We believe this is particularly important for Northern Ireland where there is a good deal of parity with England and Wales so far as substantive criminal and civil law are concerned but many differences in practice and procedure.

14.51   We have heard very powerful argument for a statutory law reform body, independent of government, which could provide an impartial and objective view of areas of law and make recommendations that the Government might include in its legislative programme. Law commissions in the other jurisdictions considered were, without exception, established on a statutory basis. Taking account of the need to develop law and practice appropriate to the circumstances of Northern Ireland, **we recommend that a Law Commission for**

Northern Ireland be established by statute to keep under review criminal and civil law, including procedure and practice, and to make recommendations to the Government on whatever changes it considers necessary or desirable. The establishment of such a Commission should not be dependent upon responsibility for criminal justice matters being devolved.

14.52   We were impressed by the working methods of the South African Law Commission, in particular its use of project committees with external experts acting as project leaders under the oversight of a Commissioner. We recognise the importance of public consultation in this field and believe that the approaches of the South African and Canadian Law Commissions provide examples of good practice.

14.53   Modern societies require law reform to work towards the clarification, simplification and publication of laws that promote respect for human rights and are responsive to the needs of the community. **We believe the functions of the Law Commission for Northern Ireland should include:**

- reviewing the current state of the law and coming forward with recommendations for reform;

- modernising and, where appropriate, simplifying and consolidating legislation;

- providing advice to the Government as to the most suitable topics for law reform and the most appropriate agencies to make a study of the options for reform;

- keeping abreast of developments in other jurisdictions, including in particular England and Wales, Scotland and the Republic of Ireland;

- working closely with Law Commissions in England and Wales, Scotland and the Republic of Ireland with a view to assessing the scope for harmonisation of the criminal law and procedure in all four jurisdictions;

- commissioning research; and

- inviting suggestions for reform and consulting as widely as possible.

14.54   **The Law Commission should consider both substantive law and procedural matters, taking account of current practice and implications for criminal and civil justice.**

14.55   **We recommend that the Commission be chaired by a High Court judge on a part-time basis.** In terms of membership of the Law Commission our attention has been focused on the need to bring in different experience and areas of legal expertise and **we recommend that membership of the Law Commission should include a senior barrister, a senior solicitor, a legal academic, and one lay person. Members should be remunerated.** From experiences of law reform bodies in other jurisdictions, it is clear that the involvement of at least one person engaged full-time on law reform greatly enhances the productivity and credibility of the organisation. However, in the context of a jurisdiction the size of Northern Ireland, we believe that it would be sensible to start with an entirely part-time membership. This can be kept under review in the light of experience and we should stress that we envisage a full-time and well-qualified secretary to the Commission, together with a full-time research officer and a full-time secretariat.

14.56   We considered to whom the Commission should be responsible and who would make the appointments to the Commission. **If a Law Commission were to be established in advance of responsibility for criminal justice being devolved, then its members should be appointed by the Secretary of State for Northern Ireland, consulting the First Minister and Deputy First Minister. In this event, the Commission should agree its programme of work with the Secretary of State and First Minister and Deputy First Minister. It should submit its reports jointly to the Secretary of State and relevant members of the Northern Ireland Executive Committee. Its reports should be tabled before the Northern Ireland Assembly and Westminster Parliament, and should be published.**

14.57   We see much merit in placing responsibility for appointments to the Commission with a senior non-political figure who would have an interest in law reform as it affects all government departments. **Once responsibility for criminal law matters is devolved, responsibility for appointing members to the Commission could pass to the Attorney General for Northern Ireland** (discussed in Chapters 4 and 15) **who would consult with departmental Ministers, as appropriate, and consider government remits for the programme. Policy responsibility for law reform matters would be assumed by the Minister responsible for justice matters.**

14.58   The details of working methods will be a matter for the Commission. However we endorse the proactive approach to consultation employed in most other jurisdictions. In the context of a project in Northern Ireland this might involve publication of a Law Commission scoping paper, followed by a period of research and of public consultation that would involve actively going out into the community to seek comments and views as well as receiving inputs from the professions and interest groups. The results of this process would be collated and incorporated in a report for government, which would include recommendations. Consideration should be given to using project teams, drawn at least in part from people outside the Commission, to take forward aspects of the work programme.

14.59   **We recommend that in developing its programme of work, the Commission should make its own suggestions and receive remits from government. In drawing up its programme of work it should also take account of views of others through a consultation process.**

14.60   Funding is clearly an important issue. **We recommend that the Law Commission should receive a sufficient budget for books and materials and to facilitate the**

commissioning of research and project work. We further recommend that the Law Commission be required to make all publications publicly accessible. A web-site facility would more widely publicise and aid distribution of the Commission's documents.

14.61   The research report[7] provides a cost analysis, based on the assumption of two full-time Commissioners, the provision of a stand-alone law library, and staffing support. They suggest annual running costs of around £660,000 with additional start-up costs of around £320,000. Our recommendation is based on the assumption that none of the Commissioners will work full-time and that the Commission may seek to use an existing law library. On this basis we estimate that annual running costs will be in the region of £500,000, and that start-up costs will be in the region of £250,000.

14.62   **We have identified a number of matters that were raised with us in the course of consultation, some of which are reflected elsewhere in the report, which we believe it would be appropriate for the Law Commission for Northern Ireland to consider as part of its early programme of work:**

- **The disclosure procedures under the provisions of the Criminal Procedure and Investigations Act 1996.**

- **Plea bargaining, focusing on issues concerning formalisation, transparency and human rights.**

- **Domestic violence, in particular how current law, policy and practice helps or hinders prevention, protection and service provision in relation to domestic violence. Such a review should not be confined to criminal procedures, but encompass family and civil remedies as well.**

- **Producing, for use by practitioners, a simple, clear and concise comparative guide to criminal law and procedure in Northern Ireland and the Republic of Ireland** (see also Chapter 17)**.**

14.63   Internal arrangements to support government in legislative matters will still be required and **in the event of criminal justice responsibilities being devolved, we recommend that responsibility for criminal law and procedure and those aspects of civil law which are currently the responsibility of the Office of Law Reform should be brought together within a new Department of Justice.**

---

7   Dickson and Hamilton, Research Report 9.

Organisation
and
Research

15 Organisation and Structure

Introduction

15.1 Our terms of reference require us to consider "… the structure and organisation of criminal justice functions that might be devolved to an Assembly, including the possibility of establishing a Department of Justice, while safeguarding the essential independence of many of the key functions in this area". They also require us to consider "… measures to improve the responsiveness and accountability of… the criminal justice system".

15.2 This chapter sets out the current organisation of criminal justice functions in Northern Ireland, and considers how they might be organised in the context of devolution of responsibility of criminal justice functions to the Northern Ireland Assembly. In doing so it draws upon what has been said already in this report in respect of elements of the criminal justice system, most notably the need to protect the independence of the judiciary and the prosecution. We consider the accountability and responsiveness of the criminal justice system. We take account of the need for structures that allow for the efficient and effective management of the system and address the important issue of tackling delay in bringing cases to trial.

15.3 We note also paragraph 7 of the Policing and Justice section of the Belfast Agreement which states:

> "The participants also note that the British Government remains ready in principle, with the broad support of the political parties, and after consultation, as appropriate, with the Irish Government, in the context of ongoing implementation of the relevant recommendations, to devolve responsibility for policing and justice issues."

15.4 We have, therefore, worked on the assumption that we should seek to bring forward proposals that are appropriate to the political and institutional context of Northern Ireland envisaged in the Belfast Agreement. We sought views in our consultation paper on whether and in what form criminal justice functions should be devolved to the Northern Ireland

Assembly, and on how those functions should be organised. We also sought views on what mechanisms agencies might use to draw out the views of the community and individual citizens on the services they provide, on what the role and nature of independent scrutiny should be, and on what more could be done to improve the accountability and responsiveness of criminal justice agencies.

15.5   We recognise that what we say in this chapter goes wider than criminal justice and addresses the administration of civil justice. Members of the judiciary are, for example, not only concerned with criminal matters; they also dispense civil justice.

Human Rights Background

15.6   There are no international human rights instruments that deal explicitly with the matter of how a criminal justice system should be structured and organised. However, the *European Convention on Human Rights* in Article 1 requires states to secure the rights and freedoms set out in the Convention. It is implicit, therefore, that states must have in place systems which enable them, for example, to protect everyone's right to life (Article 2), liberty and security of person (Article 5) and private and family life (Article 7).

15.7   In the case of *Osman v the United Kingdom*[1] the European Court noted that: "... the first sentence of Article 2(1) enjoins the state not only to refrain from the intentional and unlawful taking of life, but also to take appropriate steps to safeguard the lives of those within its jurisdiction". The Court also noted that the primary duty of a state was to secure the right to life by putting in place an effective framework of criminal law to deter the commission of offences against the person, backed up by law enforcement machinery for the prevention, suppression and punishment of breaches of the law.

15.8   Some of the instruments bear upon the administration of justice, as was noted in Chapters 4 and 5 in respect of the prosecution and judiciary (particularly in respect of the need for independence), and in Chapter 10 in relation to the administration of juvenile justice. They do not, however, provide much by way of direct guidance on how to organise and structure criminal justice systems. What is clear is that in designing criminal justice structures due care must be taken to ensure that those structures do not of themselves inhibit the state in fulfilling its obligations to protect the rights of its citizens. This suggests that the criminal justice system should be organised in such a way as to ensure that there are:

- mechanisms to develop effective criminal law;

---

1   *Osman v United Kingdom*, 28 October 1998, Reports 1998-VIII.

■ mechanisms for the prevention, detection, prosecution, adjudication and punishment in respect of crime, and that these are scrutinised regularly to ensure that their effectiveness and adherence to human rights norms are maintained and developed; and

■ mechanisms to ensure that the elements of the criminal justice system work together in a co-operative and co-ordinated way in delivering services and upholding rights and freedoms.

15.9 The avoidance of unnecessary delay is a human rights principle with direct bearing on the courts. *The European Convention on Human Rights* states that, "everyone arrested or detained... shall be brought promptly before a judge or other officer authorised by law to exercise judicial power and shall be entitled to trial within a reasonable time or to release pending trial". This is accompanied by the need to bring those deprived of their liberty speedily before a court so that the lawfulness of their detention can be tested.[2]

Organisation of the Criminal Justice System

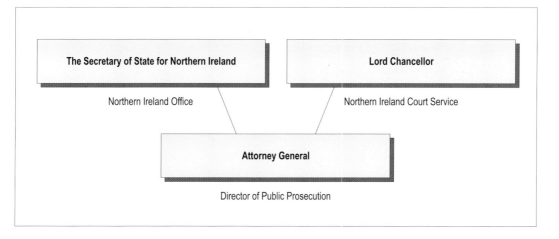

15.10 The publicly funded elements of the criminal justice system are responsible to three Ministers: the Secretary of State for Northern Ireland, the Lord Chancellor and the Attorney General.

15.11 The criminal justice system in Northern Ireland has evolved broadly in parallel with that in England. It is similar in many respects to that in the Republic of Ireland, which also has its roots in the English system. The criminal law within which it operates is a mix of common law, Acts of the Irish Parliament prior to 1800, Acts of the Northern Ireland Parliament, Acts

---

2   Livingstone and Doak, Research Report 14, sections 1.4 and 1.7.

of the Westminster Parliament, and Orders in Council made since 1972. In general, changes to the criminal law in Northern Ireland have remained in step with those in England and Wales, although some differences arise due to the distinct circumstances in Northern Ireland.

SECRETARY OF STATE FOR NORTHERN IRELAND

15.12   The Secretary of State for Northern Ireland has responsibility for the content of the criminal law in Northern Ireland and for the overall effectiveness of the criminal justice system. The Secretary of State also has responsibility for policy, legislation and the resource framework within which policing, prisons, and probation are delivered, together with policy on victims, crime prevention and community safety, and juvenile justice. The Secretary of State is responsible for the Compensation Agency, the Forensic Science Agency for Northern Ireland, State Pathology, and the provision of staff, offices and other resources for the Department of the Director of Public Prosecutions for Northern Ireland. Until 1997 the Secretary of State was responsible for considering alleged miscarriages of justice and for referring cases back to the Court of Appeal, where appropriate. On 31 March 1997 this responsibility in Northern Ireland and in England and Wales passed to the independent Criminal Cases Review Commission.

15.13   The Secretary of State is also responsible for the provision of certain facilities and services to enable sentences of the courts to be carried out, including prisons, probation and juvenile justice arrangements. The Northern Ireland Prison Service is a next steps agency within the Northern Ireland Office, with a Director General responsible to the Secretary of State for efficient and effective service provision. Probation is run by an independent Board (a non-departmental public body), appointed by and working within a strategic framework set by the Secretary of State. Juvenile justice arrangements have been the subject of recent legislative change and the introduction of a new strategic approach, intended to place more emphasis on diverting children away from the criminal justice system and custody.

15.14   In addition, under direct rule, the Secretary of State for Northern Ireland is responsible for certain aspects of civil law reform, which is delivered by the Office of Law Reform within the Department of Finance and Personnel.

THE ATTORNEY GENERAL FOR NORTHERN IRELAND

15.15   The Attorney General for England and Wales is the chief law officer of the Government, with responsibility for advising government departments and representing the Government's interest in important legal disputes. The same person fulfils the functions of Attorney General for Northern Ireland. In Northern Ireland the Attorney is responsible for the superintendence and direction of the Director of Public Prosecutions for Northern Ireland. The Attorney's functions in respect of the prosecution are set out in more detail in Chapter 4 of this report.

THE LORD CHANCELLOR

15.16   The Lord Chancellor is a Minister, the Speaker of the House of Lords, and the senior judge when that House is acting in its judicial capacity. The Lord Chancellor exercises executive functions in Northern Ireland through the Northern Ireland Court Service, which is a unified and distinct civil service of the Crown. Those responsibilities in relation to judicial and tribunal appointments are set out in Chapter 6. The Lord Chancellor is responsible for policy, legislation and resources in respect of the administration of the civil and criminal courts, for civil and criminal legal aid, and for aspects of civil law.

ACCOUNTABILITY AND INSPECTION ARRANGEMENTS

15.17   The criminal justice agencies in Northern Ireland are held accountable in a number of ways. They are accountable through their responsible Ministers to Parliament for the way in which they provide services, by way of parliamentary questions, scrutiny by select committees, and scrutiny of proposed legislation. They are accountable for the proper use of financial resources to Parliament, for which there are well-established audit systems. They are also directly accountable to the public, by way of Citizen's Charter commitments, annual reports, scrutiny by inspectorates, complaints mechanisms, and through judicial scrutiny of their actions. We have talked about these accountability mechanisms for each agency in the relevant chapter in the report.

15.18   One mechanism for achieving independent scrutiny and public accountability is through inspection. In Northern Ireland the RUC and Prison Service are subject to scrutiny by the HM Inspector of Constabulary (on a statutory basis) and HM Inspector of Prisons (by agreement) respectively. The Probation Service and juvenile justice centres are inspected by criminal justice specialists within the Social Services Inspectorate of the Department of Health and Social Services. The Forensic Science Agency for Northern Ireland is subject to inspection by the United Kingdom Accreditation Service, the body responsible for assessment and accreditation of organisations performing calibration, testing or sampling. Other agencies, such as the Northern Ireland Court Service and the Department of the Director of Public Prosecutions for Northern Ireland, are not subject to functional inspections at present, although they are subject to parliamentary scrutiny and financial audit.

INTER-AGENCY MACHINERY

15.19   In addition, there is inter-agency machinery designed to encourage co-operation and co-ordination across the criminal justice system. Ministers representing the Secretary of State for Northern Ireland, the Attorney General and the Lord Chancellor meet regularly to oversee the criminal justice system as a whole. They are advised by a Criminal Justice Board comprising the heads or senior officials of the main statutory organisations in the criminal justice system, with responsibility for developing the overall strategy for the criminal justice system and dealing with issues of inter-agency interest. Such issues include action to reduce delays in the criminal justice process and devising a strategy for developing information technology within criminal justice agencies in order to enhance the speed and quality of information flow between them. In addition the Criminal Justice Issues Group, which comprises representatives from the Bar Council, the Law Society and the judiciary, as well as the members of the Criminal Justice Board, considers important issues across the criminal justice system as a whole. The Board and the Criminal Justice Issues Group are supported by a common secretariat.

DELAY

15.20   The reduction in the time taken for court cases to be concluded is a key element in the Government's plans for improved efficiency in the criminal justice system and is being addressed through inter-agency machinery. Delay in criminal cases has been a problem in Northern Ireland and one of the tasks of the crosscutting review[3] was to examine delay and suggest how cases might be expedited.

15.21   The main recommendation of the review was that a case management approach should be adopted within the criminal justice system. In other words cases should be monitored regularly to ensure that those which seem to be slipping receive individual attention. This has required the organisations involved, for example the RUC and the DPP, to set administrative targets for each of the stages of cases for which they are responsible, including those for indictable offences triable before the Crown Court and offences tried summarily before the magistrates' courts. In addition, on foot of a practice direction from the Lord Chief Justice, the judiciary has set targets for the period from committal to arraignment and the magistracy for the time from first appearance to disposal. The targets are being reviewed year on year with a view to reducing progressively the time taken to process cases, while at the same time not allowing concern for speed to interfere with the quality of justice. As part of this process the RUC is currently developing a joint performance management system with the DPP, the

---

3   The cross-cutting review of criminal justice, examining the work of the criminal justice system across departmental boundaries, was initiated by Ministers in August 1997 as part of the Government's Comprehensive Spending Review.

Forensic Science Agency and State Pathology. This involves service level agreements between the RUC and the other bodies covering such factors as the timeliness, content and quality of materials passing between the organisations.

15.22 The review also made a number of detailed recommendations for legislative change and administrative change, for example new information technology systems for the transfer of case papers and other information. The programme of change is overseen by the Criminal Justice Board through a sub-group on which all the relevant organisations and the Law Society and Bar Council are represented.

15.23 For some years now the criminal justice organisations have been operating an administrative time-limits scheme, monitoring the time taken to bring to trial cases tried on indictment and summary cases prosecuted by the DPP, where the defendant is remanded in custody. These tend to be the more complex cases being processed through the system. In such (non-scheduled) cases the average time lapse between first court appearance at which the accused was remanded in custody and committal for trial in the Crown Court for the first half of 1999 was running at 209 days. This was made up of 106 days for the police to investigate and assemble evidence and submit the file to the DPP, 69 days for the DPP to issue a direction and 34 days between direction and committal. The average processing time from committal to arraignment (the start of proceedings in the Crown Court) was 30 days. Arraignment to trial took an average of 55 days.

Views Expressed during the Consultation Process

15.24 We heard a range of views on how criminal justice functions should be organised, on whether and in what form criminal justice functions should be devolved to the Northern Ireland Assembly, and on how the responsiveness and accountability of the criminal justice system might be improved.

THE EXTENT AND TIMING OF DEVOLUTION

15.25 There was broad support for the proposition that responsibility for criminal justice functions should, in the fullness of time, be devolved to the Northern Ireland Assembly. Very few respondents believed that criminal justice functions should not be. Most of those who commented on this issue believed that responsibility for all aspects of criminal justice should be devolved, including responsibility for:

■ policing, prisons, probation and juvenile justice;

■ criminal law and procedure;

- the administration of the courts;

- the prosecution system; and

- the selection and appointment of the judiciary.

15.26   As has already been noted in the relevant chapters, some concerns were expressed about devolution of more sensitive responsibilities such as those for judicial appointments and the prosecution system. Views on these issues were rehearsed more fully in the relevant chapters, and are not repeated here. However, there was almost universal support for the propositions that responsibility for the prosecution function should be kept separate from all other criminal justice functions and that the independence of the judiciary was of paramount importance.

15.27   There were significant differences between those who commented on when devolution of responsibility for criminal justice matters should occur. In a Northern Ireland Grand Committee debate on this Review on 8 July 1999 David Trimble MP commented that: "devolution of responsibility for criminal justice functions and associated matters is extremely important, and should be achieved as speedily as possible. It is an important aspect of the move towards the whole community in Northern Ireland taking responsibility for these matters that most directly affect it. Clearly there are sensitivities and difficulties... but I hope that the Government's policy will be to devolve as speedily as possible". We heard other views that suggested that responsibility for criminal justice issues should not be devolved until such time as the criminal justice system had been reformed by the Government. One organisation commented that "... the Assembly will have to win legitimacy over a period of years before devolution of this central state responsibility would be seen to be appropriate". We must say that we did not hear many fully considered views on this issue in the course of our consultation process. There was a general feeling, however, that criminal justice functions should be devolved at a point after responsibility for economic and social functions had been devolved.

THE ORGANISATION OF DEVOLVED FUNCTIONS

15.28   We were struck by the absence of any argument for significant change to the existing structure and organisation of criminal justice functions in advance of devolution. Where change was advocated, it was almost always premised on the assumption of criminal justice functions being devolved. The main exception to this was in respect of the prosecution function, which is discussed in Chapter 4 of this report.

15.29   Relatively few respondents expressed an opinion on how criminal justice functions should be organised post-devolution. Most of those who commented on this issue suggested that many, and perhaps all, criminal justice functions should be gathered within a single Department of

Justice. One submission noted that "... a Department of Justice is potentially very positive. The most obvious benefit would be the establishment of a highly focused, specialised and locally-oriented body". Another submission suggested that while most criminal justice functions should be brought within a single Department of Justice, responsibility for juvenile justice should fall within a Department for Youth, which would include education and care provision. One organisation, whilst generally supporting the concept of a single Department of Justice, noted that "keeping the various elements [of the criminal justice system] separate has the potential benefit that they may be less prone to adopt a unified anti-Catholic approach".

15.30   We heard evidence from the Forensic Science Agency for Northern Ireland on its relationships with other criminal justice agencies in Northern Ireland. The Agency noted that it worked mainly on behalf of the police (as was the case in most other jurisdictions) but that it also maintained a working relationship with the Department of the Director of Public Prosecutions. The Agency discussed whether there was a case for changing its status to that of a body independent of government or an integral part of the police. It concluded that while it was preferable to maintain its independence from the police, there was little to choose between remaining an executive agency and becoming a body independent of government.

15.31   Those who commented on the handling of alleged miscarriages of justice recommended that the Criminal Cases Review Commission should continue to consider cases arising from Northern Ireland. The only adverse comment made about the operation of the Commission concerned the perceived delays in processing cases. Some organisations recommended that it should be given additional funding and staff to tackle its backlog of cases.

ACCOUNTABILITY AND INSPECTION

15.32   In contrast, we heard a great deal of comment on the issues of accountability and inspection. Most of those who commented agreed that devolution of responsibility for criminal justice functions to the Northern Ireland Assembly was the key to improving accountability. Criminal justice agencies would come within the control of local politicians and would be subject to regular scrutiny by the Assembly committee structure, by the Assembly as a whole, and would also come within the ambit of the proposed Civic Forum.

15.33   We also heard a range of views from a variety of sources on other mechanisms which could strengthen the accountability of individual criminal justice agencies and the criminal justice system as a whole to the Assembly, to the community as a whole and individual members of the public. These included:

■   The publication of annual reports by each agency, setting out information on the agency's functions, its performance in relation to agreed objectives and commitments, information on the nature and outcome of complaints, and information on public and stakeholder attitudes to its performance. Some also suggested that an annual report should include information on the religious, gender and ethnic composition of the agency concerned.

■ The development and publication of standards of service that the public can expect from each agency.

■ The development and publication of codes of practice or statements of ethics for the staff of each agency.

■ The development of mechanisms by each agency to determine regularly the views of the public on the service provided by the agency concerned.

■ The development and publication of information packs by each agency on the service it provides. This was seen as a key way to inform and educate the public about the operation of the criminal justice system.

■ The commissioning and publication of research into the operation of agencies and projects within the criminal justice system.

■ The publication of information on the views of the public and users of the service.

■ The need for clear, easily understood and well publicised complaints mechanisms for each agency.

■ The involvement of the voluntary and community sectors in inter-agency machinery.

15.34   We heard a range of views in relation to the arrangements for the inspection of the criminal justice system. Most of those who commented on this issue believed that there was merit in a single criminal justice inspectorate. Those who supported the creation of a single inspectorate did so for a variety of reasons. One reason put forward most commonly was that such an inspectorate would allow thematic inspections across a number of agencies to be carried out. One submission noted that "... the various parts of the system are so dependent on each other and changes to one have such implications for others that a single properly managed and resourced inspectorate would be preferable". Most of those who favoured a single inspectorate also recommended that it should be independent of government and of the agencies that it was responsible for inspecting. One submission also suggested that it should be responsible for considering equality policy and "Targeting Social Need" analyses "of the working practice of the criminal justice system".

15.35   Not everyone favoured a single criminal justice inspectorate. Some felt that the existing inspection arrangements were adequate. Others felt that a single inspectorate could not hope to cover the very different and diverse range of services provided by criminal justice agencies and that specialist knowledge would be diluted or lost. Others felt that inspection was not an appropriate tool for some parts of the criminal justice system, such as the work of the judiciary or the courts, where it was feared that an inspectorate would compromise judicial independence. In addition, some criminal justice agencies believed that they were already subject to sufficiently rigorous third-party inspection covering all aspects of their work and that any additional layer of inspections was unnecessary. This was particularly the case in respect of the Forensic Science Agency of Northern Ireland, who argued that United Kingdom Accreditation Service scrutiny (which sets standards for the organisation and management of work), coupled with moves to develop a Council for the Registration of Forensic Practitioners in the United Kingdom (which would provide a degree of reassurance about the competence and ethical standards of forensic practitioners), obviated the need for additional inspection. Similar arguments applied to the State Pathology Department, whose staff would also become subject to scrutiny by the Council for the Registration of Forensic Practitioners.

15.36   We heard the view expressed by some that whilst inspection reports were currently made available to the public, in practice it had proved difficult in the past to obtain copies of reports. Those who commented on this issue believed that inspection reports should be routinely published, presented to the relevant Assembly committee and made easily available to the public.

15.37   The issue of delay in bringing cases to trial was raised with us, usually in general terms, on many occasions during the review, from a range of perspectives. It was a concern of the profession, the criminal justice agencies, the political parties, human rights groups and others. At the same time, there was recognition that, especially as law and procedure became more complex, speed should not be achieved at the expense of quality of justice.

Research and International Comparisons

15.38   We commissioned a review of relevant research information in respect of modelling the organisation of the criminal justice system, with particular reference to the potential devolution of criminal justice functions to the Northern Ireland Assembly. The resulting research report is published along with this report.[4] We drew upon their report, and the information we gathered in the course of our study visits, in our consideration of the options for the organisation and structure of the criminal justice system in Northern Ireland post-devolution.

15.39   We recognise, however, that the lessons we can draw from experience in other countries is limited, given the unique political and institutional context which exists in Northern Ireland. There are no ready made solutions based on the experience of other jurisdictions, although there are some pointers from which we can learn.

---

4   Walker and Telford, Research Report 18.

MODELS IN OTHER JURISDICTIONS

15.40   We saw a number of models for organising criminal justice functions in the jurisdictions we visited. To illustrate the range of existing models we describe the arrangements in a number of these jurisdictions. We first of all describe the arrangements in Scotland and the Republic of Ireland, both of which have omnibus justice departments. The arrangements in the Netherlands provide an example of a typical civil law approach, while Canada illustrates an approach within a federal jurisdiction with a mixed common law and civil law heritage. New Zealand provides a model that has recently resulted from a major reform of institutions.

SCOTLAND AND THE REPUBLIC OF IRELAND

15.41   The organisation of criminal justice functions in Scotland and the Republic of Ireland is similar in many respects, in that they both separate responsibility for prosecution from other criminal justice functions, and they both have omnibus justice departments which are responsible for most criminal justice functions.

15.42   In Scotland, responsibility for criminal justice functions is split between the Lord Advocate, who is responsible for the prosecution system and who plays a significant role in the appointment of the Scottish judiciary, and the Scottish Justice Department. The Justice Department is responsible to a Minister in the Scottish Executive, and is responsible for all criminal justice policy and procedure and for social work policy relating to criminal justice, and for the running of the Scottish prisons, through the Scottish Prison Service, which is a next steps agency. The Department is responsible for the organisation, administration and staffing of the Supreme and Sheriff Courts in Scotland, working through a next steps agency, the Scottish Courts Service. It is also responsible for the organisation of policing in Scotland.

15.43   In the Republic of Ireland most criminal justice functions come within the ambit of the Department of Justice, Equality and Law Reform. The Department is responsible for overall criminal justice policy, policing, prisons, probation services, the organisation and administration of the courts, judicial appointments, and for equality and law reform issues. The Department has recently created executive agencies to run the courts and the prisons. The independence of the judiciary is guaranteed by the Constitution of 1937. The Director of Public Prosecutions, while appointed by the Attorney General and having a consultative relationship with the Attorney, does not act under the Attorney's direction or superintendence. The Director's independence is protected by statute.

THE NETHERLANDS AND CANADA

15.44   Criminal justice functions in the Netherlands are organised in a way that is typical of the continental European civil law approach. Responsibility for policing and for the internal security of the state rests with the Ministry of Interior, while all other justice functions - including responsibility for the appointment of the judiciary and for the prosecution service - rest with the Ministry of Justice. The criminal justice system has undergone considerable change in recent years. Responsibility for policing has only recently been transferred from the Ministry of Justice to the Ministry of Interior, and the prosecution service and its relationship to the Government and parliament has been reviewed and reshaped, with a view to enhancing public accountability while strengthening the independence of prosecutorial decision making.

15.45   In Canada, which has a mixed common law and civil law heritage, both the federal government and the provinces have responsibilities for criminal justice functions. At federal level criminal justice functions are split between the Attorney General and the Solicitor General. The Solicitor General is responsible for policing and law enforcement, national security, corrections and conditional release of prisoners. Delivery of service is through a number of agencies, notably the Royal Canadian Mounted Police, the Canadian Security Intelligence Service, the Correctional Service of Canada, and the National Parole Board. A small central department provides the Solicitor General with policy advice and support. Other criminal justice functions, including overall responsibility for criminal policy and the criminal law, policy on victims and crime prevention, the appointment and training of federal judges, federal courts administration, and the federal prosecution function, fall within the remit of the Department of Justice of Canada, which is responsible to the Attorney General. A number of provinces are organised in a similar way with criminal justice functions divided between two ministries. Others, such as Alberta, combine all these functions within a single Ministry of Justice.

NEW ZEALAND

15.46   The management of the public sector in New Zealand changed radically in the years after 1985, as did its structure. Prior to 1995 justice functions were concentrated in a single Department of Justice. Responsibility for criminal justice is now spread across a number of departments, ministries and agencies. Core criminal justice functions are the responsibility of four departments: the Ministry of Justice, the Department of Corrections, the Department for Courts, and the Crown Law Office, together with the New Zealand police. Each of these organisations reports directly to a Cabinet Minister.

15.47   The Ministry of Justice provides strategic policy advice to the Government across the justice sector, focusing on constitutional law, civil justice, criminal justice and electoral operations. It also manages the system for judicial appointments, and considers alleged miscarriages of justice.

15.48   The Department of Corrections manages all custodial and non-custodial sentences imposed by the courts on offenders. It has three core elements: the Public Prisons Service; the Community Probation Service; and the Psychological Service. The Department of Social Welfare provides facilities and staffing for family group conferencing, working through the Children, Young Persons and their Families Service. The Department for Courts administers all courts and tribunals and enforces court orders relating to fines and debts.

15.49   The Crown Law Office is responsible for the criminal prosecution system and for providing legal advice to the Government. It is responsible to the Attorney General and is headed by a government official, the Solicitor General. The New Zealand police is a national police service. It is not responsible to any department of state, and reports directly to the Minister for Police. It develops its own policy and legislative proposals that are taken through Parliament by the Minister.

DELAY

15.50   In many jurisdictions the need to avoid undue delay, which we have noted in international instruments as a human right, has been a focus of government activity. In England and Wales, for example, legislation enabling the application of statutory time-limits has been in place for some time. So far these regulations have related only to indictable offences and have imposed limits only on the time that defendants spend in custody awaiting trial. More recently the Crime and Disorder Act 1998 has introduced provisions allowing different time-limits to be set in different classes of cases, for example allowing shorter time-limits for persistent young offenders. Pilots are being planned with a view to more widespread implementation in due course.

15.51   There is always a need to ensure that the pressure to dispose of cases quickly does not compromise the right to a fair trial. Furthermore, a defendant might receive a fair trial but little support or help to prevent re-offending. The development of the community court model in America was in part a response to the pressure on judges to dispose quickly of relatively minor offences, with little attention being paid to tackling the causes of criminal behaviour. We heard in a number of jurisdictions of the danger of focussing on speed of process at the expense of other considerations. For example, pressure to reduce delay could inhibit the development of restorative and reparative outcomes, given the need to contact victims and organise conferences.

Evaluation and Recommendations

15.52   Earlier in this chapter we made clear that we had worked on the assumption that we should seek to bring forward proposals that were appropriate to the political and institutional context of Northern Ireland envisaged in the Belfast Agreement. We did not see it as within our remit to consider what, if any, overall structural and organisational changes were necessary in the period leading up to devolution, however long that period might be. We do not, therefore, recommend any change to the current allocation of ministerial responsibilities in advance of devolution, although we have elsewhere in this report argued for some re-ordering of responsibilities within current portfolios. These include the substantial changes we have recommended to the prosecution service and the arrangements for the management of the Secretary of State's responsibilities for juvenile justice.

15.53   We focus on how criminal justice functions might best be marshalled within the Northern Ireland Executive and what arrangements are necessary to ensure that the elements of the criminal justice system are held accountable to the new institutions of government in Northern Ireland, to the community as a whole, and to individuals who come into contact with the criminal justice system. In our discussion of criminal justice matters we inevitably include areas, such as judicial matters and the courts' administration, which are equally relevant to the civil justice system.

EXTENT AND TIMING OF DEVOLUTION

15.54   We were struck, but not surprised, by the widespread view held amongst those we heard from in the consultation process that criminal justice functions should be devolved to the Northern Ireland Assembly. Few disagreed with the premise that the new Northern Ireland Assembly should assume responsibility for most or all criminal justice functions, although there were differences of opinion on precisely when such functions should be devolved.

15.55   We considered whether there should be a programme of devolution of criminal justice functions, with some functions being devolved at different times, or whether all criminal justice functions capable of being devolved should be devolved at the same time. We also considered elsewhere in this report whether there are specific criminal justice functions which should continue to be reserved or excepted matters indefinitely, such as responsibility for judicial appointments or the prosecution system.

15.56   We believe that there is no reason in principle to withhold from the Northern Ireland Assembly responsibility for a similar range of criminal justice functions to those devolved currently to the Scottish Parliament. That would mean broadly those criminal justice responsibilities now within the remits of the Secretary of State for Northern Ireland, the Lord Chancellor and the Attorney General. Functions excluded from the remit of the Scottish

Parliament include: national security; measures against terrorism and subversion; official secrecy; interception of communications; and nuclear security. **We recommend that responsibility for the same range of criminal justice functions as are devolved to the Scottish Parliament should be devolved to the Northern Ireland Assembly. Our preference is that they should all be devolved at the same time.**

15.57   The precise timing of devolution of responsibility for criminal justice functions will, of course, be a matter for discussion between the political parties in Northern Ireland and the British Government, and we make no firm recommendations on this. In practice, if responsibility for justice functions is to be devolved as a package then it can only be devolved once appropriate legislative provision has been made for excepted matters, including the appointment of the judiciary. This will require primary legislation by a Westminster Bill, for which time will have to be found in the legislative timetable. We recognise that it is possible to provide a legislative framework to allow for the staging of devolution of some functions.

ORGANISATION OF DEVOLVED FUNCTIONS

15.58   We envisaged in Chapter 4 the creation of a local, non-political Attorney General for Northern Ireland to carry out a range of functions, including oversight of the prosecution process and responsibility for the Law Commission (which was discussed in Chapter 14). We take as a given fact here the creation of such a figure, which would separate out responsibility for the prosecution from all other criminal justice functions. If it is decided that such an appointment is not to be made, we remain of the view that the Public Prosecution Service should be separate and freestanding. We also recall that we envisaged responsibility for community safety activity falling within the remit of the Office of the First Minister and Deputy First Minister, rather than within a department, although if this does not prove possible then these would be matters for a Department of Justice. We therefore focused our attention on how other criminal justice functions should be organised in the context of devolution. We considered two principal models: one in which all criminal justice functions are gathered together in a single omnibus Department of Justice; and a second in which justice functions are split between two departments.

15.59   In the first model all functions other than the prosecution function, responsibility for the Law Commission and judicial matters are gathered within a single Department of Justice headed by a Minister for Justice that would encompass responsibility for:

■   criminal and civil law and procedure (excluding those aspects of civil law not currently within the remit of the Office of Law Reform and the Northern Ireland Court Service);

■   policing, prisons, probation and juvenile justice;

■   policy in relation to victims and witnesses;

- policy and legislation in relation to firearms, fireworks and explosives;

- public order policy and legislation, and the Parades Commission for Northern Ireland;

- criminal injury and damage compensation;

- the administration of the courts (including coroners' courts);

- criminal and civil legal aid;

- the enforcement of judgments and other orders of the courts;

- the Forensic Science Agency for Northern Ireland and the State Pathology Service;

- funding the Judicial Appointments Commission (responsibility for the appointments would rest with the First Minister and Deputy First Minister, as recommended in Chapter 6);

- co-ordination of criminal justice research.

15.60   Given the size and spread of responsibilities of such a department there may be a need for the Minister to be assisted by a junior Minister.

15.61   The second model envisages splitting criminal justice functions between two departments. It is possible to do so in a number of ways, and we have seen a number of models in other jurisdictions. Given what we said in Chapter 12 in relation to the future management of prisons and probation, and in Chapter 10 about the management of the juvenile justice system, we suggest that in this model these functions should remain together within a single department, together with policing. Responsibility for all other justice functions would rest within a separate Department of Justice.

15.62   We recognise that other factors may influence the choice of the number and composition of departments with responsibility for justice functions, and that it is possible to conceive of models in which functions are split between more than two departments, as is the case in New Zealand. We note, however, that the difficulties of ensuring co-operation and effective co-ordination across the statutory elements of the criminal justice system are likely to become more acute as the number of departments increases. An omnibus department of the type we described above would have the advantage of minimising problems of co-ordination and would mirror the arrangements in both Scotland and the Republic of Ireland. We would counsel against creating more than one principal department with responsibility for criminal justice functions, in addition to that of the role of an Attorney General for Northern Ireland. **We recommend the creation on devolution of a single Department of Justice, headed by a Minister for Justice, bringing together all justice functions other than the prosecution, responsibility for the Law Commission and judicial matters.** Such a department would not, of course, have any role in making judicial appointments.

15.63   It will be apparent from our recommendations that we envisage a range of criminal justice services being delivered through next steps agencies, focusing on efficient and effective service delivery in accordance with the overall policy established by the responsible Minister. There will need to be a strong policy element in the core of the Department of Justice in order to advise the Minister. However, it is important to note that the agencies themselves, often with specialist professional expertise, will play an important role in the development of policy. This is particularly the case, for example, with the Prison Service where operational matters cannot be easily divorced from policy and where it is important that the Minister has access to advice from the Director General on policy matters. On the other hand, where the courts' administration is concerned, the "arms length" relationship with the Minister, usually associated with agency status, will be particularly important as a means of distancing from the executive matters in which the judiciary have an interest. Such considerations, along with accountability mechanisms, will need to be reflected in the framework documents that govern the relationship between agencies, the core department, and the Minister.

15.64   We note in passing a number of points in relation to the Forensic Science Agency of Northern Ireland and the State Pathology Department. We have already indicated where, within government, they should be placed, and we do not recommend any change in their status. We believe that it is important for the Forensic Science Agency and the State Pathology Department to be seen to be independent of the police and the prosecution. We note, however, that the location of the Forensic Science Agency, on a site that is closely associated with the police, is unfortunate and detracts from the perceived independence of the Agency from the police. We recognise the historical and security reasons for this arrangement, but **we recommend that as peace and political stability become embedded efforts should be made to find an alternative site for the Forensic Science Agency that would not be shared with the police.**

15.65   In addition, **there is scope for enhancing the management arrangements for the Agency and we recommend that a forensic science professional or academic from another jurisdiction in the United Kingdom should be invited to join the Agency's advisory board. We recommend secondments to and from other forensic science organisations to encourage professional development and discourage the development of a police or prosecution-focused culture.**

15.66   **As regards the State Pathology Department, we note its particularly heavy workload and recommend that it be reviewed to ensure that the expertise of its staff is properly deployed. We also note the limited administrative support arrangements for the State Pathology Department, and recommend that it should be strengthened to ensure that the professional staff are able to devote their time to professional tasks.** There should be sufficient administrative support to enable the Department to prepare and publish an annual report and other documents to enhance public accountability.

CRIMINAL CASES REVIEW COMMISSION

15.67   We were not aware of any pressure to create a separate and distinct Criminal Cases Review Commission in Northern Ireland. **We recommend, therefore, that the existing Criminal Cases Review Commission should continue to consider cases that involve alleged miscarriages of justice emanating from Northern Ireland.**

ACCOUNTABILITY AND INSPECTION

15.68   We noted from Strand One of the Belfast Agreement that "there will be a Committee for each of the main executive functions of the Northern Ireland Administration" and that:

"the Committees will have a scrutiny, policy development and consultation role with respect to the Department with which each is associated, and will have a role in initiation of legislation. They will have the power to:

■   consider and advise on Departmental budgets and Annual Plans in the context of the overall budget allocation;

■   approve relevant secondary legislation and take the Committee stage of relevant primary legislation;

■   call for persons and papers;

■   initiate enquiries and make reports;

■   consider and advise on matters brought to the Committee by its Minister."

15.69   We believe that the creation of such a committee for each department concerned with justice issues will provide a powerful means of holding the criminal justice system to account. If criminal justice functions are split between two or more departments there may be a need for the Assembly to consider the creation of a standing committee to consider cross-cutting issues within the criminal justice system. There may also be a role for the consultative Civic Forum that paragraph 34 of Strand One of the Belfast Agreement envisages.

15.70   In addition, Chapter 3 sets out a number of recommendations designed to enhance the accountability and responsiveness of the agencies within the criminal justice system, and of the criminal justice system as a whole. **We recommend that agency annual reports should, as a matter of course, be laid before the relevant departmental committee. In addition, if the Assembly constitutes a standing committee for the criminal justice system as a whole, we recommend that it and any departmental committees should receive and consider an annual report on the system in its entirety, prepared by the Criminal Justice Board.**

15.71   We noted the importance of inspection as a tool for holding criminal justice agencies to account for their actions and for the proper expenditure of public resources. In respect of the latter, we recognise that the Northern Ireland Audit Office will continue to play a vitally important role in holding departments and individual agencies within the criminal justice system to account for the expenditure of public funds. We also noted the views we heard in the course of the consultation process in relation to inspection. All those who commented on this issue believed that inspection of criminal justice functions was both necessary and desirable. There was some disagreement over whether individual agencies should have their own inspection arrangements or whether there should be a single, all-embracing and independent criminal justice inspectorate.

15.72   We believe that in the political and institutional context of Northern Ireland envisaged by the Belfast Agreement, and in the organisational context outlined above, the balance of argument favours the creation of a single independent criminal justice inspectorate. Therefore, **we recommend the creation of a statute-based, independent Criminal Justice Inspectorate which should:**

- **be responsible for ensuring the inspection of all aspects of the criminal justice system other than the courts;**

- **be funded by the Minister for Justice, and that the Chief Criminal Justice Inspector should be appointed by that Minister;**

- **present its inspection reports to the Minister for Justice, the responsible Minister (if the agency inspected is the responsibility of another Minister) and the relevant departmental committee or standing committee;**

- **publish its reports and make them widely and readily available;**

- **publish an annual report of its activities, present that report to the Minister for Justice, and lay it before the relevant departmental and standing committees;**

- **be responsible for advising Ministers on standards within criminal justice agencies (standard setting should remain the prerogative of Ministers);**

- **employ a range of full and part-time inspectors and buy in expertise, including that from other inspection agencies in England and Wales and Scotland, as appropriate (such as HM Inspectorate of Prisons and HM Inspectorate of Constabulary);**

- **be responsible for determining its own programme of inspections, in consultation with the relevant Ministers;**

- **carry out a range of inspections, including; periodic, cyclical and surprise inspections of systems and structures; thematic, issues-based inspections; and inspections which might require special skills (e.g. medical expertise); and**

■ work closely with other inspectorates (e.g. on Health and Safety, Mental Health, and Social Services) and with professional bodies such as the Royal College of Pathologists and the Policy Advisory Board for Forensic Pathology.

INTER-AGENCY MACHINERY

15.73 Whatever structure is eventually adopted for organising criminal justice functions in Northern Ireland there will be a continuing need for inter-Ministerial and inter-agency machinery to develop and maintain a co-operative and coherent approach to delivering the aims of the criminal justice system. This needs to occur, as at present, on three levels:

(i) at ministerial level within the Northern Ireland Executive;

(ii) at the level of heads of agencies and senior policy-makers within the devolved departments and the Public Prosecution Service; and

(iii) at the level of (ii), but involving other significant partners, such as other relevant Northern Ireland departments, sentencers, the voluntary sector, and the legal profession.

15.74 **To this end we recommend that Ministers in the Northern Ireland Executive responsible for criminal justice functions, together with the Attorney General for Northern Ireland, should meet regularly to oversee the criminal justice system as a whole. They should, in particular, agree and publish a common set of aims for the criminal justice system**, as recommended in Chapter 3.

15.75 The ministerial group will require support at official level by way of a group which is responsible for developing the overall strategy of the criminal justice system, for ensuring that the system works co-operatively and in a co-ordinated way to provide services to users and to the public, and for dealing with issues of inter-agency interest. **We recommend that support to the ministerial group should continue to be provided by the Criminal Justice Board. The Criminal Justice Board should comprise, as at present, the heads of the main statutory agencies within the criminal justice system and senior policy-makers from within the relevant departments. It should comprise:**

■ **The head of the Public Prosecution Service.**

■ **The Chief Constable of the Police Service of Northern Ireland.**

■ **A senior representative from the Attorney General's Office.**

■ **The head of the Department of Justice and of any other department with criminal justice functions.**

■ **The heads of the Prisons, Probation, Courts and Juvenile Justice Agencies.**

■ **The head of the central Community Safety Unit.**

15.76   We see a continuing need for an inter-agency group, such as the Criminal Justice Issues Group, which provides a means of co-ordinating the consideration of new needs and policy issues across the range of organisations contributing to criminal justice, and which looks forward, innovates and reviews new inter-agency initiatives. It should bind together representatives of the criminal justice agencies, including the members of the Criminal Justice Board, with representatives of other relevant Northern Ireland departments, the judiciary, the Bar Council and the Law Society. We note the important role which sentencers and the legal profession have played in taking forward the work of the Criminal Justice Issues Group and the continuing importance of their involvement in future. In addition, **we agree with those who suggested that the membership of the Criminal Justice Issues Group should be expanded to include representatives of the major voluntary sector organisations, given the important role they currently play - and will continue to play in future - in delivering criminal justice, and we so recommend.**

15.77   **We recommend that the ministerial group, the Criminal Justice Board, and the Criminal Justice Issues Group should continue to be supported by a common secretariat, which should be located within the Department of Justice.**

CASE MANAGEMENT AND DELAY

15.78   Throughout our consultation we heard calls for the speedier disposal of justice and for a reduction in the time taken to bring cases to trial. There were particular concerns about the impact of delay on people being held in prison awaiting trial, and we are conscious of the human rights implications if people are not brought to trial within a reasonable period. This is an area where the inter-agency machinery outlined above can make a major contribution.

15.79   As noted above, as a result of a review that concluded in 1998, the criminal justice system in Northern Ireland is already taking a number of steps to reduce delay. The steps include setting administrative targets for the various stages of cases linked to case management systems and joint performance management. The RUC and the DPP are the key agencies when it comes to issues of timeliness in the period up to committal. It is the intention to keep the administrative targets under review with a view to seeing whether they can be progressively reduced during the period to 2002. We note that the judiciary is playing an important role in the management of cases, especially following arraignment, with a view to ensuring that trials take place in a timely fashion. Magistrates are also actively engaged in keeping adjournments to a minimum and seeking to reduce the time taken to dispose of cases. There has been a significant and positive culture change in the courts.

15.80   We commend this work. The new system has been in operation since the beginning of the 1999 calendar year and there have been some improvements both in terms of a reduction in overall time taken and in a lower rate of failure to meet specific targets (notwithstanding the tightening of targets). However, it will take some time before we can be certain that the new arrangements are having a continuing effect. We are conscious that at a time of major change sustaining a downward pressure on time taken to bring cases to trial, without compromising on the quality of justice, will be a big challenge.

15.81 Within Northern Ireland there is already legislation (Northern Ireland (Emergency Provisions) Act 1996) enabling the Secretary of State to set statutory time-limits for scheduled offences. However, the power has not been used. There has been concern that the introduction of custody time-limits might result in persons suspected of serious offences being released on bail or acquitted. This is a particular concern in relation to terrorist cases that often rely on lengthy and detailed forensic examination to provide evidence for the prosecution. We note, however, that statutory time-limit schemes permit the limits to be extended on certain grounds. For example in England and Wales an extension may be granted under the Prosecution of Offences Act 1985 if there is "good and sufficient cause for doing so" (for example if a witness is ill on the day of trial) or if "the prosecution has acted with all due expedition" (which would enable an extension in cases where delays had been caused by the defence).

15.82 In thinking about the time taken to bring cases to trial, we are conscious of a number of considerations. There is the human rights imperative that cases be brought to trial in a reasonable time and, particularly when defendants are remanded in custody, there are obvious reasons for wanting determination of guilt or innocence and sentencing to take place as soon as possible. But there are other factors to bear in mind. For example the longer the time that elapses between an incident and a witness giving evidence, the more likely it is that problems of recall will arise. Delay can increase the pressure on victims and witnesses who may be concerned about a court appearance; and it can also increase the distress suffered by victims as a result of the offending behaviour.

15.83 In the light of all these considerations we conclude that the arrangements introduced in Northern Ireland after the cross-cutting review, including the extended administrative time-limits scheme, should be allowed to run, but that they should be monitored closely. There remains considerable scope for improvement. **We recommend the introduction of legislation that will enable statutory time-limits to be introduced in Northern Ireland, should that be judged to be necessary.** If the administrative scheme proves not to be having the desired effect, that might be a trigger for the introduction of time-limits; such statutory limits might also be considered for classes of case where delay is particularly damaging. Further, **we recommend that in addition to setting target time-limits within which cases should be completed, attention should be paid to the average time taken to process cases at the relevant stages.** This will help ensure continued downward pressure on completion times for all cases, not just those that might be the most difficult.

ORGANISED CRIME

15.84   Several people raised with us concerns about the possible future development of organised crime in Northern Ireland. A number of factors might contribute to this including an increase in drugs related crime, some ex-paramilitaries turning to crime for personal gain, and the spread of organised crime from other jurisdictions. Countering organised crime requires intelligence and detective work, financial expertise, an effective legal framework, co-operation between agencies and with the private sector, and, above all, co-ordination with ground-level community safety activity. Increasingly, it also places a premium on international co-operation. To facilitate an effective approach in dealing with this threat **we recommend the establishment of an inter-agency group in Northern Ireland tasked with developing a strategic and co-operative framework for countering organised crime. The core of such a group might be the Department of Justice, the police, Customs and Excise, the Public Prosecution Service and the central Community Safety Unit.**

16 Research and Evaluation

Introduction

16.1 The capacity for research and evaluation is indispensable in a criminal justice system that aspires to be responsive, effective and forward looking. Research into crime levels and trends informs Ministers and policymakers about the effectiveness of the system and assists them in devising new and innovative approaches for the future. It helps them target programmes on types of crime and geographical areas where the need is greatest. Of equal importance is the use of evaluation to assess the impact of policies, programmes and schemes and their value for money so that decisions can be taken on whether to continue with them and also as a basis for spreading best practice. Research has a crucial part to play in accountability mechanisms, through providing tools for the monitoring of outcomes against performance.

16.2 Research and evaluation are essential tools for assessing the effectiveness of the criminal justice system and provide the basis for making improvements. In Chapter 3 we have set out the principles and values that we believe should inform decisions taken about the criminal justice system. In this chapter we look at the function of research and the structures that are necessary to provide adequate research and evaluation.

16.3 The need for adequate evaluation of criminal justice programmes is recognised in international human rights instruments. For example, Article 9(d) of the *United Nations Guidelines for the Prevention of Juvenile Delinquency* (the Riyadh Guidelines), Rule 30 of the United Nations *Standard Minimum Rules for the Administration of Juvenile Justice* (the Beijing Rules) and Rule 20 of the *United Nations Standard Minimum Rules for Non-Custodial Measures* (the Tokyo Rules) all emphasise the need for policies, programmes and strategies to be based on monitoring and evaluation.

16.4 The value of research has been demonstrated to us from many perspectives in the course of our review, and it is relevant that we have chosen to publish 18 research papers alongside our report. In the remainder of this chapter, we examine the research capacity in Northern Ireland and its organisation.

Current Arrangements in Northern Ireland

16.5   In Northern Ireland, the two main sources of research experience and expertise on criminal justice matters and crime prevention matters lie within government and the universities.

16.6   Within government, responsibility for social research in all departments lies with the Northern Ireland Statistics and Research Agency (NISRA), which is an executive agency within the Department of Finance and Personnel. It provides research and statistical services directly and purchases services from outside in order to assist policy makers and inform debate. In the criminal justice system, NISRA staff are based in the Northern Ireland Court Service, Probation Service, Police Authority for Northern Ireland, the RUC and the Criminal Justice Directorate of the Northern Ireland Office. In addition, we should note that the Forensic Science Agency for Northern Ireland and the State Pathology Department carry out research within their own specialities.

16.7   The Northern Ireland Office has seven NISRA researchers and statisticians, together with support staff, in its Statistics and Research Branch. They are responsible for producing a variety of publications including a *Commentary on Northern Ireland Crime Statistics* each year and a bi-annual *Digest of Information on Northern Ireland Criminal Justice System*, which are widely used and well received. The table opposite indicates some of the most recent publications.[1]

16.8   The Northern Ireland Court Service produces annual judicial statistics and a variety of data is published in the annual reports of the Chief Constable of the Royal Ulster Constabulary and the Northern Ireland Prison Service.

16.9   The University of Ulster and Queen's University both have criminal justice research capacities, including the Institute of Criminology and Criminal Justice within the School of Law at Queen's University, and researchers from both institutions have assisted us in our research programme. The number of experienced criminologists and researchers on crime prevention and criminal justice within Northern Ireland, however, is relatively limited.

---

1   The last three documents listed are available at http://www.nics.gov.uk/nio. The other documents are available from Statistics and Research Branch, Northern Ireland Office, Massey House, Stoney Road, Belfast.

Statistics and Research Branch Publications

Title	Last Published
A Commentary on Northern Ireland Crime Statistics 1997	May 1998
Gender and the Northern Ireland Criminal Justice System	December 1997
Criminal Justice in Northern Ireland – Key Statistics 1997	October 1998
Digest of Information on the Northern Ireland Criminal Justice System – 3	April 1998
Juveniles and the Northern Ireland Criminal Justice System	February 1997
Northern Ireland Statistics on the Operation of the Prevention of Terrorism Act	Quarterly Publication
Sexual Offending in Northern Ireland	May 1997
Statistics on the Operation of the Northern Ireland (Emergency Provisions) Act	Quarterly Publication
Drugs in Northern Ireland – Some Key Facts 1992-1998	November 1998
Preliminary Research Findings from the 1994/5 Northern Ireland Crime Survey Research Findings 1/96	June 1996
Fear of Crime and Likelihood of Victimisation in Northern Ireland – Research Findings 2/96	November 1996
Changing Patterns of Drug Use in Northern Ireland – Some Recent Survey Findings – Research Findings 1/97	June 1997
Use of Bail and Levels of Offending on Bail in Northern Ireland – Research Findings 1/98	March 1998
The Northern Ireland Prison Population in 1998 – NIO Statistical Bulletin 1/99.	December 1999
Fear of Crime and Victimisation in Northern Ireland – NIO Research Findings 1/99	December 1999

16.10   The voluntary sector has also been a source of expertise, for example through the Centre for Independent Research and Analysis of Crime established in 1988 by the Extern Organisation. Some examples of the work for which the independent sector and universities have received funding include: reviews of prosecution process; legislation relating to changes to the "right of silence"; delay in the Northern Ireland criminal justice system; evaluation of prison programmes; a community crime survey; a study of self-reported delinquency; and an analysis of long-term trends in crime in Ireland. Current projects in receipt of funding include the evaluation of projects that aim to address the offending patterns of persistent young offenders and a pilot scheme to divert mentally disordered offenders from the formal criminal justice system.[2]

16.11   Given the relatively small size of Northern Ireland's jurisdiction, NISRA staff and policy makers have been alive to the importance of drawing lessons from research carried out elsewhere and in this context Home Office research and statistical reports have been particularly helpful. Also, when putting research work out to tender, agencies are well aware of the need to attract interest from academic institutions and others outside Northern Ireland, while at the same time doing all they can to support and enhance the local research base.

---

2   For details of this research contact the Statistics and Research Branch at the Northern Ireland Office.

Views Expressed During the Consultation Process

16.12   During our consultation exercise a number of references were made to research. It was seen as a necessity if we were to:

- assess the levels and impact of crime and its causes, so that strategies and policies could be properly directed to where they would have the most effect;

- provide the tools to enable evaluation to take place;

- measure the effectiveness of the criminal justice system in meetings its aims and objectives therefore constituting an important means of providing accountability; and

- support equity monitoring.

16.13   Another theme that emerged was the desire for a strong independent research capacity in Northern Ireland. This was seen as of value not only to enable government to buy in research but also because it made for a healthy environment if academic institutions and the voluntary sector were able independently to initiate research. Some commented on the need for considered and informed interpretation of research data.

16.14   Some pointed to the danger that raw data, taken in isolation or out of context, could mislead or produce over-simplistic results. This was not presented as an argument against research, but rather in support of the view that publications of statistics should be accompanied by informed commentary.

16.15   Submissions from a number of groups highlighted specific areas where there was a need for research. These included research into the impact of the current law on domestic violence, the operation of the juvenile justice centres, women and children's experience of the criminal justice system and the effectiveness of early interventions for mentally disordered offenders.

16.16   As we have noted in Chapter 3 the argument was also advanced for the collection of data on the background of people working in the criminal justice system and of the people being processed through it. It was argued that the aims of the criminal justice system set out in the Belfast Agreement emphasised equal treatment for all. Therefore, gathering data on the experience of different groups, whether defined through religious affiliation, gender, sexual orientation, marital status, class or disability, was one way in which the system could be held accountable.

Experience in Other Jurisdictions

16.17   A particularly useful aspect of the visits we undertook to other jurisdictions was the opportunity to talk directly with people who were involved in the latest research into criminal justice issues. For example, Canada has a commitment to developing policy from a solid research base and their emphasis on the reintegration of offenders emerged following research into the effectiveness of various strategies of intervention. In the Netherlands there has been a policy for several years of evaluating its crime prevention initiatives and a proportion of the funding for these initiatives has been set aside in order to support evaluation. Similarly in New Zealand and Australia restorative justice programmes are the subject of long-term evaluation by independent, university-based researchers.

16.18   Internationally, the most striking trend that we identified in this area was the focus on evaluation. In Canada and New Zealand service providers, whether statutory or voluntary sector, would be expected to include evaluation in their business plans supporting any bid for project funding.[3] The same approach is being adopted in England and Wales where 10% of the £250 million being invested by the Home Office in its three year crime reduction programme (see Chapter 11) is to be devoted to research and evaluation.

Evaluation and Recommendations

16.19   In undertaking this review we felt it was essential to have a full range of up to date research on the issues facing Northern Ireland in addressing crime. For that reason we conducted an audit of existing research and where gaps were identified we commissioned additional work. We have published our research that we hope will be a useful tool for academics, policymakers, voluntary agencies and others with an interest in this area.

16.20   The Government and the public need accurate and up-to-date statistics and research data in order to be able to gauge trends in crime and the effectiveness of the system as a whole and of particular types of intervention. This is essential if policies are to be well directed and if proper accountability is to be secured. An effective research strategy requires co-operation between the criminal justice agencies in sharing of information and there is a need for a common approach to classifying and recording data. Individual agencies have their own research needs, but it should be clearly understood that agencies do not "own" information which, subject to the requirements of confidentiality in the interests of justice or to protect individuals, should be in the public domain. We tend to agree with the report of the cross-cutting comprehensive spending review on criminal justice which concluded that the Criminal Justice Board should co-ordinate the criminal justice research programme annually

---

3   In Canada, www.merx.cebra.com lists all available Government funds.

and ensure proper access to its products. **We recommend that the Criminal Justice Board should be tasked with taking forward further work on the harmonisation of statistical categories across the criminal justice system and ensuring co-operation between agencies in sharing information. In all planning and framework documents, a duty should be placed on agencies to share information, provided that protocols are in place to ensure that this does not harm the interests of justice or enable individuals to be publicly identified.**

16.21   In Chapter 3 we examined the need for a set of guiding aims and principles for the criminal justice system and the need for an appropriate range of indicators was noted. For example, if work is being directed towards reducing the fear of crime it is important to develop meaningful indicators of the level of fear and whether that level is changing. Similarly the aim of a fair and equitable system requires equity monitoring. We have explained our approach to equity monitoring in Chapter 3. This will require the development of an information technology system capable of tracking cases and disposals to support research and evaluation in the future.

16.22   We see an ever-increasing need for well presented research and statistical information for the following reasons:

- to enable policy decisions and funding to be targeted on the basis of identified need;

- the policy of linking funding to evaluation;

- the need to monitor a range of indicators to assess how far the system is meeting its aims;

- the likelihood of an increased focus on crimes that are not related to terrorism; and

- the changes recommended in our report will need evaluation.

16.23   This last point is particularly important. As a result of our recommendations we expect major change and innovation in several areas, such as approaches to juvenile offending, community safety and prosecution processes. In principle, any major change in criminal justice practice requires evaluation. Funding is vital to sustain research. We note that the Home Office is setting aside major sums for evaluation of its Crime Reduction Programme. **We recommend that evaluation should be an integral part of business planning for the development of new policies and programmes and that provision for evaluation should be included in the funding of crime reduction projects. Such evaluation will need to be addressed in a proportionate manner and, especially where small sums are involved, it might not necessarily always involve the use of academic researchers or consultants. However, we have no doubt that if evaluation and the other drivers for research identified above are to be taken seriously, then there will be a need to increase the criminal justice research capacity in Northern Ireland.**

16.24   The existing Statistics and Research Branch within the Northern Ireland Office provides a variety of services to the NIO and the rest of the criminal justice system through:

- the provision of statistics and statistical analysis;

- undertaking research;

- co-operating with other organisations in providing research; and

- commissioning research and evaluation.

We recommend that the Statistics and Research Branch of the Northern Ireland Office should have responsibility for the collation of statistical information across the criminal justice system.

16.25   The challenge will be maintaining a pool of expertise in Northern Ireland that will be available to undertake research for both the Government and universities and colleges. Research capacity is currently underdeveloped, the size of the jurisdiction making it difficult to sustain a range of expertise. Researchers working for NISRA tend to move between departments and specialisms. While this may be necessary from a career development perspective, it can militate against the development of in-depth expertise in such areas as criminal justice. We note the efforts made by NISRA to ensure that a level of experience on criminal justice matters is sustained amongst their staff working within the NIO and the criminal justice agencies and hope that they will pay particular attention to this in the future. **In order to enhance the critical mass of criminal justice research expertise within government and to build on links with outside research institutions, we recommend the use of secondments and staff exchanges between government and outside research institutions. Further, we recommend that government and outside researchers should work together to build up the pool of research capabilities, and work collaboratively on such matters as research projects, seminars, conferences and training.** In adopting such an approach, government and the universities would be building on the efforts already being made by a number of individuals amongst their own statistics and research staff. Funding for research bursaries would be an option worth pursuing further.

16.26   We have already noted the importance of a small jurisdiction making use of research promoted and undertaken by its larger neighbours. **We recommend that some funding be targeted towards fostering co-operation between researchers through joint conferences and seminars, and suggest that specific research projects might be undertaken on an all-island basis.**[4]

16.27   There are clearly resource implications in some of this, and they are extremely difficult to assess. **We recommend that discussions take place between those in government responsible for justice matters, NISRA, the Department of Higher and Further Education, Training and Employment and the universities with a view to developing a costed research strategy.**

---

4   See chapter 17.

Structured Co-operation

17 Structured Co-operation

Introduction

17.1   Our terms of reference invite us to address and bring forward proposals relating to "the scope for structured co-operation between the criminal justice agencies on both parts of the island". In this chapter we set out some of the structures under which criminal justice co-operation might occur. We then make some suggestions on particular areas where we believe there is an opportunity for increased structured co-operation between Northern Ireland and the Republic of Ireland.

17.2   We have not attempted to list all the areas where co-operation occurs, or might occur in the future, many of which are or can be addressed through informal working arrangements. The development of opportunities will be a joint matter between those involved in criminal justice in Northern Ireland and the Republic of Ireland. We feel it is important to note that there are also opportunities for co-operation in a broader European Union framework and within these islands.

Human Rights

17.3   Both the United Kingdom and Ireland are member states of the European Union, where values are founded on a shared commitment to human rights and respect for such regional and international instruments such as the *European Convention on Human Rights* and the *International Convention on Civil and Political Rights*. At the European Council meeting held at Tampere, Finland in October 1999 there was agreement to draw up a draft charter of fundamental rights of the European Union.[1] This was recognition of the close connection between the protection of rights and the creation of an area of freedom, security and justice in the European Union.

---

1   Presidency Conclusions, Tampere European Council, 15 and 16 October 1999.

17.4   The intention is to foster co-operation but also ensure that co-operation between the member states of the European Union is subject to the protection of rights, such as the right to asylum and the right to privacy. Both of these areas raise issues when considering co-operation between jurisdictions on criminal justice matters. The right to asylum, set out in Article 14 of the *Universal Declaration of Human Rights*, may not be invoked in the case of prosecutions genuinely arising from non-political crimes; thus human rights protections should not mean that those who have committed a crime are able to avoid prosecution by crossing to another jurisdiction. A right to privacy has implications for cross-border co-operation in that information must not be shared between jurisdictions without regard for the right to privacy of the individual.

17.5   As noted in Chapter 3, the British Government is incorporating the *European Convention on Human Rights* into Northern Ireland law. The Government of Ireland is at present considering the incorporation of the Convention into Irish law. The written Irish Constitution already provides human rights guarantees, which we understand from the Irish Government are equivalent to, or in many cases stronger than, those set out in the Convention. As provided for in the Belfast Agreement, both Governments are establishing Human Rights Commissions with similar mandates and remits; legislation for this purpose is at present before the Dáil. The Belfast Agreement also provides for a joint committee of the two Human Rights Commissions, North and South.

Current Arrangements

17.6   Co-operation on criminal justice matters between North and South has been developing over many years, both on a formal basis and as a result of informal arrangements which have grown up out of contact between policymakers and agencies in both jurisdiction. One example of this co-operation was the Law Enforcement Commission, which resulted in the enactment of the Criminal Jurisdiction Act 1975 and, in Ireland, of the Criminal Law (Jurisdiction) Act in 1976. From 1985 to 1999, the Anglo-Irish Agreement provided the principal framework for this co-operation. Under the Agreement, an Intergovernmental Conference and a joint secretariat were established. The remit of these institutions included security and related matters, legal matters, including the administration of justice, and the promotion of cross-border co-operation. These institutions ceased to exist following the entry into force of new arrangements that flowed from the Belfast Agreement.

17.7   Co-operation in the field of justice and home affairs is an area that has been developing rapidly at the European Union level. The member states of the Union are committed to its development as an area of freedom, security and justice by making full use of the possibilities offered by the Treaty of Amsterdam. Some of the implications for criminal justice co-operation were stated at the Tampere European Council in October 1999 as follows:

"The enjoyment of freedom requires a genuine area of justice, where people can approach courts and authorities in any Member State as easily as their own. Criminals must find no way of exploiting differences in the judicial systems of Member States. Judgments and decisions should be respected and enforced throughout the Union, while safeguarding the basic legal certainty of people and economic operators. Better compatibility and more convergence between the legal systems of member states must be achieved."[2]

17.8   The United Kingdom and Ireland are also members of the Council of Europe, which provides an additional framework for co-operation in criminal justice matters, particularly in the area of legal co-operation. Both the United Kingdom and Ireland are parties to a number of Council of Europe conventions, including: the *European Convention on Mutual Assistance in Criminal Matters*; the *European Convention on the Transfer of Sentenced Persons*; the *European Convention on Laundering, Search, Seizure and Confiscation of Proceeds from Crime*; and the *European Convention on the Suppression of Terrorism*.

17.9   Co-operation within both of these frameworks will continue to provide opportunities for the development of co-operation between North and South, through the use of agreed instruments and programmes. Moreover, membership of these bodies is fully compatible with the development of closer bilateral relationships, provided that such co-operation is in keeping with developments within the European Union and the conventions to which both states are parties.

MUTUAL ASSISTANCE

17.10   Legal co-operation thus constitutes a common interest for all the countries in the European Union. It can occur on a number of levels. One mechanism is mutual assistance in criminal matters, which aims to make it easier to obtain evidence from other countries, to reinforce agreements allowing investigations and to develop a permanent framework for exchanges of information between investigators and judicial authorities in different countries, where appropriate.

17.11   Both the United Kingdom and Ireland are party to the 1959 Council of Europe *Convention on Mutual Legal Assistance in Criminal Matters,* which provides for reciprocal assistance on matters such as the provision of evidence and extracts from judicial records and the serving of writs. The Criminal Justice (International Co-operation) Act 1990 provides a legal basis for the United Kingdom to give such practical assistance to judicial and prosecuting authorities in another jurisdiction and to accept such assistance. This can take various forms, including the service of process in the United Kingdom on behalf of another jurisdiction, such as the delivery of summonses, the transfer of a United Kingdom prisoner to give evidence which

---

2   Presidency Conclusions, Tampere European Council, 15 and 16 October 1999, paragraph 5.

has been requested by another jurisdiction, and the authorisation of searches for material relevant to an investigation in another jurisdiction. In Ireland, the legal basis on which mutual assistance is provided is the Criminal Justice Act 1994. In 1998, the United Kingdom and Ireland signed an Agreement on Mutual Assistance in Relation to Criminal Matters, which supplements existing international instruments in this field. Both parties agree to grant each other assistance in investigations and proceedings, including the tracing, restraint and confiscation of the proceeds and instruments of crime. The Agreement will come into force when both parties have completed the necessary constitutional formalities.

MUTUAL RECOGNITION

17.12   Mutual recognition of decisions and enforcement of judgments is a more far-reaching proposal, and is a principle that has been endorsed as the cornerstone for judicial co-operation within the European Union:

> "Enhanced mutual recognition of judicial decisions and judgements and the necessary approximation of legislation would facilitate co-operation between authorities and the judicial protection of individual rights. The European Council therefore endorses the principle of mutual recognition which, in its view, should become the cornerstone of judicial co-operation in both civil and criminal matters within the Union. The principle should apply both to judgements and to other decisions of judicial authorities." [3]

17.13   Mutual recognition could be applied in a variety of areas. For example it could allow evidence gathered in one Member State to be admissible before the courts of other member states, the freezing of proceeds of crime which have been removed to another country or the return of fugitives.

17.14   The backing of warrants is a practical example of mutual recognition between the United Kingdom and Ireland. Both countries have legislated so that warrants for arrest in one state will be backed in the other to simplify the process of bringing fugitives, who have crossed the border, back to the jurisdiction in which they have been accused or have been sentenced. [4] This provides a more flexible procedure than traditional forms of extradition.

OPPORTUNITIES FOR STRUCTURED CO-OPERATION UNDER THE BELFAST AGREEMENT

17.15   The Belfast Agreement establishes a new set of relationships within the island of Ireland and provides a framework for the development of structured co-operation between the criminal

---

3   Presidency Conclusions, Tampere European Council, 15 and 16 October 1999, paragraph 33.

4   Backing of Warrants (Republic of Ireland) Act 1965.

justice agencies on an all-island and cross-border basis. In addition, there are numerous possibilities for co-operation between criminal justice agencies on both parts of the island through agreed European structures.

17.16 The British-Irish Intergovernmental Conference brings together the British and Irish Governments to promote bilateral co-operation at all levels on all matters of mutual interest within the competence of both Governments. The Belfast Agreement sets out the role of the British-Irish Intergovernmental Conference, as follows:

- The Conference will bring together the British and Irish Governments to promote bilateral co-operation at all levels on all matters of mutual interest within the competence of both Governments.

- In recognition of the Irish Government's special interest in Northern Ireland and of the extent to which issues of mutual concern arise in relation to Northern Ireland, there will be regular and frequent meetings of the Conference concerned with non-devolved Northern Ireland matters, on which the Irish Government may put forward views and proposals. These meetings, to be co-chaired by the Minister for Foreign Affairs and the Secretary of State for Northern Ireland, would also deal with all-island and cross-border co-operation on non-devolved issues.

- Co-operation within the framework of the Conference will include facilitation of co-operation in security matters. The Conference will also address, in particular, the areas of rights, justice, prisons and policing in Northern Ireland (unless and until responsibility is devolved to a Northern Ireland administration) and will intensify co-operation between the two Governments on the all-island and cross-border aspects of these matters.[5]

17.17 The North/South Ministerial Council has also been established under the Belfast Agreement to develop consultation, co-ordination and action within the island of Ireland on matters of mutual interest within the competence of the Administrations, North and South. Following devolution of criminal justice issues, sectoral or cross-sectoral meetings of the North/South Ministerial Council might be convened on criminal justice matters. The Agreement sets out the role of the North/South Ministerial Council which is:

(i) to exchange information, discuss and consult with a view to co-operating on matters of mutual interest within the competence of both Administrations, North and South;

(ii) to use best endeavours to reach agreement on the adoption of common policies, in areas where there is mutual cross-border and all-island benefit, and which are within the competence of both Administrations, North and South, making determined efforts to overcome any disagreements;

5   *The Belfast Agreement*, Strand Three, British-Irish Intergovernmental Conference, paragraphs 2, 5 and 6.

(iii)   to take decisions by agreement on policies for implementation separately in each jurisdiction, in relevant meaningful areas within the competence of both Administrations, North and South;

(iv)   to take decisions by agreement on policies and actions at an all-island and cross-border level to be implemented by the bodies to be established as set out in paragraphs 8 and 9 below [of the Strand Two section of the Belfast Agreement].[6]

17.18   The Agreement states that consideration is to be given to the establishment of an independent consultative forum appointed by the two Administrations (Dublin and Belfast), representative of civil society, comprising the social partners and other members with expertise in social, cultural, economic and other issues. This forum might have a role to play in discussing all-island and cross-border co-operation after criminal justice issues are devolved to the Northern Ireland administration.

17.19   In addition to the North/South relationship the Belfast Agreement recognised the importance of East/West relationships. The British-Irish Council, consisting initially of the two Governments, devolved institutions in Northern Ireland, Scotland and Wales, with the Isle of Man and Channel Islands, will exchange information, discuss, consult and use best endeavours to reach agreement on co-operation on matters of mutual interest. As with the North/South Ministerial Council, specific sectoral or cross-sectoral meetings of the British-Irish Council are envisaged. Criminal justice issues, such as crime reduction or anti-drug strategies, might be addressed in such meetings.

Views Expressed during the Consultation Process

17.20   Although cross-border and all-island co-operation to tackle crime did not feature prominently in formal, written submissions to the Group, this issue received widespread support at our consultation seminars, where it was discussed in some detail. There was a recognition that issues such as registration of sex offenders, combating drugs, motoring offences and post-release supervision all had cross-border or all-island aspects. Joint inspectorates, interchanges between court staff North and South and joint training were also suggested with a view to exchanging best practice. Some of those attending seminars also argued for a harmonisation of criminal justice policy and law between the two jurisdictions, possibly through an all-Ireland law commission. In general terms there was a concern that offenders should not be able to escape across the border and thereby frustrate justice.

17.21   Some of the agencies and groups that came to talk to us noted that links between the two jurisdictions could be fruitful, particularly in the area of staff training or exchanges. For

---

6   *The Belfast Agreement,* Strand Two, paragraph 5.

example the Probation Board for Northern Ireland engages in joint training events and the Social Service Inspectorate in Northern Ireland has provided advice on setting up a similar body in the Republic of Ireland. However, it was pointed out that opportunities for such activity were limited by the differing qualifications and legislative regimes on either side of the border.

17.22   We were also made aware of the informal contacts that take place where ideas on tackling common problems are shared. One example was the contact between the Northern Ireland Court Service and their Irish counterparts on issues such as court design and information systems. Similar contact exists between the Judicial Studies Board in Northern Ireland and the Judicial Studies Institute in Dublin.

17.23   There was a suggestion from one group that co-operation across boundaries needed to be set in the context of the work towards eventual harmonisation at European Union level. They argued for harmonisation of jurisprudence with the aim of ensuring similar rights and safeguards, as well as offences and punishments, North and South.

17.24   From the political parties support for co-operation was expressed from a number of different perspectives. For example some focused on operational co-operation and co-ordination in order to improve the effectiveness of the fight against crime; this was addressed both from a North/South perspective, given the existence of the land border, and on an East/West basis as a means of improving co-operation throughout these islands. Others argued for a harmonisation of law and all Ireland structures, including the possibility of an all Ireland Constitutional Court and a joint inter-departmental committee of criminal justice officials. There was a general welcome for the attention being paid to co-operation on justice and home affairs issues within the European Union.

Evaluation and Recommendations

PRINCIPLES

17.25   The land border between Northern Ireland and its neighbour, the Republic of Ireland, in one sense creates a challenge to be met, for example in the area of effective communication. It also presents an opportunity to be grasped in the interests of developing effective criminal justice strategies and responses. It is essential that there is consultation and co-operation to prevent criminals from taking advantage of the existence of two adjacent jurisdictions, and in furtherance of the joint interest of all of us on these islands in securing justice.

17.26   In formulating the recommendations that follow we have therefore been guided by the principle that co-operation across boundaries should occur wherever it is necessary or useful. We foresee a strengthening of such co-operation between Northern Ireland and the Republic of Ireland taking account of the European Union framework.

17.27   As well as co-operation and co-ordination in combating criminal behaviour, there is also scope for working together in the prevention of crime and on community safety issues and in dealing with offenders after conviction. In some cases there may be a case for seeking harmonisation of procedures between North and South in order to facilitate effective co-operation. However, there is also a need to take account of and facilitate effective joint working with the other jurisdictions of the United Kingdom. In some areas we should be prepared to welcome diversity of practice in different jurisdictions and be prepared to learn from best practice in each.

STRUCTURES FOR CO-OPERATION

17.28   As already pointed out, the Belfast Agreement provides for political institutions within which bilateral co-operation can be developed further. Whether criminal justice co-operation is best dealt with in the British-Irish Intergovernmental Conference, the North/South Ministerial Council or the British-Irish Council will depend on whether criminal justice functions have been devolved and on the nature of the issues being addressed by these institutions.

17.29   There is also the new dynamic behind increasing co-operation between States within the European Union in the field of justice and home affairs with the aim of creating a single area of freedom, security and justice. These developments present a major opportunity for Northern Ireland, the only part of the United Kingdom with a land border with another State, to tackle crime and its causes more effectively through co-operation across the border.

17.30   **We suggest that a group of criminal justice policymakers from the two jurisdictions be established. The purpose of such a group would be to identify and advise on the opportunities for co-operation at government level and between the criminal justice agencies North and South, taking account also of the need for effective co-operation with other parts of these islands. It would also take forward consideration of the recommendations of this review on structured co-operation. In its work, the group would take account of the impact of developments at the European Union level and the opportunities these afford for enhancing bilateral co-ordination and co-operation.** This group should report to the British-Irish Intergovernmental Conference on matters that are not devolved and, on relevant matters, to the British-Irish Council. To the extent that criminal justice matters are devolved to the Northern Ireland Executive, it would also report to the North/South Ministerial Council.

17.31   In addition to co-operation between the governments and their respective agencies, it is important to note the opportunities for co-operation between other parts of the criminal justice system. For example many community groups addressing the causes of crime, members of the legal profession and academics and researchers, already have cross-border or all-island links. These might be developed further and new opportunities sought.

17.32   Given the complexity and importance of the issues involved, we did not have the time to develop firm proposals for cross-border co-operation. However, we have sought to identify those areas where the two jurisdictions might benefit from enhanced co-operation and the machinery for considering these matters further.

EXCHANGE AND INTERCHANGE

17.33   At one level of co-operation, there is the sharing of best practice, staff exchanges and the pooling of resources in specific areas. We believe that such exchange should occur between the two jurisdictions on this island and is beneficial in creating an outward looking criminal justice system.

17.34   Several criminal justice agencies commented to us that developing some aspects of joint training, including conferences and the sharing of good practice, would be useful. We also note the recommendations of the Independent Commission on Policing for structured co-operation between the two police services in training, and for a programme of long term personnel exchange. **We recommend that the scope for the joint delivery of training, education (including continuing professional development) and the exchange of good practice on criminal justice issues should be examined.**

17.35   Consultations on this would involve agencies, the voluntary sector and academic institutions in producing creative ways to facilitate joint working. We believe that joint training is justified, because two small jurisdictions would benefit from pooling resources, and in order to foster greater understanding of the law and procedures in the two jurisdictions. For this latter reason **we also recommend that consideration be given to the scope for regular personnel exchange between agencies such as probation, prosecution, prisons, courts and criminal justice policymakers.** Equally it will be important to foster and develop such opportunities between criminal justice agencies in Northern Ireland and those in the rest of the United Kingdom.

17.36   It was pointed out to us that differences in the standards applied and qualifications required in the two jurisdictions act as a barrier to joint training (such as courses leading to initial professional qualifications) and personnel exchange. **We recommend that consideration be given to recognition of qualifications and the possibility of harmonising standards between the two jurisdictions, while recognising the importance of compatibility between Northern Ireland and other parts of the United Kingdom.**

17.37   As we note in Chapter 16, there is scope for a more developed approach to research on criminal justice issues in both jurisdictions. We believe that co-operation in this field is important because there are similar features in the criminal trends in the two jurisdictions as well as some notable differences and much could be learned through comparative study. Recorded crime levels in both Northern Ireland and the Republic of Ireland have historically been much lower than in other European countries.

17.38   It is not possible for a jurisdiction the size of Northern Ireland to sustain a large enough pool of expertise to conduct the wide variety of research and evaluation that we believe should be carried out on a regular basis. There is therefore a strong case for drawing on expertise available in other jurisdictions. **We recommend fostering co-operation between researchers through joint conferences and seminars, and suggest that specific research projects might be undertaken on an all-island basis.** For such co-operation to occur research funds must be made available for joint projects and money should be allocated for joint conferences and seminars.

17.39   We note the formation of the National Crime Council (in Ireland) and have recommended in Chapter 11 the creation of a Community Safety Unit. The arguments for co-operation in training and research also point to the need to share good practice and work towards developing a common approach to tackling the causes of crime. According to the Tampere European Council, "the exchange of best practices should be developed, the network of competent national authorities for crime prevention and co-operation between national crime prevention organisations should be strengthened".[7] **We recommend that the central Community Safety Unit should develop close links with its counterparts in the Republic of Ireland, Scotland, England and Wales, and more widely.**

17.40   We would like to make a special mention of drug related crime in the context of cross-border co-operation. We heard a concern expressed in several towns we visited at the possibility of an increase in drug related crime. In this area cross-border co-operation is especially important and we note that criminal justice agencies have developed a particular expertise in dealing with drugs problems. The drug problem is significantly different in the two jurisdictions but much can be learnt by working together to tackle drug related criminal activity. **We endorse close liaison between the two jurisdictions in sharing information about trends and what works in education and prevention in relation to the misuse of drugs.**

OPERATIONAL CO-OPERATION

17.41   A number of issues arise from the fact that Northern Ireland and the Republic of Ireland are separate jurisdictions sharing a land border which is crossed and re-crossed regularly as part of people's normal lives. Economic, social and family ties straddle the border. So too does

---

7   Presidency Conclusions, Tampere European Council, 15 and 16 October 1999, paragraph 42.

criminal activity. This poses particular problems for the criminal justice agencies. As we have noted above, there is already considerable co-operation between agencies on both sides of the border, but there are some specific areas where we suggest that further work might be undertaken.

17.42   In Chapter 13 we make a number of recommendations aimed at ensuring that victims and witnesses are properly supported by the criminal justice system. However, we are conscious that the victim of, or the witness to, a crime in Northern Ireland may live in the neighbouring jurisdiction (and *vice versa*). This raises issues about how victims and witnesses are to be kept informed about and consulted on the progress of cases, and about arrangements for providing protection, support and counselling. **We recommend that both jurisdictions consider the cross-border dimension with a view to developing reciprocal arrangements for victim and witness support, particularly in relation to providing information, protection, and counselling.**

17.43   A number of issues may arise where a person from one jurisdiction is prosecuted and sentenced in the other. Similar problems may arise where offenders wish to change domicile.

17.44   Mechanisms enabling prisoners released from custody in one United Kingdom jurisdiction to be supervised in another were introduced in the Crime (Sentences) Act 1997. However there are currently no mechanisms that allow the continued supervision of released prisoners outside the United Kingdom. Nor are there mechanisms to allow the supervision of individuals given non-custodial disposals. Although people subject to supervision or serving non-custodial sentences in Northern Ireland may be allowed to travel to the Republic of Ireland and might even undertake programmes in the other jurisdiction, there is no ready mechanism for enforcement unless the offender is in Northern Ireland.

17.45   Where an offender subject to a community sentence in Northern Ireland is normally resident in the Republic of Ireland or has good reason for moving there, it would be preferable to facilitate him or her. But equally it is unsatisfactory if as a result he or she would avoid serving part of the sentence or lose the opportunity for support aimed at rehabilitation and the prevention of further offences. Moreover, there may be circumstances where the most satisfactory programme for an offender is one that operates in the other jurisdiction.

17.46   Remedying the situation will not be easy. Not only are there issues around the continued enforcement of sentences imposed in one jurisdiction but carried out in another, but there is also the fact that different disposals are available, with different arrangements for enforcement, North and South. However, similar problems were encountered in the three United Kingdom jurisdictions in relation to supervision, which were eventually overcome. **We recommend that the issue of developing mutual arrangements for continued enforcement of non-custodial sentences and post-custodial supervision should be addressed. Arrangements for accessing programmes available in the other jurisdiction should also be considered.**

17.47   **Specifically in the context of the new juvenile justice arrangements** (see Chapters 9 and 10) **we suggest that there should be flexibility to allow the use of cross-border facilities for youth conference orders.** We note that, at a local level, projects already exist which take referrals from both sides of the border. For example the voluntary group Extern West and the North Western Health Board (Donegal, Leitrim and Sligo) have developed a range of services for young people at risk, including a youth support programme which receives referrals from the Garda Síochána as well as from social services in Northern Ireland.

17.48   Under the *Convention for the Transfer of Sentenced Persons,* which was ratified by the Republic of Ireland in 1995, it is possible for prisoners to be repatriated from the United Kingdom to the Republic of Ireland and *vice versa.* There have been a number of transfers in both directions. In general the arrangements work well, although there remain problems, not unique to movements between the Republic of Ireland and the United Kingdom, when because of different remission or release rules, the repatriation of a prisoner might result in a reduction in the period of time served.

17.49   The Convention arrangements are applicable where a prisoner intends to reside permanently in the receiving jurisdiction. However, it has been suggested to us that there may be other circumstances where movement between the Irish jurisdictions might be appropriate. This could be to facilitate visits by relatives, particularly in cases where the nearest prison to a person's home was in the other jurisdiction. Temporary transfers are commonplace between the United Kingdom jurisdictions and are regularly used to allow prisoners to be visited by relatives. They may also be used to allow prisoners to visit close relatives who are ill. A similar mechanism to allow temporary movement between Northern Ireland and the Republic of Ireland would be a practical response to a humanitarian concern. **We recommend that consideration be given to facilitating the temporary transfer of prisoners between Northern Ireland and the Republic of Ireland.**

17.50   The collection and application of information lies at the heart of the investigation and prosecution of criminals. Access to information, under particular circumstances, is already governed by the Criminal Justice (International Co-operation) Act 1990.

17.51   The field of forensic science provides two examples of areas that might benefit from greater links North and South. At present an offenders' DNA database operates in Northern Ireland as in the rest of the United Kingdom. This proves valuable in identifying suspects for crimes. However, there is no comparable system in the Republic of Ireland. **We suggest that discussion of the development of relevant forensic science databases and the scope for exchanges of information should take place under the structures for co-operation.**

17.52   Co-operation across the border could also enable criminal justice agencies to access services in the other jurisdiction. For example, the forensic science laboratory in Dublin has developed particular expertise in techniques for sampling automobile paint types for the benefit of criminal investigations. In two small jurisdictions it might be beneficial to develop centres of expertise which would be made available either side of the border. Encouragement is being given to such a strategy on a Europe wide basis. This is an area where there is potential benefit from links between criminal justice services throughout these islands. **We recommend that the possibility of widening access to services such as forensic science and pathology across jurisdictional boundaries be investigated.**

17.53   Registers of sex offenders and for child protection purposes have been set up under recent Northern Ireland legislation. During the consultation process we heard public concern that the effectiveness of such registers could be undermined by the ability of individuals who have committed offences in the Republic of Ireland to move to Northern Ireland without any notification of their offences. The Government of Ireland has recently published a Bill providing for a notification procedure or tracking system for convicted sex offenders. This will provide the opportunity for greater protection of the public in both jurisdictions from such offenders, for co-ordinating an approach to sex offender registers, and for sharing information between the authorities in the two jurisdictions. **With a view to sharing information between the authorities in the two jurisdictions, we recommend that the possibility of co-ordinating an approach to dangerous offender registers be given consideration.** Clear protocols would need to be drawn up on the use and contents of these registers, so that they do not contravene data protection and privacy legislation.

MUTUAL RECOGNITION AND HARMONISATION

17.54   We have set out the principles that we believe should govern the harmonisation of law and practice between Northern Ireland and the Republic of Ireland. It is with this in mind that we make the following suggestions.

17.55   There is a range of arguments in favour of a harmonisation of law between jurisdictions. From the point of view of law enforcement a more uniform system would reduce the possibility of criminal activity, at whatever level, benefiting from differences in the law. Similarly, the accused, victims and witnesses would be assured of rights and safeguards irrespective of which side of the border a crime occurred.

17.56   The development of criminal law in both jurisdictions has been largely incremental. The variety of statutes and common law principles that apply can make it difficult to be certain of the precise content and meaning of the law.[8] In Chapter 14 we look at law reform in more detail. The problem of a lack of clarity in law is especially difficult for criminal justice practitioners dealing with cases with a cross-border aspect. Furthermore disparities and lack of clarity in law and practice between jurisdictions can lead to delays in the criminal justice process.

---

8   See McCutcheon and Quinn, (1998), *Codifying Criminal Law in Ireland,* Statute Law Review, 131, 143.

17.57   **We recommend that consideration be given to inviting the Law Commission, which we have recommended for Northern Ireland, to co-operate closely with the Commissions in the other three jurisdictions in these islands with a view to promoting the harmonisation of aspects of criminal law and procedure in all four jurisdictions.**

17.58   We recognise that this will be a long-term project. More immediately, **we recommend that consideration be given to producing, for use by practitioners, a simple, clear and concise comparative guide to criminal law and procedure, North and South.**

17.59   We wish to comment on the specific issue of reporting restrictions where we feel there is a particularly strong case for reaching agreement between the two jurisdictions on a joint approach. We have in mind situations where a judge makes an order restricting reporting in order to prevent the prejudicing of a trial. Similarly reporting restrictions can be important to protect the rights of third parties, witnesses, victims and defendants. For example the report *Speaking up for Justice* noted that reporting restrictions were not enforceable consistently throughout the United Kingdom.[9] When witness intimidation might be an issue, any restrictions on the reporting of proceedings in England and Wales would need to apply equally in Scotland and Northern Ireland if they were to be effective. Provisions to achieve this were incorporated into the Youth Justice and Criminal Evidence Act 1999.

17.60   The issue of reporting restrictions in Northern Ireland being made ineffective due to its proximity to the Republic of Ireland is a serious concern. The circulation of newspapers on both sides of the border is commonplace and broadcasts of television and radio from the other side of the border can easily be received. **We recommend that there should be discussion within the structures for co-operation on how reciprocal arrangements might be developed to ensure the effectiveness of reporting restrictions.**

---

9   *Speaking up for Justice, Report of the Interdepartmental Working Group on the Treatment of Vulnerable or Intimidated Witnesses in the Criminal Justice System* (1998) Home Office, London: HMSO, chapter 11 and paragraph 8.22.

Recommendations
and
Appendices

Summary of Recommendations

The following is a list of all the recommendations in this report:

Human Rights and Guiding Principles

1   We recommend that human rights issues should become a permanent and integral part of training programmes for all those working in criminal justice agencies, the legal professions and the relevant parts of the voluntary sector. [para. 3.25]

2   We endorse the Criminal Justice Board aims for 1999/2000 as a good model for the criminal justice system-wide set of aims: [para. 3.28]

Aim A

To dispense justice fairly and efficiently and to promote confidence in the criminal justice system

(i)   Provide fair and just criminal processes and outcomes.

(ii)   Improve service delivery by enhancing levels of effectiveness, efficiency and co-operation within the criminal justice system.

(iii)   Make the criminal justice system as open, inclusive and accessible as possible and enhance and promote public confidence in the administration of justice.

Aim B

To contribute to the reduction of crime and the fear of crime

(i)   Work co-operatively to help reduce crime.

(ii)   Reduce numbers of persons re-offending and frequency of re-offending for persistent offenders.

(iii)   Reduce levels of fear of crime.

---

3   We recommend that the aims of the criminal justice system be published, together with a criminal justice plan outlining measures to be taken in support of them and appropriate performance indicators. An annual report on progress in implementing the plan should also be published. [para. 3.29]

4   We recommend that, whatever machinery is devised for administering criminal justice matters after devolution, it should have as a primary task the development of a concerted and proactive strategy for securing a "reflective" workforce in all parts of the system. [para. 3.35]

5   We recommend that the Criminal Justice Board and its research sub-committee be tasked with developing and implementing a strategy for equity monitoring the criminal justice system, as it affects categories of people, in particular by community background, gender, ethnic origin, sexual orientation and disability; whilst ensuring that this is done in a way that does not compromise judicial independence. [para. 3.38]

6   We recommend that the outcome of equity monitoring should be published on a regular basis, to the maximum extent possible without risking the identification of the community background of individuals. [para. 3.41]

7   As part of our strategy for developing transparency and accountability mechanisms, we recommend the publication of statements of ethics for each of the criminal justice agencies covering all those employed or holding office in the criminal justice system. [para. 3.45]

8   If an organisation were, by its policy or its actions, clearly committed to acting contrary to the law or the interests of the criminal justice system, then it would be for the criminal justice agencies to make clear that their employees were not permitted to belong to such an organisation. [para. 3.47]

9   We agree with the Special Rapporteur on the Independence of Judges and Lawyers that government has a responsibility to provide the machinery for an effective and independent investigation of all threats made against lawyers and note the role of the Police Ombudsman if such allegations relate to the actions of police officers. Further, we endorse his recommendation that training seminars should be organised to enable police officers and members of other criminal justice agencies to appreciate the important role that defence lawyers play in the administration of justice and the nature of their relationship with their clients. [para. 3.53]

10   We recommend the continuation of bursaries to ensure that entry to the legal professions is open to people of talent from all sections of the community, regardless of means. [para. 3.55]

11   We recommend that lawyers should receive appropriate training in human rights principles before starting to practise. [para. 3.56]

12   We suggest that there would be some benefit in the compilation by the Law Society of a list of experts in particular fields that could be drawn on by the defence. [para. 3.60]

13   We recommend research into the impact of PACE at the stage of police questioning. [para. 3.63]

14   We recommend a public information and education strategy for the criminal justice system. This might include the following features, some of which are already in place:

-    The production and distribution of guides to various aspects of criminal justice, targeting specific groups such as witnesses, victims, children, minority groups and defendants.

-    The prominent display of mission statements for each criminal justice agency.

-    The publication of statements of principles showing how the system as a whole will address specific issues, such as the treatment of victims, racial discrimination or cross-agency working.

-    The publication by all agencies of codes of practice in accessible language.

-    The publication by all agencies of annual reports, which include objectives, indicators and an account of performance.

-    The publication of statistical and research material in accessible form.

-    Consideration of innovative methods for increasing public understanding such as open days at courts for schools, colleges and the public, and the creation of videos explaining aspects of the criminal justice system.

-    The inclusion of a criminal justice module in the school civics curriculum. [para. 3.67]

15   The need for awareness of criminal justice issues should be considered as part of the current review of the Northern Ireland curriculum. [para. 3.68]

16   All parts of the criminal justice system should be covered by complaints mechanisms that are well publicised, easily accessible and understood, administered with due sensitivity and expedition and which, where appropriate, have an independent element. The workings of the complaints mechanisms should receive coverage in annual reports and, in those parts of the system subject to inspection, be inspected. [para. 3.70]

The Prosecution

17   We recommend that in all criminal cases, currently prosecuted by the DPP and the police, responsibility for determining whether to prosecute and for undertaking prosecutions should be vested in a single independent prosecuting authority. [para. 4.127]

18   We recommend that the investigative function should remain the responsibility of the police and not be subject to external supervision. [para. 4.130]

19   We recommend that the powers contained in Article 6(3) of the Prosecution of Offences (Northern Ireland) Order 1972 be retained and that the head of the prosecution service should make clear publicly the service's ability and determination to prompt an investigation by the police of facts that come into its possession, if these appear to constitute allegations of the commission of a criminal offence, and to request further information from the police to assist it in coming to a decision on whether or not to prosecute. [para. 4.131]

20   We recommend that Article 6(3) of the 1972 Order be supplemented with a provision enabling the prosecutor to refer a case to the Police Ombudsman for investigation where he or she is not satisfied with an Article 6(3) response. [para. 4.132]

21   We recommend that a duty be placed on the prosecutor to ensure that any allegations of malpractice by the police are fully investigated. [para. 4.133]

22   We recommend that it be a clearly stated objective of the prosecution service to be available at the invitation of the police to provide advice on prosecutorial issues at any stage in the investigative process. [para. 4.135]

23   We suggest that, where a prosecutor has been extensively involved in advising the police on prosecutorial matters at the investigative stage, in order fully to safeguard the independence of the prosecution process consideration should be given to the possibility of arranging for the decision to prosecute to be made or scrutinised by another member of the prosecution service. [para. 4.136]

24   We recommend that where the police prefer a "holding" charge under Article 38(7) of the Police and Criminal Evidence (Northern Ireland) Order 1989, a prosecutor should be seized of and be responsible for the presentation of the case before a magistrates' court in accordance with the provisions of Article 47 of the Order. [para. 4.138]

25   It should be the prosecutor's sole responsibility to formulate and determine the charge that is presented to the court. [para. 4.138]

26   The prosecutor should have legal responsibility for the application to the magistrates' court for remand, including the presentation of all supporting evidence. [para. 4.138]

27   We recommend that consideration be given to amending the Police and Criminal Evidence (Northern Ireland) Order 1989 to enable a prosecutor, on reviewing the case, to withdraw the charges before the court appearance. [para. 4.139]

28   We recommend that (if the law is changed in the way we suggest), until the prosecutor has determined whether to proceed with the remand application, the fact of the arrest and the name of the person detained should not be publicised. [para. 4.139]

29   We recommend that the prosecutor should assume full responsibility for the case between the point of charge (or summons) and trial, including tracking progress of the case, advising

the police on the evidence required to secure conviction and deciding on what matters should be disclosed to the defence. [para. 4.141]

30   We suggest that the timing of commencement of legislation that will flow from our recommendations should be planned so as to ensure that all necessary resources, preparation and training are in place and completed before procedural changes are introduced. [para. 4.142]

31   We believe that the present disclosure provisions should be reviewed and suggest in Chapter 14 that this might be one of the matters for consideration by a Law Commission. [para. 4.143]

32   We recommend that consideration be given to introducing simplified procedures for transferring cases to the Crown Court in Northern Ireland, while ensuring safeguards for a defendant who wishes to argue that there is no case to answer. Such a development could be accompanied by a major effort further to reduce time taken to bring cases to trial. [para. 4.144]

33   We recommend that once the police at divisional level decide that they wish to proceed and judge that they have sufficient evidence to warrant prosecution, the facts of the case should be sent to the prosecutor. In order to facilitate the process, consideration should be given to the development of standard forms, with the information fields necessary for purposes of issuing a summons, which could be e-mailed or faxed to the prosecutor. [para. 4.146]

34   We recommend that in summons cases arrangements be made to ensure that the facts of the case are passed to the prosecutor by a police officer who is close to and familiar with the investigation. [para. 4.147]

35   We envisage moving towards a position where it is the norm for legally qualified staff of the prosecution service to present cases at magistrates' courts (including committals), while retaining the option of briefing independent counsel when appropriate. [para. 4.149]

36   We recommend that caution guidelines should be agreed between the police and the prosecution service. Statistics should be kept and the practice kept under review, with particular attention being paid to consistency of approach and to ensuring that cases are dealt with expeditiously. [para. 4.151]

37   We recommend that prosecutors be enjoined positively to consider the diversion option in their consideration of cases. The options available to them might be:

- referral back to the police with a recommendation to caution;

- diversionary options, for example mentally disordered offenders or drug users being referred to treatment or young offenders being offered programmes to address offending behaviour; and

- the making of arrangements for restorative interventions. [para. 4.152]

38   We think it right for the prosecutor to have the ability to review the decision not to prosecute if the offender fails to follow through the arrangements for diversionary activity, treatment or restorative agreements. [para. 4.153]

39   We recommend that consideration be given to introducing the prosecutorial fine in Northern Ireland. [para. 4.154]

40   It will be necessary for the prosecution service, together with the police, to engage with the community and other agencies and service providers about what is involved in the diversionary process and to seek to arrive at a clear understanding of what diversionary schemes and options may be available at the local level. [para. 4.155]

41   We recommend that outreach to the community and inter-agency working be a stated objective of the prosecution service. [para. 4.156]

42   We recommend that political responsibility for the prosecution system should be devolved to local institutions along with other criminal justice functions, or as soon as possible after devolution of such functions. [para. 4.158]

43   We recommend that consideration be given to establishing a locally sponsored post of Attorney General who, inter alia, would have oversight of the prosecution service. We see the Attorney General as a non-political figure drawn from the ranks of senior lawyers and appointed by the First Minister and Deputy First Minister. We would suggest a fixed term appointment, with security of tenure, say for five years, which would not be affected by the timing of Assembly terms. [para. 4.160]

44   We recommend that the formulation in section 27 of the Scotland Act 1998 be adopted in that, although not a member of the Assembly, the Attorney should be enabled by Standing Orders to participate in Assembly business, for example through answering questions or making statements, but without voting rights. [para. 4.161]

45   There should be no power for the Attorney General to direct the prosecutor, whether in individual cases or on policy matters. [para. 4.162]

46   We recommend that legislation should: confirm the independence of the prosecutor; make it an offence for anyone without a legitimate interest in a case to seek to influence the prosecutor not to pursue it; but make provision for statutory consultation between the head of the prosecution service and the Attorney General, at the request of either. [para. 4.163]

47   We recommend that it be made clear on the face of legislation, as in section 27 of the Scotland Act 1998, that the Attorney could decline to answer questions on individual cases where to do so might prejudice criminal proceedings or would be contrary to the public interest. [para. 4.163]

48   We recommend that the head of the prosecution service should be accountable to the appropriate Assembly Committee for financial and administrative matters relating to the running of service. [para. 4.163]

49   We recommend that, where information is sought by someone with a proper and legitimate interest in a case on why there was no prosecution, or on why a prosecution has been abandoned, the prosecutor should seek to give as full an explanation as is possible without prejudicing the interests of justice or the public interest. It will be a matter for the prosecutor to consider carefully in the circumstances of each individual case whether reasons can be given in more than general terms and, if so, in how much detail, but the presumption should shift towards giving reasons where appropriate. [para. 4.167]

50   We recommend that the head of the prosecution service be required by statute to publish the following:

- an annual report.

- a code of practice outlining the factors to be taken into account in applying the evidential and public interest tests on whether to prosecute; and

- a code of ethics, based in part on the standards set out in UN Guidelines. [para. 4.169]

51   We recommend that the prosecution service should be subject to inspection, with a significant independent input. [para. 4.170]

52   We recommend that the Criminal Justice Inspectorate, which we propose in Chapter 15, be given the responsibility for buying in the professional expertise necessary to carry out inspections. [para. 4.171]

53   We recommend that the Criminal Justice Inspectorate be under a statutory duty to arrange for the inspection of the prosecution service, report to the Attorney General on any matter to do with the service which the Attorney refers to it and also report the outcome of inspections to the Attorney General. [para 4.171]

54   We recommend that the Criminal Justice Inspectorate should include in its annual report a review of inspection activity and its outcomes in relation to the prosecution service. [para. 4.171]

55   Details of complaints procedures for the prosecution service should be publicly available and included in the service's annual report, along with an account of the handling of complaints throughout the year. [para. 4.172]

56   We recommend that an independent element be introduced into the procedures where the complainant is not satisfied with the initial response and where the complaint is not about the exercise of prosecutorial discretion. [para. 4.172]

57   The Criminal Justice Inspectorate should audit the operation of the prosecution service's complaints procedures on a regular basis. [para. 4.172]

58   We recommend that the Department of the Director of Public Prosecutions be renamed the Public Prosecution Service for Northern Ireland. [para. 4.174]

59   We recommend that the appointment process for the head of the Public Prosecution Service and deputy be through open competition, with a selection panel, in accordance with procedures established by the Civil Service Commissioners for Northern Ireland. These appointments would be made by the Attorney General for Northern Ireland. Appointments would be for a fixed term, or until a statutory retirement date. There should be statutory safeguards to ensure that removal from office by reason of misconduct or incapacity would be possible only after a recommendation to that effect coming from an independent tribunal. [para. 4.176]

60   We recommend that the Public Prosecution Service should establish local offices from which the bulk of prosecutorial work in their respective areas would be conducted. The boundaries of such offices should be coterminous with police and court boundaries, which in turn are based on district council areas. [para. 4.178]

61   We recommend that each of these offices should be headed by a senior prosecutor of sufficient status for decisions on most prosecutions to be delegated to the local offices. [para. 4.178]

62   External recruitment of new staff should be subject to open competition, in accordance with fair employment and equal opportunities best practice. A substantial recruitment exercise would provide the opportunity to attract applicants from a range of diverse backgrounds, including defence lawyers and people from all parts of the community, with a geographical spread across Northern Ireland. [para. 4.180]

63   Consideration should be given to some posts being the subject of fixed-term contracts and to offering financial assistance to a limited number of students seeking professional qualifications, on the basis that they might start their career within the Public Prosecution Service. [para. 4.180]

64   We recommend the appointment of a senior manager as head of Corporate Services to work to, and alongside, the head of the Public Prosecution Service. This post would have particular responsibility for driving the change agenda and ensuring the efficient and effective management of what will be a larger and more dispersed organisation than is the case at present. [para. 4.181]

65   We recommend that at the earliest possible stage in establishing the Public Prosecution Service training needs should be identified and the necessary resources deployed to meet them. [para. 4.182]

66   We recommend that those who are considering the resource implications and the organisational issues arising from our proposals in respect of the prosecution function should examine the Glidewell Report, with a view to seeing whether there are lessons to be learnt from the experience of England and Wales. [para. 4.183]

The Judiciary

67   We recommend that primary Westminster legislation should make explicit reference to the requirement for an independent judiciary and place a duty on the organs of government to uphold and protect that independence. [para. 6.82]

68   Merit, including the ability to do the job, thus providing the best possible quality of justice, must in our view continue to be the key criterion in determining appointments. [para. 6.84]

69   It should be a stated objective of whoever is responsible for appointments to engage in a programme of action to secure the development of a judiciary that is as reflective of Northern Ireland society, in particular by community background and gender, as can be achieved consistent with the overriding requirement of merit. [para. 6.85]

70   We endorse the view that extensive experience of advocacy should not be regarded as a prerequisite of success in a judicial capacity and recommend that practice and/or standing requirements for recruitment to all levels of the bench should not differentiate between barristers and solicitors. [para. 6.89]

71   We recommend that consideration be given to consolidating and amending the legislation relating to eligibility criteria for judicial appointments with a view to shifting the emphasis to standing (i.e. period since being called to the Bar or admitted as a solicitor) rather than practice. Time spent in lower judicial posts should also be recognised for eligibility purposes. [para. 6.90]

72   In our view it should be clear that progression from one judicial tier to another is regarded as an accepted form of appointment, provided that it takes place on the basis of merit as part of open competition. [para. 6.91]

73   We recommend the enactment of legislation enabling responsibility for judicial appointments in Northern Ireland to be devolved on an agreed basis at a date to be determined by the Government in the light of the prevailing circumstances. This would of necessity be primary Westminster legislation. The legislation would include provisions establishing the machinery and procedure by which appointments were to be made. [para. 6.95]

74   On devolution, political responsibility and accountability for the judicial appointments process should lie with the First Minister and the Deputy First Minister. [para. 6.96]

75   For the appointment of the Lord Chief Justice and Lords Justices of Appeal, responsibility for making recommendations to Her Majesty The Queen would lie with the Prime Minister, as now, but on the basis of recommendations from the First Minister and the Deputy First Minister. [para. 6.96]

76   We suggest that consideration be given to including in the primary Westminster legislation that provides for the transfer of judicial matters of a provision that no vote, resolution or Act of the Assembly on judicial matters should be valid unless it has cross community support, as defined by section 4(5) of the Northern Ireland Act 1998. [para. 6.97]

77   We recommend that legislation enabling responsibility for judicial appointments to be devolved should include provision for the establishment of a Judicial Appointments Commission. [para. 6.102]

78   As for membership of the Commission, we envisage a strong judicial representation drawn from all tiers of the judiciary (including a representative of the lay magistracy – see Chapter 7) and nominated for appointment by the Lord Chief Justice after consultation with each of those tiers. The Lord Chief Justice or his nominee would chair the Commission. In line with practice elsewhere, there would be one representative nominated by the Law Society and one by the Bar Council. In total the Commission might consist of around five judicial members, two from the professions and four or five lay members. [para. 6.103]

79   The lay members of the Commission should be drawn from both sides of the community, including both men and women. This could be achieved through a legislative provision along the lines of section 68(3) of the Northern Ireland Act 1998 which provides that the Secretary of State should, so far as practicable, secure that the Northern Ireland Human Rights Commission is representative of the community in Northern Ireland. [para. 6.104]

80   The First Minister and Deputy First Minister would appoint the nominees of the Lord Chief Justice and the professions and would secure the appointment of lay members through procedures in accordance with the guidelines for public appointments (the Nolan procedures). [para. 6.104]

81   The Commission should be responsible for organising and overseeing, and for making recommendations on, judicial appointments from the level of High Court judge downwards. [para. 6.105]

82   Working through an Appointments Unit, the Commission would organise its selection panels which, for appointments at deputy resident magistrate and above, would always include at least one member of the judiciary at the tier to which the appointment was to be made and a lay person. The selection panel would shortlist, take account of the available information on the candidates, and conduct interviews with a view to making recommendations to the Commission. [para. 6.105]

83 We recommend that for all judicial appointments, from lay magistrate to High Court judge, and all tribunal appointments, the Commission should submit a report of the selection process to the First Minister and Deputy First Minister together with a clear recommendation. [para. 6.106]

84 The First Minister and Deputy First Minister would be required either to accept the recommendation or to ask the Commission to reconsider, giving their reasons for doing so; in the event of their asking for a recommendation to be reconsidered, they would be bound to accept the second recommendation. The First Minister and Deputy First Minister would then:

- in respect of High Court and county court judges, and resident magistrates, advise Her Majesty The Queen to appoint the recommended candidate;

- in respect of appointment of deputy county court judges and deputy resident magistrate, and of appointments below the level of resident magistrate, make the appointment. [para. 6.106]

85 We recommend that the First Minister and Deputy First Minister should consult with the Judicial Appointments Commission over the procedure to be adopted in appointments to the positions of Lord Chief Justice and Lord Justice of Appeal and submit such procedure to the Prime Minister for approval. The same principles of transparency and appointment on merit should apply as with other appointments. [para. 6.109]

86 The Judicial Appointments Commission would require a fully resourced administrative structure in the form of a Judicial Appointments Unit separate from the Court Service (or Department of Justice) but staffed by officials drawn from it. This Unit, under the supervision of the Commission, would assist the Commission in:

- establishing criteria for appointment which provide for the level of technical and legal competence required by particular posts and the personal qualities necessary for members of the judiciary, including an awareness of social and human rights issues;

- organising the selection processes which would include open advertising, published criteria for appointment and structured interviews for all appointments from High Court judges downwards;

- ensuring that selection panels had before them all the information on which to base decisions, including the results of consultation with the senior judiciary and professional associations;

- publishing detailed information on all aspects of the appointments system in Northern Ireland, along the lines of *Judicial Appointments*, the Lord Chancellor's Department publication for England and Wales;

- publishing an annual report on the appointments process;

- developing a strategy of equal opportunity and outreach designed to broaden the pool of potential applicants in a way that maximised the opportunity for men and women from all parts of the community to secure appointments; and

- identifying and, where possible, addressing factors which might make it more difficult, or constitute a disincentive, for qualified candidates from particular parts of the community to apply for appointment. [para. 6.111]

87   There should remain a role for formal written consultation with the senior judiciary and the heads of the legal profession in respect of candidates for appointment as county court judge and above. For the sake of ensuring transparency and fairness, the results of such consultation should be made available to the selection panels for these posts, who would consider them along with all other relevant information. [para. 6.112]

88   We consider that the present practice of asking for named referees for lower tier appointments should be extended to include candidates for appointment as High Court or county court judges and suggest that consideration be given to including an element of self-assessment in application forms for judicial appointments. [para. 6.112]

89   We recommend that those responsible for judicial appointments should engage in discussions with the Bar Council and Law Society about equal opportunity issues and their implications for the judicial appointments process. The Equality Commission should be asked to assist with these discussions. [para. 6.113]

90   Efforts should be made to stimulate interest in becoming a judge, especially in sectors which are under represented or where historically applications have been disproportionately low. [para. 6.114]

91   We are attracted to the idea of developing a database of qualified candidates interested in securing judicial appointment, and we recommend that this idea be considered further. [para. 6.115]

92   We recommend that consideration be given to introducing a small number of part-time appointments. [para. 6.116]

93   We recommend that consideration be given to finding a satisfactory way, with the assistance of proxy indicators if necessary, of assessing for statistical purposes the religious and ethnic background of applicants for judicial posts and of those who wish to be included in the database. There would also need to be assessment for statistical purposes of the ethnic background of applicants. This information would not be available to those involved in the selection process [para. 6.120]

94   We recommend that those elements of our appointments strategy which do not require legislative change be adopted for implementation at an early stage and be operated within the existing structures. Early steps should also be taken to establish a dedicated Judicial Appointments Unit within the Northern Ireland Court Service to assist the Lord Chancellor

and the Lord Chief Justice in their duties within the current judicial appointments process. [para. 6.122]

95   We recommend the early appointment of a person or persons of standing to oversee and monitor the fairness of all aspects of the existing appointments system and audit the implementation of those measures that can be introduced before devolution. Such a person or persons should not be a practising member of the legal profession, should be independent of the judicial system and government, and should have the confidence of all parts of the community. They should have access to all parts of the appointments process and report annually to the Lord Chancellor. That report should be published. [para. 6.123]

96   We recommend that, on appointment, members of the judiciary be required to swear on oath along the following lines:

> I, [ ], do swear [or do solemnly and sincerely and truly affirm and declare] that I will well and faithfully serve in the office of [ ], and that I will do right to all manner of people without fear or favour, affection or illwill according to the laws and usages of this realm. [para. 6.128]

97   We think that the membership of the Board, drawing representation from each judicial tier, is about right, although an academic input might bring benefits. [para. 6.131]

98   We believe that the Board should produce an annual report on its activities and on its training plans for the judiciary. It should continue to be supported by an administrative secretariat. [para. 6.131]

99   We think that the Judicial Studies Board should develop a prioritised training plan, with members of the judiciary making the major contribution but also taking account of the views of the professions and other stake-holders. [para. 6.132]

100   We recommend that the Judicial Studies Board pay particular attention to maximising the benefits to be secured from co-operation with England and Wales, Scotland and the Republic of Ireland. [para. 6.133]

101   We believe that induction training should be mandatory. [para. 6.134]

102   We think that training is more likely to have a beneficial effect and secure the necessary commitment if it is developed by the judiciary for the judiciary on a voluntary basis. The Judicial Studies Board should monitor closely the progress of voluntary training and the degree of participation in it. [para. 6.134]

103   We endorse the current arrangements that give full-time judges and magistrates tenure during good behaviour until a statutory retirement age. [para. 6.136]

104   We recommend that removal from office of a judge or lay magistrate should only be possible on the basis of the finding of a judicial tribunal constituted under statutory authority and

convened by the First Minister and Deputy First Minister or the Lord Chief Justice, that a magistrate or judge was unfit for office by reason of incapacity or misbehaviour. [para. 6.136]

105   We recommend that a complaints procedure be devised and published. This would make clear that complaints about the exercise of judicial discretion could only be addressed through the judicial (i.e. the appeal) process, essential if judicial independence is to be maintained. Complaints about conduct or behaviour would be the ultimate responsibility of the judiciary, although, as now, officials in the Court Service could be tasked with dealing with the administration of such matters. [para. 6.137]

106   We recommend that for the most serious complaints which appear to have substance, including those which might merit some form of public rebuke or even instigation of the procedure for removal from office, the Lord Chief Justice should have the option of establishing a judicial tribunal to inquire into the circumstances and make recommendations. [para. 6.137]

107   We recommend that consideration be given to drawing up a statement of ethics which might be annexed to the annual report of the Judicial Appointments Commission. [para. 6.138]

108   On remuneration we recommend that judges' salaries continue to be fixed by reference to their equivalents in England and Wales, which are within the remit of the Senior Salaries Review Body. [para. 6.139]

109   We recommend that the Lord Chief Justice should have a clearly defined position as head of the whole judiciary (including the lay magistracy) in Northern Ireland. [para. 6.141]

110   We recommend that legislation be passed to redesignate resident magistrates as district judges (magistrates' courts). [para. 6.142]

Lay Involvement in Adjudication

111   We fully endorse the principle of jury trial in cases tried on indictment at the Crown Court. [para. 7.3]

112   We do not believe that a sufficiently strong case has been made at present to warrant change from the current system whereby a professional magistrate sitting alone adjudicates at summary adult trials. [para. 7.48]

113   We strongly endorse the view that efforts should be made to make the system more responsive to community concerns and to encourage lay involvement in an informal capacity. We make recommendations elsewhere about opening up the courts to the public and we believe that the judiciary could make a significant contribution to this. Participating in various

types of discussion fora, facilitating court visits and seeking out the views of the public on the way in which the system works should significantly reduce the likelihood of their being "out of touch" and should enhance confidence generally. [para. 7.49]

114   We strongly endorse the continued involvement of lay panellists in youth courts. [para. 7.50]

115   We do not think that lay people should any longer have the power to extend the period during which a suspect might be held in custody by the police, hear committal proceedings or adjudicate on a range of complaints against adults. There should however continue to be a role for suitably trained lay justices in presiding over special courts for first remand hearings. [para. 7.52]

116   We recommend that lay people should continue to have a role in hearing complaints with a view to issuing summonses and warrants. [para. 7.53]

117   We recommend that all lay appointees empowered to fulfil judicial functions should be designated as lay magistrates. [para. 7.55]

118   We recommend that a system be devised whereby lay magistrates would be formally authorised to perform each of the three functions only following appropriate training. We would envisage training being the responsibility of a sub-committee of the Judicial Studies Board. Current members of the Juvenile Lay Panel will already have received structured training and we envisage that they would therefore be eligible for re-appointment as lay magistrates without the need for a selection process in their case; it will of course be necessary to appoint significant numbers of additional lay panellists to provide for the expanded jurisdiction of the youth courts. [para. 7.56]

119   We envisage appointments to the position of lay magistrate being made using the same mechanism as used for other members of the judiciary. The selection procedure should, however, draw upon the advice of local committees, as now, which should include a mix of existing magistrates and representatives of outside interests, including people with a community focus. The objective should be to secure the appointment of magistrates on the basis of publicly available criteria through advertisement and a proactive effort to secure nominations from organisations in the community including, for example: the private sector, voluntary and community organisations, churches and other local groups. There should be a retirement age of 70 for lay magistrates. [para. 7.57]

120   It should be for the body responsible for courts' administration to organise the attendance of lay magistrates at court to enable them to fulfil their functions and stand-by rotas in case they are needed out of hours. [para. 7.58]

121   We recommend that the quality and impact of lay involvement, especially in the youth court and in the county court, be monitored and evaluated as a possible basis for extending the work of lay magistrates. [para. 7.61]

122   We think that there are aspects of jury trials that should be reviewed including, inter alia, measures to prevent intimidation of jurors, and the role of juries in particular classes of case. [para. 7.66]

Courts

123   We recommend an independent review into the law and practice of inquests in Northern Ireland. [para. 8.36]

124   We believe that the courts in Northern Ireland should operate efficiently but also effectively and in a way that promotes confidence in the criminal justice system. [para. 8.41]

125   The courts' administration should contribute to and be fully involved in the co-ordinated strategy of public education and information about the criminal justice system. [para. 8.45]

126   We endorse the current efforts of the Northern Ireland Court Service to provide information to the public and recommend that this work is developed further. [para. 8.46]

127   Information points in courthouse reception areas should include a range of leaflets explaining what goes on in courts, while the internet and video might be used to disseminate information. [para 8.46]

128   Visits to courts should continue to be encouraged as a way of increasing community awareness and understanding. [para. 8.46]

129   We recommend the establishment of court user groups across Northern Ireland inclusive of the judiciary, the professions, criminal justice agencies, and voluntary organisations representing victims and witnesses. We also suggest that consideration be given to means of sharing best practice between such groups. [para. 8.47]

130   We see the Criminal Justice Issues Group as a body bringing together the judiciary, the heads of the main criminal justice agencies, the legal profession and the voluntary sector to promote good practice throughout the system. [para. 8.47]

131   We recommend that it should be an objective for all court buildings to have appropriate reception, waiting and consultation areas for those attending court, with adequate refreshment facilities and proper access for the disabled. Consideration should also be given to the need to accommodate and staff information points, witness support facilities and other community services as considered appropriate in the local area. [para. 8.49]

132   We recommend that the layout of courtrooms should take account of the needs of the judge and those attending court to have good lines of sight and be able to hear the proceedings. [para. 8.50]

133   Courtrooms should have the appropriate degree of formality, and be designed to minimise the risk of jury or witness intimidation. We also recommend research into audibility, layout and procedure in the courts throughout Northern Ireland to highlight any simple improvements that might be made. We note the importance of those participating in court speaking clearly. [para. 8.50]

134   Local court user groups will have a role in making suggestions for and monitoring improvements in facilities with reference to agreed standards. [para. 8.51]

135   We recommend the simplification of dress worn in court and an end to the wearing of wigs except on ceremonial occasions. [para. 8.52]

136   We recommend that steps be taken to ensure the language used in the criminal courts is easily understood by lay people. [para. 8.53]

137   We endorse the work that is currently under way in drawing up a common list of interpreters to be used for victims, witnesses and suspects. [para. 8.54]

138   We recommend that consideration of the use of the Irish language in courts be taken forward in the wider context of the development of policy on the use of Irish in public life generally. [para. 8.56]

139   In line with the assessment of security risk, the Court Service should assume full responsibility for security at its courthouses, for jury keeping and for the reception and provision of information for court users. [para. 8.58]

140   We recommend that the Court Service should have the responsibility, in consultation with the police, for drawing up policy in relation to countering intimidation of jurors, witnesses, victims and other members of the public on court premises and for ensuring that the policy is implemented. [para. 8.59]

141   We recommend that there should be no change in the arrangements for displaying the Royal Coat of Arms on the exterior of existing courthouses. However, in order to create an environment in which all those attending court can feel comfortable we recommend that the interior of courtrooms should be free of any symbols. We recommend that the flying of the Union flag at courthouses should continue to be in line with flag flying practice at other government buildings which are the responsibility of the Secretary of State for Northern Ireland. These practices would become subject to any decision of the Assembly on devolution of responsibility for courts administration. [para. 8.62]

142   We believe that the declaration of "God Save The Queen" on entry of the judiciary to the court is unnecessary and we recommend that this practice should end. [para. 8.63]

Restorative and Reparative Justice

143   We recommend the development of restorative justice approaches for juvenile offenders. [para. 9.53]

144   We recommend that restorative justice schemes for young adults (i.e. those between 18 and 21 years of age inclusive) and adults be piloted and evaluated carefully before final decisions are made on whether and how they might be applied across Northern Ireland as a whole. [para. 9.54]

145   We recommend that in Northern Ireland the police continue to have the option of issuing informal warnings or cautions to juveniles. [para. 9.59]

146   We recommend that restorative justice should be integrated into the juvenile justice system and its philosophy in Northern Ireland, using a conference model (which we term a "youth conference") based in statute, available for all juveniles (including 17 year olds, once they come within the remit of the youth court), subject to the full range of human rights safeguards. [para. 9.60]

147   We recommend that a Northern Ireland system should focus on:

- reparative justice and meeting the needs of victims, so giving them a real place in the youth conference, rather than just regarding it as a means to reform the offender;

- rehabilitative justice, where what is important is the prevention of re-offending by the young person, so that the youth conference focuses on offending behaviour;

- proportionality, rather than pure retributive justice;

- reintegrative shaming, where the offender acknowledges the harm done, but where the youth conference clearly separates the offender from the offence and focuses on the potential for reintegrating the offender into the community in the plan and on the prevention of re-offending;

- repairing relationships which have been damaged or broken by crime;

- devolving power to youth conference participants (see below for discussion of who those participants might be) to create the youth conference and the plan, but requiring subsequent approval for the plan from the court for cases which have gone to court (see below in relation to police/prosecution referrals);

- encouraging victims to bring one or more supporters (who might be, but need not necessarily be, a member of Victim Support);

- encouraging offenders to bring significant others (especially their families, but also particular members of the community important to them) to the youth conference, but not placing such a strong emphasis on the responsibility of the family to deal with offending as is done in New Zealand. [para. 9.62]

148   Even where there is a need for custody or a traditional criminal justice community sanction (such as probation, community service or a compensation order), we recommend that these should be capable of being combined with other elements within a youth conference order (allowing a number of elements to be incorporated into a plan, not all of which can be combined at present). [para. 9.63]

149   We recommend that a court-based youth conferencing scheme should operate on the basis of court referrals, with the youth conference resulting in a report to the court which contains a draft plan. If approved by the court, the plan will form the basis for the court disposal. Court-ordered referrals should be required after guilt has been admitted or determined, but before disposal. They should be discretionary for offences that are triable only on indictment. [para. 9.65]

150   Where the court orders a youth conference, we recommend that there should be no requirement to request a pre-sentence report, so as to avoid introducing a further cause of delay. [para. 9.66]

151   Every effort should be made by the conference co-ordinators to contact victims, to encourage them to attend and to organise conferences in such a way as to facilitate the attendance of victims. [para. 9.68]

152   Victims should be able to be accompanied at the conference by a supporter (or, at the discretion of the co-ordinator, more than one supporter – a restriction on numbers would be inappropriate, especially in the case of child victims). [para. 9.70]

153   If the victim does not wish to attend the conference, then he or she should be offered the alternative of submitting a written statement (describing the effect of the offence and indicating whether an apology, reparation or compensation would be received positively). [para. 9.71]

154   If victims do not wish to attend a youth conference that should not prevent it from going ahead. Victims should not have a veto on conferences taking place. [para. 9.71]

155   We recommend that in Northern Ireland, for purposes of attendance at youth conferences, "family" should be viewed in its broad context to include those, such as church or youth leaders, who play a significant role in the offender's life. [para. 9.72]

156   We recommend that the following should always take part in a youth conference:

   ▪ the co-ordinator;

   ▪ the juvenile and the juvenile's parents or guardians; and

   ▪ either a police officer or prosecutor. [para. 9.76]

157   We recommend that the following may participate in the youth conference:

- the victim (if he or she agrees) and the victim's supporters;

- significant others relevant to the offender (at the co-ordinator's discretion);

- a defence solicitor or barrister (where this is wished by the offender or his or her guardian); and

- where appropriate, professionals such as probation and social services, who can provide information to the conference about possible options for the plan and about the offender's background (but only as information providers and at the co-ordinator's discretion). [para. 9.77]

158   We recommend that the youth conference co-ordinator should have the same type of monitoring and breach powers as probation officers in relation to monitoring probation orders and their requirements. If offenders do not complete their plans in their entirety or, in the judgement of the co-ordinator, sufficiently, then breach proceedings would start. [para. 9.79]

159   We recommend that the youth conference and youth conference co-ordinators should be housed within a separate arm of the Department of Justice or one of its agencies. [para. 9.82]

160   We recommend that the development of restorative justice, and in particular the development of the menu of national and local programmes and projects which the youth conference can draw upon, should be driven at both national and local level. [para. 9.85]

161   We recommend that a national level inter-agency body responsible for youth conferencing should be established; it might be a sub-group of the Criminal Justice Board. It could have responsibility for ensuring the availability of programmes across Northern Ireland to support community sanctions, restorative justice generally, and youth conferences in particular. It should deal with the accreditation and setting of standards for restorative justice, including those that apply to community restorative justice schemes, and encourage the spreading of good practice. [para. 9.85]

162   We recommend that youth conference co-ordinators should take the lead in developing networks and inter-agency arrangements in local areas, and should co-ordinate the development of a local menu of programmes and options that might form part of a youth conference order. They should develop close links with a variety of organisations and groups with an interest in youth conferences in local areas, including funders, programme providers, community groups, sentencers, the police, probation, social services and education authorities. [para. 9.86]

163   We recommend that priority be given to establishing facilities for court-referred youth conferences, and that the system be expanded to provide for police and prosecutor referrals more slowly. [para. 9.87]

164   We believe that in the longer term, as resources permit, youth conference co-ordinators should assist with pre-court conferences as part of a diversionary strategy. [para. 9.90]

165   We think it is important that, when resources permit, youth conferences, as with other forms of diversion, should be available through prosecutor referral as well as police referral. [para. 9.92]

166   For prosecutor referrals, the right to prosecute should remain until the plan has been completed. In the case of police referrals the co-ordinator should monitor the implementation of any agreed plan and report back to the police, but the police should not have the option of proceeding further. [para. 9.93]

167   We recommend that the courts' sentencing powers be reviewed to facilitate the possibility of restorative interventions, including the formal payment of compensation before sentence is finally passed. [para. 9.94]

168   We believe that community restorative justice schemes can have a role to play in dealing with the types of low-level crime that most commonly concerns local communities. However, we recommend that community restorative justice schemes should:

(i)   receive referrals from a statutory criminal justice agency, rather than from within the community, with the police being informed of all such referrals;

(ii)   be accredited by, and subject to standards laid down by the Government in respect of how they deal with criminal activity, covering such issues as training of staff, human rights protections, other due process and proportionality issues, and complaints mechanisms for both victims and offenders;

(iii)   be subject to regular inspection by the independent Criminal Justice Inspectorate which we recommend in Chapter 15; and

(iv)   have no role in determining the guilt or innocence of alleged offenders, and deal only with those individuals referred by a criminal justice agency who have indicated that they do not wish to deny guilt and where there is prima facie evidence of guilt. [para. 9.98]

Juvenile Justice

169   We recommend that in drawing up legislation flowing from this Review, the Government should develop, agree and incorporate a clear statement of the aims of the juvenile justice system in Northern Ireland and a statement of the principles which should guide those who exercise the powers conferred by the legislation with due regard to the international human rights standards to which the United Kingdom has given commitment. [para. 10.66]

170   We recommend that children aged 10-13 inclusive who are found guilty of criminal offences should not be held in juvenile justice centres, and that their accommodation needs should be provided by the care system. [para. 10.69]

171   We recommend that 17 year olds be brought within the ambit of the youth court. [para. 10.70]

172   In the particular circumstances of Northern Ireland we recommend that it should continue to be the practice for 17 year olds to be remanded and sentenced to the young offenders centre. [para. 10.72]

173   We recommend that the staff at the young offenders centre pay particularly close attention to the 17 year olds in their care and be prepared to take special measures, including the provision of separate accommodation, for any who are assessed as being vulnerable or immature. [para. 10.72]

174   We recommend that a form of community service should be developed for those under 16 years of age, with a maximum period of service of 40 hours. The service to be undertaken should be tailored to the needs of juveniles of that age group and be of a nature most likely to maintain and promote the development of the juvenile in responsible, beneficial and socially acceptable ways. The arrangements should be piloted and evaluated rigorously. [para. 10.74]

175   We recommend the introduction of reparation orders in Northern Ireland. [para. 10.75]

176   We recommend:

    (i)   the piloting and evaluation of bail information and support schemes to provide the courts with information and advice to assist them with making bail and remand decisions in respect of individual juveniles;

    (ii)   the development of bail hostel accommodation specifically for juveniles, particularly within Belfast;

    (iiii)   that those remanded in custody should be assessed as quickly as possible to determine the nature of the regime required, including the degree of supervision; and

    (iv)   that remands in custody should be for the shortest period of time possible. [para. 10.78]

177   We recommend that Lisnevin juvenile justice centre be closed. [para. 10.79]

178   We endorse the development of further diversionary mechanisms based on a partnership approach and recommend that any savings arising from the rationalisation of the juvenile justice estate should be reallocated to diversionary programmes and other community-based sanctions for juveniles. [para. 10.87]

179   We recommend also the development of prosecutor-driven diversionary schemes for juveniles, including the power to refer back for a police caution and the development of agreed guidelines on good practice in diversion at police and prosecutor level. [para. 10.87]

180   In respect of juveniles, we recommend that the Government should commission independent research into the effects of the Criminal Evidence (Northern Ireland) Order 1988 on juvenile defendants as a matter of urgency, and that the findings of that research should be published. [para. 10.89]

181   We recommend that those who volunteer to act as appropriate adults should receive training by a wide range of agencies, to include training on the needs of those who have learning or other disabilities, or who are suffering from a mental disorder, and children's rights and broad human rights awareness. [para. 10.90]

182   In respect of the operation of the youth court we recommend that:

     (i)   Guidelines should be developed for the layout and operation of the youth court, emphasising the need for all the participants in court to sit at the same level, the need for all participants to be able to hear what is being said in court, the need for simple and plain language to be used during the proceedings, and the need for the defendant and his or her parents to be given opportunities to participate and express themselves freely.

     (ii)   Defence and prosecution advocates should be encouraged, through professional education and development, to enhance their expertise in respect of handling juvenile cases and their awareness of the human rights instruments and jurisprudence as they relate to juveniles. This should not interfere with the juvenile's right to the lawyer of his or her choice. Professional and lay members of the bench should receive similar training under the auspices of the Judicial Studies Board.

     (iii) In the light of the outcome of evaluation, the child witness scheme should be made available at all criminal court venues in Northern Ireland, including youth courts.

     (iv) Efforts to deal with delays in cases being brought before the youth court should continue.

     (V)   Given the need to tackle delay and the impact of extending the jurisdiction of youth courts to include 17 year olds, there should be an examination of youth court sittings and consequential implications for magistrates' courts. [para. 10.94]

183   We recommend that the Government should consider carefully the implications of judgments of T & V v United Kingdom for the operation of the juvenile justice system in Northern Ireland. [para. 10.95]

184   We make the following recommendations in respect of the complaints mechanisms and inspection arrangements:

     (i)   Complaints mechanisms should be reviewed as a matter of urgency to ensure that they conform to the *United Nations Rules for the Protection of Juveniles Deprived of their Liberty*, and to ensure that they include an independent element.

(ii)   On admission to a juvenile justice centre, all juveniles should, as now, be given a copy of the rules governing the juvenile justice centre and a written description of their rights and obligations in a language they can understand, together with a description of the ways in which they can make complaints, as well as the address of public or private agencies and organisations which provide legal assistance.

(iii)   For those juveniles who have difficulty in understanding the written guidance, the guidance should, as now, be explained to them.

(iv)   All agencies providing facilities and services for juvenile offenders, including juvenile justice centres, should come within the remit of the Criminal Justice Inspectorate, in respect of those services or facilities.

(v)   Each juvenile justice centre should have a local advisory committee that brings in local professional and community representatives, including representatives of nearby residents. [para. 10.98]

185   We recommend the creation of a next steps agency which would take on responsibility for the range of responsibilities which fall to the current Juvenile Justice Board as are set out in Article 56(5) of the Criminal Justice (Children) (Northern Ireland) Order 1998. [para. 10.101]

186   We recommend that the development of juvenile justice policy should be separate from the functions of the juvenile justice agency and should be a matter for a separate unit in the department within which the agency is placed. That unit should be responsible for advising the Minister in relation to policy and legislative proposals. The unit should also be responsible for developing a strategy for the delivery of juvenile justice services, and should develop and publish aims, standards and performance indicators. [para. 10.102]

187   We recommend that an overarching Probation, Prisons and Juvenile Justice Advisory Board be adopted. [para. 10.103]

188   We recommend that, pending devolution, political responsibility for the juvenile justice system should remain with the Secretary of State for Northern Ireland and that policy and legislative advice should continue to be provided by the Northern Ireland Office. After devolution, we believe that ministerial responsibility should lie with whichever Minister is responsible for prisons and probation. [para. 10.104]

189   We recommend the use of research as a basis for developing an informed juvenile justice policy. We recommend that all new initiatives and legislation should be routinely monitored and subject to rigorous and independent evaluation. [para. 10.105]

190   We recommend that in developing policy and practice the views of the public and of young people in particular should be taken into account. To achieve this, innovative approaches to consultation should be developed, and consideration should be given to how best to seek out the views of young people. [para. 10.106]

191   We also recommend that, to enhance public confidence in the juvenile justice system, a communication strategy be developed to advertise successes, develop public awareness of existing practice and new initiatives, and to provide information to sentencers on the availability of programmes and other community disposals. [para. 10.106]

Community Safety

192   We recommend that the aim of a community safety strategy in Northern Ireland should be to create the conditions which promote an inclusive partnership-based approach in developing community safety initiatives between relevant agencies, voluntary groups, the private sector and local communities, with a view to reducing crime, the fear of crime and enhancing community safety. [para. 11.51]

193   We recommend the development of a Northern Ireland community safety strategy based upon extensive consultation with relevant agencies, political structures, and the voluntary, private and community sectors. [para. 11.51]

194   We recommend that in developing a community safety strategy for Northern Ireland specific consideration be given to:

-    offences against women, particularly domestic violence;

-    child abuse;

-    interventions in relation to youth offending;

-    the needs of ethnic minority communities;

-    drug, substance and alcohol abuse;

-    street violence, low-level neighbourhood disorder and anti-social behaviour;

-    car crime; and

-    reducing criminality (i.e. addressing the factors which lie behind criminal behaviour). [para. 11.52]

195   We recommend that there should be no presumption that any particular body should always take the lead in individual community safety projects. [para. 11.58]

196   Rather than District Policing Partnerships we recommend that:

-    Community Safety and Policing Partnerships (CSPPs), chaired by local authority elected members, should be established.

■ The role and remit of the CSPP should be set out in statute, supplemented by good practice guidelines.

■ The membership of the CSPP should be as recommended by the Policing Commission for District Policing Partnership Boards, with a majority of elected members, and with independent members selected to represent business and trade union interests and to provide expertise in matters relating to community safety. We suggest that consideration be given to inviting councils to seek nominations through bodies such as Chambers of Commerce, Business in the Community, the Northern Ireland Committee of the Irish Congress of Trade Unions and the Northern Ireland Council for Voluntary Action. The District Partnership Boards, currently in place to administer European funding, provide a useful model.

■ The CSPP should prepare a local community safety strategy based on local crime profiles, people's worries about crime locally, and the availability of local services.

■ When carrying out this wider community safety role, the CSPP should consult widely in the community and work in partnership with community, statutory, and voluntary agencies; on the statutory side, the police should be involved along with others such as the Probation Service, the Public Prosecution Service, social services, education, health and the Northern Ireland Housing Executive.

■ It should be open to the CSPP to invite other relevant agencies to the monthly public meetings envisaged in recommendation 36 of the Policing Commission Report.

■ The CSPP should submit an annual report of its activities in relation to community safety to the district council or councils to which it relates, and then to the Policing Board and the central Community Safety Unit (which is referred to below) for their information. [para. 11.61]

197   We recommend that there should be a central Community Safety Unit responsible for:

■ developing a community safety strategy for Northern Ireland;

■ providing a focus for the promotion and co-ordination of community safety throughout government, the voluntary and the private sectors;

■ developing effective and innovative public consultation mechanisms in developing community safety policy, including the development of mechanisms to engage the Civic Forum;

■ encouraging initiatives, by funding and evaluating pilot projects, at the local level, and by making crime mapping information available to local partnership bodies;

■ setting the monitoring and funding requirements for centrally-funded projects;

■ spreading good practice and mainstreaming successful demonstration projects;

■ advising Ministers on community safety policy; and

■ publishing an annual report setting out progress against strategic objectives, funding activity and the contributions of departments and agencies towards community safety objectives. [para. 11.64]

198   We recommend that the Community Safety Unit should develop guidance packs, covering such issues as:

■ advice for developing local schemes;

■ training manuals;

■ publicity and "how to consult" guides;

■ crime audit guides and assistance;

■ help and guidance in relation to monitoring and evaluation; and

■ advice on preparing bids for funding. [para. 11.65]

199   We recommend that a central Community Safety Unit be staffed by a team of people who bring a range of knowledge and experience to bear, including knowledge of community safety, wider government social and economic policy, finance, research and evaluation, and training issues. There would be merit in some staff working in the team on a secondment basis, from the police and probation for example, and at least one research officer should be included. It should be headed by someone of sufficient stature to command respect and confidence within and beyond government in Northern Ireland. In addition, given the acknowledged expertise developed within the Community Safety Centre, we recommend that it and its staff be integrated into the team. [para. 11.68]

200   We recommend that, until such time as responsibility for criminal justice issues is devolved to the Northern Ireland Assembly, the Community Safety Unit should be located within the Northern Ireland Office. [para. 11.69]

201   On devolution, we recommend that the Community Safety Unit be located within the Office of the First Minister and Deputy First Minister. If that proves impracticable then it should be located within a justice department; but steps should be taken through central machinery to ensure that community safety is addressed on a co-ordinated, inter-departmental basis. Committing departments and agencies to contributing to an annual report on community safety would be one way of encouraging such an approach. [para. 11.70]

202   We recommend the creation of a non-statutory and advisory Community Safety Council, which should comprise representatives from local partnership bodies together with representatives of the relevant departments and statutory agencies, and should be supported by the Community Safety Unit. [para. 11.71]

203   We also recommend that relevant agencies should have a clear statutory responsibility for helping to prevent crime and reduce the fear of crime and to contribute to community safety. Relevant agencies might include the Probation Service, social services, education and health authorities, and the Public Prosecution Service. [para. 11.72]

204   Based on what we have seen elsewhere, we recommend that the Community Safety Unit should have a budget to fund demonstration projects, to fund projects which are of a scale or geographic extent beyond the capabilities of local partnership arrangements, for the production and dissemination of good practice guides, and to provide seed-corn funding for the administration and implementation of local partnership projects and arrangements. We further recommend that the arrangements for funding new initiatives should include a requirement that a percentage of the funds allocated be devoted to evaluation of the project. [para. 11.73]

205   We make the following recommendations:

- That district councils be given the power to contribute an amount initially up to the equivalent of a rate of 3p in the pound, for the purpose of funding community safety initiatives.

- The legislation containing the power to raise such funds and authorising expenditure on community safety matters should on its face, or through regulations, contain clear guidelines about the raising of such funds and the use to which they might be put. For example, expenditure should be based on a clearly established analysis of local crime as defined in the local community safety strategy.

- CSPPs should be encouraged to seek funds from other sources, including the private sector.

- CSPPs should be able to seek a limited amount of funding from the central Community Safety Unit. Such funding might be provided on a matching basis, thus providing the CSPPs with an incentive to seek alternative sources of funds, whether from district council funds, the private sector or elsewhere. [para. 11.75]

206   We recommend that the Community Safety Unit should draw up funding guidelines as a matter of priority. [para. 11.76]

Sentences, Prisons and Probation

207   We recommend that the current sentencing framework for adults be reviewed to establish whether it could adequately accommodate restorative interventions where appropriate and, if not, to consider what changes might be made in order for it to do so. [para. 12.52]

208   We recommend that it should be a recognised function of the Probation Service to provide aftercare and support, including supervision, to discharged prisoners and that the service should be adequately resourced to this end. Our expectation is that the Prison and Probation Services should work together to prepare release packages for prisoners. These arrangements should be evaluated with a view to considering whether compulsory supervision should be introduced. [para. 12.56]

209   We recommend that judges when sentencing should explain in greater detail and in simple language the impact of the sentence, including the fact that, with remission, the offender may be eligible for release having served half the sentence and that time spent in prison awaiting trial may count towards the period served. [para. 12.60]

210   We recommend that the current Life Sentence Review Board be replaced by an independent body that is not part of the Northern Ireland Prison Service or the proposed Department of Justice. Its membership should include individuals with an expertise in psychiatry or psychology and it should have a judicial input that would enable it to act as a tribunal for dealing with discretionary and Secretary of State's pleasure cases. Its membership might also include individuals with expertise in criminology. [para. 12.64]

211   In relation to all indeterminate sentence cases, including mandatory life sentence cases, we recommend that judges when sentencing should be required to set a period for retribution and deterrence (equivalent to the tariff set in England and Wales). In most cases the period would be a fixed term of years, although it must be envisaged that some offences might be so serious that a whole life period would be appropriate. The period would be announced in open court and would be appealable. Once this period had been served, it would be the responsibility of the independent body to determine, primarily on grounds of risk, when the prisoner should be released. [para. 12.65]

212   We recommend that the practice of Board of Visitors adjudication should end. [para. 12.69]

213   We understand that the Prison Service, RUC and DPP are currently considering a protocol that would guide the prison authorities on the circumstances in which the RUC and DPP should be brought in to deal with prison offences, and we recommend that this protocol be speedily completed and published. [para. 12.75]

214   We recommend some increase in the penalty available to governors, which would need to be consistent with European Court findings (including in relation to cases currently before the European Commission). [para. 12.75]

215   We recommend that a mechanism be set up to oversee programmes in both prisons and the community with a view to ensuring continuity and consistency, and also ensuring that evaluations are published and, where appropriate, form the basis for the roll-out of successful schemes. [para. 12.80]

216   We conclude that electronic monitoring is a technique that should be kept under review in the light of developing experience elsewhere, including in England and Wales. It is an issue which could be remitted to the Criminal Justice Issues Group. [para. 12.83]

217   We suggest that consideration be given to recruiting a small number of non-executive members to the management board of the Service. They might be selected on the basis of the particular managerial skills that they would bring to the board. [para. 12.91]

218   We recommend that prison governors should be expected to consider programmes of outreach into nearby communities. [para. 12.92]

219   We attach great importance to the training of prison staff in cultural awareness; furthermore, given the extent of change being experienced by the Service, we endorse the view that particular emphasis should to be given to training in new roles and skills to enhance the ability of prison officers to work effectively with prisoners. [para. 12.93]

220   We consider that this would be an opportune time for the Northern Ireland Prison Service to look at its uniform requirements. [para. 12.94]

221   The Probation Service must, on the basis of it being able to demonstrate value for money and efficient working, be properly resourced to reflect its workload and its continuing need to support voluntary organisations working alongside it. [para. 12.102]

222   We recommend that, on devolution of criminal justice matters, the Probation Service be reconstituted as a next steps agency. This would mean that responsibility for probation services would lie directly with the relevant Minister, on the same basis as the Prison Service. Both agencies would be supported by small management boards comprising senior staff. [para. 12.103]

223   A senior officer of the Probation Service should sit on the prisons management board and a senior prisons official should sit on the probation management board. [para. 12.103]

224   We recommend that the responsible Minister be supported by an advisory board which would advise on all matters to do with probation, prisons and juvenile justice. It would comprise the heads of the three organisations and members with an interest in correctional and related matters, drawn from the voluntary and community sector, children's organisations and social and related services. [para. 12.104]

225   The advisory board would assist the Minister in considering strategic and policy issues, determining priorities, setting standards and monitoring service delivery. The board would have a special interest in ensuring co-ordination and co-operation on the delivery of services where appropriate. [para. 12.104]

226   The framework document determining the relationships between the Probation Agency and the core department should make clear that operational decisions in relation to individual

cases are entirely a matter for the professional staff. It should also make clear that, although these decisions may be scrutinised in the course of inspection, neither administrative civil servants in the core department nor the Minister would play a part in them, unless consulted by the professionals. [para. 12.105]

227   We recommend that particular consideration be given to the following:

- staff exchanges between the organisations;

- joint training programmes; and

- joint approaches to the development of offending behaviour programmes that can be delivered in the custodial and community settings, together with arrangements for accrediting, monitoring and evaluating them (with evaluations being published). [para. 12.106]

Victims and Witnesses

228   The interests of victims should feature in the codes of practice and plans of all criminal justice organisations that interface with them, and in the criminal justice plan that we advocate for the system as a whole. [para. 13.38]

229   We recommend that a sub-group of the Criminal Justice Issues Group should maintain a specific focus on victims issues, should monitor and evaluate the new arrangements and should report regularly. It should include both statutory and voluntary agencies that are concerned with the provision of criminal justice services to victims. [para. 13.40]

230   The possibility of a victims' advocate should be considered again in the future if new arrangements on behalf of victims are seen not to be working effectively. [para. 13.40]

231   We recommend that the agency which has lead responsibility for working with victims at particular points in the criminal justice process should be clearly delineated. [para. 13.41]

232   We recommend that the lead role in ensuring the provision of information and explanation to victims and seeking their views be taken by the police until such time as the case is passed to the prosecutor, that is until a suspect is charged or a summons issued (although as a matter of practicality it is recognised that the police will have a significant role until the file is received in the prosecutor's office). The lead role (including notifying the victim of the outcome of the case in the courts) would subsequently be taken by the prosecutor until the case is finished in the courts. The prosecutor would also lead on any issues arising out of an appeal. [para. 13.42]

233   Where a custodial sentence was imposed, the Prison Service would then take the lead. Where a non-custodial sentence was imposed, and the victim had an interest in being kept informed, the Probation Service would take the lead. [para. 13.42]

234   In the case of a diversionary measure which involves victims, the agency or body responsible for implementation would have responsibility for informing victims about the progress and, where contact between victim and offender is envisaged, for taking steps to ensure the safety of victims. [para. 13.42]

235   Each lead agency should have a clearly advertised point of contact. [para. 13.42]

236   We recommend that the criminal justice agencies in Northern Ireland should build on their existing commitments in the Code of Practice for victims, in which they undertake to provide information at various stages in the criminal justice process (although not if it is against the wishes of the victim). The provision of information should not be limited to cases that the criminal justice system might classify as "serious". [para. 13.45]

237   We recommend that it should be for the lead agency to ensure the necessary information is made available, although it may be appropriate for the information to be passed through or provided by a third party. [para. 13.45]

238   We recommend that wherever possible victims should be informed and consulted about the development of their cases. But when and how to consult them, particularly those who are witnesses, must be a matter for the professional judgement of the prosecutor. [para. 13.47]

239   On balance and subject to our overriding recommendation that when and how to consult must be a matter for the professional judgement of the prosecutor, we recommend that the general rule, building on the Director of Public Prosecutions' current practice, should be for victims to be consulted about important changes in the way that "their" case is being handled. We also recommend that information about such changes should be actively offered rather than the victim having to request it, although we accept that it might not be possible to consult victims in certain circumstances, for example, if they are not at court when decisions have to be taken. [para. 13.51]

240   We recommend that practice be reviewed to ensure that the prosecutor who will be responsible for a wider range of cases than hitherto considers the effect of the crime on the victim and makes certain that those acting on behalf of the prosecution, including independent practitioners, bring all relevant information to the attention of the court and up-date it regularly. This would include not only information from the victim but also information from others, for example medical professionals, who would be able to advise on the effect on the victim or on similar cases. We consider it important that the responsibilities of the prosecutor in this regard be given due prominence in relevant publications of principles and codes of practice. [para. 13.55]

241   We draw attention to the importance of maintaining the duty of prosecuting advocates to challenge allegations about victims made by the defence in absence of supporting evidence. [para. 13.56]

242   We recommend three changes in practice relating to the giving of information about the release, or likely release date, of prisoners:

- Where an offender is sentenced to custody and where the victim wishes, the Prison Service should be responsible for explaining the impact of the sentence including the likely release date and the likely arrangements for temporary release. It should be the responsibility of the prosecutor to check whether the victim wishes to use this service and if so to put the victim in touch with the Prison Service.

- Where information about release is requested by the victim, the Prison Service should be required to give it, provided the prisoner is not put at risk.

- The Prison Service should put in place formal mechanisms to deal with concerns expressed by victims about safety, particularly in relation to temporary release. [para. 13.59]

243   We recommend that publicly funded witness support schemes should be made available at all Crown Court and magistrates' courts venues. Children should be included in such arrangements on a basis determined in the light of the outcome of evaluation of the current pilot scheme. [para. 13.62]

Law Reform

244   We recommend that a Law Commission for Northern Ireland be established by statute to keep under review criminal and civil law, including procedure and practice, and to make recommendations to the Government on whatever changes it considers necessary or desirable. The establishment of such a Commission should not be dependent upon responsibility for criminal justice matters being devolved. [para. 14.51]

245   We believe the functions of the Law Commission for Northern Ireland should include:

- reviewing the current state of the law and coming forward with recommendations for reform;

- modernising and, where appropriate, simplifying and consolidating legislation;

- providing advice to Government as to the most suitable topics for law reform and the most appropriate agencies to make a study of the options for reform;

- keeping abreast of developments in other jurisdictions, including in particular England and Wales, Scotland and the Republic of Ireland;

- working closely with Law Commissions in England and Wales, Scotland and the Republic of Ireland with a view to assessing the scope for harmonisation of the criminal law and procedure in all four jurisdictions;

- commissioning research; and

- inviting suggestions for reform and consulting as widely as possible. [para. 14.53]

246   The Law Commission should consider both substantive law and procedural matters, taking account of current practice and implications for criminal and civil justice. [para. 14.54]

247   We recommend that the Commission be chaired by a High Court judge on a part-time basis. [para. 14.55]

248   We recommend that membership of the Law Commission should include a senior barrister, a senior solicitor, a legal academic, and one lay person. Members should be remunerated. [para. 14.55]

249   If a Law Commission were to be established in advance of responsibility for criminal justice being devolved, then its members should be appointed by the Secretary of State for Northern Ireland, consulting the First Minister and Deputy First Minister. In this event, the Commission should agree its programme of work with the Secretary of State and First Minister and Deputy First Ministers. It should submit its reports jointly to the Secretary of State and relevant members of the Northern Ireland Executive Committee. Its reports should be tabled before the Northern Ireland Assembly and Westminster Parliament, and should be published. [para. 14.56]

250   Once responsibility for criminal law matters is devolved, responsibility for appointing members to the Commission could pass to the Attorney General for Northern Ireland who would consult with departmental Ministers, as appropriate, and consider government remits for the programme. [para. 14.57]

251   Policy responsibility for law reform matters would be assumed by the Minister responsible for justice matters. [para. 14.57]

252   We recommend that in developing its programme of work, the Commission should make its own suggestions and receive remits from government. In drawing up its programme of work it should also take account of views of others through a consultation process. [para. 14.59]

253   We recommend that the Law Commission should receive a sufficient budget for books and materials and to facilitate the commissioning of research and project work. We further

recommend that the Law Commission be required to make all publications publicly accessible. [para. 14.60]

254   We have identified a number of matters that were raised with us in the course of consultation, some of which are reflected elsewhere in the report, which we believe it would be appropriate for the Law Commission for Northern Ireland to consider as part of its early programme of work:

- The disclosure procedures under the provisions of the Criminal Procedure and Investigations Act 1996.

- Plea bargaining, focusing on issues concerning formalisation, transparency and human rights.

- Domestic violence, in particular how current law, policy and practice helps or hinders prevention, protection and service provision in relation to domestic violence. Such a review should not be confined to criminal procedures, but encompass family and civil remedies as well.

- Producing, for use by practitioners, a simple, clear and concise comparative guide to criminal law and procedure in Northern Ireland and the Republic of Ireland. [para. 14.62]

255   In the event of criminal justice responsibilities being devolved, we recommend that responsibility for criminal law and procedure and those aspects of civil law which are currently the responsibility of the Office of Law Reform should be brought together within a new Department of Justice. [para. 14.63]

Organisation and Structure

256   We recommend that responsibility for the same range of criminal justice functions as are devolved to the Scottish Parliament should be devolved to the Northern Ireland Assembly. Our preference is that they should all be devolved at the same time. [para. 15.56]

257   We recommend the creation on devolution of a single Department of Justice, headed by a Minister for Justice, bringing together all justice functions other than prosecution, responsibility for the Law Commission and judicial matters. [para. 15.62]

258   We recommend that as peace and political stability become embedded efforts should be made to find an alternative site for the Forensic Science Agency that would not be shared with the police. [para. 15.64]

259   There is scope for enhancing the management arrangements for the Agency and we recommend that a forensic science professional or academic from another jurisdiction in the United Kingdom should be invited to join the Agency's advisory board. We recommend secondments to and from other forensic science organisations to encourage professional

development and discourage the development of a police or prosecution-focused culture. [para. 15.65]

260   As regards the State Pathology Department, we note its particularly heavy workload and recommend that it be reviewed to ensure that the expertise of its staff is properly deployed. We also note the limited administrative support arrangements for the State Pathology Department, and recommend that it should be strengthened to ensure that the professional staff are able to devote their time to professional tasks. [para. 15.66]

261   We recommend that the existing Criminal Cases Review Commission should continue to consider cases that involve alleged miscarriages of justice emanating from Northern Ireland. [para. 15.67]

262   We recommend that agency annual reports should, as a matter of course, be laid before the relevant departmental committee. In addition, if the Assembly constitutes a standing committee for the criminal justice system as a whole, we recommend that it and any departmental committees should receive and consider an annual report on the system in its entirety, prepared by the Criminal Justice Board. [para. 15.70]

263   We recommend the creation of a statute-based, independent Criminal Justice Inspectorate which should:

- be responsible for ensuring the inspection of all aspects of the criminal justice system other than the courts;

- be funded by the Minister for Justice, and that the Chief Criminal Justice Inspector should be appointed by that Minister;

- present its inspection reports to the Minister for Justice, the responsible Minister (if the agency inspected is the responsibility of another Minister) and the relevant departmental committee or standing committee;

- publish its reports and make them widely and readily available;

- publish an annual report of its activities, present that report to the Minister for Justice, and lay it before the relevant departmental and standing committees;

- be responsible for advising Ministers on standards within criminal justice agencies (standard setting should remain the prerogative of Ministers);

- employ a range of full and part-time inspectors and buy in expertise, including that from other inspection agencies in England and Wales and Scotland, as appropriate (such as HM Inspectorate of Prisons and HM Inspectorate of Constabulary);

- be responsible for determining its own programme of inspections, in consultation with the relevant Ministers;

- carry out a range of inspections, including; periodic, cyclical and surprise inspections of systems and structures; thematic, issues-based inspections; and special inspections which might require special skills (e.g. medical expertise); and

- work closely with other inspectorates (e.g. on Health and Safety, Mental Health, and Social Services) and with professional bodies such as the Royal College of Pathologists and the Policy Advisory Board for Forensic Pathology. [para. 15.72]

264   We recommend that Ministers in the Northern Ireland Executive responsible for criminal justice functions, together with the Attorney General for Northern Ireland, should meet regularly to oversee the criminal justice system as a whole. They should, in particular, agree and publish a common set of aims for the criminal justice system. [para. 15.74]

265   We recommend that support to the ministerial group should continue to be provided by the Criminal Justice Board. The Criminal Justice Board should comprise, as at present, the heads of the main statutory agencies within the criminal justice system and senior policy-makers from within the relevant departments. It should comprise:

- The head of the Public Prosecution Service.

- The Chief Constable of the Police Service of Northern Ireland.

- A senior representative from the Attorney General's Office.

- The head of the Department of Justice and of any other department with criminal justice functions.

- The heads of the Prisons, Probation, Courts and Juvenile Justice Agencies.

- The head of the central Community Safety Unit. [para. 15.75]

266   We agree with those who suggested that the membership of the Criminal Justice Issues Group should be expanded to include representatives of the major voluntary sector organisations, given the important role they currently play - and will continue to play in future - in delivering criminal justice, and we so recommend. [para. 15.76]

267   We recommend that the ministerial group, the Criminal Justice Board, and the Criminal Justice Issues Group should continue to be supported by a common secretariat, which should be located within the Department of Justice. [para. 15.77]

268   We recommend the introduction of legislation that will enable statutory time-limits to be introduced in Northern Ireland, should that be judged to be necessary. [para. 15.83]

269   We recommend that in addition to setting target time-limits within which cases should be completed, attention should be paid to the average time taken to process cases at the relevant stages. [para. 15.83]

270   We recommend the establishment of an inter-agency group in Northern Ireland tasked with developing a strategic and co-operative framework for countering organised crime. The core of such a group might be the Department of Justice, the police, Customs and Excise, the Public Prosecution Service and the central Community Safety Unit. [para. 15.84]

Research and Evaluation

271   We recommend that the Criminal Justice Board should be tasked with taking forward further work on the harmonisation of statistical categories across the criminal justice system and ensuring co-operation between agencies in sharing information. [para. 16.20]

272   In all planning and framework documents, a duty should be placed on agencies to share information, provided that protocols are in place to ensure that this does not harm the interests of justice or enable individuals to be publicly identified. [para. 16.20]

273   We recommend that evaluation should be an integral part of business planning for the development of new policies and programmes and that provision for evaluation should be included in the funding of crime reduction projects. Such evaluation will need to be addressed in a proportionate manner and, especially where small sums are involved, it might not necessarily always involve the use of academic researchers or consultants. However, we have no doubt that if evaluation and the other drivers for research identified above are to be taken seriously, then there will be a need to increase the criminal justice research capacity in Northern Ireland. [para. 16.23]

274   We recommend that the Statistics and Research Branch of the Northern Ireland Office should have responsibility for the collation of statistical information across the criminal justice system. [para. 16.24]

275   In order to enhance the critical mass of criminal justice research expertise within government and to build on links with outside research institutions, we recommend the use of secondments and staff exchanges between government and outside research institutions. Further, we recommend that government and outside researchers should work together to build up the pool of research capabilities, and work collaboratively on such matters as research projects, seminars, conferences and training. [para. 16.25]

276   We recommend that some funding be targeted towards fostering co-operation between researchers through joint conferences and seminars, and suggest that specific research projects might be undertaken on an all-island basis. [para. 16.25]

277   We recommend that discussions take place between those in government responsible for justice matters, NISRA, the Department of Higher and Further Education, Training and Employment and the universities with a view to developing a costed research strategy. [para. 16.27]

Structured Co-operation

278   We suggest that a group of criminal justice policymakers from the two jurisdictions be established. The purpose of such a group would be to identify and advise on the opportunities for co-operation at government level and between the criminal justice agencies North and South, taking account also of the need for effective co-operation with other parts of these islands. It would also take forward consideration of the recommendations of this review on structured co-operation. In its work, the group would take account of the impact of developments at the European Union level and the opportunities these afford for enhancing bilateral co-ordination and co-operation. [para. 17.30]

279   We recommend that the scope for the joint delivery of training, education (including continuing professional development) and the exchange of good practice on criminal justice issues should be examined. [para. 17.34]

280   We recommend that consideration be given to the scope for regular personnel exchange between agencies such as probation, prosecution, prisons, courts and criminal justice policymakers. [para. 17.35]

281   We recommend that consideration be given to recognition of qualifications and the possibility of harmonising standards between the two jurisdictions, while recognising the importance of compatibility between Northern Ireland and other parts of the United Kingdom. [para. 17.36]

282   We recommend fostering co-operation between researchers through joint conferences and seminars, and suggest that specific research projects might be undertaken on an all-island basis. [para. 17.38]

283   We recommend that the central Community Safety Unit should develop close links with its counterparts in the Republic of Ireland, Scotland, England and Wales, and more widely. [para. 17.39]

284   We endorse close liaison between the two jurisdictions in sharing information about trends and what works in education and prevention in relation to the misuse of drugs. [para. 17.40]

285   We recommend that both jurisdictions consider the cross-border dimension with a view to developing reciprocal arrangements for victim and witness support, particularly in relation to providing information, protection, and counselling. [para. 17.42]

286   We recommend that the issue of developing mutual arrangements for continued enforcement of non-custodial sentences and post-custodial supervision should be addressed. Arrangements for accessing programmes available in the other jurisdiction should also be considered. [para. 17.46]

287   Specifically in the context of the new juvenile justice arrangements we suggest that there should be flexibility to allow the use of cross-border facilities for youth conference orders. [para. 17.47]

288   We recommend that consideration be given to facilitating the temporary transfer of prisoners between Northern Ireland and the Republic of Ireland. [para. 17.49]

289   We suggest that discussion of the development of relevant forensic science databases and the scope for exchanges of information should take place under the structures for co-operation. [para. 17.51]

290   We recommend that the possibility of widening access to services such as forensic science and pathology across jurisdictional boundaries be investigated. [para. 17.52]

291   With a view to sharing information between the authorities in the two jurisdictions, we recommend that the possibility of co-ordinating an approach to dangerous offender registers be given consideration. [para. 17.53]

292   We recommend that consideration be given to inviting the Law Commission, which we have recommended for Northern Ireland, to co-operate closely with the Commissions in the other three jurisdictions in these islands with a view to promoting the harmonisation of aspects of criminal law and procedure in all four jurisdictions. [para. 17.57]

293   We recommend that consideration be given to producing, for use by practitioners, a simple, clear and concise comparative guide to criminal law and procedure, North and South. [para. 17.58]

294   We recommend that there should be discussion within the structures for co-operation on how reciprocal arrangements might be developed to ensure the effectiveness of reporting restrictions. [para. 17.60]

Appendix A

Political Parties and Others who gave Written Submissions or Position Papers to, or who met the Criminal Justice Review Group

Alliance Party of Northern Ireland

Amnesty International

Institute of Professional Legal Studies, Queens University, Belfast

Antrim Borough Council

Ards Borough Council

Association of Justices of the Peace for Northern Ireland

Association of the Bar of the City of New York

Ballymena Borough Council

Banbridge District Council

(The General Council of) The Bar of Northern Ireland

British Irish Rights Watch

Committee on the Administration of Justice

The Conservative Party

Council of H.M. County Court Judges in Northern Ireland

Criminal Justice (Children) Lobby Group

Mr D Buchanan

Financial Crime Services Unit, RUC

Democratic Unionist Party

Director of Public Prosecutions

(Dr Fred Browne, Consultant Forensic Psychologist) Knockbracken

Mental Health Services South & East Belfast Trust

Eastern Drugs Co-Ordination Team

ECONI (Evangelical Contribution of Churches)

Extern Organisation

Forbairt Feirste

Forensic Science Agency of Northern Ireland

Francis Rafferty & Co, Solicitors

Glenshane Community Development Ltd

GM Vard (Irish Marxist)

[Include] Youth

Institute of Directors (Northern Ireland Region)

Irish American Unity Conference

Professor Josine Junger-Tas

Criminal Justice Services Division, NIO

Criminal Justice Policy Division, NIO

Law Commission

Law Society of Northern Ireland

Lenadoon Community Forum

Lisburn Borough Council

Lisnevin Juvenile Justice Centre

MENCAP in Northern Ireland

Mourne Unionist Association

NIACRO

(Muckamore Abbey Hospital) North & West Belfast Health & Social Services Trust

North Down Borough Council

North-Eastern Education and Library Board

Northern Health and Social Services Board

Northern Ireland Court Service

Northern Ireland Juvenile Courts Association

Northern Ireland Prison Service

Northern Ireland Resident Magistrates' Association

Northern Ireland Women's Aid Federation

NSPCC Northern Ireland

Office of Law Reform, DFP

Pobal

Police Federation for Northern Ireland

Probation Board for Northern Ireland

Professor Wilfried Schärf, University of Capetown

Professor Howard Zehr, Mennonite University of Virginia

Progressive Unionist Party

Quaker House Penal Affairs Group

Rathgael Juvenile Justice Services

Relatives for Justice

Royal Ulster Constabulary

ESRC Violence Project, School of Public Policy, Economics & Law, University of Ulster

Mr Sean Mulrine

Sinn Féin

Sir Louis Blom-Cooper QC

Social Democratic and Labour Party

Social Services Inspectorate

Sophy Bryson

St Patrick's Youth Justice Services

Standing Advisory Commission on Human Rights

T J Ritchie

The Superintendents' Association of Northern Ireland

The Workers Party

Mr Tim Chapman

Tommy McCready JP

Ulster Unionist Party

United Campaign Against Plastic Bullets

Victim Support Northern Ireland

Witness Support Scheme, Victim Support Northern Ireland

Northern Ireland Women's Coalition

Northern Ireland Human Rights Commission

Lawyers' Committee for Human Rights

Desmond Perry, Resident Magistrate

Newry & Mourne District Council

Fermanagh Solicitors' Association

Appendix B

Criminal Justice Review Research Reports

	Title	Author
1	Attitudes to Crime, Crime Reduction and Community Safety in Northern Ireland	Kristine Amelin, Michael Willis, Colette Blair and Debbie Donnelly
2	Attitudes to the Criminal Justice System in Northern Ireland	Kristine Amelin, Michael Willis and Debbie Donnelly
3	Participation in the Criminal Justice System in Northern Ireland	Kristine Amelin, Michael Willis and Debbie Donnelly
4	Crime Reduction/ Reducing Criminality	Colette Blair
5	Judicial Appointments	Colette Blair
6	Prisons and Probation	Colette Blair
7	Review of the Community Safety Centre and a Crime Reduction Strategy for Northern Ireland	Adam Crawford and Colette Blair
8	Community Safety Structures: An International Literature Review	Adam Crawford and Mario Matassa
9	Re-Forming Law Reform in Northern Ireland	Brice Dickson and Michael Hamilton
10	Restorative Justice Options for Northern Ireland: A Comparative Review	Jim Dignan and Kerri Lowey
11	Lay Involvement in Adjudication	Sean Doran and Ruth Glenn
12	Attitudes to the Criminal Justice System	Seamus Dunn, Valerie Morgan and Helen Dawson
13	Community Safety: Partnerships and Local Government	Dermot Feenan
14	Human Rights Standards and Criminal Justice	Stephen Livingstone and Jonathan Doak
15	Criminal Justice Co-operation Across Shared Land Borders: The Republic of Ireland and Northern Ireland	S. K. Nijhar
16	Criminal Prosecutions Procedure and Practice: International Perspectives	Keith Bryett and Peter Osborne
17	Juvenile Crime and Justice – A Review	David O'Mahony and Ronan Deazley
18	Designing Criminal Justice: The Northern Ireland System in Comparative Perspective	Neil Walker and Mark Telford

Appendix C

Seminars

Date	Venue	Location
6th May 1999	Balmoral Conference Centre	Belfast
7th May 1999	Balmoral Conference Centre	Belfast
12th May 1999	Killyhevlin Hotel	Enniskillen
13th May 1999	Seagoe Hotel	Craigavon
20th May 1999	Galgorm Manor	Ballymena
21th May 1999	Everglades Hotel	Londonderry
27th May 1999	Canal Court Hotel	Newry
28th May 1999	Mellon Country Inn	Omagh
24th June 1999	Interpoint Centre	Belfast